Religion in the Lives of English Women,
1760–1930

Religion in the Lives of English Women, 1760-1930

EDITED BY GAIL MALMGREEN

INDIANA UNIVERSITY PRESS
Bloomington and Indianapolis

Manufactured in Great Britain

Library of Congress Cataloging in Publication Data

Religion in the lives of English women, 1760–1930.
   Includes bibliographies and index.
   1. Women in Christianity—England—History.
2. Women and religion—England—History. 3. England—Religion.
I. Malmgreen, Gail.
BR755.R45 1986   274.2′08′088042   86-45172
ISBN 0-253-34973-7

1 2 3 4 5 90 89 88 87 86

Contents

For
Anna, Elizabeth, Abigail, and Charlotte Paskow
many paths, one spirit

Preface

My first debt of gratitude is the obvious one — to the contributors. Finding them was a challenge, working with them was rewarding, and getting to know them as friends was a lasting bonus of the project. By common effort we managed to lighten the burdens and deflect some of the frustrations of breaking new ground.

It is difficult to measure what this work owes to Constance Buchanan and the community embodied in the Woman's Studies Program at Harvard Divinity School. They offered every kind of support and encouragement, in a spirit of love and fellowship, and they insisted that the religious history of women must be reclaimed from the shadows. To a historian that kind of urgency on the part of potential readers is rare, and irresistible.

Others helped in many ways. Henry Abelove, Karen Greenspan, Jim Obelkevich, Malcolm Thomas, Martha Vicinus and Chris Waters were generous with advice and assistance. The Wesley Historical Society (Yorkshire), Cambridge University Press, and the editors of *Victorian Studies* and the *Journal of Ecclesiastical History* gave permission to reprint material originally published by them. Dr John Walsh and Mrs Goodith Heeney kindly agreed to allow Brian Heeney's essay to be included here. The Ashmolean Museum, the Tate Gallery, Leeds City Art Gallery and Temple Newsam House and Sotheby's provided illustrations and gave permission to reproduce paintings in their collections. Paula Dubin, Margaret Evans and Christine Sullivan helped to prepare the manuscript.

Without the faith and confidence of Joan Catapano of Indiana University Press this project might never have begun, and would certainly not have been finished. And Richard Stoneman of Croom Helm was the exemplary editor, always patient with the intricacies

of orchestrating the work of authors so widely scattered on both
sides of the Atlantic.

G.M.

Chapter 1

Introduction

Gail Malmgreen

One measure of the vitality of feminist scholarship over the past two decades has been its willingness to link up with the greater world outside academia. In the best tradition of radical intellectual movements it has offered a new vision of human potential and an altered sense of our historical past. But every era of scholarship has its favourite lines of approach. And religion has so far been a somewhat neglected element in the women's history revival. Feminist historians who are secular in outlook can readily project backward their own concern with issues of women's health, work and wages, literary creativity or domestic relations, but they may find it harder to see the feminist component in nineteenth-century temperance or missionary movements. And those most interested in spirituality have not always been historically inclined; some contemporary feminists have spoken and written as if the tradition of women's sacred wisdom is a direct legacy from ancient (even prehistoric) times to the present — with little of consequence happening in between.

It is disappointing, though perhaps not surprising, that the studies which are cornerstones of scholarship in modern British church history, the works of Owen Chadwick or W. R. Ward, for example, Edward Norman's *History of Roman Catholicism in England*, or Rupp and Davies's *New History of Methodism*, should have almost nothing to say about women. If only George Eliot had been more orthodox, Charlotte M. Yonge more brilliant, or Catherine Booth more respectable, women might have found at least a niche in the standard texts.

The work of a new generation of social historians of religion, among them Hugh McLeod, Alan D. Gilbert and Thomas Laqueur, has unfortunately done little more to extend our understanding of women. The sources on which they have most relied —

1

official surveys such as the Ecclesiastical Census of 1851 and denominational records, national and local — are maddeningly uninformative on matters of gender. We have no idea, yet, how women's religious beliefs and practices might be correlated with social class, age, marital status, geography or educational background. But there are signs that a more comprehensive approach to the study of religion and society is possible, and on the way.

In the study of women and religion American historians have had the advantage of an earlier start. The result has been a harvest of valuable theses and monographs, as well as the reference guides and general texts to support teaching and further research.[1] This is not to say that British resources are entirely lacking. As the wide-ranging footnotes to this volume attest, there is earlier work to build on — beginning with Olive Anderson's ground-breaking article on feminism and preaching.[2] Particular areas have been brightly illuminated — through Frank Prochaska's work on women and philanthropy, Martha Vicinus's recent writing on women's religious communities, Elizabeth Jay's penetrating discussion of religious fiction, and James Hopkins's study of Joanna Southcott;[3] and there is an encouraging crop of work in progress. Still, the current state of knowledge is very uneven. Quaker and Methodist women have been relatively well served, while the historiography of Roman Catholic laywomen, for example, is all but non-existent.

Even the most basic facts about sex ratios in church membership and participation are unknown. We do not know either what proportion of all believers were women, or what proportion of all women were believers. Recent studies have demonstrated that for most American denominations, over the period from the mid-seventeenth to the first quarter of the nineteenth century, church membership shows a persistent female majority of between 60 and 70 per cent.[4] For England such calculations are difficult, in part because the Church of England, as a catch-all communion enjoying the privileges of an official monopoly, was not concerned with keeping membership lists. What little evidence has been gathered so far suggests similarities to the American pattern.[5] Indeed there are further complications. Mere membership or even attendance figures are not necessarily indicators of commitment or activism — far less a measure of inner belief. It is likely that there was, in England as in America, a 'feminisation' of religion, consequent in part on the increasing separation of church and state. Religion was consigned to women's sphere; as Mary Maples Dunn has put it, 'To be a good woman was to be a good Christian. But to be a good man was to be a good citizen, active, competitive, self-confident.'[6] Yet the details, the particularities of the English case, are still a mystery.

If feminist historians ignore religion, or confine themselves to the wilder fringes of female spirituality, we will have forfeited our understanding of the mental universe of the no doubt substantial majority of women who were believers. What was the nature of women's private devotions? Were women's religious beliefs consistently different from those of men? Does it make sense to speak of female-identified theologies in the eighteenth or nineteenth century, as it does in the twentieth? Can we discern a distinctively female ethical voice in the past, as Carol Gilligan has in the present? To begin to answer such questions we must look afresh at women's published speculative and didactic writing; but in addition we must turn to the fiction and poetry, diaries, letters and memoirs, where women's voices are most clearly heard.

This is not to take issue with the emphasis labour and social historians have placed on the themes of class, wealth and social/political empowerment. The religious history of women cannot, should not, be separated from history *tout court*. One has only to recall that women's pastoral work was almost always unpaid work, that a female preacher could far more easily come by an audience than a church of her own to preach in, that the hierarchical structure of some religious communities clearly reflected the class divisions of the outer world. Marriage and child-rearing, even for the stalwart revivalists of Primitive Methodism, severely restricted women's freedom to travel and teach — however powerful their 'call' might have been.

A class-bound Victorian domestic ideology of female service and self-abnegation, confused and confusing in its effects, fuelled the multifarious projects of female philanthropy and social improvement which male commentators like Dickens alternately ridiculed and sentimentalised. Religious rescue-workers who set out so energetically to reclaim the lost usually had little comprehension of the material and cultural world of the labouring classes, and only a hazy sense of what was to be done with the 'fallen' once they were saved. Feminist critic Anne Smith has asked to what extent the history of modern feminism must be seen as 'part of the . . . historically inevitable process of divvying up the power and the spoils of power more equally between the sexes in the middle class'.[7] It is a fair question, and one that may be extended to women's religious activism.

A recurring theme in this volume is the intimate interrelationship between religious and political life. Both abolitionism and temperance posed threats to male pocketbooks as well as principles, and were opposed accordingly in Parliament. In an atmosphere of virulent anti-Catholicism nunneries could be seen as potential conduits of papal influence and priestly intrigue, and both Wesleyan Methodism and Salvationism were at first considered serious threats to both civil order and the privileges of the Establishment. The Queen's preferences in matters of ecclesiastical patronage had political repercussions. Woman's disfranchisement could be, and was, interpreted as an infringement of her spiritual, as well as her temporal, rights and duties.

Borrowing techniques from anthropology and sociology, such historians as Keith Thomas and James Obelkevich have revealed a world of popular spirituality that flourished beyond (often below) the confines of church or chapel, and connected with religious institutions only partially and intermittently. In this world, where custom could outweigh formal teaching and leadership owed more to local loyalties than to denominational certification, wise women and prophetesses loomed large. Clearly one source of the success of Ann Carr and her co-workers lay in their ability to act as brokers between the world of popular piety and the more structured faith of the chapels. But there is a great deal more to be learned about the precise nature of the interactions and transactions involved.

To recapture the religious beliefs of ordinary women is a daunting assignment, but why should the more accessible figures, including those women most closely connected to and intimately involved with the official church, still be so little known? Brian Heeney and others have looked at the social profile of the Victorian clergy, but what of clergy sisters, wives and daughters? If the cleric was a species of gentleman, were his female relations then gentlewomen? What part did such women take in pastoral work? Did the sexes tend to agree on matters of doctrine and worship? How many Mrs Arabins were there to every Mrs Proudie; how many Mrs Collinses to every Mrs Elton?

The close identification of many devout women with male relatives or mentors put them in an ambiguous position — *in* but not quite *of* ecclesiastical life. An instructive example is Elizabeth

Wordsworth, whose father was Canon of Westminster and later Bishop of Lincoln. As her biographer puts it,

> She made [her father's] interests her own, filling her letters with long accounts of such functions as Church Congresses, and endless discussion of current ecclesiastical problems and controversies, but writing always with the faintest hint of self-mockery . . . [She] was always her father's chief assistant in the enormous task of writing a commentary on the entire Bible.[8]

Obviously some women found a strong vicarious appeal in attachment to a male cleric. Others made their faith a means of escape from domestic confinement, or a statement of individual identity. Religious commitment and expression was, after all, an approved outlet for female assertiveness — within limits. We may speculate as to the nature of the personal odyssey which led William Gladstone's sister to become a Roman Catholic, or William Morris's sister to be the head of Anglican sisterhood.

Feminist historians should not forget that women took to the public platform on behalf of religion long before they were stirred by politics; that women left the home in droves to conduct Sunday schools and prayer-meetings long before they campaigned for professional training; and that religious writing offered middle-class women a chance to be self-supporting even before the heyday of the great female novelists. Jane Lewis, whose recent book on *Women in England, 1870–1950* includes no sustained discussion of religion, alludes slightingly to the 'evangelical tradition, which, in the early and mid-nineteenth century had proved as successful as science in containing women'.[9] Hannah More (and Catherine Booth) would have been surprised to hear it! As Margaret Maison's discussion of hymn-writing demonstrates, religious publishing was a welcome and congenial outlet for talented women in acute need of a steady income. The religious market was vast, and, significantly, of the best-known writers of religious fiction nearly half were women.[10] Colin Dews's Female Revivalists found in their mission not only an alternative to marriage but a way of life that was quite independent of male supervision and authority.

Late Victorian women reformers from Florence Nightingale to Emily Davies and Millicent Fawcett, whatever their private views may have been, were obliged to pay heed to and make compromises with the religious assumptions of their supporters. Most English feminists were seeking, not to break free from religion, but to purge it of the oppressive accretions of centuries of patriarchal misinterpretation; hence the 'new woman' was often a new religionist. It is useful to recall the initial feminist appeal of Salvationism and the enthusiasm with which some feminists embraced novel, and usually female-created, spiritual philosophies — for Annie Besant it was Theosophy, for Christabel Pankhurst Seventh-Day Adventism, for many others Christian Science.

Quaker and other nonconformist women were among the first to speak out for women's equality, their feminism a direct outgrowth of their liberal faith; but by the late nineteenth century, as Catherine Prelinger's and Brian Heeney's essays suggest, religious feminism was taking its cues from, and trailing behind, the secular feminist movements. Lilian Shiman's study of women and temperance demonstrates that certain sections of British womanhood were quite receptive to radical innovation exported from America; but the 'do everything' faction in the temperance movement was a minority, and in the end cautious respectability prevailed. The religious feminist tradition in England seems to have lacked the extremes of exuberance and combativeness found in Americans like suffragist and Methodist minister Anna Howard Shaw. When asked, during a lecture in 1896, 'Why does the Scripture say there shall be no marriage in heaven?' Shaw replied, 'Ah, my dear friends [and she drew a long sigh], some one has answered that by saying, because there will be no men there.'[11] This is a far cry from the tone of Josephine Butler, Margaret Lucas or Maude Royden. The difference is epitomised by the early success of vociferous demands for female ordination in America, and the fact that ordained women from several denominations played leading roles in the American women's movement.[12]

The pursuit of women's religious history requires new categories of analysis, and its reconstruction will ultimately revise our total understanding of religious history. Historians will, for instance, be made to look more closely at the broad question of the relationship of lay and clerical components in the life of any church. Traditional demarcations between lay and clerical roles, official bodies and informal networks, liberal and conservative stances, and orthodox teaching and popular belief are likely to be unhelpful, even misleading, where women are concerned.

Perhaps the most important task confronting the historian of women's spirituality is to keep alive the central paradox, the complex tension between religion as 'opiate' and as an embodiment of ideological and institutional sexism, and religion as transcendent and liberating force. It is surely neither possible nor necessary to weigh up, once and for all, the gains and losses for women of religious commitment.[13] What is clear is that the dealings of organised religion with women have been richly laced with ironies and contradictions. Female preaching, as Dr Johnson knew, was something that was never done well; but when the success of female revivalists began to encroach alarmingly on the prerogatives of male clergy, rules had to be made against it.

Nineteenth-century feminists were very well aware of the monstrous hypocrisy inherent in a Victorian ideal which paid effusive homage to women's higher spiritual nature and special nurturing mission, and then proceeded to deny women legal control over the religious or secular training of their own children. Ecclesiastical bodies sometimes reached heights of absurdity in their efforts to channel and control women's spiritual impulses. A Church of England Congress meeting at Reading in 1883 devoted its opening session to 'Women's Work'; a large audience, preponderantly female, listened to papers by an array of male notables: Professor Acland on 'District Visitors', Mr Talbot, MP, on 'Mission Women', the Dean of Chester on 'Deaconesses', and others. Archdeacon Emery, permanent secretary of the Congress, pointed out that 'the ladies concerned in the general subject thought they should have been allowed to read papers . . . but the Bishop and the Committee had decided otherwise'. This session, the press commented, was especially well attended because a concurrent one, on 'Purity' and 'The Prevention of the Degradation of Women and Children', was closed to women![14] That a July 1985 synod of the Church of England should have bestowed a measure of pastoral status on deaconesses — a hundred years late, and still hedged with limitations — is a poignant commentary on progress in the Church, and a reminder of the fathomless patience of churchwomen.

The pace and impact of secularisation — the overall decline of religion as a cultural and political force which so troubled Victorian clerics — may well have been different for women than for men. But women were affected, and profoundly. For women of the class and generation of Mrs Tonna and Mrs Barbauld, religious publishing was virtually the only available career, and for political pamphleteer Elizabeth Heyrick the religious platform was the obvious platform. But by the end of the nineteenth century options for women had expanded immeasurably. In terms of the numbers attracted, neither the revival of sisterhoods nor the deaconess movements can be considered notably successful. Much more impressive is the strength of religious ideals of womanly sacrifice and service in determining the tone and structure of the new secular professions for women — in particular nursing and teaching, where norms of celibacy were widely approved, both within and outside the professional community. Perhaps women were less thoroughly 'secularised' than men; this is another question that awaits exploration. The motivation for Salvationists working with unwed mothers, for temperance lecturers, or for deaconesses confronting the ills of the urban slums was religious, but other influences — particularly the revelations and techniques of social science — were at work on them as well. Where women's movements were concerned, there was no all-out antagonism between the new science and religion. Religiously-based reforms such as temperance and the campaign for 'social purity' quite happily appropriated popular scientific theories of eugenics and 'moral hygiene'. The progressive spirit in lay politics also had its reverberations in church and synagogue affairs. One legacy of the suffrage movement, reinforced by wartime dislocations, was a small but tenacious feminist current within the churches — a movement very much stronger and more confident today.

This anthology brings specialists in women's studies and religious studies together in a joint enterprise, seeking to open up a new vista across disciplinary lines. Only by putting religion back into women's history can we attain a full understanding of the 'female world of love and ritual' which Carroll Smith-Rosenberg evokes so powerfully. When church history penetrates beyond the serried ranks of bishops and rabbis, priests, preachers and theologians, it will lay bare another sort of church. In *this* church, as readers of Barbara Pym's novels or of the records of sick-visitors and Sunday-school teachers will know, women were far from invisible.

The essays collected here do not address every question that could be asked about the religion of Englishwomen. For the most part they concentrate, not on the interior world of belief, but on the public expression of religion, and on religion as an engine of social action. In so doing they provide evidence on both sides of the debate about the separateness of 'women's culture'. They demonstrate that religion was many things for women, a shelter, an escape, a consolation, a justification, a discipline, an inspiration, and, on occasion, an arena for rebellion against the prescriptions of male authority and conventional morality. In the mutually supportive networks of female co-workers in early Methodism, in the distinctive radicalism of some female abolitionist groups, in the sisterhoods and deaconess communities, we may think we glimpse a 'woman's world' in embryo. Yet the long-term fate of such groups is sobering and reveals their ultimate subordination to restrictions imposed from outside. Susan Casteras's unsparing examination of the nun image in Victorian art chronicles a triumph of social myth over female reality. By means of the artists' impressively 'realist' visions, public curiosity was satisfied and anxiety allayed, while the truth of the matter retreated under a barrage of propaganda.

To what extent did women's spiritual impulses and religious vocations, however expressed, persist in a more or less hostile environment as sources of strength, self-definition, and accomplishment? Now the question has been posed. Answering it will require a new angle of vision, and the work of many hands.

Notes

1. See especially Evangeline Thomas, *Women's Religious History Sources: A Guide to Repositories in the United States* (New York, 1983); Janet W. James (ed.), *Women in American Religion* (Philadelphia, 1980); and Rosemary R. Ruether and Rosemary S. Keller (eds), *Women and Religion in America* (New York, 1981); Mary F. Bednarowski, 'Outside the Mainstream: Women's Religion and Women Religious Leaders in Nineteenth-Century America', *Journal of the American Academy of Religion*, XLVIII (1980), pp. 207–31; and Gayle G. Yates, 'Spirituality and the American Feminist Experience', *Signs*, IX (1983), pp. 59–72.

An exception to the dearth of such material for Britain is Dale A. Johnson's documentary collection, *Women in English Religion, 1700–1925* (New York, 1983), which has not, however, been widely available.

2. O. Anderson, 'Women Preachers in Mid-Victorian Britain: Some Reflexions on Feminism, Popular Religion and Change', *The Historical Journal*, XII (1969), pp. 467–84.

3. See F. K. Prochaska, *Women and Philanthropy in Nineteenth Century England* (Oxford, 1980); M. Vicinus, *Independent Women: Work and Community for Single Women, 1850–1920* (Chicago and London, 1985), Ch. 2; E. Jay, *The Religion of the Heart: Anglican Evangelicalism and the Nineteenth-Century Novel* (Oxford, 1979); and J. K. Hopkins, *A Woman to Deliver Her People: Joanna Southcott and English Millenarianism in an Era of Revolution* (Austin, Tex., 1982).

4. The statistical evidence is summarised in essays by Mary M. Dunn, Gerald F. Moran, and Mary P. Ryan in J. James (ed.), *Women in American Religion*; and in Richard D. Shiels, 'Feminization of American Congregationalism, 1730–1835', *American Quarterly*, XXXIII (1981), pp. 46–62.

5. My study, in progress, of eighteenth-century Methodist membership lists from

Lancashire and Cheshire indicates an average of 55% female membership for smaller communities, and a rise to nearly 70% in urban centres like Manchester and Stockport by the end of the century; but these figures are still tentative.

6. M. M. Dunn, 'Saints and Sisters', in James (ed.), *Women in American Religion*, p. 39.

7. *New Statesman*, 23 August 1985, p. 25.

8. Georgina Battiscombe, *Reluctant Pioneer: A Life of Elizabeth Wordsworth* (London, 1978).

9. J. Lewis, *Women in England, 1870–1950* (Bloomington, Ind., 1984), p. 89.

10. See M. Maison, *The Victorian Vision: Studies in the Religious Novel* (New York, 1961), Appendix.

11. Unidentified clipping, Library of Congress, Susan B. Anthony Scrapbook, no. 34.

12. Nancy A. Hardesty, *Women Called to Witness: Evangelical Feminism in the Nineteenth Century* (Nashville, Tenn., 1984) is a recent study arguing for the primacy of evangelical influences in American feminism.

13. Opposing viewpoints in this debate are sharply focused in an exchange between Joan Iverson and Julie Dunfey on women and Mormonism, in *Feminist Studies*, X (1984), pp. 505–36.

14. *Women's Suffrage Journal*, 1 November 1883, p. 201.

Chapter 2

'Thine, Only Thine!' Women Hymn Writers in Britain, 1760–1835

Margaret Maison

Feminist poets in eighteenth-century Britain lamented the condition of women, seeing them as miserable slaves of that 'haughty tyrant Man',[1] powerless puppets, ignorant nincompoops,

> Debarr'd from Knowledge, banished from the Schools,
> And with the utmost Industry, bred Fools.[2]

Women, they claimed, were accorded the status of cloistered idiots, and Anglican attitudes, on the whole, did not favour the rehabilitation of these severely handicapped members of society. St Paul was widely quoted, and female subservience and inferiority were frequently proclaimed from the pulpit by clerics who, while grudgingly admitting that women had souls, insisted that they should read nothing but scriptures and sermons, and show passive obedience, first to their fathers and then to their husbands, in all matters great and small.

Dissent from orthodoxy, however, often involved dissent from these sexist stances, and it is refreshing to observe how many women of Nonconformist persuasion enjoyed an exceptional measure of liberty, equality and fraternity in religious activities throughout the eighteenth century. They not only participated in the movements of the time, but also, on occasion, took leading roles. The redoubtable Selina, Countess of Huntingdon (1707–91) set up her own chapels, appointed her own clergy, opened her own seminary and compiled her own psalms, hymns and doxologies.

In Moravian and Wesleyan groups women acted as missionaries, musicians, choristers and organisers of conferences and communities. Methodist women even braved masculine ridicule by preaching, convinced, unlike Dr Johnson, that this was a perfectly acceptable vocation for women, since, as George Eliot's delightful

11

eighteenth-century preacher Dinah Morris maintained, 'It isn't for men to make channels for God's spirit as they make channels for the water-courses, and say, "Flow here, but flow not there".'[3]

The Holy Spirit flowed through the female pen as well as the female voice, and women were moved to write tracts, pamphlets and missionary letters. They launched magazines, did useful editing and translating work, popularised such fascinating literary genres as letters from the dead to the living, and poured forth a steady stream of hymns and devotional verse.

Although royal permission had been granted for hymns to be sung in Church of England services as far back as 1559 by a sovereign who was both a woman and a hymn writer, conservative Anglicans, who clung to their psalms and their prejudices, and dismissed much of popular hymn-singing as flamboyant and undignified, were only gradually won over.

It was the Moravians, with their musical, charismatic, ecumenically-minded leader Count Nicolaus Ludwig von Zinzendorf, who revitalised hymn-singing, transforming its image into one of vigour and spontaneity, a heartfelt expression of love and praise and trust in Christ, a profound experience in which women were included as a matter of course. Both Zinzendorf's first and second wives were hymn writers. The Moravians saw the importance of music as a universal language and an aid to evangelism. They did not share that dislike of instrumental music and the opposition to organs that characterised some British Nonconformist groups. Their passionate enthusiasm kindled the fires of musical devotion in Britain, and by the end of the century hymns were a recognised part of worship for all British Christian congregations with the exception of the Society of Friends.

Hymns were published in leaflets and broadsheets and small collections, often in the form of tiny oblong volumes, sometimes with separate tune books. The tunes came from innumerable sources — old psalms and carols, traditional airs, ballads, jigs and folksongs of different countries, from operas, oratorios and Masses, and from the works of contemporary composers, including such great names as Handel, Haydn and Bach. (Women did not shine here: they appear to have confined themselves to words rather than melodies.)

In the eighteenth century hymns were composed for private worship as well as public, for cottage as well as church, for chamber and closet as well as chapel, hospital, school and open-air congregation. Hymns were for all occasions and could be sung anywhere: Madame Guyon and her maid sang hymns in prison, harvesters sang in the fields, children sang in the nursery, and the Moravians sang lustily on board ship, especially when the going got rough. Nor was it even necessary to sing the hymns; insomniacs recited them on their restless pillows, invalids whispered them in the sick room, and Mary Fletcher, the evangelical prophetess of Madeley, read hymns aloud to her dying husband. Hymns enjoyed an extensive circulation and many were written expressly for domestic consumption rather than congregational use.[4]

Their extraordinary popularity gave women welcome opportunities for authorship. Icy hostility to Christian ladies as writers melted in the sunshine of sacred song, and those three giants of eighteenth-century hymnology, Isaac Watts and the two Wesleys, John and Charles, all encouraged, influenced and were influenced by women hymn-writers and hymn-singers.

Watts, as is well known, fell in love with Elizabeth Singer, afterwards Mrs Rowe, whose religious writings, including hymns, were famous far beyond her immediate Dissenting circle. Although Watt's proposal to the 'Heavenly Singer' was refused, they kept up a close friendship throughout her marriage and widowhood, and their relationship was satirised by the poet Edward Young:

Charm'd with her Learning, with what Rapture he
Hangs on her Bloom, like an industrious Bee,
Hums round about her, and with all his Power
Extracts sweet Wisdom from so fair a Flower![5]

The Wesleys extracted sweet wisdom from a considerable number of fair flowers. Their mother Susanna always began and ended her children's lessons with hymns, and led the hymn-singing at her devotional gatherings in the kitchen, attended by children, servants, neighbours and friends. Their sister Mehetabel wrote religious verse of a high order. The Wesley brothers did not hesitate to include hymns by women in their collections, and John was so impressed by the Moravian writers Anna Nitschmann and Anna Dober that he translated their hymns into English in the 1730s.

The most distinguished woman hymn writer of eighteenth-century Britain was neither Moravian nor Methodist but Baptist. The General Baptists were slow to accept hymn-singing in their churches, but the Particular Bapists, with John Bunyan and his singing pilgrims as their splendid example, proved far more receptive. It is perhaps unfortunate that one of their earlier women hymn writers, Mrs Anne Dutton (1698–1765), produced nothing but rubbishy doggerel. Mrs Dutton was a kind of eighteenth-century Mrs Jellyby, who bombarded African Negro converts and other innocent victims with her letters (thirteen volumes of these missives were published) and sent her husband to America to sell her tracts. Her hymns are mere clumsy expressions of Calvinist theology; witness her description of the Holy Spirit:

He is as Sovereign in his Love,
    As Son and Father be;
And when he on the Elect moves,
    He is an Agent free.[6]

To compensate we have the hymns of Anne Steele (1717–78), one of the brightest stars in the firmament of Baptist hymnody, hailed by the historians as the 'mother' of English women hymn writers.[7] She was born in Broughton, Hampshire, where her father and great uncle were Baptist ministers. Her health was delicate; she had consumptive tendencies and never fully recovered from a childhood hip injury received in a horse-riding accident. Her mother died when she was three, and a stepmother and stepsister brought conflicts and tensions into the household, which, although the subject of constant prayer, were not resolved for some time.

At the age of twenty she became engaged. Help and release seemed at hand, but all turned to tragedy when her fiancé was drowned while swimming in the River Avon the day before the wedding. After this Anne Steele remained at home, leading a life of peaceful retirement in her quiet village. Her stepmother died in 1760, and her father, to whom she was deeply attached, in 1769. Outward tranquillity concealed depths of pain, frustration and suffering as she progressed along her 'pathway of affliction' to God.[8]

Her book of verse was published in two volumes in 1760, under the pseudonym of 'Theodosia'. All profits went to charity, the Bristol Education Society receiving a large share from the 1780 edition. Her father, who had encouraged her in her religious writings, had slight misgivings when it came to publication. 'I pray God to make it useful and keep her humble', he wrote in his diary.[9] (The eighteenth century considered pride of authorship particularly perilous for the female sex. Even John Wesley was capable of writing to an aspiring woman poet, 'MY DEAR MAIDEN, BEWARE of pride, beware of flattery.'[10])

Anne Steele's hymns echo the attractive simplicity, spontaneity and ardour of Watts and the Wesleys, with added notes of feminine sensitivity and introspection. The love and praise of God, the pleasures of 'grateful rapture,'[11] and the joys of a close personal relationship with Jesus Christ come across strongly. Christ is frequently addressed in the language of a lover:

> Dear centre of my best desires,
>   And sov'reign of my heart,
> What sweet delight thy name inspires!
>   What bliss thy smiles impart!

                    *   *   *

> Too oft, alas, my passions rove,
>   In search of meaner charms;
> Trifles unworthy of my love
>   Divide me from thy arms.[12]

He is pictured as supremely and irresistibly beautiful, with a radiant face, a 'blissful smile',[13] and 'lovely melting eyes'.[14]

> Should nature's charms, to please the eye,
>   In sweet assemblage join,
> All nature's charms would droop and die,
>   Jesus, compar'd with thine.[15]

But He is also the crucified Saviour, with 'bloody sweat, like drops of rain'.[16] Anne Steele, influenced by the popular Wesleyan and Moravian hymns, places much emphasis on His blood and wounds, and on the groans and agonizing cries of His crucifixion. Fortunately she does not share the Moravians' taste for slaughtered Lamb and their fondness for the erotic and sometimes ridiculous imagery of kissing, embracing and entering the 'nail-holes' of Christ's body; her contemplation of Christ's sufferings is more balanced and reflective:

> Those healing hands with blessing fraught,
> Nail'd to the cross with pungent smart!
> Inhuman deed! Could no kind thought
> To pity move the ruthless heart?[17]

A sense of her own unworthiness, together with that deep consciousness of sin so characteristic of her faith, reveals itself in her hymns; her literary landscape, like that of Watts, is heavily populated with worms. There are 'sinful worms',[18] 'rebellious worms',[19] and this earth is in fact a 'nest of worms'.[20] The vanity of human wishes is emphasised again and again: the gilded snares and the 'illusive dreams'[21] of the world offer no lasting pleasure. Even rural retirement, held by the eighteenth century to be so conducive to virtue, can lose its attractions, as the author knew from personal experience:

> O Happiness, thou pleasing dream,
>   Where is thy substance found?
> Sought thro' the varying scenes in vain,
>   Of earth's capacious round.

*　　*　　*

> The busy town, the crowded street,
>   Where noise and discord reign,
> We gladly leave, and tir'd, retreat,
>   To breathe and think again.

> Yet if retirement's pleasing charms
>   Detain the captive mind,
> The soft enchantment soon dissolves;
>   'Tis empty all as wind.

> Religion's sacred lamp alone,
>   Unerring points the way,
> Where happiness for ever shines
>   With unpolluted ray.[22]

Anne Steele's outlook was influenced by her ill health, and by the sorrows and disappointments that she endured. Sanctified suffering, resignation to God's will, and trust in God as the great physician and healer are constant themes of her verse, and she set the fashion for women's hymn-writing for invalids that lasted for over a century. There were a great many women invalids in those days, confined to bed or sofa, afflicted by illnesses beyond the scope of contemporary medical knowledge, and, when lovingly nursed and cared for, often attaining a surprising longevity. For them Anne Steele prescribes prayer and the reading of the

Holy Scriptures. Her most famous hymn, beginning 'Father of Mercies', tells of the therapeutic effects of reading the word of God:

> Here springs of consolation rise,
>   To cheer the fainting mind,
> And thirsting souls receive supplies,
>   And sweet refreshment find.
>
> Here the Redeemer's welcome voice
>   Spreads heavenly peace around,
> And life and everlasting joys
>   Attend the blissful sound.[23]

This hymn proved very popular with the Victorians, sung to the tune of 'Southwell' by H. S. Irons, organist of Southwell Minster. A good hymn, of course, could achieve inter-ecclesiastical as well as international approval, and Anne Steele's work found its way into a variety of hymnals, including the official Anglican *Hymns Ancient and Modern*, first collected in 1861.

The invalid hymn-singers were helped to face the prospect of death with serenity and even cheerfulness. Anne Steele's verse reflects the significant shift in attitudes towards death in the mid-eighteenth century. Just as, in sculpture, the death's head motif on gravestones was gradually replaced by cherubs, urns, and willows, so too in literature, the emphasis on grisly physical details, adverse last judgments, hellish torments and bottomless pits gave way to a more optimistic and joyful approach. The king of terrors became a divine messenger, a lover, a herald of heaven, and death was celebrated more widely as a triumph and a victory.

Few women were able to go as far as Charles Wesley did in his extravagant enthusiasm for corpses:

> Ah, lovely Appearance of Death!
>   No Sight upon Earth is so fair;
> Not all the gay Pageants that *breathe*
>   Can with a dead Body compare.[24]

They preferred to focus their emotions on the delights of hope and heaven. A very popular eighteenth-century funeral hymn, frequently used in Britain and America, was written by Cowper's aunt, Judith Madan (1702–81), who used the 'Glass of Faith' to look upwards:

> In this World of Sin and Sorrow,
> Compass'd round with many a Care,
> From Eternity we borrow
> Hope that can exclude Despair:
> Thee, triumphant GOD and SAVIOUR!
> In the Glass of Faith we see:
> O assist each faint Endeavour!
> Raise our earth-born Souls to Thee![25]

Anne Steele's funeral hymns, although less crisply expressed, show a similar bright resilience:

> While to the grave our friends are borne,
>   Around their cold remains,
> How all the tender passions mourn,
>   And each fond heart complains!
>
> But down to earth, alas in vain
>   We bend our weeping eyes;
> Ah! let us leave these seats of pain,
>   And upward learn to rise.
>
> Hope chearful smiles amid the gloom,
>   And beams a healing ray,
> And guides us from the darksome tomb,
>   To realms of endless day.[26]

The absence of illness in a future life was often stressed, and the absence of the British winter was also considered a highly desirable prospect to frail Christians shivering in their inadequately heated homes. A hymn adapted from Anne Steele's 'Reflection on a Winter Evening', beginning 'Stern winter throws his icy chains', became extremely popular:

> But while to this low world confin'd
>   Where changeful seasons roll,
> My blooming pleasures will decline,
>   And winter pain my soul.

O happy state, divine abode,
    Where spring eternal reigns;
And perfect day, the smile of God,
    Fills all the heav'nly plains![27]

Anne Steele's hymns, simple sensitive, personal, and radiating
the glow of a *Herzensreligion*, found a warm response in Britain
and America; Dr Julian listed seventy-five still in common use in
the 1890s, and a paperback edition of them appeared in 1967 to
mark the two hundred and fiftieth anniversary of her birth. Her
impact on her contemporaries was considerable and she had a great
many imitators, especially among those who favoured the hymn as
a closet companion.

Steele may well have influenced Elizabeth Scott (1708–76),
daughter of a Norwich independent minister, who went to America
in 1751 and married Elisha Williams, a former Rector of Yale. Her
hymns in Ash and Evans's Bristol *Collection* (1769) show a similar
concern with the pains and problems of her personal life:

Why, oh my Heart, these anxious Cares?
Why these tumultuous sickening Fears?
Why thus all pensive and forlorn,
Dost thou thy thickening Troubles mourn?[28]

The famous *Songs in the Night* (1780), by 'a young woman under
heavy afflictions', also echoes many of Anne Steele's themes. The
author was Susanna Harrison (1752–84), a domestic servant and
Congregationalist, who became bedridden with a spinal disease.
She, like Anne Steele, sees God as the supreme healer:

How vain are all the drugs and skill
    Of great physicians here!
If God denies a blessing still
    I languish in their care.[29]

She too has a 'longing to be dissolved' and looks forward to death
as the most attractive form of women's liberation:

Come Death, thou welcome messenger, appear,
    I would embrace thee with extended arms,
T'untie the silken bands that hold me here,
    Instead of horror, thou shalt come with charms.[30]

Anne Steele's work also appealed to the Bluestockings, and one of her admirers was the evangelical Anglican Hannah More (1745–1833), who visited her at Broughton and composed a poem to commemorate the occasion. Hannah More's prolific literary output included only a handful of hymns. Her 'Morning Soliloquy' much liked by Dr Johnson, castigates the vice of sloth, and another points out the equal opportunities martyrdom offers to both sexes:

> E'en a woman — women, hear,
> Read in Maccabees the story!
> Conquer'd nature, love and fear,
> To obtain a crown of glory.[31]

Steele's influence is more apparent in the work of another hymn-writing *bas-bleu*, Anna Laetitia Aikin, later Mrs Barbauld (1743–1825). Brought up in intellectual Dissenting circles (her father was a tutor at the distinguished Warrington Academy), she could read like an adult before she was three; and, despite the usual paternal hesitation over 'imparting to females any tincture of classical learning',[32] she mastered Greek and Latin with ease. She married a Dissenting minister and they kept a small school, but her husband's fits of violence and insanity caused painful problems and culminated in his suicide in 1808. Mrs Barbauld continued to occupy herself with literary and educational work; her reputation was high, and she and Hannah More were considered by many to be the most eminent women of their time.

Her *Devotional Pieces* (1775) contains a plea for the renewal of warmth and zeal in psalm-singing and includes an interesting essay on devotional taste in which the author expresses her regret that 'the living voice of the people, the animating accompanyments of music' and 'the exulting movements of pious joy'[33] are not more widely used in public worship. Those claiming that devotional writers are 'apt to run into the language of love' are reprimanded:

> Love borrows the language of Devotion, for the votaries of that passion are fond of using those exaggerated expressions, which suit nothing below the divinity; and you can hardly address the greatest of all Beings in a strain of more profound adoration than the lover uses to the object of his attachment.[34]

Those who disapprove of 'romantic excesses' in worship are

similarly dismissed: 'All the warm and generous emotions are treated as romantic by the supercilious brow of a cold-hearted philosophy.'[35]

Mrs Barbauld was clearly on the side of sensibility in its clash with Stoicism — an eighteenth-century battle that included some lively skirmishes among the Bluestockings. Elizabeth Carter had sounded a stirring trumpet call through her translation of Epictetus in 1758, while her friend the educationalist Hester Chapone deplored such stoical leanings and resisted all efforts to convert the human heart into a 'flint'. Mrs Greville's 'Ode to Indifference' was often quoted by the supporters of idealised apathy, and the Stoicism of Epictetus enjoyed a considerable vogue in Britain for many decades.[36]

Sensibility was even more popular. This supremely desirable quality for eighteenth-century bosoms included, at its best, sympathy, compassion, tenderness, humanitarianism and a perceptive appreciation of nature. At its worst it involved an excess of tears, blushings, palpitations, swoonings, fever, insanity, agonies of joy as well as sorrow, and an unfortunate tendency to melt into the slops of sentimentality. Henry Mackenzie's best-selling novel *The Man of Feeling* (1771), one of the most tear-stained stories of the century and certainly one of the most influential, gained an impressive victory for the votaries of the tender heart and the streaming eye.

Sensibility inspired more women hymn-writers than Stoicism did, and Mrs Barbauld did not hesitate to portray her ideal Christian as a Man of Feeling:

Blest is the man whose softening heart
    Feels all another's pain;
To whom the supplicating eye
    Was never raised in vain.

Whose breast expands with generous warmth
    A stranger's woes to feel;
And bleeds in pity o'er a wound
    He wants the power to heal.[37]

Friendship between kindred spirits sharing exquisite sensibility and Christian devotion also merited a hymn from her pen:

How blest the sacred tie that binds
In union sweet according minds!
How swift the heavenly course they run,
Whose hearts, whose faith, whose hopes are one!

*   *   *

Their streaming tears together flow
For human guilt and mortal woe;
Their ardent prayers together rise,
Like mingling flames in sacrifice.

*   *   *

Nor shall the glowing flame expire
When nature droops her sickening fire;
Then shall they meet in realms above,
A heaven of joy — because of love.[38]

Both these hymns survived throughout the Victorian age, the former acquiring the title of 'Christian Charity' and the latter having its original title of 'Pious Friendship' altered to the rather less appropriate 'Christian Fellowship'.

But Mrs Barbauld scored her greatest success with her charming *Hymns in Prose for Children* (1781). Explaining her preference for prose, she wrote in her preface that, in spite of the 'condescension' of Watts's Muse in his hymns for the young, 'it may well be doubted whether poetry ought to be lowered to the capacities of children, or whether they should not rather be kept from reading verse till they are able to relish good verse'.[39] She claimed that the ''measured prose' of her pieces was 'nearly as agreeable to the ear as a more regular rhythmus'.[40]

Her fifteen hymns, composed in alternate parts and intended for recitation, were an attempt to impress upon children the power and presence of God in every situation, in life, in death, in family matters and, above all, in nature:

Every field is like an open book; every painted flower hath a lesson written in its leaves.

Every murmuring brook hath a tongue; a voice is in every whispering wind.

They all speak of him who made them; they tell us, he is very good.[41]

The young reader is addressed directly as 'child of reason', 'child of the earth' or 'child of mortality', with simple word-pictures of the village green, of hens, geese and lambs, butterflies, flowers and trees. The cosy and the cosmic are nicely balanced and the idea of the immensity of God's power in space and time well adjusted to the juvenile mind. This little book, favourite reading for adults as well as children, ran into dozens of editions, was translated into several languages, and was even 'versified' by a clerical poetaster in 1865 (the result was dismal).

As the Romantic movement gathered strength, the last two decades of the eighteenth century saw the triumph of sensibility in women's literature. The nymph Indifference, severely shaken by Mackenzie, was put to flight by Charlotte Smith's best-selling *Elegiac Sonnets and Other Essays* (1784), which opened the floodgates to vast outpourings of tear-soaked verse, dripping with disillusion and dark with escapist longings and death-wishes. A plaintive piety, a vague romantic melancholy, crept like mildew over much of women's hymn-writing, and the numbers of fainting hearts, distressed souls, drooping spirits, feeble voices and invalids in 'low and languid' states,[42] given over to 'moaning and sick sighs',[43] increased alarmingly. Steele's *Songs in the Night* went through edition after edition, and closet hymns and chamber hymns became more popular than ever.

Only occasionally did courage and cheerfulness break in, and it is a relief to find a dry eye in the hymns of Helena Maria Williams (1762–1827). Miss Williams, a radical journalist, novelist, historian of the French Revolution, and a self-confessed devotee of sensibility,[44] whose tears formed the subject of Wordsworth's first published poem in 1787, managed to address her Maker with true Christian confidence:

My lifted eye without a tear
   The lowring storm shall see;
My stedfast heart shall know no fear —
   That heart shall rest on thee.[45]

Eliza Daye (*fl.* 1798), who was often confined to her room with sickness, took heart in a similar strain:

Tho' from his house his chast'ning hand
   Withheld my languid frame,
His altar in my heart shall stand
   And there I'll bless his name.[46]

Persistent fortitude characterises the hymns of Maria Frances Cecilia Madan, afterwards Mrs Cowper (1726–97), a daughter of the poet Judith Madan. Her life was overshadowed by more than its fair share of 'dark events', but a brave spirit shines through her best-known hymn 'The Consolation':

Ere first I drew this vital breath,
   From Nature's prison free,
Crosses in number, measure, weight,
   Were written, Lord, for me.
But Thou, my shepherd, friend and guide,
   Hast led me kindly on,
Taught me to rest my fainting head
   On Christ, the 'corner-stone'.

So comforted and so sustain'd,
   With dark events I strove,
And found them, rightly understood,
   All messengers of love;
With silent and submissive awe
   Ador'd a chastening God,
Rever'd the terrors of his law,
   And humbly kiss'd the rod.[47]

But many Christian women found the task of being 'silent and submissive' a burdensome one, and fell more than half in love with easeful death, as the gateway not to oblivion but to paradise. The Baptist Maria de Fleury shared Susanna Harrison's longings for liberation:

I'm fetter'd and chained up in clay,
I struggle and pant to be free,
I long to be soaring away,
My GOD and my SAVIOUR to see.[48]

Women followed Anne Steele in denouncing the deceptive nature of sublunary enjoyments. Mrs Cowper insisted that the world offered 'poison in golden cups'[49] and Mrs Anne Flowerdew (1759–1830), an Islington schoolmistress writing hymns in the 1790s, expressed her disillusion on more than one occasion:

Fondly and eager I pursue
   Some fresh delusive bliss,
The airy phantom mocks my grasp,
   And flies my fond embrace.[50]

The only satisfactory alternative, they found, was to embrace Jesus, and female invalids and insomniacs welcomed Jesus to their bedsides, if not to their beds. Jesus as the Heavenly Bridegroom was a well-established figure in mystical tradition, and kissing the rod may have had subconscious erotic undertones, but few women ventured as far as Madame Guyon in their conjugal commitments to Christ as a tender loving husband, whose presence gave such pleasure in the night.

Madame Jeanne-Marie Bouvier de la Motte Guyon (1648–1717), the famous French mystic and quietist, was the only Catholic woman hymn-writer widely acclaimed in eighteenth-century Britain. (Catholic disabilities at home made for an absence of the native product.) British Protestants of all varieties applauded this 'truly pious' soul, whose virtues proved that 'even the cloud of Romish superstition does not preclude the rays of the sun of righteousness.'[51] In 1776 John Wesley, in his preface to a short biography of this inspiring figure, praised her 'most fertile imagination' and her 'vast impetuosity of spirit', but pointed out 'that capital mistake, which runs thro' all her writings, that God never does, never can purify a soul, but by inward or outward suffering. Utterly false!'[52]

Reading the work of so many British women hymn-writers, one wonders if they too were not guilty of that 'capital mistake'. Too few availed themselves of sensibility's more positive advantages, and too few seemed able to cope with more extrovert subjects. There was a poor response, for example, to the challenge of the missionary hymn. A striking exception was Mrs Voke of Gosport (*fl.* 1795), who repeatedly urged the 'favor'd Briton' to proclaim his Redeemer's name to the 'untaught heathen' and the 'unlearn'd savage' in spirited hymns much approved by the Victorians. Mrs Voke also gave her country a rap on the knuckles in a hymn which was not so generally appreciated:

Britain hath long enjoy'd
   The precious written word;
And careless Britons long abused
   The goodness of the Lord.[53]

It is perhaps even more disappointing that so few women followed Mrs Barbauld in writing hymns for children, although there was a growing demand, especially with the rise of the Sunday schools at the end of the eighteenth century. Watts's *Divine Songs Attempted in Easy Language, for the Use of Children* (1715) still reigned supreme. Neither Cennick nor Charles Wesley could match them, and Mrs Darwall's efforts for charity children succeeded only in striking a chilling note:

> See the helpless infant band,
>   Born to penury and grief.[54]

Indeed, as Jane Taylor observed, Watts's hymns were 'so beautiful and so universally admired that they almost discourage, by their excellence, a similar attempt, and lead the way where it appears temerity to follow.'[55]

Fortunately Jane (1783–1824) and her elder sister Ann, later Mrs Gilbert (1782–1866), made the attempt, with pleasing results. The sisters belonged to a large and lively literary family of Independent persuasion. Both parents were deeply concerned with educational matters: their mother, Ann Taylor, supplied *Practical Hints to Young Females*, and their father Isaac, minister and engraver, wrote such works as *Advice to the Teens* and *Bunyan Explained to a Child*. The whole family set great store by habits of industry, good temper and 'Christian cheerfulness'.[56] Watts was revered, and hymn-singing vigorously practised. Isaac rose daily at six to pray aloud and sing hymns for an hour. Even when his voice was 'cracked with age' his family could hear the 'cheerful though quaking notes' coming from his closet.[57]

It was the sisters' own 'hearty affection for that interesting little race, the race of children'[58] that inspired their celebrated poetry for infant minds and their much-loved rhymes for the nursery. Generation after generation of children became familiar with such characters as Meddlesome Matty, Dirty Tom, Greedy Richard and Dutiful Jem, together with a variety of quarrelsome dogs, conceited wasps and disobedient fish, all adorning a tale and pointing a moral.

The authors blended entertainment and instruction with delightful simplicity and humour; they made morality attractive, and their views on mental illness and racial toleration, together with their opposition to hunting, shooting and fishing, placed them well ahead of their time. Edith Sitwell, introducing a new edition of their work in 1925, described its effect on her: 'These poems do not raise, at least in this infant mind, any wish to be the reverse of virtuous', and she praised their 'comfortable domestic certainty that virtue will be triumphant'.[59]

The sisters followed up these early successes with *Hymns for Infant Minds* (1808) and *Original Hymns for Sunday Schools* (1812), which indicate the same comfortable certainty and inspire the same agreeable desire for virtue. Their pleasant and perceptive approach to religion and character-building made them instant and lasting best-sellers. Like Watts, they banished all extravagances of thought and expression, making 'the sacrifice of poetry to simplicity wherever they stood opposed'.[60] They avoided all forms of party spirit or sectarian controversy, thus rendering the hymns suitable for all Christian children. (The expression of thankfulness for being 'a happy English child'[61] grates on the twentieth-century ear, but the ecumenical tone offers some compensation for insularity.)

The hymns aim to give the child an awareness of God's immense power and protection, and the idea of His omnipresence is beautifully conveyed:

If I could find some cave unknown,
　Where human feet had never trod,
Yet there I could not be alone;
　On every side there would be GOD.[62]

The idea of eternity too is expressed most effectively:

Days, months and years must have an end;
　Eternity has none:
'Twill always have as long to spend
　As when it first begun![63]

Rules of conduct for the Christian child are simple and straightforward. The importance of industry and concentration cannot be overstressed, especially in matters of Bible reading and prayer. God is aware of everything that goes on in the child's mind: there is even a hymn 'Against Wandering Thoughts'. Truthfulness is vital, self-conquest must be practised, and anger and impatience rooted out. Jane's famous hymn, sung to Haydn's music, tells how to do it:

> When for some little insult given
>> My angry passions rise,
> I'll think how JESUS came from Heaven,
>> And bore his injuries.[64]

Pride too must be eradicated, and Ann's 'The Way to Find Our Pride' and 'The Way to Cure Pride', in rhyming couplets (to be memorised rather than sung), form a masterly exercise in self-examination and a trustworthy guide to the attainment of Christian humility.

Filial duty looms large and even includes the duty of consoling one parent over the loss of another — a heroic task for a small child. Ann, who had a slightly morbid attitude to death, managed to control it in her hymns, where a no-nonsense, no-horrors approach to mortality is taken. Mamma tells her child:

> These hands and feet and busy head,
>> Shall waste and crumble quite away;
> But though your body shall be dead,
>> There is a part which can't decay.[65]

The child must be prepared to face the facts of death in the family. Only God knows the details of time and place.

> He knows the point, the very spot,
>> Where each of us shall fall;
> And whose shall be the earliest lot,
>> And whose the last of all.[66]

But the good child has nothing to fear: the loved ones around him/her will 'form a family anew, Unbroken, in the skies'.[67]
Hell is explained as

>> a state of endless woe,
> Where unrepenting sinners go:
> Tho' none that seek the SAVIOUR'S grace
> Shall ever see that dreadful place.[68]

This is an improvement on Watts, whose hell of devils and darkness, fires and chains, was highly conducive to infant nightmares.

The sisters' Sunday school hymns continued in this vein. Hymns of gratitude for instruction, particularly after a sermon, appear as a commendable gesture of juvenile courtesy, and later editions include a charming hymn for the teachers, asking God to bless their labours in training children 'for the sky', and expressing the hope that

> Ne'er may Satan
> Plunder Zion's nursery.[69]

These hymns of Ann and Jane Taylor, known, it is claimed, on four continents, encouraged large numbers of female imitators whose temerity was usually stronger than their talents, although by this time less temerity was required: the increase in the number of magazines and periodicals, especially for young people, enabled women to publish hymns with greater ease and independence than ever before, and the growing tolerance of the Established Church towards hymn-singing caused Anglican ladies to come forward and offer their new contributions towards hymnody for the young.

Anne Houlditch, later Mrs Shepherd (1809–51), a country rector's daughter who wrote religious novels, gave us that ever-popular children's hymn 'Around the Throne of God in Heaven'; Elizabeth King, later Mrs Mills (1805–29), wrote another favourite 'We speak of the realms of the blest'; and Dorothy Ann Thrupp (1779–1847) produced rather commonplace jingles that fortified Zion's nurseries for many years.

Zion's sickrooms too were still struggling against Satan. A steady stream of hymn-writing continued to be poured forth by the 'afflicted' women of the early nineteenth century — the consumptives, the sufferers on sofas, the guilt-ridden, anguished and exhausted souls, devoted to their Bibles, to Young's *Night Thoughts*, and to soothing doses of laudanum.

There were more 'songs in the night';[70] there were more appeals from the feverish and the restless:

> Lord of my life! be with me now
> While sleep forsakes my throbbing brow,
> And in resistless billows lost,
> My weary soul seems tempest tost,

wrote 'Charlotte Elizabeth' [Tonna] (1790–1846), a Norwich rector's daughter, victim of delicate health, deafness, and a disastrous first marriage.[71]

> There were more longings to be dissolved:
> Asleep in Jesus! blessed sleep,
> From which none ever wakes to weep,[72]

cried the Scottish Colonel's wife Mrs Margaret Mackay (1802–87) in a hymn which found great favour among 'weak and weary invalids'.[73]

The Baptist Maria Horsey, later Mrs Saffery (1773–1858), whose hymns show 'the deep gloom of mortal things',[74] knew where to shed her tears:

> Oh! Let the tear of anguish flow,
>   Thou pitying Saviour, on thy breast,
> For want, and weariness, and woe,
>   Are welcome to that gentle rest.[75]

'I weep, but not rebellious tears', confessed Caroline Bowles (1786–1854), whose temperament was of a melancholy cast even before she married the ageing poet Robert Southey and endured the unhappiness of hostile stepchildren and a senile partner.

> As link by link was rent away,
>   My heart wept blood, so sharp the pain,
> But I have lived to count this day
>   That temporal loss eternal gain.
> For all that once detained me here
> Now draws me to a holier sphere.[76]

For Mary Ann Roscoe (1795–1845) there was more fatigue than pain in the process:

> When human hopes and joys depart,
> I give thee, Lord, a contrite heart,
> And, on my weary spirit steal,
> The thoughts that pass all earthly weal.[77]

Caroline Fry, later Mrs Wilson (1787–1846), was a convert from atheism (at twenty she 'hated the very name of God'[78]) and died of consumption after many years of ill health. She tried hard to see the silver lining and the possibilities of 'affliction leading to glory'. In her popular hymn of that name she reminded Christians that

> Full oft the clouds of deepest woe
>   So sweet a message bear,
> Dark though they seem, 'twere hard to find
>   A frown of anger there.
> For loving is the hand that strikes,
>   However keen the smart,
> If sorrow's discipline can chase
>   One evil from the heart.[79]

It is somewhat surprising that these Christian women, mourning and weeping in a vale of tears and enduring 'sorrow's discipline' so painfully, did not have more frequent recourse, in their hymns, if not in their lives, to the Holy Spirit, the acknowledged Comforter. This deficiency was remedied by the Anglican Harriet Auber (1773–1862), who lived in retirement and in 1829 published a volume containing attractive versions of the psalms that became popular in both Britain and America. 'The want of suitable Hymns for public worship has long been seriously felt by members of the Established Church',[80] she wrote in her preface. Fortunately for posterity, she included in the collection some original hymns of her own, one of which, with its gently, controlled, calming effect, enhanced by the beautiful music supplied by the Victorian composer, J. B. Dykes, has become a minor classic among hymns. The first two verses set the tone:

> Our blest Redeemer, ere He breathed
>   His tender last farewell,
> A Guide, a Comforter bequeathed
>   With us to dwell.
>
> He came in semblance of a dove,
>   With sheltering wings outspread,
> The holy balm of peace and love
>   On earth to shed.[81]

Harriet Auber's regret at the dearth of good Anglican hymns was shared by Reginald Heber, who became Bishop of Calcutta and author of the missionary masterpiece, 'From Greenland's Icy

Mountains'. He tried unsuccessfully to get a collection of hymns authorised by Anglican authorities in 1820, and he felt strongly that the Church of England was losing out to the Nonconformists in the matter of sacred song.

Heber's interest in hymn-writing was communicated to his close friend and fellow Anglican author, Mrs Felicia Hemans, née Browne (1794–1835), whose poetic reputation in the 1820s soared to amazing heights.[82] Idol of the reciters, queen of the annuals and albums, friend of Scott and Wordsworth, she was unquestionably the most popular and influential woman poet that England had ever known. Her eager readers appeared to be totally intoxicated by her verse, which mingled romantic melancholy and sensibility with an intense feeling for nature, a love of domesticity (with the accent on affections rather than passions), and a fervent Christian spirit.

Her life was unhappy. A brief broken marriage left her, at the age of twenty-four, with five young sons to bring up, and although rural retirement in Wales with an adored mother (whose husband had also deserted her) provided a measure of consolation and inspiration, her mother's death in 1827 shattered her again. A frail invalid, she continued to enchant the public, her vivacious intelligence, delicate sensitivity and dazzling beauty proving almost as captivating as her writings.

Hemans produced a great deal of religious verse, and, influenced by Heber, popularised what Dr Louis Benson called the 'poetic' or 'literary' hymn,[83] an expression of heightened feelings and vivid imagination, with rich imagery and flowing rhythms, the incense of devotion gaining an added fragrance from the Romantic movement. Her spectacular successes gave new impetus to women's writing, especially within the Anglican communion. She broke with the old convention, still prevalent in some quarters, of Christian women writing anonymously or under pseudonyms and devoting their profits to church funds and charities; she used her own name, and her poetry had to help pay for her sons' education.

Her early hymns were written for children, and sent to America, where one of her most enthusiastic admirers, Professor Andrews Norton of Harvard, father of the scholar Charles Eliot Norton, arranged for their publication in Boston in 1827. A London edition appeared in 1833 and a Dublin one in 1834.

Mrs Hemans followed the Barbauld and Taylor tradition of presenting nature as God's handiwork, as in 'The Nightingale' ('The Child's Evening Hymn'):

When twilight's gray and pensive hour
Brings the low breeze and shuts the flower,
And bids the solitary star
Shine in pale beauty from afar;

When evening's primrose opes to shed
Soft fragrance round her grassy bed;
When glow-worms in the wood-walk light
Their lamp to cheer the traveller's sight;—

At that calm hour, so still, so pale,
Awakes the lonely nightingale,
And from a hermitage of shade,
Fills with her voice the forest glade.[84]

Such hymns as these delighted adults as well as children for many decades, but it was her approach to God through her own personal sorrows that struck deeper chords and made an overwhelming appeal to so many nineteenth-century women. Although not a feminist, Mrs Hemans was particularly concerned with the sufferings of women. She believed that, however educated and liberated women might be, they could rarely detach themselves from their natural affections — from sexual love, from family feelings, and, above all, from their maternal instincts. Women were thus inevitably and hopelessly vulnerable; their best course was to accept it all as a kind of martydom and practise Christian fortitude in the traditional manner.

Her belief in a female destiny closely linked to tragedy and tears, and her own experience of the failure of professional triumphs to secure private happiness, led her to sympathise with such characters as Madame de Stael's poetess Corinne, who found that neither fame nor intellect could compensate for a wounded heart. Weary of her role as *femme célèbre*, Mrs Hemans constantly preached that genius in a woman was so often only a splendid misfortune, and a brilliant career little more than a dazzling degradation.

Echoes of her disillusion resound in her hymn-writing. We hear them in 'The Italian Girl's Hymn to the Virgin' (Catholic devotion to the Mother of God enabling a woman-to-woman supplication):

Oh! 'tis not well, this earthly love's excess!
    On thy weak child is laid
The burden of too deep a tenderness.

*   *   *

I tremble with a sense
Of grief to be; I hear a warning low —
    Sweet mother! call me hence!
This wild idolatry must end in woe.

    The troubled joy of life,
Love's lightning happiness, my soul hath known;
    And, worn with feverish strife,
Would find its wings: take back, take back, thine own![85]

Only in 'A Poet's Dying Hymn', published in *Blackwood's* in 1832, do we detect gleams of serenity and resignation:

That I have loved — that I have known the love
    Which troubles in the soul the tearful springs,
Yet, with a colouring halo from above,
    Tinges and glorifies in all earthly things,
Whate'er its anguish or its woe may be,
Still weaving links for intercourse with thee:
                    I bless thee, O my God![86]

Death was an obsessive theme with Mrs Hemans, her preoccupation with times and places of death, funerals, graves, departed spirits, and prospects of family reunions in heaven made her the poet of the bereaved *par excellence*. Her exquisite lyric and much-loved hymn, 'The Hour of Death', laments the fact that death is an event for all seasons:

    Leaves have their time to fall,
And flowers to wither at the north wind's breath,
    And stars to set — but all,
Thou hast *all* seasons for thine own, O Death![87]

Mrs Hemans's maternal instincts were strong (few poets in our language have written so sensitively on the pleasures and pains of motherhood), and deaths of children, heart-rending in their poignancy and frequency, feature prominently in her verse and form the subject of a fine 'Funeral Hymn' from 'The Burial of an Emigrant's Child in the Forests'):

Where the long reeds quiver,
   Where the pines make moan,
By the forest river,
   Sleeps our babe alone.
England's field-flowers may not deck his grave,
Cypress shadows o'er him darkly wave.

Woods unknown receive him,
   Midst the mighty wild;
Yet with God we leave him,
   Blessed, blessed child!
And our tears gush o'er his lovely dust,
Mournfully, yet still with hearts of trust.[88]

Hemans's own sons all survived to manhood, but her elder sister had died of a 'decline' at eighteen, and it was the memory of this that prompted one of her shortest and best-known hymns 'A Dirge' (from her dramatic poem 'The Siege of Valencia'), which was used for her own memorial tablet in St Ann's Church, Dublin. The mood of buoyant hope and almost brisk confidence was a rare one for her:

Calm on the bosom of thy God,
   Fair spirit! rest thee now!
E'en while with ours thy footsteps trod,
   His seal was on thy brow.

Dust, to its narrow house beneath!
   Soul, to its place on high!
They that have seen thy look in death
   No more may fear to die.[89]

Hemans's care for her dying mother produced the poignant 'Hymn by the Sickbed of a Mother' with its concluding plea:

By thy meek spirit, Thou, of all
   That e'er have mourn'd, the chief —
Thou Saviour! if the *stroke* must fall,
   Hallow this grief![90]

But it was the death of Scott in 1832 that inspired a hymn which became, in an abbreviated form, more popular than any other she had written. The hymn as a cry for help, so dear to women hymn-writers, is used effectively here, and Mrs Hemans's frequently expressed belief and trust in the fatherhood of God (doubtless enhanced by her own and her sons' fatherless condition) give the hymn its spiritual and emotional strength:

> O Father! in that hour,
> When earth all succouring power
>   Shall disavow;
> When spear and shield and crown
> In faintness are cast down —
>   Sustain us, Thou!
>
> By Him who bow'd to take
> The death-cup for our sake,
>   The thorn, the rod;
> From whom the last dismay
> Was not to pass away —
>   Aid us, O God!
>
> Tremblers beside the grave,
> We call on thee to save,
>   Father divine!
> Hear, hear, our suppliant breath!
> Keep us, in life and death,
>   Thine, only thine![91]

Mrs Hemans's death in 1835 in no way diminished the popularity of her hymns and religious verse. For most of the Victorian age she was acclaimed as a kind of literary saint, and her example spurred on countless women to seek employment through the 'consecrated pen'.

The pre-Victorian women hymn-writers had blazed a notable trail, aided by the spirit of ecumenism and romanticism, and the explorations of sensibility and introspection that sprang from the early Evangelical revival. Their work marks a significant break-through in women's writing.

Often they wrote as women to women, about women's concerns and difficulties, their pains and problems, their hopes and aspirations. They wrote, too, as laywomen and not as theologians; it remained for the Oxford Movement to persuade women to widen the scope of their religious and literary activities, and to produce that amazing hybrid, the 'theological romance'.

For the women of the eighteenth and early nineteenth centuries a simpler medium sufficed, and hymn-writing supplied a praiseworthy vocation that even Anglican fathers, husbands and clerics came to accept and encourage, an opportunity for women to find a voice in religious matters and to use their talents in the service of God and in the advancement of humanity towards ideals of Christian perfection.

Notes

1. 'Pastora to Captain Fido on his Last Epistle', in J. Brereton, *Poems* (London, 1744), p. 272.
2. A Lady [Lady Mary Chudleigh], *The Ladies Defence; or, the Bride-woman's Counsellor Answer'd* (London, 1701), p. 14.
3. See Eliot's *Adam Bede*, Ch. 7, 'A Vocation'.
4. Relevant works on hymns and hymn-writers include: J. Miller, *Our Hymns: Their Authors and Origin* (London, 1865); J. Julian, *A Dictionary of Hymnology* (London, 1892): L. F. Benson, *The English Hymn* (New York, 1915); C. S. Phillips, *Hymnody Past and Present* (London, 1931); C. H. Phillips, *The Singing Church* (London and Oxford, 1945; rev. edn. 1979); E. Routley, *Hymns and Human Life* (London, 1952): M. Frost (ed.), *Historical Companion to Hymns Ancient and Modern* (London, 1962).
5. E. Young, *Love of Fame, the Universal Passion* (London, 1725–8), Satire V, 'On Women', lines 385–8.
6. 'The Love of the Spirit', in A. Dutton, *A Narration on the Wonders of Grace* (London, 1734), p. 78.
7. E. Routley, *Hymns and Human Life* (London, 1952), p. 206.
8. Preface (signed J. R. B.) to *Hymns by Anne Steele* (London, 1967), p. xxi.
9. J. Sheppard, 'Memoir', in Anne Steele, *Hymns, Psalms and Poems* (London, 1863), p. xii.
10. A. R. Collinson, *Memoir of Mrs. Agnes Bulmer* (London, 1837), p. 4.
11. 'Christ Dying and Rising', in Theodosia [Anne Steele], *Poems on Subjects Chiefly Devotional*, 2 vols (London, 1760), I:184.
12. 'Jesus the Best Beloved', ibid., p. 163.
13. 'Life and Safety in Christ Alone', ibid., p. 55.
14. 'Meditating on the Redeemer's Sufferings', ibid., p. 181.
15. 'Christ the Supreme Beauty', ibid., p. 155.
16. 'Redeeming Love', ibid., p. 10.
17. 'Meditating on the Redeemer's Sufferings', ibid., p. 181.
18. 'The Heavenly Guest', ibid., p. 67.
19. 'On a Stormy Night', ibid., p. 24.
20. 'Desiring a Taste of Real Joy', ibid., p. 112.
21. 'The Favour of God the Only Satisfying Good', ibid., p. 30.
22. 'Searching after Happiness', ibid., p. 25. (Some versions have 'seeking'.)
23. 'The Excellency of the Holy Scriptures', ibid., p. 135.

24. 'On Sight of a Corpse', in [C. Wesley], *Funeral Hymns*, 1st Series (London, 1746), p. 7.

25. 'A Funeral Hymn', published in her son Martin Madan's *Collection of Poems and Hymns* (London, 1763), p. 177.

26. Also called 'A Funeral Hymn', in *Poems on Subjects Chiefly Devotional*, I:74.

27. 'Reflection on a Winter Evening', ibid., II:121.

28. 'Trust in God under the various Calamities of Life', Hymn 238 (signed 'S'), in J. Ash and C. Evans (eds), *A Collection of Hymns, adapted to Public Worship* (Bristol, 1769), p. 234.

29. Hymn 92, in *Songs in the Night; by a Young Woman Under Heavy Afflictions* [Susanna Harrison], 4th edn (Ipswich, 1788), p. 91.

30. Hymn 89, 'Longing to be Dissolved', ibid., p. 87.

31. 'The True Heroes: or the Noble Army of Martyrs', in H. More, *Poetical Works* (London, 1835), p. 485.

32. *The Works of Anna Laetitia Barbauld, with a Memoir by Lucy Aikin*, 2 vols (London, 1825), I:vii. See also C. L. Balfour, *A Sketch of Mrs. Barbauld* (London, 1854); and B. Rodgers, *Georgian Chronicle* (London, 1958).

33. [Mrs. A. L. Barbauld], *Devotional Pieces Compiled from the Psalms and the Book of Job: To which are Prefixed, Thoughts on the Devotional Taste, on Sects and on Establishments* (London, 1775), p. 49.

34. Ibid., p. 23.

35. Ibid., p. 4.

36. It even became prescribed reading for theological students. See *The Christianity of Stoicism* (Carmarthen, 1818), by the Bishop of St David's [Thomas Burgess].

37. Hymn IV, in A. L. Aikin, *Poems* (London, 1773), p. 121.

38. 'Pious Friendship', in *The Works of Anna Laetitia Barbauld*, I:333.

39. Mrs Barbauld, *Hymns in Prose for Children* (23rd edn, London, 1820), pp. v–vi.

40. Ibid., p. vi.

41. Ibid., p. 59.

42. 'A Sunday Evening's Hymn in Sickness', in E. Daye, *Poems on Various Occasions* (Liverpool, 1798), p. 245.

43. 'Song in the Night', in *Original Poems, on Various Occasions by a Lady* [M. F.C. Madan] (London, 1792), p. 107.

44. 'To Sensibility', in H. M. Williams, *Poems* (London, 1786), p. 21.

45. 'A Hymn', ibid., p. 99.

46. 'A Sunday Evening's Hymn in Sickness', in Daye, *Poems*, p. 245.

47. 'The Consolation', in [Madan], *Original Poems*, p. 21.

48. 'An Hymn', in M. de Fleury, *Divine Poems and Essays on Various Subjects* (London, 1791), p. 95.

49. 'The Soul', in [Madan], *Original Poems*, p. 30.

50. 'Future Happiness. A Support under Afflictions', in A. Flowerdew, *Poems on Moral and Religious Subjects* (London, 1803), p. 93.

51. H. Moore, *The Life of Mrs. Mary Fletcher, of Madeley* (Birmingham, 1817), p. xxiiii.

52. J. Wesley, *An Extract of the Life of Madam Guion* (London, 1776), preface, p. vii.

53. 'The Slumbering Professor Roused', in *Poems, Inscribed to the Missionary Society by their Friend* [Mrs Voke] (Southampton, 1796), p. 47. (Dr Julian mistakenly calls her Mrs Vokes.)

54. 'Hymn, sung by the Charity-Children, Walsall', in Mrs Darwall, *Poems on Several Occasions* (Walsall, 1794), p. 117. Mrs Darwall's husband, an Anglican

vicar, was a lively exception to the rule of apathy: he composed hymns and campaigned for a faster style of singing in church.

55. The Authors of 'Original Poems', 'Rhymes for the Nursery', etc. [A. and J. Taylor], *Hymns for Infant Minds* (London, 1808), Advertisement to the 1st edition, p. v.

56. Essay on 'Mirth and Cheerfulness', in *The Contributions of Q.Q. to a periodical work, by the late Jane Taylor*, 2 vols (London, 1824), I:279.

57. J. Gilbert (ed.), *Autobiography and Other Memorials of Mrs. Gilbert (formerly Ann Taylor)* (London, 1874), p. 10.

58. Several Young Persons [A. and J. Taylor and others], *Original Poems for Infant Minds* (London, 1804), preface, p. iii.

59. Jane and Anne [*sic*] Taylor, *Meddlesome Matty and Other Poems for Infant Minds*, with an introduction by Edith Sitwell (London, 1925), pp. xi–xii.

60. *Hymns for Infant Minds*, Advertisement to the 1st edition, p. v. Subsequent references are to the 9th edition (London, 1817).

61. 'A Child's Hymn of Praise' (by Ann), ibid., p. 1.

62. 'Thou God, Seest Me' (by Ann), ibid., p. 33.

63. 'Time and Eternity' (by Ann), ibid., p. 50.

64. 'Against Anger and Impatience' (by Jane), ibid., p. 24.

65. 'About Dying' (by Ann), ibid., p. 32.

66. 'To a Little Sister on her Birth-day' (by Ann), ibid., p. 35.

67. Ibid., p. 36.

68. 'Upon Death' (by Ann), ibid., p. 79.

69. 'A Public Hymn for the Teachers', in A. and J. Taylor, *Original Hymns for Sunday Schools* (stereotype edn, London, *c.* 1822), p. 35.

70. By Agnes Bulmer (1775–1837).

71. 'Thoughts at Night', in Charlotte Elizabeth, *Osric: A Missionary Tale; with the Garden and Other Poems* (Dublin, 1825), p. 49. Her full name was Charlotte Elizabeth Browne, and she was married first to Captain George Phelan and then to the Rev. Lewis Tonna. Charlotte Elizabeth, *Personal Recollections* (London, 1841); L. Balfour, *A Sketch of Charlotte Elizabeth* (London, 1854).

72. 'Asleep in Jesus', sometimes called 'Sleeping in Jesus', first published in *The Amethyst*, 1832.

73. Mrs Mackay, *Thoughts Redeemed; or, Lays of Leisure Hours* (Edinburgh, 1854), preface, p. iii.

74. 'Thought before Sunset', later called 'Evening Hymn', in M. G. Saffery, *Poems on Sacred Subjects* (London, 1834), p. 184.

75. Untitled hymn, ibid., p. 139. Sometimes called 'Silent Prayer'.

76. 'I Weep, but not Rebellious Tears', later called 'For the Aged', in C. B. Southey, *Poetical Works* (Edinburgh and London, 1867), p. 285. The Victorians appreciated this even more than the celebrated 'Mariner's Hymn'.

77. 'In Trouble and Affliction', in [M. A. Roscoe], *Poems for Youth* (London, 1820), p. 48.

78. T. S. Dickson, *Caroline Fry, A Story of Grace* (London, 1908), p. 6.

79. C. Fry, *Poetical Catechism* (London, 1821), p. 22.

80. H. Auber, *The Spirit of the Psalms* (London, 1829), preface, p. ix.

81. Ibid., p. 147.

82. There is some controversy about the year of her birth. Her sister gives it as 1793, but her brothers favour 1794; some early verse, meticulously dated, offers further evidence for 1794. On her life, see *The Works of Mrs. Hemans; with a Memoir of her Life, by her Sister* [Harriet Hughes], 7 vols (Edinburgh and London, 1839); H. F. Chorley, *Memorials of Mrs. Hemans* (London, 1836); and P. Trinder, *Mrs. Hemans* (Cardiff, 1984).

83. Benson, *The English Hymn*, p. 437.

84. 'The Child's Evening Hymn', in F. Hemans, *Poems* (Edinburgh and London, 1849), pp. 532–3.

85. 'The Italian Girl's Hymn to the Virgin', ibid., p. 449.

86. 'A Poet's Dying Hymn', ibid., p. 584.

87. 'The Hour of Death', ibid., p. 375.

88. 'The Burial of an Emigrant's Child in the Forests', ibid., p. 581.

89. 'The Siege of Valencia', ibid., p. 290.

90. 'Hymn by the Sickbed of a Mother', ibid., p. 487.

91. 'The Funeral Day of Sir Walter Scott', ibid., p. 586.

Chapter 3

Elizabeth Heyrick: Radical Quaker

Kenneth Corfield

In 1823 the Society for the Mitigation and Gradual Abolition of Slavery was formed in London, and in the next few years numerous local societies were established by like-minded men in towns throughout England. In 1825 three women's anti-slavery societies were formed, at Birmingham, Sheffield and at Calne in Wiltshire; by the end of the decade there were over forty others.[1] The first part of this essay deals with the efforts that English women made in the abolitionist cause, and with the work of one woman in particular, the Leicester Quaker Elizabeth Heyrick, an interesting but neglected figure. She is mentioned in several accounts of the abolitionist movement as the author of a bold pamphlet, *Immediate not Gradual Abolition of Slavery* (1824), which criticised the main Society's more cautious and limited policy. But historians have paid less attention to the way she sustained her demands. She wrote four pamphlets demanding immediate emancipation for the slaves in 1824 alone, and three more by 1828; and while she was not the only advocate of an immediate solution, she was the most insistent.[2] It has also gone unnoticed how other women adopted a similarly radical position and expressed their views independently of the male anti-slavery societies whose mere 'auxiliaries' they were supposed to be. A fuller survey of Elizabeth Heyrick's abolitionist ideas and of the women who shared them should therefore help to understand the emergence of immediatism in anti-slavery thought, and provide further opportunity to discuss the importance and implications of women's anti-slavery work in general. Such activity was one of the few avenues open to women of conscience in early nineteenth-century society, but Heyrick did not confine herself either to attacking slavery or to the charitable concerns often undertaken by women of her religious persuasion or well-to-do background. Between 1815 and 1830 she wrote over twenty

41

pamphlets, putting forward radical opinions on various social, economic and political subjects.[3] Heyrick's ideas are discussed in the second part of the essay.

I

Elizabeth Heyrick was born in December 1769, and was the eldest daughter of John and Elizabeth Coltman. Her father and brothers were wealthy manufacturers in the Leicester hosiery trade, and both her parents pursued genteel literary and cultural interests. By religion, they were Dissenters. Visitors to the house included John Wesley, who once preached a sermon there, and Dr Priestley. Mr Coltman senior was described as 'a warm friend' to religious and civil liberty, and among the family's collection of curiosities were the autographs of Tom Paine and Franklin, and Washington's greatcoat, which a more distant relative had been given while fighting for the Americans in the war of independence.[4]

When Elizabeth married John Heyrick, a relation of the Macaulay family, in 1789 she was already disposed by her own upbringing to share their anti-slavery views.[5] There are also early signs that she had broader sympathies: in 1769 her brother wrote to her saying that he shared her concern for negro slaves, 'however we may disagree respecting the freedom of white men'.[6] The factor which was to be most influential in determining the future course of her life was the sudden death of her husband in 1797. Their marriage had been passionate but stormy. 'How they lived together I know not,' wrote a friend, 'it was always either my plague or my darling.'[7] Mr Heyrick was a possessive husband and was 'so tenacious of her affections' that he 'secluded her from all society' and forbade her to see even her parents.[8] Yet she was devastated by his death and underwent a spiritual crisis which saw her resolve to give up 'all ungodly lusts . . . to like anything was an immediate reason for its being sacrificed'.[9] It was this resolve that led her to become a Quaker, in 1798 or 1799, and to take up philanthropic and, later, anti-slavery activity.

Heyrick began her anti-slavery work in 1824 when, with her friend Susannah Watts, she canvassed the population of Leicester against the use of slave-grown sugar. In the same year she wrote four tracts advocating the boycott of West Indian produce as the 'certain' means of effecting the immediate abolition of slavery, and until her death in 1831 this remained her greatest goal, both as a propagandist and in her capacity as a district treasurer for the Birmingham female anti-slavery society. As a Quaker Heyrick saw slavery as an offence against the laws of God, and so the refusal of its products provided not only a test of anti-slavery sentiment but a means whereby people impatient with the failure of gradualist attempts to improve the slaves' conditions could hope to destroy the evil system at a stroke.[10] This was a weapon which the poorer classes were best fitted to wield, she maintained, not only because the rich were too few and too neglectful of their duty to abolish slavery in this way, but because the poor 'have themselves tasted of the cup of adversity'.[11] Looking to the exertion of such individual virtue, Heyrick criticised the Anti-Slavery Society's attempts to secure a revision of the protective import tariffs that made free-grown East Indian sugar dearer than the West Indian variety; unrealistically, she wanted people to substitute it for slave-grown sugar regardless of cost and saw 'nothing Utopian' in expecting them to do so 'were East India double the price'.[12] Indeed she welcomed the sacrifice that this involved. Christianity could not be professed cheaply, she wrote, and 'heroic and painful acts' were necessary in order to show the people's capacity to be moved by high moral considerations rather than by self-interest, to 'separate the doers from the mere hearers of the word'.[13] As for the timing of abolition, Heyrick argued that the slaveholders' stubborn opposition even to gradual reforms had removed any reason to treat them in a conciliatory way, and that delay would only worsen the slaves' condition since, with the ultimate prospect of emancipation hanging over them, the owners would exploit their property more harshly meanwhile.[14]

But more essentially Heyrick felt it was the fundamental sinfulness of slavery that demanded it be crushed at once. Gradual emancipation was 'the very master-piece of satanic policy', she insisted.[15] Righteousness demanded no compromise with evil, and there must be 'no lukewarm propositions of mercy . . . no mutilated offerings on the altar of duty'.[16] Heyrick none the less recognised that almost all abolitionists supported a gradualist policy, and she criticised them for it, denying Henry Brougham's view that the slaves were not yet fit for freedom.[17] In 1826 Heyrick and another abolitionist, James Stephen, both called on electors to support parliamentary candidates who would pledge themselves to vote for emancipation, but she went beyond him in wanting that pledge to be for the immediate termination rather than the mitigation of slavery.[18] She was equally emphatic about denying slaveholders' claims to compensation for their slaves, and maintained that it was the slaves themselves who should be compensated.[19] It went with this kind of moral absolutism that Heyrick gave no thought to any system of apprenticeship, and apparently never considered details of the slaves' future position once they were freed. Emancipation would be a simple act of righteousness, and it was not necessary to look beyond it.

Among historians of the abolitionist movement, David Brion Davis has described Heyrick's advocacy of immediate emancipation in 1824, but sees the shift from gradualism occurring around 1830–1 when, he writes, the Society 'took its cue from men like [James] Stephen, [Andrew] Thomson, and Joseph Sturge'.[20] Howard Temperley and Betty Fladeland have similarly observed that the movement acquired a new militancy at that time.[21] It is certainly true that in spite of Heyrick's efforts between 1824 and 1828 the male abolitionist leaders adhered to their gradualist policy. This was what Buxton, Clarkson, Zachary Macaulay and Wilberforce all wanted. 'No man can wish . . . for immediate emancipation; it can only be done gradually,' declared William Allen,[22] while James Cropper, reputedly embarrassed by Heyrick's pamphlets, was still looking in 1829 to a plan for freeing the slaves in thirty years.[23] 'The Abolitionists . . . almost universally have given up in hopeless despair the present existing race of slaves as unfit subjects for general emancipation,' wrote another campaigner in 1827.[24] By contrast, there was an identifiable group of female abolitionists who followed Heyrick's lead and demanded immediate freedom for the slaves before their male counterparts did. Davis rightly suggests that the 'decline of faith in gradualism' was related to support for the boycott of slave-grown goods in the 1820s;[25] in fact, it was exactly those women who most enthusiastically encouraged the sugar boycott who also demanded immediate abolition, while their male leaders were more cautious about the timing of emancipation and preferred other means of achieving it. Thus in Sheffield, where the female anti-slavery society had 'principally directed' its operations to recommending the use of free-grown sugar, 'immediate and total' abolition was called for in the Society's annual report for 1826.[26] In February 1827 the committee bought and distributed 2,000 copies of Heyrick's *No British Slavery* containing the same message.[27] Suggestions that the sugar boycott would be ineffective and immediate emancipation disastrous were alike refuted by the Sheffield women, and they regretted the objections heard from respected male abolitionists who 'shrank back' from seeking an immediate solution.[28] They were, they said, reluctant to criticise those whom they would normally regard with humility, but in this instance, 'We ought to obey God rather than man . . . on principles like these the simple need not fear to confront the sage, nor a female society to take their stand against the united wisdom of the world'.[29] Many of the Sheffield female society's members, like its treasurer Mary Rawson, had husbands or brothers in the separate men's society, most of whom supported only gradual emancipation. The philanthropist Samuel Roberts recalled that at an early meeting of the society he 'stood alone' in advocating immediate action, and although he was soon joined by James Montgomery he admitted that in 1828 their views still put them in a minority.[30] But the women reiterated their view that abolition must take place 'without reserve, without limitation, without delay'.[31]

Probably the first female anti-slavery association to take up Heyrick's radical position was the one based on Salisbury and Calne in Wiltshire. Since 1825 it had organised a vigorous campaign in the county against slave-grown goods, stating that slavery could only be ended by the refusal of these 'bloodstained articles'.[32] Its members distributed copies of Heyrick's pamphlets and complained at the colonies' resistance to reforms. They dismissed petitioning Parliament as 'a wholly fruitless task', criticised abolitionists who were satisfied with a partial mitigation of slavery, and condemned gradualism as 'continued rebellion against God'.[33] Here too the women were ahead of local, as well as national, male abolitionist opinion. Their first call for immediate emancipation came in 1825 in a 'Letter to a Friend', written by the association's Quaker founder, Mrs Martha Gundry; its recipient might well have been Elizabeth Heyrick, for she quoted from it in a tract of 1826.[34] By comparison, meetings of male anti-slavery societies in Salisbury, Calne, Melksham, Marlborough, Warminster, Bath and Bristol during February 1826 all took the 'melioration' and 'ultimate extinction' of slavery as their aims, and emphasised 'that they wish these things to be *gradually* accomplished'.[35] And the women's association in Wiltshire was quite proud to distinguish its views from more cautious ones:

Men may propose only gradually to abolish the worst of crimes, and only mitigate the most cruel bondage, [wrote Mrs Gundry] 'but why should we countenance such enormities? . . . we must not talk of gradually abolishing murder, licentiousness, cruelty, tyranny . . . I trust no Ladies' Association will ever be formed with such words attached to it.'[36]

In fact, the female society set up at Birmingham in 1825 did call for the 'amelioration' of slavery in successive annual reports, but it too was demanding immediate emancipation in April 1830, four months before the men's auxiliary society in Birmingham adopted the principle, and was even threatening to withhold funds from the main Anti-Slavery Society pending *its* support for the idea.[37] The women were 'anxious not to compromise their own principles, nor . . . sanction anything which falls short of Right,' wrote their secretary Lucy Townsend, and would 'appropriate £50 to the London Gentleman's Anti-Slavery Society when they are willing to give up the word "gradual" in their title and not to recur [*sic*] in any terms of approbation to the Resolutions of . . . 1823, which . . . would only serve to legalize Iniquity'.[38] Their protest did not have to last very long, for on 15 May 1830 an amendment in favour of immediate emancipation was carried at a meeting of the Anti-Slavery Society in London, and in July the Society's secretary Thomas Pringle wrote to thank the Birmingham women for their donation of £50.[39] Since neither set of minutes gives any indication as to whether the women's resolution was discussed by the London committee, it cannot be established that their protest had any definite effect, but the fact that such action was considered is testimony to their determination and independence. As for women in Heyrick's native Leicester, they formed a district branch of the Birmingham female society and left no separate record of their opinions, though Heyrick's strong views were certainly not shared by the men's anti-slavery society in Leicester, with her brother and brother-in-law among its officers. The society's only extant report (1824) is an early one, but its statement that 'we should deprecate an immediate emancipation almost as much as the planters themselves' seems a commitment to caution that would be slow to change.[40]

By 1831 there were at least forty-seven female anti-slavery associations in Britain.[41] In Birmingham, Sheffield and Wiltshire women had adopted a stance that put them, by varying degrees, ahead of local male abolitionists and of the nationally-known leaders of the movement. How many of the other female societies held these radical ideas could be shown if more of their reports and minute-books came to light, but by 1829 women were demonstrably active in promoting sugar boycotts at Worcester, Colchester, London, Peckham and Edinburgh;[42] since this kind of protest usually meant dissatisfaction with gradualist notions, it might be reasoned that these societies, too, shared Heyrick's arguments. At any rate, women's early support for immediate abolition of slavery was clearly recognised by Charles Orpen, director of the Hibernian Negro's Friend Society in Dublin. His society, he affirmed in 1831, stood for 'full, free, instantaneous, total, unconditional emancipation'; by comparison, English abolitionists had not gone sufficiently far. 'But,' he added, 'many of the Ladies' Associations, in England, are in great measure free from these censures.'[43] Orpen was in touch with the female societies in Birmingham and Calne, and his praise for them and criticism of the 'usual policy of the Gentlemen's Anti-Slavery Societies' also took in the 'grand moral principle' of refusing slave produce, which he charged the latter with neglecting. The women, he said, had 'taken the lead in just general principles'.[44]

How was women's support for immediate abolition regarded by male anti-slavery leaders in England? Might it have influenced some eventually to adopt the same position? A eulogistic survey of Elizabeth Heyrick's life written in 1862 suggested vaguely that her pamphlets were 'the means of converting some who had great influence in high places to the truth and justice of her views'.[45] These might have included George Stephen, who in 1834 recommended her first tract as still relevant to the continuing campaign against apprenticeship in the West Indies.[46] Her ideas might also have persuaded Joseph Sturge, who became privately converted to immediate emancipation earlier than most and who later praised Heyrick for being first to expose the 'delusion' of a gradual solution.[47] But Sturge also stated that Heyrick's pamphlets had little effect at first, except to make her regarded as 'an amiable enthusiast and visionary'; other abolitionists, he suggested, took a less kind view and 'despised' her.[48] The Anti-Slavery Committee obtained twelve copies of her *Immediate not Gradual Abolition of Slavery* in 1824 '[for] any member who may apply for them', and there is some evidence that the committee discussed her draft of a later work, for which Macaulay took her to task. He apparently had thought she 'acquiesced in his views' and would change her pamphlet accordingly.[49] But Heyrick's arguments were repeated unchanged in subsequent pamphlets; they were clearly too strong for the Society, and later abolitionist journals which recalled her ideas with approval testified to the hostility she sometimes met. She was 'considered a fanatic' said *The Slave*, 'and stigmatized even by faithful abolitionists as a woman of one idea, and that idea . . . incorrect and injudicious'.[50] Heyrick was mentioned in very few abolitionists' memoirs or accounts of the movement, the *Anti-Slavery Reporter* mentioned her only once, and then briefly, during the 1820s,[51] and neither that journal nor the Society's committee noticed her death in 1831. As for the female societies that shared her ideas, their meetings were not described at any length in the *Reporter*, their opinions were not recorded there, and their annual reports were not discussed by the committee. When Charles Orpen pointed out the more advanced views of 'many of the Ladies' Associations in England', the committee merely made its standard note that 'letters from Dr. Orpen of Dublin were read and disposed of'.[52]

Heyrick's memory was not eclipsed completely: after the Emancipation Act became law a woman in Leicester recalled that she was celebrated there in 1834 as 'the undaunted, persevering, and eloquent advocate' of immediate abolition, and that Heyrick's and her friend Susannah Watts's names 'were illuminated in the town'.[53] But overall the evidence suggests that female abolitionists had little influence in persuading men to shift their ground and press for immediate emancipation; and it would be unwise to take Daniel O'Connell's 1833 pronouncement that 'the women of England have led the way . . . at your command we have done our duty and slavery is at an end' as anything but a rhetorical flourish.[54] David Brion Davis was probably nearer the truth when he wrote that in moving towards 'immediatism' the Anti-Slavery Society 'took its cue' around 1830 from men like Stephen, Thomson, and Sturge. In doing so, however, the Society clearly ignored views that some female abolitionists had held for several years.

In contrast to the hostility or indifference of contemporary male abolitionists in England, Heyrick's views were more warmly remembered by other women. Her 'spirit-stirring appeals' were described in 1847 by anti-slavery women in Birmingham.[55] Her example was celebrated by the Newcastle Quaker Anna Richardson, who in the 1840s and 50s pursued the free-produce cause in her journal *The Slave* with something of Heyrick's own earlier passion, and in 1853 an address presented to Harriet Beecher Stowe from women in Surrey recalled Heyrick as the first to propose immediate abolition of slavery.[56] Women also wrote the two known accounts of her life, in 1862 and 1895.[57] As well, Heyrick's writings were better received by abolitionists in the United States than in England. *Immediate not Gradual Abolition of Slavery* was reprinted in its first American edition before the end of 1824. It made an instant impression on Benjamin Lundy, who 'at once adopted its views' and serialised the pamphlet in his journal *Genius* during 1826 and 1827.[58] He particularly enjoyed Heyrick's forthright language, so 'unlike the milk-and-water style of some writers on this side of the Atlantic'.[59] William Lloyd Garrison was another who praised her work, while the black abolitionist Frederick Douglass described her as 'the woman to whom I owe everything'; and William Jay atrributed his own conversion to the anti-slavery cause to her writings.[60] But most interestingly, Heyrick was an example to the American abolitionist and feminist Lucretia Mott, and this added to the latter's resentment at women being excluded as delegates from the World's Anti-Slavery Convention in London in 1840; before the convention began she attended an informal gathering at which immediate emancipation was discussed and 'gave them to understand that this originating with E. Heyrick, — a woman, when the convention should be held in America we should not contemplate the exclusion of women'.[61]

For many observers, however, Heyrick's bold work flew in the face of standard notions of female capacity. Because she had the courage to overstep the boundary lines restricting her sex, wrote a (female) friend, she was 'in danger of gaining the epithet "masculine" . . .'[62] The 'vigorous style' of her *Immediate not Gradual Abolition of Slavery* gave the impression that it 'emanated from one of the other sex', and it was quoted in the House of Commons 'as the work of a gentleman'.[63] The Bristol Quaker Anthony Swain, who knew that Heyrick was the author, described the pamphlets' 'powerful . . . cogent, superior style' and asked, 'is it possible that any woman could write in that manner?'[64] And the critical reviewer of her anonymously published *No British Slavery*, which recommended a boycott of slave-grown sugar, attacked it in *John Bull* in 1824 for being the disguised work of an East India merchant, declaring that 'nothing was wanting but the fellow's name and number of his shop'.[65] Indeed, *all* of women's anti-slavery work was likely to evoke uneasiness from male observers, even close colleagues in the struggle. William Wilberforce was characteristically worried by it, telling Macaulay that 'for ladies to meet, to publish, to go from house to house stirring up petitions' were things unsuited to the female character 'as delineated in Scripture'.[66] Other men, however, would have agreed with William Allen that women were at least well fitted for the task of keeping the nation's homes and tea-tables clear of slave-grown goods.[67] In general, their anti-slavery efforts drew fulsome praise from male abolitionists. Daniel O'Connell's congratulations have already been quoted, and George Stephen gave female societies a similarly glowing report: 'they did everything,' he wrote in 1834, 'they formed the cement of the whole Antislavery building'.[68] It is difficult, though, not to see such praise as at least faintly patronising, and that was probably the tone that most commonly described men's reactions to women's efforts. Few men were willing to go beyond that. Few supported women's claim to be admitted as delegates to the Anti-Slavery Convention in 1840 — O'Connell was a hesitant exception — and most preferred them to sit quietly in the upstairs gallery. And George Stephen's lavish praise of women's activity can be set against more negative comments elsewhere in his letters. The female societies, he wrote in October 1830, were sometimes 'inactive and inefficient'.[69] In the following month he left a successful meeting with male abolitionists at Oakham and went on to Leicester where, he said somewhat dismissively, 'our meeting was quite of a different character . . . it was only an assembly of about 150 Ladies of the place . . . so I told my usual tale of horror'.[70]

How did women who undertook anti-slavery work respond to criticism, and how did they view their work themselves? Heyrick's friend Susannah Watts wrote in verse to answer a charge that 'ladies who were zealous' in the abolitionist cause 'were brazen-faced': they had 'To blunt the shafts of manly wit, / To ward off censure's galling hit, / And keep reproach aloof', she said, and they needed to be made of 'invulnerable brass'.[71] Watts was none the less quite clear that women who thus involved themselves were 'peculiarly impelled . . . to step out of their usual sphere,'[72] and such apologies for their efforts were heard regularly. Women were repeatedly at pains to describe their anti-slavery work as proof that even the 'weak and feeble' of the world could be God's chosen instruments of justice, and they often belittled their work and devalued its possible influence. 'As a Female Anti-Slavery Association we are sensible of the little we can do to promote this great cause,' declared the Sheffield Ladies' Anti-Slavery Society in 1829.[73] Calls for more women to join the societies reassured potential supporters that there was 'nothing presumptuous' about their efforts and maintained that anti-slavery work was a religious and not a political question,[74] while the things that often attracted women to the cause and the kind of tasks they undertook were alike consistent with their acceptance of a confined social role. Slavery damaged home and family life, and female societies often had the protection of women and child slaves as their special concern, while their campaign against slave-grown goods recommended itself as a 'quiet' and 'unpolitical' task to which women were suited by their 'softer' domestic virtues.[75] And although women in at least three anti-slavery societies expressed radical ideas about abolition and were quite conscious of taking an independent stance ahead of male abolitionist opinion, this implied no similarly radical attitude to the social or political position of their own sex. Women in Sheffield were apologetic and deferential in their criticism of men who sought a gradual solution, and although in Calne they were prouder to distinguish their more advanced ideas, women who held these views always stressed that they were simply 'obeying God's command', for to tolerate slavery was to displease Him. At Calne the ladies who criticised gradualism and organised a country-wide boycott of slave produce were still anxious about 'preserving the delicacy of the female character'.[76] The Birmingham female society, barely qualifying similar opinions, thought that women could use their influence 'in the minor departments (as they are usually called) of household affairs' to keep West Indian sugar out of their homes.[77] Such sentiments were still being expressed during the later free labour campaign of the 1840s and 50s: it offered an exception to the rule, women in Manchester felt, that when faced by evil 'man must work and woman must weep'.[78] And even Elizabeth Heyrick felt this way, offering apologies for the 'feeble efforts' of women, while expressing the belief that 'the great purposes of infinite wisdom are often accomplished through weak instruments'.[79]

There were certainly some women, like Anne Knight and Elizabeth Pease, whose advocacy of freedom for slaves led them on to claims for their own emancipation, and the feminist activity of abolitionists in the United States is particularly well known.[80] But just how typical this was of female abolitionists in England remains open to argument. The historian Sheila Rowbotham has written that the connection with feminism 'has probably been greatly underestimated',[81] but the views held by the women in the anti-slavery societies examined here do little to strengthen that suggestion, at least in so far as they made no explicit claims for their sex's rights. On the other hand, the tasks of fund-raising, petitioning and public canvassing that women undertook in the course of their anti-slavery work gave them an experience of business and committee procedures that they might not otherwise have learned in nineteenth-century England. By performing duties and expressing ideas which did not take them into any exclusively male domain some women acquired a greater sense of self-confidence, too — Martha Gundry of Calne, for example, with her letter of 1825, and Mary Rawson of Sheffield, who in 1838 resisted attempts by the men's society to interfere with the female society's proceedings. The women would welcome assistance, she wrote, 'from fellow-labourers in the same important cause' but wished 'respectfully, but most distinctly, to remind the Gentlemen's Committee that they represent an entirely independent Society'.[82] The clearest such expression of confidence in the performance of a 'female mission' that would not infringe on male preserves was made by Elizabeth Heyrick. She felt that women were 'happily excluded . . . from the turmoils of ambition . . . and the cares of legislation', yet could strongly influence public opinion and practice 'without violating that retiring delicacy which constitutes one of their loveliest ornaments'.[83] The beginnings of the struggle against slavery had required qualities 'peculiar to the stronger sex', but to continue it in the face of the public apathy of the time, she wrote in 1828, and to 'array against slavery a general system of decisive practical discouragement' was 'indispensably' the special work of women.[84]

II

Elizabeth Heyrick herself was much more than an abolitionist. She was said to be interested in 'every subject that had the remotest relation to the cause of social and political liberty', and the woman who wrote this sketch of her life in 1862 also described her as 'one of the noblest pioneers of social liberty, not only for her own sex, but for mankind at large'.[85] How far this claim is supported by the evidence of Heyrick's own writings is the question which motivates the second part of this essay, but she was certainly more than the 'woman of one idea' of contemporary comment. She wrote at least twenty-one pamphlets, among them a series of tracts on social, economic and political matters, expressing ideas that few contemporaries, and fewer historians, have noticed she possessed.

Until 1817 Heyrick had been engaged only in the kind of philanthropic concerns that Quaker women habitually undertook. She had established a school, campaigned against cruelty to animals, visited prisons, and advocated penal reform. Some of her actions were unusual — she stopped a bull-baiting contest at Bonsall in Derbyshire by buying the doomed animal and having it led to safety, and she spent summers living in a shepherd's cottage outside Leicester eating only potatoes in order to see how Irish migrant labourers managed.[86] But the causes she took up at first were not particularly surprising. Her writings before 1817 comprised two tracts on bull-baiting and four general appeals to Christian moral principles.[87] In these, however, she expressed a fundamental sense of righteousness that determined her later attacks on slavery and made her criticise much of the social and political system in Britain as well. It was also through her interest in penal reform that she came to consider the plight of the poor at home, and while this was a road which many Quakers took, Heyrick's criticisms, and some of her solutions, went unusually far.

In pamphlets published in 1817 and 1819 Heyrick's attention shifted from the local sufferings of the Leicester framework-knitters to the condition of the working class in the country as a whole.[88] She insisted that their poverty was not accidental but was caused by the greed of the rich, whom she accused of 'grinding the faces of the poor'.[89] It was 'the spirit of the slave trade' that had reduced them to their present state, and she repeatedly made the point that West Indian slavery and the condition of the English poor alike were due to the same 'sordid passion', a 'LUST OF WEALTH'.[90] She saw the vices of the poor as the result rather than the cause of their sufferings, attacking the prison system for making worse criminals out of offenders drawn to steal by hardship, and condemning the hypocrisy of hanging a man for petty theft 'whilst robberies en masse which impoverish . . . millions' went unpunished.[91] The government, she wrote, was headed by 'a prime minister of Mammon' responsible for greater devastation than 'even the plains of Waterloo' displayed.[92] It protected the interests of the rich with Corn Laws and defended even their pleasures with Game Laws, while the poor were 'wrung to the very dregs'; it was quick to silence expressions of popular discontent, she wrote in 1819, yet did nothing to relieve its cause.[93] Heyrick saw the immiseration of the poor as something that was being *done to* them, and she attacked contemporary theories of political economy in whose name it took place. The relief provided under the Poor Laws was so scanty as to be a 'slow poison' to its recipients, while its administrators were 'applauded . . . for saving the pockets of [their] parishioners'.[94] But Heyrick blamed the huge increase in the poor rates that had none the less occurred on the employers' refusal to pay just wages, and above all she attacked the 'pernicious dogma' that wages should find their own level.[95]

Heyrick's proposed remedy for these ills was made 'in defiance of the maxims of political economy' that she felt had produced them.[96] She stated a belief in the rights of the labouring classes to a decent life and demanded their protection by the direct intervention of the legislature to raise wages and 'fix a minimum upon them', so that 'the workman . . . should be guarded . . . against encroachments of the master'.[97] 'The Rights of Man — the Rights of Woman — the Rights of Brutes — have been boldly advanced,' she wrote, 'but the Rights of the Poor still remain unadvocated'.[98] The government had passed Corn Laws to protect the landed interest and must interfere now in defence of labour, she asserted. Wages must be increased without encroaching on workers' hours of rest, indeed there should follow a reduction in working hours to twelve instead of sixteen a day; and Heyrick used characteristic language in expecting it to be done immediately, declaring 'there must be no timid, reluctant half-measures . . . no gradual emancipation'.[99] In 1817 she had still hoped that employers would increase wages voluntarily, but by 1819 she argued that only legislative action, and not private charity, could make this provision, and anticipated the objections of 'high political authority, from which it has been thought there is no appeal' by denying that such intervention was either impracticable or harmful to commerce.[100] Rather, by shortening the hours of those who were in work, it would provide jobs for others and thus reduce the poor rates.[101] But Heyrick principally justified her case on the grounds that the labouring classes formed 'the largest, the most important body in the community', and with the affirmation in 1819 that 'Labour ought to be considered in the eye of the law as PROPERTY; the poor have no other, and it should be regarded as sacred.'[102] The poor man's labour was his only means of subsistence, she said, and the law must provide severe penalties 'to guard it from embezzlement'.[103] Heyrick wrote this two years after the appearance in 1817 of David Ricardo's *Principles of Political Economy*, and like many radical writers she seized on his theory of value and used it to attack the developing capitalist system for denying human labour its just reward.

Heyrick restated her ideas in several shorter tracts between 1823 and 1826, by which time she had also begun her anti-slavery work and renewed her efforts for penal reform and for the protection of animals. These writings, too, contained criticism of the exploitation of British workers. In 1823, for example, she compared the treatment of horses with that of human labourers.[104] She blamed their treatment and the treatment of slaves alike on 'the higher ranks of society' and condemned the racial and social arrogance of the type of Englishman who 'imagines that men of his own country, of his own colour, of his own rank in society, are the distinguished favourites of Heaven'.[105] In 1824 she attacked the new Vagrancy Law as exhibiting the same heartless treatment of the dispossessed that she had condemned before, and in 1826 she again condemned the government's failure to protect workers' 'labour and ingenuity', although this was the source 'from whence the rich derive all their riches'.[106]

In between, Heyrick had welcomed the repeal of the Combination Laws and supported a strike by workers in the Leicester hosiery trade. One long strike by the framework-knitters had already ended in defeat, but in 1825 they came out again and Heyrick criticised the employers' refusal to meet their demands; she believed the repeal of the Combination Laws had given the men a chance to raise their wages and that the employers were now obstructing it. She saw the strike as the workmen's only remedy, and felt that by refusing to return to work without better terms in spite of great hardship they were 'discovering that same spirit of constancy, perseverance, and fortitude, which when displayed by other classes . . . is extolled as heroic'. She reminded the employers in Leicester that it was the right of 'free-born Britons' to withdraw their labour, and criticised attempts to break the strike by prosecutions and the use of blacklegs, who 'betray . . . and incur the contempt of their comrades'.[107] One of the leading members of what she called this 'hostile combination' of local employers was her brother, John Coltman; he was an 'unbending advocate' of *laissez-faire* and had opposed the framework-knitters' every attempt to raise their wages.[108] Heyrick herself sympathised not only with their trade-union activity but with other recent protests they had made, remembering the Luddites hanged for frame-breaking at Leicester in 1817 and criticising the laws that made such action a capital felony.[109]

Although Heyrick was concerned to defend the rights of labour in general, some further investigation of her ideas in their local setting is in order. She was writing at a time when framework-knitters in Leicester and the Midlands were facing a savage reduction in their living standards. According to William Felkin, the leading contemporary authority on the hosiery trade, their wages had fallen by 1819 to as little as four shillings a week for sixteen to eighteen hours daily labour, and they were 'not receiving enough to sustain nature'.[110] What lay behind this was the systematic removal in the early years of the nineteenth century of the laws that had formerly regulated the trade, and against such a background Heyrick's calls for that protection to be restored echoed those already made by men like Gravener Henson of Nottingham and the Radical MP Peter Moore, and by the framework-knitters themselves.[111] Since 1811 they had made repeated requests for a minimum wage. They criticised the inconsistency of a Parliament that would legislate to keep up the price of corn but not the price of labour in terms that Heyrick might have borrowed from them; and they argued, as she did, that improved wages would bring about a twelve-hour day. But whether they were in turn aware of her pleas in defence of labour is uncertain. Heyrick's labour writings probably had a much smaller circulation than the best known of her anti-slavery works, and they seem to have received little notice from contemporaries in general.[112] It was not her ideas that William Felkin remembered from the period around 1819, but the less far-reaching plan for a fund to help unemployed framework-knitters put forward by Robert Hall, a local preacher.[113] By the 1860s there seemed no point in seeking wage legislation from a Parliament devoted to *laissez-faire* principles, but the proposal was still realistic when Heyrick was writing; the victory of free competition was still incomplete, and her ideas recalled the paternalist code of the eighteenth century which had protected wages and standards.

With many critics of the new economic order Heyrick shared a nostalgia for a past that was only partly idealised in memory. Her sympathy with Luddites derived from a deep dislike of a manufacturing system which 'condemns rational intelligences to . . . the same dull round of mechanical drudgery'.[114] Since the country had exchanged its agricultural for a commercial character and machinery was introduced into domestic manufactories, she thought, 'simplicity, contentment, virtue, and happiness [had] deserted the land'.[115] She regretted the loss of the labourer's 'honest independence' and questioned whether changes which brought so much misery could be called progress.[116] Anxious to revive the spiritual element that she felt society had lost, she was moved above all by the sentiments she drew from her Quakerism; she saw every question as fundamentally religious, and the greatest ones as stark contests between good and evil, truth and sin. She talked about 'righteousness' in her anti-slavery and labour tracts alike, repeatedly stating that 'righteousness exalteth a nation', and passed apocalyptic judgements on all who failed this test: 'if governments be corrupt, they must be consumed . . . if nations be depraved, they must be destroyed'.[117] She was convinced that her causes were also God's. She criticised Malthus's doctrines because they suggested that the Lord would allow His creatures to starve if their numbers multiplied too far, and attributed the greed of the rich to 'our fallen nature', which she blamed in turn on the 'deadly venom' spread by 'the powers of darkness'.[118] She argued that the case for fixing just wages was sanctioned by 'Divine Law', against which political economists with their 'pagan philosophy' had no appeal, and in general she wanted the 'spirit of trade' to be replaced by the 'maxims of *Christian* economy'.[119] One of the attractions she found in Quakerism lay in its emphasis on self-denial (this was at the heart of her campaign against slave produce and showed in her sympathy with striking workers making sacrifices for their future good). Because Christianity had lost these 'self-denying austerities', she thought, it had become 'diluted' and 'neutralized'.[120] Heyrick therefore looked back to the self-sacrifice and egalitarianism that was latent in original Christian belief, and coupled it with the anti-slavery idea that God's blessing reached even the lowest, whether slave or free. She reminded people that 'Christianity is still an equalizing principle' and that their God remained 'the equal Father of all'.[121]

Taken together, Heyrick's fierce dislike of industrialism, her criticism of social inequalities, and some of her particular proposals for society's improvement seem an impressive set of radical credentials. But how 'radical' was she by comparison with other writers and activists of the 1820s and 30s? Recent studies have shown how women like Anne Knight, Frances Morrison, Eliza Macaulay and Fanny Wright went from anti-slavery work to critiques of social and economic relations and of relations between the sexes.[122] Did Heyrick share their socialist and feminist views? Her biblical zeal separated her from the more extreme 'infidel' elements in Owenism, but a nonconformist conscience could provide a base for political radicalism of various kinds in the nineteenth century, and Heyrick must be placed in that context.

Although Heyrick believed fundamentally that the rich and poor were all 'children of one Parent', she did not translate this idea into schemes for levelling society. It meant simply obedience to 'the divine principle of loving our neighbour as ourselves'; if the rich failed this test of righteous conduct they would suffer divine retribution from 'the dread interdict of Him . . . who casteth down all oppressors'. Heyrick had stated that workers owned nothing but their labour and demanded its protection, but she did not draw the Owenite conclusion that they were therefore entitled to the full value of what they produced. She argued only for fixing a 'just' or a 'living' wage and made no criticism of the principle of employers' profits, saying it was necessary to resist 'exorbitant demands for the remuneration of labour' as well as employers' attempts to cheapen it.[123] Similarly, although in 1825 she supported the workers' right to strike, she did not believe that the interests of capitalist and labourer were by definition mutually opposed, and in general she saw the relationship between them only in terms of 'masters' and 'men'. The few surviving letters from her correspondence with close relatives suggest that she accepted her wealthy family's employment of domestic servants quite naturally, while wanting them to be generously treated.[124]

Heyrick's regard for the personal ties that had formerly bound society together inclined her to a paternalistic view of political subjects. In the tracts she wrote in 1817 and 1819 she thought that the proper treatment of poverty would 'extinguish popular commotions' and convince the people 'that their governors are also their friends and protectors'.[125] She criticised middle-class supporters of parliamentary reform for their opposition to the idea of wage legislation, and accused them of using the issue of Reform to deflect popular clamour away from themselves, maintaining that 'annual parliaments' and 'equal representation' would be 'but a shadow' to the poor, from which they would not benefit without a more fundamental change in the 'sordid, unfeeling' philosophy of the times.

By 1826 Heyrick was more critical of the ruling class's abuse of political power and had decided that the measures she wanted for the protection of labour were not to be had from a Parliament elected mainly 'by aristocratical influence'.[126] She did not follow these criticisms, however, with any calls to change the system of representation.

Heyrick's most radical political sentiments were expressed in pamphlets written in the mid-1820s. In 1826 she dealt with the controversial Leicester election of that year. She regretted the defeat of the popular Radical candidate and condemned the devious tactics employed against him by the town's oligarchical Tory corporation.[127] She stated her support for Catholic Emancipation (a major issue in the election), criticising the exclusion from Parliament of 'our Catholic fellow-subjects' and put her faith in the 'free and fearless' expression of public opinion as the means of checking such abuses.[128] The boycott of slave produce had shown how 'the common people of England' could make their wishes felt if governments would not act; it would teach governments that they could not resist the force of public principle, and lead to further changes, at least indirectly:[129] 'the people having once discovered their power to reform abuses,' she wrote in 1824, 'the government will perceive that they may be disposed to exercise it in other quarters, and will . . . determine to anticipate the people'.[130]

Notwithstanding such views, Heyrick did not demand Reform; she did not call for a wider or more democratic franchise and made no statement of popular political rights. She simply outlined ways of ensuring that even an unreformed Parliament would carry out its duties to the people. In 1826 she asked electors to return a new Parliament more favourable to 'universal philanthropy' by refusing to vote for candidates with unacceptable opinions.[131] The idea of testing candidates' anti-slavery opinions was a currently common one, but Heyrick also wanted electors to have other questions in mind. She insisted that no one vote for any defender of slavery, because such men would exploit British labourers too, or for any supporter of the Corn Laws, or of blood sports, or boxing. This would be achieved, she added, '*in spite of* rotten boroughs, unequal representation, ministerial influence, &c., &c.'[132] She thought such things were wrong but did not believe it essential to change them; rather, she always believed in the possibility of re-awakening the conscience of the rich to an awareness of their Christian duties, and she was concerned for their salvation as well as for the physical welfare of the poor.[133]

A recent biographer of Elizabeth Fry has said that she never took up the cause of women's rights because she 'desired no more freedom than the freedom to work for ennobling causes'.[134] The same seems true of Elizabeth Heyrick. Her writings contain no statement of feminist principles. Indeed, in a tract written in 1811 she took a conservative view of the roles of the sexes. 'If public offices, political transactions, commercial exertions be the province of man,' she wrote, 'the education of children, the order and economy of the family, and the business of creating the pleasures of home, all devolve upon women.'[135] But she also believed that in matters of social conscience women had a decisive part to play, and in both word and deed during the 1820s she exemplified that idea of 'female mission' through which, as historians like Alex Tyrrell have shown, women were able to obtain recognition outside the purely domestic sphere.[136] She provided other women with an example to admire at a time when the rights of their sex were being actively considered. Heyrick had devoted her energies to anti-slavery and labour issues, to Catholic Emancipation and Corn Law repeal, to penal reform and the protection of animals, and on some of these questions her ideas went beyond ordinary philanthropy. She belonged to the same Quaker milieu as both Elizabeth Fry and Anne Knight, and she shared with them a view of the world that was fundamentally religious. She went further than Fry in the range of her activity and in the solutions she advanced, without having the socialist and democratic goals that Knight pursued.

There is still much that remains unknown about Elizabeth Heyrick. Her personal diaries and correspondence with leading anti-slavery figures have reportedly been lost, and only a few contemporaries wrote anything about her.[137] None the less, she was clearly a remarkable figure. Most of her writing and humanitarian endeavour was undertaken when she was already in her fifties. It was predicted that she would make a good speaker,[138] though there is no evidence that she ever took her causes onto a public platform. She was the strongest and most uncompromising advocate of the immediate abolition of slavery. To that end she recommended a form of popular direct action in which women should take the lead, and there were identifiable groups of women who followed her example. She was a consistent supporter of penal reform, and towards the end of her life William Allen wrote to seek her support for moves to abolish capital punishment.[139] Finally she was a passionate critic of the new industrial age and its values. She challenged the economic orthodoxy of the day, criticising the 'pessimism' of Malthusian dogma and the heartlessness of *laissez-faire* principles, and defended labour by her demands for a legal minimum wage and her support for trade unions. One of the pamphlets she wrote attacking the greed of early capitalism provoked the same kind of surprise as some of her anti-slavery writings: it was 'a difficult subject for a woman to write upon; it would be difficult even for a man', said one observer.[140] But when she died in 1831 another friend praised 'the correctness of her views on Political economy'. She had taught, he felt, that 'the modern grinding system' was a 'truly anti-Christian practice'.[141] This writer was typical of those few friends, relatives and fellow Quakers who remembered Heyrick's work and admired it. As an abolitionist, as a social critic, and as a champion of the oppressed in general, she deserved wider recognition.

Notes

1. *Account of the Receipts and Disbursements of the Anti-Slavery Society for the Years 1829 and 1830: With a List of the Subscribers* (London, 1830). The same source lists twice as many male anti-slavery societies.
2. Heyrick's anti-slavery pamphlets were: *Immediate not Gradual Abolition of Slavery; or an Inquiry into the Shortest, Safest, and Most Effectual Means of Getting Rid of West Indian Slavery* (London, 1824); *An Enquiry Which of the Two Parties is Best Entitled to Freedom? The Slave or the Slave-holder?* (London, 1824); *An Appeal Not to the Government but to the People of England on the Subject of West Indian Slavery* (London, 1824); *No British Slavery; or, an Invitation to the People to Put a Speedy End to It* (London, 1824); *Letters on the Necessity of a Prompt Extinction of British Colonial Slavery* (London, 1826); *Appeal to the Hearts and Consciences of British Women* (Leicester, 1828); *Apology for Ladies' Anti-Slavery Associations* (London, 1828).
    Other calls for immediate abolition were made by the Sheffield philanthropist Samuel Roberts, and in pamphlets like: Anthropos, *The Rights of Man, (not Paine's) but the Rights of Man in the West Indies* (London, 1824), and Anon., *Reasons for Preferring Immediate to What is Called Gradual Emancipation* (London, 1825).
3. As well as the seven anti-slavery pamphlets listed in note 2, Heyrick wrote the following: *The Warning. Recommended to the Serious Attention of All Christians, and Lovers of Their Country* London ([c. 1806]); *Instructive Hints in Easy Lessons for Children* [c. 1810]; *A Christmas Box for the Advocates of Bull-Baiting* (London, 1809); *Bull-Baiting: a Village Dialogue Between Tom Brown and John Simms* (London, 1809); *Familiar Letters Addressed to Children and Young Persons of the Middle Ranks* (London, 1811); *Plain Tales; or, the Advantages of Industry* (London, [c. 1816]); *Exposition of One Principal Cause of the National Distress, Particularly in Manufacturing Districts, With Some Suggestions for its Removal* (London, 1817); *Enquiry Into the Consequences of the Present Depreciated Value of Human Labour. In Letters to Thos. Fowell Buxton, Esq., M.P.* (London, 1819);

Cursory Remarks on the Evil Tendency of Unrestrained Cruelty; Particularly on that Practised in Smithfield Market (London, 1823); *Protest Against the Spirit and Practice of Modern Legislation as Exhibited in the New Vagrant Act* (London, 1824); *A Letter of Remonstrance from an Impartial Public to the Hosiers of Leicester* (Leicester, 1825); *Animadversions on the Late Contested Election for the Borough of Leicester* (Leicester, 1826); *Appeal to the Electors of the United Kingdom, on the Choice of a New Parliament* (London, 1826).

Two other tracts were attributed to Heyrick: *On the Advantages of a High Remunerating Price for Labour* (Leicester, 1825; see below, note 109), and *Letters of a Recluse* (published posthumously?). On the latter see C. H. Beale, *Catherine Hutton and Her Friends* (Birmingham, 1895), p. 214. I have been unable to trace a copy of the latter tract. Both Beale's account and Smith's (supp., p. 187) coincidentally state that Heyrick wrote only '18' pamphlets altogether, but the two lists do not contain all the same titles. Many of the tracts listed here are in a volume lettered 'Heyrick's pamphlets' in the East Midlands collection of the University of Nottingham Library; also in the volume 'Pamphlets Printed by Thomas Combe of Leicester' in the Leicestershire local studies collection, Leicester Public Library. I am grateful to the librarian, Mr A. W. Stevenson, for his help in tracing these, and to Mr Mike Thompson, a former fellow MA student at Birkbeck College, for sharing his extraordinary bibliographical knowledge.

4. This biographical information is drawn from Anon., *A Brief Sketch of the Life and Labours of Mrs. Elizabeth Heyrick* (Leicester, 1862). (In Friends Library, Tracts, vol. 511, no. 14); C. H. Beale, *Catherine Hutton and Her Friends*, esp. pp. 123–4, 186–217; the Hutton-Beale family papers in Birmingham Reference Library; the Coltman family MSS in the Leicestershire County Record Office; and W. Gardiner, *Music and Friends* (London, 1838), I:61, 114.

5. The first evidence of her anti-slavery views is contained in the poetry her husband wrote about her in the 1790s, e.g. 'To the Sympathetic, an African Picture', in J. Heyrick, *First Flights* (London, 1797). (In Leicestershire local studies collection.)

6. Samuel Coltman to Elizabeth Heyrick, 1796, in Coltman Family MSS, 15 D 57 f. 34.

7. Unsigned letter dated 1802, ibid., f. 387.

8. Ibid., f. 387; and Beale, *Catherine Hutton*, p. 190.

9. Coltman family MSS, f. 387.

10. *Immediate not Gradual Abolition, passim.* The campaign against slave-grown goods is described more fully in K. Corfield, 'English Abolitionists and the Refusal of Slave-Grown Goods, 1780–1860' (MA thesis, University of London, 1983).

11. *No British Slavery*, p. 6.

12. *Letters on the Necessity*, p. 107.

13. Ibid., p. 169.

14. Ibid., p. 7.

15. *Immediate not Gradual Abolition*, pp. 8, 24.

16. *Apology for Ladies' Anti-Slavery Associations*, p. 7.

17. *An Enquiry Which of the Two Parties is Best Entitled to Freedom?*, p. 5.

18. *Letters on the Necessity*, p. 153. James Stephen, in the same year, only asked candidates to support the 'progressive termination' of slavery: *Address to the Electors and People of the United Kingdom* (London, 1826), p. 81.

19. *Letters on the Necessity*, p. 183–219.

20. D. B. Davis, 'The Emergence of Immediatism in British and American Anti-slavery Thought', *Mississippi Valley Historical Review*, XLIX (1962), pp. 220–1.

21. H. Temperley, *British Anti-Slavery, 1833–1870* (London, 1972), pp. 12–18; and B. Fladeland, *Men and Brothers; Anglo-American Antislavery Co-operation* (Urbana, Ill., 1972), pp. 165–83.

22. *Proceedings of the First Anniversary Meeting of the Anti-Slavery Society on 25 June 1824* (London, 1824), p. 107.

23. Minutes of the Society for the Mitigation and Gradual Abolition of Slavery, Rhodes House Library, Oxford, MSS Brit. Emp., s.20, E2/3, p. 6, 3 March 1829; and K. Charlton, 'James Cropper and Liverpool's Contribution to the Anti-Slavery Movement', *Trans. Hist. Soc. of Lancashire and Cheshire*, CXXIII (1972), pp. 64–5.

24. T. S. Winn, *A Speedy End to Slavery in Our West India Colonies* (London, 1827), p. 2.

25. Davis, 'Emergence of Immediatism', p. 226.

26. *Second Report of the Sheffield Female Anti-Slavery Society* (Sheffield, 1827), pp. 3, 6; and the Society's Minute Book, entry for January 1826. (Both in John Rylands Library, Manchester.)

27. Sheffield Female Anti-Slavery Society Minute Book (Rylands MS 743), 13 February 1827, pp. 13–14.

28. *Second Report of the Sheffield Female Anti-Slavery Society*, p. 6.

29. Ibid., pp. 4–6, 8–11.

30. S. Roberts, *The Autobiography and Select Remains of the Late Samuel Roberts* (London, 1849), p. 3; and *Omnipotence as Exemplified in the History of the Abolition of Slavery* (Sheffield, 1833), p. 8. Roberts and Montgomery together edited *The Negro's Friend, or the Sheffield Anti-Slavery Album* (1826), dedicated to immediate abolition.

31. *Fifth Annual Report of the Sheffield Ladies' Anti-Slavery Society* (Sheffield, 1830), p. 11; and Minute Book, p. 46.

32. *Third Annual Report of the Ladies' Association for Salisbury, Calne, Melksham, Devizes and their Respective Neighbourhoods in Aid of the Cause of Negro Emancipation* (Calne, 1828), p. 17.

33. Ibid., p. 17; and *Fourth Annual Report* (Calne, 1829), pp. 6–7.

34. Martha Gundry, *Letters to a Friend* (1825), quoted in Heyrick, *Letters on the Necessity*, p. 164.

35. Reports in *Devizes and Wiltshire Gazette*, 9 and 16 February 1826.

36. Gundry, *Letters to a Friend*.

37. *Annual Reports* (1826–30) of the Female Society for Birmingham, West Bromwich, Wednesbury, Walsall, and their Respective Neighbourhoods for the Relief of British Negro Slaves (Birmingham, 1826–30); the Society's Album (1826–8); and the Minute Book of the men's society in Birmingham (see entry for 16 August 1830). All in Birmingham Reference Library.

38. The women passed this resolution on 8 April 1830. MS Minute Book of Birmingham Ladies' Society for the Relief of British Negro Slaves, 1825–52, p. 100. Birmingham Reference Library.

39. Ibid., 23 December 1830. (Minute refers to Pringle's letter dated 28 July.)

40. Leicester Auxiliary Anti-Slavery Society, *An Address to the Public on the State of Slavery in the West India Islands* (London, 1824), p. 11. Betty Fladeland, (*Men and Brothers*, p. 179) incorrectly refers to this pamphlet as the work of women (including Heyrick) in Leicester, but the names of the 18 men who made up the Society's committee are clearly printed at the front of the address, and Heyrick would never have subscribed to such gradualist notions.

41. *Account of the Receipts and Disbursements of the Anti-Slavery Society for the Years 1829 and 1830; with a List of the Subscribers* (London, 1830); and *Account of the Receipts . . . for 1831* (London, 1831).

42. *Anti-Slavery Reporter*, no. 4 (September 1825); no. 14 (August 1826); and vol. I, no. 7 (new series) (July 1853). Also Heyrick, *Apology for Ladies' Anti-Slavery Associations*, p. 15.

43. C. E. H. Orpen, *The Principles, Plans and Objects of the Hibernian Negro's Friend Society, Contrasting with those of the Previously Existing Anti-slavery*

Societies (Dublin, 1831), pp. 1–2.

44. Ibid., pp. 4, 6, 7, 14.

45. Anon., *A Brief Sketch of the Life and Labours of Mrs. Elizabeth Heyrick* (Leicester, 1862), p. 20.

46. George Stephen to Anne Knight, 14 November 1834. In Knight Family papers, Friends Library, Box W.

47. Joseph Sturge, *A Visit to the United States in 1841* (London, 1842), p. 56.

48. Ibid., p. 56.

49. Anti-Slavery Society Minutes, Rhodes House Library, E2/1, 8 Dec. 1824, p. 145; and E2/2, 21 Sept., 5 Oct. and 19 Oct. 1825.

50. *The Slave*, no. 32 (August 1853). See also, for example, *British Friend*, VIII (April 1849).

51. *Anti-Slavery Reporter*, no. 32 (January 1828).

52. Anti-Slavery Society Minutes, 19 Jan. 1831, Rhodes House Library, E2/3, p. 77.

53. 'Short Account of Susanna Watts' Life', MS written by Clara Parkes, 2 February 1865, in 'Scrapbook Compiled by Susanna Watts', Leicestershire local studies collection.

54. O'Connell is quoted in F. Thistlethwaite, *America and the Atlantic Community, Anglo-American Aspects 1790–1850* (New York, 1959), p. 122.

55. *22nd Annual Report of the Birmingham Ladies' Negro's Friend Society* (Birmingham, 1847), p. 17.

56. *The Slave*, no. 32 (August 1853); *Anti-Slavery Reporter*, vol. I, no. 7 (new series) (July 1853).

57. The earlier of the two, Anon., *A Brief Sketch*, was used by Catherine Hutton Beale for her own account of Heyrick's work, *Catherine Hutton and Her Friends* (see pp. 186–217).

58. B. Lundy, *The Life, Travels, and Opinions of Benjamin Lundy* (Philadelphia, 1847), pp. 216, 306, 308; and M. L. Dillon, *Benjamin Lundy and the Struggle for Negro Freedom* (Urbana, Ill., 1966), pp. 106–8.

59. Dillon, *Benjamin Lundy*, pp. 107–8.

60. F. B. Tolles (ed.), *Slavery and 'The Woman Question'. Lucretia Mott's Diary of Her Visit to Great Britain to Attend the World's Anti-Slavery Convention of 1840* (Haverford, Pa., 1952), p. 24, n 1; and Sturge, *A Visit*, p. 56. I am grateful to Professor Sidney Kaplan for the reference to Frederick Douglass.

61. Tolles (ed.), *Slavery and 'The Woman Question'*, pp. 23–4.

62. Anon., *A Brief Sketch*, pp. 3–4.

63. Ibid., p. 20.

64. Sarah Pennock Sellers, *David Sellers, Mary Pennock Sellers* (Philadelphia, 1936), p. 45.

65. *John Bull*, vol. IV, no. 48 (29 November 1824).

66. R. I. and S. Wilberforce, *The Life of William Wilberforce, by His Sons* (London, 1838), V:264–5.

67. William Allen, *The Duty of Abstaining from West India Produce. A Speech Delivered at Coach-makers' Hall* (London, 1792), p. 23.

68. George Stephen to Anne Knight, 14 November 1834. In Knight Family papers, Friends Library, Box W.

69. Stephen to Knight, 8 October 1830.

70. Stephen to Knight, 5 November 1830.

71. MS scrapbook of Susanna Watts, dated 11 February 1834, in Leicestershire local studies collection.

72. Ibid.

73. *Sheffield Ladies' Anti-Slavery Association, Fourth Annual Report* (Sheffield, 1829), p. 10.

74. Sheffield Ladies' Association for the Universal Abolition of Slavery, *An Appeal to the Christian Women of Sheffield* (Sheffield, 1837), p. 13, and their petition (1838). Both in John Rylands Library.

75. Ibid.

76. *Second Report of the Ladies' Association for Calne, Melksham, . . .*, p. 4.

77. *Second Report of the Female Society for the Relief of British Negro Slaves for Birmingham . . .*, p. 16.

78. Manchester Ladies' Free Grown Cotton Movement, notice, *c.* 1849, in John Rylands Library.

79. Heyrick, *Appeal to the Hearts and Consciences of British Women*, p. 3; *Apology for Ladies' Anti-Slavery Associations*, pp. 3–5, 11.

80. For Anne Knight, see Gail Malmgreen, 'Anne Knight and the Radical Sub-Culture', *Quaker History*, LXXI (Fall 1982), pp. 100–13. For Elizabeth Pease and other campaigners, especially in America, see Thistlethwaite, *America and the Atlantic Community*, Ch. 4.

81. S. Rowbotham, *Hidden from History* (London, 1973), p. 48.

82. Sheffield Ladies' Association for the Universal Abolition of Slavery, John Rylands Library, MS 743, f. 63.

83. Heyrick, *Appeal to the Hearts and Consciences of British Women*, p. 3.

84. Ibid., p. 4. On the whole question of the 'feminisation' of philanthropic activity, see Alex Tyrrell, ' "Women's Mission" and Pressure Group Politics in Britain, 1825–1850', *Bulletin of the John Rylands Library*, LXIII (Autumn 1980), pp. 194–230.

85. Anon., *A Brief Sketch*, p. 4.

86. Ibid., pp. 11–15.

87. See note 3 above.

88. *Exposition of One Principal Cause of the National Distress*; and *Enquiry into the Consequences of the Present Depreciated Value of Human Labour. In Letters to Thos. Fowell Buxton, Esq., M.P.* These two pamphlets, published anonymously, contain passages virtually identical in sentiment and language. The second (hereafter cited as *Letters to Buxton*) was Heyrick's reply to Buxton's *Enquiry into the System of Prison Discipline* (London, 1818).

89. *Exposition of . . . the National Distress*, p. 16.

90. Ibid., pp. 3–4, 8.

91. *Letters to Buxton*, pp. 14–15, 23–5, 107.

92. *Exposition of . . . the National Distress*, p. 2.

93. *Letters to Buxton*, pp. 14–15, 23–5, 107.

94. Ibid., p. 78.

95. Ibid., pp. 10, 102.

96. Ibid., p. 105.

97. Ibid., p. 50; see also pp. 80, 112–13; and *Exposition of . . . the National Distress*, pp. 8, 31.

98. *Exposition of . . . the National Distress*, p. 21.

99. Ibid., p. 29; *Letters to Buxton*, p. 113.

100. *Letters to Buxton*, pp. 80, 102.

101. Ibid., pp. 113–15.

102. Ibid., pp. 62, 10.

103. Ibid., pp. 65, 86.

104. *Cursory Remarks on the Evil Tendency of Unrestrained Cruelty*, p. 22.

105. Ibid., p. 13.

106. In *Protest Against the Spirit and Practice of Modern Legislation*; and *Appeal to the Electors of the United Kingdom*, p. 7.

107. *A Letter of Remonstrance . . . to the Hosiers of Leicester*, pp. 7–15.

108. Coltman's hostility to the workers' demands is described in A. Temple

Patterson, *Radical Leicester* (Leicester, 1975), and in the *Leicester Journal*, 24 June 1825.

109. *A Letter of Remonstrance*, p. 12. Heyrick remembered five Luddites being hanged; in fact there were six (Patterson, *Radical Leicester*, p. 114). Heyrick may also have been responsible for producing a second pamphlet criticising the Combination Laws and supporting the right to strike; it consisted entirely of extracts from an article in the *Edinburgh Review* (1824) by the economist J. R. McCulloch, and was published in Leicester in 1825 under the title *On the Advantages of a High Remunerating Price for Labour*. Heyrick was named as the author in Joseph Smith's *Descriptive Catalogue of Friends' Books* (London, 1867), I:444.

110. W. Felkin, *A History of the Machine-Wrought Hosiery and Lace Manufacturers* (Cambridge, 1867), pp. 441–2.

111. E. P. Thompson, *The Making of the English Working Class* (Harmondsworth, 1968), esp. pp. 565–9, 579–91.

112. Heyrick's *Letters to Buxton* was mentioned, by title only, in the lists of new publications printed in the *Quarterly Review*, XX (July 1819) and the *Edinburgh Review*, XXXII (October 1819), and by Robert Hall, who knew her well, in his *A Reply to the Principal Objections Advanced by Cobbett and Others* . . . (Leicester and London, 1821). A copy of Heyrick's pamphlet was presented to the factory reformer, Michael Sadler, with the significant inscription, 'rare tract'. (Copy in Goldsmith's Library, London.)

113. Felkin, *A History*, p. 442.

114. *Letters to Buxton*, p. 96.

115. *Exposition of . . . the National Distress*, pp. 5–6.

116. Ibid., p. 6; *Letters to Buxton*, p. 34.

117. *The Warning*, p. 23; cf. ibid., p. 9, *Letters to Buxton*, p. 87, and *Appeal to the Electors*, p. 16.

118. *Letters to Buxton*, pp. 74, 84.

119. Ibid., pp. 10, 103–9.

120. *Exposition of . . . the National Distress*, pp. 18–19.

121. Ibid., pp. 18, 28; *Letters to Buxton*, p. 8.

122. See Malmgreen, 'Anne Knight', and *Neither Bread nor Roses: Utopian Feminists and the English Working Class, 1800–1850* (Brighton, 1978); also Barbara Taylor, *Eve and the New Jerusalem: Socialism and Feminism in the Nineteenth Century* (London, 1983).

123. *Exposition of . . . the National Distress*, pp. 15–16; *Letters to Buxton*, pp. 47, 50.

124. For example, Samuel Coltman to Elizabeth Heyrick, 11 October 1818, Coltman Family MSS, 15 D 57, f. 136.

125. *Letters to Buxton*, p. 23; *Exposition of . . . the National Distress*, p. 36.

126. *Exposition of . . . the National Distress*, pp. 1–3, 11, 31–2; *Appeal to the Electors*, p. 7.

127. *Animadversions on the Late Contested Election*, pp. 4–10. Heyrick was not the only woman to be outraged at the Leicester Corporation's behaviour. Her friend Catherine Hutton called it 'a disgrace to the age', and, although she held very conservative views about women's domestic role, wrote privately that 'this flagrant injustice . . . almost makes me a politician'. C. Hutton to Anne Coltman, 25 March 1827, in Hutton-Beale MSS, vol. 79, f. 281, Birmingham Reference Library.

128. *Animadversions*, pp. 6, 15–16.

129. *An Enquiry Which of the Two Parties is Best Entitled to Freedom?*, pp. 22, 26–7.

130. *An Appeal not to the Government but to the People*, p. 12.

131. *Appeal to the Electors*, p. 15.

132. Ibid., p. 16 (my emphasis).

133. *Letters to Buxton*, pp. 28–30.

134. June Rose, *Elizabeth Fry* (London, 1980), p. 184.

135. *Familiar Letters*, p. 31.

136. Alex Tyrrell, ' "Women's Mission" '.

137. On the loss of Heyrick's other writings, see Beale, *Catherine Hutton and Her Friends*, pp. 194, 211.

138. In 'A Hasty Sketch of the Coltman Family' (1802), Coltman Family MSS, f. 387.

139. Beale, *Catherine Hutton and Her Friends*, p. 109.

140. Catherine Hutton to Anne Coltman, 18 June 1818, in Coltman Family MSS, f. 409.

141. James Smith to S. Coltman, 6 November 1831, in Coltman Family MSS, f. 218. Heyrick died on 18 October 1831. She received the briefest of mentions in the obituary columns of the *Leicester Chronicle* and the *Leicester Journal* (both 22 October 1831); the *Journal* did no more than describe her as 'relict of the late John Heyrick, junr. Esq.' In its next issue (29 October 1831), the *Chronicle* carried a 500-word letter about her work from a local friend, who felt that the paper had not done her justice.

Chapter 4

Ann Carr and the Female Revivalists of Leeds*

D. Colin Dews

In the eighteenth-century Methodist revival, female preachers played a small but not insignificant part. For women to have been accepted as preachers in Methodism was a considerable achievement, in view of John Wesley's High Church principles and Oxford background, and it required a broad reappraisal of the role of women in the Church.

Initially, Wesley gave little credence to any person who had not received Episcopal ordination, a system totally debarring females.[1] He first began to modify this view when he came to recognise the gifts to be contributed by local preachers and then went on to appreciate the part to be played by 'pious females' able to call sinners to repent.[2] Abel Stevens, writing in 1876, went so far as to argue that 'Wesley's incorporation of female agency in his practical system has been one of the most effective causes of the surprising success of Methodism.'[3] The Pauline tradition of the New Testament, as originally accepted by Wesley, denied the right of women to preach in public and did not allow them to be priests. Yet, in extraordinary cases, especially in Corinth, Paul appears to have made some exceptions.[4]

A letter from Wesley to Mrs Sarah Crosby in 1761 seems to mark his acceptance of women praying and exhorting in public: 'Hitherto, I think you have not gone too far. You could not well do less. . . . I do not see that you have broken any law. Go on calmly and steadily.' The same letter revealed some of the difficulties Wesley faced in making this decision and at the same time anticipated potential criticism, for he confessed, 'You lay me under a great difficulty. The Methodists do not allow of women preachers; neither do I take upon me any such character.'[5]

Gradually Wesley's pragmatism overcame his theological objections, and by 1777 he had developed a more positive attitude.

68

In another letter to Mrs Crosby he explained,

> The difference between us and the Quakers in this respect is
> manifest. They flatly deny the rule itself, although it stands clear
> in the Bible. We allow the rule; only we believe it admits of some
> exceptions.[6]

What emerged was that a woman with an extraordinary call
could be acknowledged as a preacher but was not to itinerate.
Women were acceptable because they were a means of converting
sinners, and one advantage of employing female preachers in this
respect was that they were free to devise their own methods of proclaiming the Gospel. Indeed, some of those with strong personali-
ties developed an approach to preaching which brought results
which a more stereotyped ministry would have been unable to
achieve, although there were inherent dangers in this, as the Leeds
Primitive Methodists were to discover in the 1820s.[7]

I

By the time of Wesley's death in 1791 there was an established
tradition of female preachers in the Leeds area. One of those
instrumental in this aspect of evangelism was Mrs Sarah Crosby
(1729–1804), who was born near Leeds and was converted in
October 1749. In February 1757 she was deserted by her husband
and later in the year moved to London where she was soon living
with two more Methodists, Mrs Sarah Ryan and Mary Clark. They
came into contact with Mary Bosanquet (1739–1815), and in
March 1763 Crosby and Ryan moved into the Bosanquets' Leytonstone home to form a Christian community based on prayer, Bible
study and preaching; they were also to include an orphanage and a
school in their work.[8]

Mary Bosanquet came from a well-to-do family but soon distributed a considerable part of her wealth in Christian charity. By
June 1768 the Leytonstone community was in financial difficulties
and in that month moved north to Cross Hall, Morley, to the south
of Leeds in the adjacent parish of Batley. Sarah Ryan, already ill
when the move was made, died a short time later and her place was
taken by Ann Tripp. The community continued at Cross Hall until
1781 when the premises and stock were sold prior to the marriage

of Mary Bosanquet to the Reverend John Fletcher (1729–85) at Matley Parish Church and her subsequent removal to Madeley.[9]

These women had pioneered female preaching in the Leeds area and of this group Sarah Crosby was almost certainly the first authorised woman preacher within Methodism.[10] She was preaching by 1761, before the formation of the Leytonstone community, and on her removal to Cross Hall began to preach extensively throughout the West Riding. Her health was already deteriorating at the break-up of the Cross Hall community in 1781 but she appears to have continued preaching. Finally in 1793 she moved to a small house in Leeds adjoining the Boggard Chapel, where she and her female companions acquired the nickname 'The Female Brethren'.[11]

The acceptance of women as preachers by the end of the eighteenth century may have been stronger in some places than others. It is very likely that in Leeds, for example, Methodists were relatively receptive to women preachers because of the tradition built up by Sarah Crosby. Others active in the area included Elizabeth Ritchie of Otley (1754–1835), who sometimes accompanied Wesley on his journeys and was closely connected with Crosby's work. Another town which appears to have developed a tradition of female preachers was Nottingham, where Mrs Mary Tatham (1764–1837) was particularly active. Her uncle was David Strickland of Leeds and she was married in the town's parish church in February 1787. Mary Tatham's preaching may have reflected a Quaker background, for her mother had been disinherited by the sect for 'marrying out'.[12]

Despite a widespread acceptance of female preachers, not all Methodist leaders were enamoured of them or the part they played in revivals. The Reverend John Pawson (1737–1806), President in 1793, wrote about the revival which swept the Leeds Circuit in 1794:

> The Leeds people shame themselves. They are uncommonly turbulent . . . and they are trying to disturb other Circuits as well as their own. I believe the women are the principal mischief makers. Miss Ritchie is as bad as the worst of them.[13]

Further criticism of the 'Female Brethren' was to come from Thomas Hannam, a Leeds local preacher heavily involved in the events which were to lead to the formation of the Methodist New

Connexion. In 1796 a room called Bethel was being used by the more liberally minded Methodists in the town; here the sacraments were celebrated. Hannam commented: 'Mr. Benson has promised to preach at Bethel on Thursday next, but, we have but little reliance upon him, as he is biased [*sic*] by the "Female Brethren".'[14]

There was during this decade, in the aftermath of Wesley's death, a search for order and structure in Wesleyan Methodism as it moved from being a society of people in connection with Wesley within the Church of England to a Church in its own standing. This process continued for about fifty years and one major issue was the concept of the ministry. What emerged in Wesleyan Methodism was the growing importance of both the Connexion principle and the itinerancy, with the 'pastoral office' supported by ordination. The minister was no longer simply a travelling evangelist, the agent of special missions.[15] It was inevitable that if Wesleyan Methodism was developing its own concept of the 'pastoral office', then the role of female preachers would come under examination. By 1835 Conference was strongly disapproving of female preachers, although women could still act as class leaders and give testimonies at class meetings.[16]

There was something of a 'last ditch stand' to retain female preachers, particularly from those who believed in their effectiveness in revivals as agents of conversion. The emerging champion was the Rev. Zechariah Taft (d. 1848) who married Mary Barritt, another notable female revivalist preacher. From the 1790s, when the Conferences were held either in Leeds or Manchester, she would go to meet those preachers particularly sympathetic towards female preachers, especially the Rev. William Bramwell (1759–1818) who, along with Ann Cutler (1759–95), nicknamed 'Praying Nanny', had been instrumental in the great revival which broke out in the West Riding in 1793, soon after his appointment to the Dewsbury Circuit.[17]

Taft based his case for female preachers on one of Wesley's own maxims: 'God owns them in the conversion of sinners, and who am I that I should withstand God.'[18] He conceded, however, that females had to have an 'extraordinary' call to preach, whereas men required only an 'ordinary' call, and that while women could become local preachers, they could not fully enter the pastoral office.[19]

Regardless of the effectiveness of Taft's pen in championing the cause of female preachers and the fact that his wife was a remarkable evangelist, as early as the 1820s it was clear that Wesleyan Methodism had finally rejected the use of women as preachers. Instead, the initiative passed to the Primitive Methodists and the Bible Christians, both basically lay-created churches without a formal view of the ministry, except that it was really one of a travelling evangelist. Both saw the potential, as had Bramwell and Taft, of using women in soul-saving conversions. Revivalist by nature, neither had any fundamental objection to female preachers nor were they against women entering the itinerancy, at least in the early years of the two Connexions.

II

Primitive Methodism in Leeds originated at Wesley Chapel, Meadow Lane, with a band of fourteen people led by Samuel Smith who had come to the town from Denton in Lancashire in 1812. This band of young men prepared a plan for prayer meetings and gospel services in various parts of the town. Early in 1819 they read in a Hull newspaper of a new sect which had come over from Lincolnshire and had opened a chapel in Mill Street; in May they further learned that these 'Ranters' had a preaching station at Ferrybridge. It was agreed finally that James Verity (who had come to Leeds from Wakefield in 1817 and as a sculptor was then currently working on Bramwell's tomb) and James Atkinson should both go to Ferrybridge; this they did and so first came into contact with Primitive Methodism. On returning to Leeds, Verity, a local preacher, was criticised for preaching for the Ranters in Ferrybridge and for this was suspended as a class leader at Wesley; at this, almost the whole class withdrew.

A suggestion that this particular group should join the Ranters was initially rejected, but in September it was agreed to write to Hull inviting one of the preachers to visit them in Leeds with a view to helping in the work. Prior to William Clowes's first visit to Leeds on 24 November 1819, they had already opened seven preaching places, and had three classes and seven local preachers; on the following day they were formally made a Primitive Methodist society within the Hull Circuit.[20] Just over a year later, on Sunday, 31 December 1820, a former factory at Hill House Bank was opened as a preaching room. Bills were posted in the town announcing the opening services; preachers on the day included two women, Miss Sarah Eland and Mrs Hannah Woolhouse.[21]

Sarah Eland, sometimes called Healand, was born at Hutton Rudby, where both her parents were Wesleyan members; she was converted at the New Year's Day Covenant Service, 1802, and soon became a good influence on the village. She first came into contact with Primitive Methodism when she visited some relations in Hull and there in 1818 came into contact with Ann Carr. For five years Sarah Eland was to travel as a preacher in several Midland and Northern counties until 1824 when, after the Conference, she married the Rev. John de Putron (d. 1859 *ae*. 71), a Wesleyan minister who had spent ten years working among the French Canadians; after their marriage they went to live in the Channel Islands.[22]

Hannah Woolhouse, the wife of Richard Woolhouse, a Hull Wesleyan and by trade a sack and soil-cloth manufacturer (or possibly a furniture broker), was, herself, emerging as a notable female preacher at this time, despite local Wesleyan opposition. The Woolhouses exemplified tensions developing within Wesleyan Methodism at this time. Clearly both were revivalists by inclination and in the tradition of Bramwell; their acceptance of Wesleyan Methodism was becoming increasingly uncomfortable. Both husband and wife were Wesleyan class leaders. Mrs Woolhouse had a desire to preach but received no encouragement from the Hull Wesleyans to do this. It was to Primitive Methodism that they were to turn and in that body found full expression for their beliefs and methods, Richard Woolhouse subsequently having much to do with the introduction of Primitive Methodism into Hull.[23]

III

Ann Carr was born at Market Rasen, Lincolnshire, on 4 March 1783, the youngest of the twelve children of Thomas and Rebecca Carr.[24] When Ann was five years of age her mother died, and she was then brought up by her Congregationalist aunt. At eighteen Ann Carr was seriously ill for three months, possibly suffering from a combination of shock and a nervous breakdown following the death of the person whom it was anticipated she would one day have married, even though they were not engaged. This illness suddenly ended when she attended a prayer meeting and was converted. Her conversion was an important turning-point in her life, for she became first a Wesleyan Methodist and then a preacher.[25]

Sarah Eland first noted Ann Carr in Hull during 1818, seeing her originally in the public band meeting at Waltham Street Wesleyan Chapel. At the close of the service the two women returned to the Woolhouse home, and there Sarah Eland invited Ann Carr to accompany her to Skirlaugh. The invitation was duly accepted on condition that Eland would then go with Carr back to Market Rasen.

As a result of this meeting between Ann Carr and Sarah Eland, and their return to Lincolnshire, three hundred members were added in the Market Rasen Circuit and the revival spread to the Louth Circuit. This revival in Lincolnshire took place about the time when Primitive Methodism began to penetrate the county, and their societies particularly benefited from the preaching of these two women in such places as Caistor, Market Rasen, Teally and Walesby. Here is another example of Primitive Methodism gaining from fringe Wesleyan revivalist activity and, not surprisingly, the Wesleyans reacted to Ann Carr by putting pressure on her not to receive the Ranters lest she be removed as leader of her two classes; to avoid a division she subsequently moved to Hull.

During the summer of 1818 Sarah Eland accompanied Ann Carr on a visit to Nottingham. It was not Eland's first visit to the town for she had been there at the end of the previous August when she had gone with Mrs Woolhouse from Hull. Her husband frequently visited the Midlands and Nottingham on business and there, in 1817, had met Robert Winfield who was then pioneering Primitive Methodism in the area. His admiration for the Primitive Methodists was further influenced by the preaching of the Rev. John Harrison at Broad Marsh in the town. It was because of Woolhouse's contact with Primitive Methodism in Nottingham that his wife and Sarah Eland had gone to the town to see the revival then taking place. The chronology of events is far from clear at this period and it is possible that Ann Carr had also paid a previous visit to Nottingham, but what now attracted both her and Sarah Eland to the town was the growing reputation of Sarah Kirkland (1794–1880) as a Primitive Methodist preacher.

Sarah Kirkland had been born at Mercaston in Derbyshire and, under the preaching of the Rev. William Bramwell in her parents' home, became convinced of sin. After a time the local Wesleyan society died out, but the memories and tradition of Bramwell's revivalist activities appear to have continued, and so when Hugh Bourne visited the village in 1811 he was invited to preach in the Kirkland home. Primitive Methodism now took root and Sarah Kirkland was received into membership in 1813 and 'on plan' in September 1814, quickly becoming a successful preacher. At the end of the following year Robert Winfield invited her to accompany him to mission Nottingham, and they arrived on Christmas Day to a background of Luddite disturbances; in the ensuing February she became the Connexion's first female travelling preacher and extended the work to Bulwell, and then to Ilkeston and Hucknall Torkard.[26]

It was on 16 June, probably in 1816 (but the year may not be correct), that Ann Carr set off from Market Rasen for Nottingham with the intention of meeting Sarah Kirkland and arrived two days later. There she attended a place of worship in a large millroom, presumably the middle room of the disused Broad Marsh factory, at that time being used by the Ranters. Having attended the Quarterly Meeting on the previous day, she preached to a large, open-air company at Dick's Garden on 24 June.[27]

The Quarter Day saw Ann Carr being invited to spend a month visiting the Nottinghamshire colliers, but she delayed acceptance as she had a prior engagement at Burlington Quay (Bridlington) and then had to return to Market Rasen. She was soon back in Nottingham, however, and on 16 July attended a union camp meeting — so called because it drew its preachers from ministers of different denominations — in a spacious field near Nottingham Forest. Her mission to the miners began on 22 July and continued until 14 August, during which time she preached at Brinsley, Bulwell, Cotmanhay, Eastwood, Hucknall and Ilkeston.

Ann Carr, already a successful Wesleyan revivalist female preacher, was increasingly being drawn into Primitive Methodism where she was one of a number of similarly minded women. It was probably at this stage that she felt obliged to leave Market Rasen to avoid a division. It was to Hull she came and there in 1818 came into contact with the Woolhouses and Sarah Eland. During the summer of 1818 Mr Woolhouse heard William Clowes preach in the open air at Leicester and took the opportunity to invite him to undertake a mission in Hull; the December Quarterly Meeting of the Nottingham Circuit agreed to this. Initially, Winfield was appointed to the station, but before he could go he had broken with

Primitive Methodism and taken the path which was finally to see him as a local preacher in the Methodist New Connexion. Clowes arrived in Hull on Friday, 15 January; success quickly came, for the foundation-stone of Mill Street Chapel was laid on Friday, 12 April 1819.[28] The main foundation-stone was laid by Ann Carr who, trowel in hand, preached from the stone. She was described as having a powerful voice and a commanding manner when she preached on this occasion. Not surprisingly, the neighbourhood was quite excited by a female, open-air preacher.[29]

Hull quickly emerged as an important centre for Primitive Methodist expansion in the North. The March 1819 Quarterly Meeting of the Nottingham Circuit sent John Harrison and his wife, the preacher Sarah Kirkland, whom he had married on 11 August 1818, to Hull. The first camp meeting there, attended by Clowes, Harrison, and others, was held on Sunday, 30 May; such was the speed of progress that at the Nottingham Circuit's June Quarter Day Hull was made the head of a new circuit.[30] But the work of John and Sarah Harrison was to be brief. In 1820 she gave birth to a child; the following year her husband died. She was to marry again in 1825, William Bembridge becoming her new partner. She then ceased to travel and took the status of a local preacher in the Belper Circuit.[31]

IV

Regardless of the long tradition of female preachers in Leeds, dating back to the time of Sarah Crosby and continued by Mary Bosanquet, Elizabeth Ritchie and others, and despite the successful work of Ann Cutler in Bramwell's revivals, women were now becoming unacceptable as Wesleyan local preachers. The spirit of revivalism and the use of female preachers were passing to the Primitive Methodists, who now took up the initiative. The young but growing Connexion certainly attracted persons who had some connection with the work of Bramwell; Sarah Kirkland was of this type. It also attracted those in Wesleyan Methodism who, after Bramwell's death, had continued his revivalist tradition; John Verity and his band in Leeds were such a group and the Woolhouses and their associates in Hull were another.

Perhaps it was coincidental but it seems significant, in view of the long-established tradition of female preaching around Leeds, that when the Leeds Primitive Methodist Circuit was formed from Hull Circuit in June 1821 Ann Carr, Sarah Eland, and Martha Williams who had recently joined them were appointed to the new circuit. Their precise status is far from clear. Their names did not appear on the Hull Circuit plan for May to July 1820 (with Leeds as part of the Circuit) nor on that for June to September 1821 (with Leeds heading a Branch). Possibly they were free-lancers, acting as revivalists, under the authority of the Circuit. Certainly they could attend the Quarterly Meeting for it was noted that their presence led to business becoming complicated.

The three women appear to have been very popular in the Leeds Circuit, but they soon became involved in controversy. Some of the societies were anxious to have one of these women as their preacher, and they were willing to comply; sometimes, when a man was planned to preach, he would arrive to find one of the women already taking his place. This was totally unacceptable as the women were clearly not accepting the discipline of the plan and not surprisingly it led to many complaints. The matter was raised at the Quarterly Meeting but the women insisted that they did not wish to be planned but preferred to be allowed to go where they wished. This the Quarterly Meeting was not prepared to permit; as a result the women left and a secession took place.[32]

It was probably this same dispute to which Hugh Bourne referred in an admonitory letter to a preacher during the Leeds Conference, 1823:

> These women were suffered to go loose from circuit to circuit, and one of the larger circuits not only connived at them, but actually encouraged them. At first they appeared to be useful, but after a time the evil overbalanced the good; and finally they acted in a most treacherous manner and made great savage of religion in one circuit.[33]

Primitive Methodism, in part a response to Wesleyan discipline which limited revivalist methods, had, paradoxically, been forced almost into a similar position of defending its own discipline, by the exertions of these three female preachers.

V

Those who seceded from the Primitive Methodists within the Leeds

Circuit quickly adopted a Methodist framework. 'A Sabbath Day Plan for the Female Revivalists in the Leeds Circuit' was soon published and contained the names of about eighteen preachers and exhorters, both male and female. Their first Leeds meeting place was a large room at Spitalfields on the Bank — possibly that same Hill House Bank room occupied by the Primitive Methodists prior to the erection of their Ebenezer Chapel, Quarry Hill — and here the Female Revivalist Society was formed and their first Quarterly Meeting held. Subsequently, a large room in George's Court, George Street, was rented for £30 per annum and they remained there for three years, presumably until the Leylands Chapel in Regent Street was opened in 1825. The evidence of these buildings suggests that the secession took place in 1822.[34]

Ann Carr was the leader of the Revivalists, assisted by Martha Williams; Sarah Eland did not stay with them very long as she married in 1824. Martha Williams's background had similarities to that of Ann Carr. Williams had been born in Nottingham and was converted at the age of twelve during Bramwell's great revival in the town. This revival had begun in December 1799 by the joint efforts of Bramwell and Mary Barritt; it had resulted in about 800 being added to the society. Her spiritual experience was further enriched in 1814 when the Irish Wesleyan revivalist, the Rev. Gideon Ousley (d. 1839), preached in the Circuit. In 1819 she became a preacher and began to travel, visiting some six of the largest counties.[35]

The foundation-stone of Ann Carr's Chapel in the Leylands, a fast-growing area of Leeds notorious for slum housing and poverty, was laid on 7 March 1825. The ground floor was occupied by shops and cottages, and the large upper room used for religious meetings. The indenture for the purchase of the land from Abram Rhodes, Christopher Smith and John Hebblethwaite, merchants of Leeds, was not signed until 11 October 1825. Altogether, 867 sq. yds of land were purchased for £216 15s and, in addition to the chapel premises, seven cottages were erected; one of these provided a home for Ann Carr and the rent from the others was an investment income. Was it coincidental or not that the adjoining cottages were situated in the appropriately named Saint Street?[36]

A commonly held view was that Ann Carr was a person of means possessing property in her own right. It was further suggested that about the time she came to Leeds her aunt died, leaving her some property which, after paying off her father's debts, left her a balance of £800. It was also reputed that Martha Williams had means and contributed liberally to the sect.[37] Although there may have been some truth in these claims, the evidence suggests that this view is not totally accurate. To finance the erection of the Leylands Chapel it was necessary to obtain a mortgage of £650 from William Taite of Boston Spa, with an option of a further £50 if required. On 11 April 1834, a new mortgage for £1,000 had to be obtained from Taite, who was now living in York; he retained £700 in payment of the original mortgage and Ann Carr received the remaining £300.[38]

Both Ann Carr and Martha Williams were very popular and greatly respected among the working classes with whom they worked, and yet they were essentially different in personality. Ann Carr was a robust-looking woman, bold, courageous and energetic, her preaching being characterised by zeal, correctness and sincerity rather than by eloquence and culture; in contrast, Martha Williams was quiet and unassuming, gave the impression of an educated woman and was described as a young lady of culture and refinement.[39] Ann Carr was the most frequent speaker at their meetings, often held in the open air.

A little is known of some of the others connected with the Leeds Female Revivalists. Sarah Hales (1800–56) had been born in Leek, Staffordshire of 'ungodly parents'; there she began to attend the Wesleyan Sunday School, where she learned to read. She came to Leeds after being forced to leave home following persecution for her religious beliefs; here she was converted by the Female Revivalists. She later became one of the first Primitive Methodists in Leek, and her name appeared as a preacher on the Ramsor plan, which included Leek, in 1827; she married Isaac Birchenough in 1837.[40] Another was Leeds-born Mrs Caroline Wordsworth (1820–68) who in her youth had attended Ann Carr's Chapel but at nineteen began to attend the newly built Rehoboth P.M., Park Lane, where she became a Sunday-school teacher for the select class. In 1842 she moved to an 'important situation' in Huddersfield where she united with the Primitive Methodists; four years later she married a Mr R. Wordsworth, Barnsley Town Missionary and a local preacher.[41]

The Leylands Chapel, in the midst of a vast slum and in the valley bottom, close to the Sheepscar Beck then notorious as an open sewer, was in marked contrast to the opulent Brunswick Chapel, higher up the hillside, also opened in 1825. The contrast became even more marked. Brunswick, with its rich trustees, soon to have an organ and emerging as a place for only the 'best' preachers, was before long reducing the number of free seats for the poor and hiding those who remained behind a screen; the Leylands Chapel was for the poor.

Not surprisingly the Leylands Chapel became, in terms of nineteenth-century society, a centre for relief and work among the destitute. This included a prosperous Sunday school and a Sick Society. More important was the connection with the fledgling temperance movement which had originated in the 1820s when Irish and Scottish evangelists imported the idea of an anti-spirits association from America. Leeds was at the forefront of this movement, the Leeds Temperance Society being formed in September 1830. It moved from a 'temperance' to a 'total abstinence' society in June 1836, when the pledge was introduced. Soon after, the Leeds Youth Temperance Society was formed for all those under twenty-one who would sign a declaration to abstain. Among their objectives was the holding of regular public meetings, and the Leylands branch of this Society met at Ann Carr's Chapel. Carr was a keen temperance advocate and in May 1837, for example, was promoting the cause in Hull, where the Rev. John Stamp had founded the Primitive Methodist New Connexion run on strict teetotal lines.[42]

The Leylands Chapel appears to have been the main centre for the growing work of the Female Revivalists, but they gradually obtained other premises. A Chapel was opened at Brewery Field, Holbeck in 1826 and a large school room was taken in Jack Lane, Hunslet in 1837.[43] In addition there were societies at Stanningley and Morley.

Support for the Female Revivalists came from all the town's Nonconformist and Methodist congregations, excluding the Primitive Methodists. Perhaps the most influential of Carr's many supportive friends was the Rev. John Ely of East Parade Congregational Chapel. Others who preached at both Chapel and Sunday-school anniversaries were the Rev. Thomas Gulland from the Wesleyans, the Rev. J. E. Giles of South Parade Baptist, James Sigston of the Protestant Methodists and others from the Methodist New Connexion and Quakers.[44] The Female Revivalists' popular lovefeasts attracted persons from various denominations.

The attitude of the Primitive Methodists towards the Female Revivalists was, not surprisingly, decidedly cold. From their viewpoint Ann Carr and the other two women had refused to accept

Connexional discipline and had caused a secession within the Leeds Circuit. The events at Morley, for example, must have left a sour taste in a Connexion struggling to make progress. A Primitive Methodist chapel had been opened in the village by William Clowes as early as 1821, but the dissension in 1826 over 'the female part of the congregation imbibing the notions of Ann Carr' resulted in the almost total destruction of the society and the loss of the chapel when Samuel Middlebrook, the mortgagee, sold it to Isaac Crowther (1769–1850), a rich Wesleyan cloth manufacturer, and it passed into Wesleyan use. It took until 1830 for the Primitive Methodists to re-establish their cause in the village but in 1835 Hugh Bourne was able to preach at the opening of a new Ebenezer Chapel.[45]

The Female Revivalists held regular prayer meetings and at times an atmosphere of emotional excitement was generated akin to some forms of contemporary Pentecostalism. During these meetings a small section would become so excited that they would rise to their feet and jump upright in a most energetic manner until exhausted; it was not unknown for worshippers to jump about until perspiration streamed down their faces. There is evidence that local Primitive Methodism disapproved of this kind of behaviour for which the Revivalists were nicknamed 'Jumping Ranters' or 'Jumpers'. For example, the Quarterly Meeting held on 8 December 1834 at Quarry Hill Chapel resolved: '[that] John Ellis of Daw Green [Dewsbury] be recommended to the District Committee on condition that if he comes among us he desists from jumping'.

It is quite likely that anybody having any connection with the Female Revivalists, and who was also a Primitive Methodist, was disciplined. The Quarterly Meeting of 6 December 1835 noted: 'J. Sheard's case of going to the Jumpers and joining in their mode of worship be overlooked for this time as he promises not to go there again while among us.' On another occasion, at the Quarter Day held on 5 March 1837, a much firmer line was taken, when it was agreed that: 'Aspinall come of[f] the plan general [neglect?] of duty and having his name on the Jumpers plan.'[46]

VI

In October 1840 Ann Carr went to Nottingham to visit friends but took ill on her return to Leeds in the following November. Perhaps she was already ill then, for her will was signed on 14 October and it bequeathed to Martha Williams the cottages and chapels both at Regent Street in the Leylands and at Brewery Field, along with the school at Hunslet, on the understanding that she would continue the work. Just before Ann Carr's death on Monday, 18 January 1841, an agreement was reached with the Wesleyans allowing them to continue the work after her death, and consequently a codicil was added enabling Martha Williams to sell the various premises. The trustees for the will were John Hill, a Leylands baker, and George Cooper, a farmer from Harehills.[47]

Her funeral was held on Thursday, 21 January at Woodhouse Cemetery. The service was conducted by the Rev. J. Rawson of the Cemetery Chapel, and the Rev. J. Scales of Queen Street Congregational Chapel gave the address. On the following Sunday funeral sermons were preached by Rawson at both Regent Street and the Brewery Fields Chapels. The next day, Monday, a large congregation assembled at the Lady Lane Wesleyan Methodist Association Chapel to hear Scales give an appropriate address.[48] Later a large gravestone was erected and still survives, being retained when the cemetery was landscaped in the 1960s.

The death of Ann Carr was further marked by Martha Williams who published a posthumous autobiography and an anonymous poem, 'Lines on the Death of Ann Carr' (Leeds, February 1841). Perhaps Carr's connections with Leeds were best summarised by a tribute to her in the *Leeds Times*:

> She was woman of extraordinary firmness and decision of character . . . The fervency of her religious enthusiasm was calculated to work powerfully upon uncultivated minds, putting a strong check upon the developments of licentiousness in its grosser and more revolting form . . . She was for thirty-four years a constant and laborious preacher . . . The respect entertained for her was evinced by the thousands who followed her to her last resting-place.

Significantly, autobiography, poem and tribute all failed to record her contribution to the early growth of Primitive Methodism in Leeds. This appears to have remained a delicate subject even after her death.

Ann Carr's death left the problem of continuing the work she had begun. On 1 February 1842 an agreement was made between the Wesleyan Methodists and Martha Williams, Carr's executor, allowing the Leylands Chapel and schoolroom to be taken over by the Wesleyans for an annual rental of forty pounds. The schoolroom was then re-let to the Leeds (First Brunswick) W. M. Circuit Sunday School Committee for ten pounds per annum.[49]

Meanwhile, probate had been granted on 9 June 1841, but it was not until 15 November 1844 that Martha Williams, by this time residing in Nottingham, was able to sell the Regent Street premises. They were purchased for £820 by a number of persons — the actual ownership now becomes very complicated — of whom John Gibson, a Leeds accountant, appears to have been the main one. Although £1,000 was still owed to Taite for the mortgage taken out in 1834, he accepted £820 and cancelled the outstanding debt. This act of generosity by Taite was not the only one, for there were other outstanding debts; help in their liquidation came from Nonconformists and Methodists, excluding the 'Prims'. An attempt by Williams to sell the library to the local Wesleyan Sunday School Committee had to be rejected because it was 'contrary to rule'.[50]

The Wesleyans found the Leylands Chapel in need of repair and decoration and, despite remedying these defects, the cause declined. After two years expenditure was greater than income and the Wesleyan society was soon in financial difficulties. Pew lettings, and by implication the resulting income, began to fall, being 127 (1842), 87 (1843) and finally 34 on closure (May 1853).[51] Even so, the Ecclesiastical Returns, 1851, showed congregations of 190 in the morning and 250 at night on the day of the Census.[52] Congregations were almost certainly much larger than the pew-lettings — free seats were 120 (1842) and 234 (1851), and such an impoverished area must have included many unable to afford the lettings. In April 1853, with the society in decline, the Wesleyans decided to abandon the chapel and to transfer the work to the nearby Darley Street Wesleyan Day School, which was now entered on the plan as a preaching place.[53]

VII

As we have seen, there is good evidence to suggest that by the time Primitive Methodism came to Leeds there was already a tradition of female preachers going back to the time of Wesley. The great West Riding Revival of the 1790s, centered on Bramwell, spread to other parts of the country and showed that female preachers could be instrumental in converting persons to Christ. It was this background, encompassing both female preachers and ranterism, which was gradually being abandoned by Wesleyan Methodism as it built its 'Brunswicks' and 'Hanovers', symbolic of social and political respectability.

Primitive Methodism, youthful and energetic, with a rough, unthought-out but practical theology, in which conversion of the sinner was all-important and order and respectability almost totally irrelevant, became a natural home for women preachers, of whom Sarah Kirkland was the first of many. To people such as Ann Carr, a Wesleyan 'called-to-preach' in a male-dominated world, the 'Ranters' offered an opportunity for fulfilment. And yet, Primitive Methodism, for all its flexibility, was forced into parting with Ann Carr because even that Connexion found it necessary to set limits to the extremes to which they could allow their preachers to go in the work of revivalism and conversion.

The emerging Female Revivalists revealed a female-dominated sect, unusual in a society which allowed women to play only a severely limited role and offered them few rights. The sect's success was almost completely dependent on the dynamic personality of Ann Carr, in contrast to the more 'cultured' personality of Martha Williams. Not surprisingly, despite a mixture of almost Pentecostalist fervour in worship and a crude programme of social relief, the sect collapsed on the death of Carr.

Undoubtedly, the Leylands slum of the 1820s was not an easy area for orthodox Christianity, church or chapel, to survive; it is to the credit of Ann Carr that she made some impact among the working classes. Wesleyans and Primitive Methodists both attempted to work in the district but found less success than the Female Revivalists. As the century progressed religion in the Leylands became increasingly polarised between the Jewish synagogue and the Irish Catholics. At least, this was nearly the case; Anglo-Catholics also managed to make some impression. And, in an area today consisting of factories and warehouses, it is the Salvation Army Barracks which still maintains the Christian presence.

Notes

*This essay was originally published in D. C. Dews (ed.), *From Mow Cop to Peake, 1807–1932* (Wesley Historical Society, Yorks., 1982) and is based in part on Ch. VII of the author's M.Phil. thesis, 'Methodism in Leeds from 1791 to 1861' (University of Bradford, 1984).

1. Zecharia Taft, *Bibliographical Sketches of the Lives and Public Ministry of Various Holy Women . . . in the Church of Christ* (London, 1825), I:i.

2. Ibid., I:ii.

3. A. Stevens, *The Women of Methodism* (London, 1876), p. 13. For the general history of women in early Methodism, see also Earl Kent Brown, *Women of Mr. Wesley's Methodism* (New York, 1983); Maldwyn Edwards, *My Dear Sister* (Manchester, [1981]); Paul Wesley Chilcote, 'John Wesley and the Women Preachers of Early Methodism' (PhD thesis, Duke University, 1984); and Deborah M. Valenze, 'Prophetic Sons and Daughters: Popular Religion and Social Change in England, 1790–1850' (PhD thesis, Brandeis University, 1981).

4. Thomas M. Morrow, *Early Methodist Women* (London, 1967), p. 15.

5. John Wesley to Sarah Crosby, 14 February 1761, in J. Telford (ed.), *The Letters of the Rev. John Wesley A.M.* (London, 1931), IV:133. Strictly speaking, Mrs Crosby was an 'exhorter' rather, in that she did not preach from a text.

6. John Wesley to Sarah Crosby, 2 December 1777, in Telford (ed.), *Letters*, VI:290–1.

7. Leslie F. Church, *More about the Early Methodist People* (London, 1949), p. 150.

8. Frank Baker, 'John Wesley and Sarah Crosby', *Wesley Historical Society Proceedings*, XXIV (1949–50), pp. 76–7; Morrow, *Early Methodist Women, passim.*

9. Baker, 'John Wesley', p. 77; P. S. Forsaith, 'John Fletcher of Madeley', *Wesley Historical Society (Yorks.) Bulletin*, XXXVIII (April 1981), p. 8; Morrow, *Early Methodist Women, passim.*

10. Baker, 'John Wesley', p. 76.

11. Ibid., pp. 78–81; Morrow, *Early Methodist Women*, p. 27.

12. J. Beaumont, *Memoirs of Mrs. Mary Tatham of Nottingham* (London, 1938).

13. John Rylands Library, Manchester, Methodist Church Archives (hereafter cited as MCA), 658c, Tyerman MSS, vol. III, p. 254. John Pawson (Liverpool) to Charles Atmore (Halifax), 4 December 1794.

14. MCA, Hobhill MSS Collection. Thomas Hannam (Leeds) to Alexander Kilham (Alnwick), 22 January 1796.

15. John H. S. Kent, *Jabez Bunting: The Last Wesleyan. A Study in the Methodist Ministry after the Death of John Wesley* (London, 1955), pp. 38–9.

16. Church, *More about the Early Methodist People*, p. 137.

17. Ibid., pp. 163–6; A. S. Wood, 'After Wesley: Expansion in Yorkshire Methodism, 1791–1800', *Wesley Historical Society (Yorks.), Bulletin*, XXXVI (April 1980), pp. 3–4.

18. Taft, *Biographical Sketches*, II:iii.

19. Ibid., II:vi.

20. *The Journals of William Clowes* (London, 1844), p. 169; W. Beckworth, *A Book of Remembrance, Being Records of Leeds Primitive Methodism* (London, 1910), pp. 9–15; George Herod, *Biographical Sketches of Some of Those Preachers Whose Labours Contributed to the Origination and Early Extension of the Primitive Methodist Connexion* (London, nd), pp. 437–40.

21. Wakefield M. D. Libraries, Cryer Collection, bill for the opening services at Hill House Bank; Beckworth, *A Book of Rembrance*, p. 40.

22. Taft, *Biographical Sketches*, II:175–99; *Wesleyan Methodist Magazine* (1860), p. 835.

23. H. B. Kendall, *The Origin and History of the Primitive Methodist Church* (London, nd), I:361–2.

24. Ibid., II:69, incorrectly gives the date of her birth as 1738.

25. M. Williams, *Memoirs of the Life and Character of Ann Carr; Containing an Account of Her Conversion to God, Her Devoted Labours, and Her Happy Death* (Leeds, 1841), pp. 13–18.

26. Herod, *Sketches of Preachers*, pp. 306–21.

27. Williams, *Memoirs*, pp. 28–9.

28. Kendall, *Origin and History*, I:373; J. Petty [Rev. J. MacPherson], *The History of the Primitive Methodist Connexion, from Its Origin to the Conference of 1860. . . .* (London: 1880), pp. 83–7.

29. Williams, *Memoirs*, p. 25, gives the date of the foundation-stone laying as 18 June. Could this be the date of the opening? Kendall, *Origin and History*, I:373.

30. Herod, *Sketches of Preachers*, p. 323; Petty, *Primitive Methodist Connexion*, p. 91.

31. Herod, *Sketches of Preachers*, pp. 332–4.

32. G. Allen, *A History of Primitive Methodism in Leeds (1818–88)* (Leeds, 1888), p. 6.

33. Beckworth, *A Book of Remembrance*, p. 51.

34. Taft, *Biographical Sketches*, II:290; Williams, *Memoirs*, p. 72.

35. Taft, *Biographical Sketches*, I:172–4.

36. Leeds City Council, Deeds and Documents, no. 3452. (These have since been transferred from the Civic Hall to the ownership of the West Yorkshire County Council, Wakefield.)

37. Beckworth, *A Book of Remembrance*, p. 50; *Leeds Mercury*, 18 March and 7 October 1893.

38. Mortgage details have been obtained from the deeds.

39. *Leeds Mercury*, 18 March 1893.

40. Taft, *Biographical Sketches*, I:172–4.

41. *Primitive Methodist Magazine* (1870), pp. 428–9.

42. Brian Harrison, *Drink and the Victorians* (London, 1971), *passim*; B. Harrison, 'Temperance Societies', *Local Historian*, VIII (1968), p. 135; Williams, *Memoirs*, p. 91; *The Temperance Worker*, XLII (1897), *passim*.

43. Williams, *Memoirs*, p. 76, gives some indication of the cost of providing some of the premises:

Leylands: chapel and house	(1,704)	
,, : school and library	(440)	2,144
Brewery Field: chapel and outbuildings		695
Hunslet: school room		420
Legal fees		80
		£3,339

44. Ibid., appendix 5.

45. W. Smith, *The History and Antiquities of Morley* (London, 1876), p. 194.

46. Leeds City Archives (hereafter cited as LCA), Leeds P. M. Circuit Minute Book, 1827–37.

47. A copy of the will is included with the Leyland Chapel deeds; another copy is available at the Borthwick Institute, York.

48. Williams, *Memoirs*, p. 138.

49. LCA, Leeds (First/Brunswick) W. M. Circuit Sunday School Committee Minute Book, 1842–66.

50. Ibid.

51. LCA, Leeds Leylands W. M. Chapel Pew and Sittings Letting Book, 1842–53.

52. Public Record Office, HO/129/501. Leylands W. M. Chapel Return.
53. LCA, Leeds (East) W. M. Circuit and Brunswick Trust Minute Book, 1827–57; Leeds, Brunswick W. M. Leaders Meeting Minute Book, 1828–77.

The Leylands Chapel after the departure of the Wesleyans was occupied by a number of bodies. It was used as a Temperance Hall, a Girls' Ragged School, a Congregationalist Mission, and, briefly, a Primitive Methodist Chapel; when the Primitive Methodists left in 1870, it became St Bridget's Roman Catholic Church. Finally and appropriately, it became a synagogue in 1893, survived slum clearance at the turn of the century, and was sold to the Leeds Corporation in 1927 when required for the widening of Regent Street.

Two more of Ann Carr's chapels, at Brewery Field and at Hunslet, came into Wesleyan ownership after her death. The Hunslet premises may only have continued in use for a short time; those at Brewery Field were replaced in 1892 by the Mint Wesleyan Mission, Holbeck, and here closure finally came in the early 1970s.

Chapter 5
Queen Victoria and Religion

Walter L. Arnstein

I

If Queen Victoria had not embodied, to a significant degree, the complex of assumptions and attitudes that we continue to label 'Victorian', the adjective would presumably not have taken such firm root in the language. And indeed, in her prudery, her personal sense of duty and her domesticity (her desire to constitute, with Albert and her children, the model family of the land), the adjective would appear to describe the Queen. But what of religion? As the late George Kitson Clark reminded us, 'it might not be extravagant to say of the nineteenth century that probably in no other century, except the seventeenth and perhaps the twelfth, did the claims of religion occupy so large a part in the nation's life . . .'[1] 'No one will ever understand Victorian England,' wrote Sir Robert Ensor, 'who does not appreciate that among the highly civilized, in contradistinction to more primitive, countries it was one of the most religious the world has known.'[2] How did the personality, the views, and the influence of Queen Victoria fit into the religious life of her kingdom?

The question has been treated in detail only once, in *The Religious Life and Influence of Queen Victoria* by Walter Walsh, published a year after her death by a faithful evangelical Anglican who assiduously combed the published letters and newspaper reports in order to confirm that the monarch had ever been a devout Protestant and that 'in the history of the world since the birth of Christianity a more truly God-fearing Sovereign never sat on any earthly throne.'[3] The historian of our day may draw upon much more. Since the appearance of Walsh's volume, more than a dozen major biographies of Victoria have been published, as have scores of memoirs by men and women who knew her. Most valuable of all, in revealing the private as opposed to the public Victoria, are the letters the Queen wrote regularly to her eldest daughter, the Crown Princess of Prussia.[4] Those letters, along with some of the memoirs of her attendants and her religious counsellors,[5] significantly supplement the Queen's daily journal as transcribed and edited by her youngest daughter, Princess Beatrice. The original was destroyed.[6]

The Victorian religious revival has often been described as a middle-class phenomenon, and the unique Religious Census of 1851[7] confirms that a pattern of weekly Sunday worship was far more prevalent among middle-class church and chapel-goers than among the denizens of urban slums. Victoria in turn has sometimes been described as a 'middle-class Queen', a notion supported by Lord Salisbury, the last of the Queen's ten prime ministers, in his public obituary: 'I always felt that when I knew what the Queen thought, I knew pretty certainly what view her subjects would take, and especially the middle class of her subjects.'[8] Other observers have noted that a woman who ate off gold plates in giant palaces and who associated far more often with aristocrats and servants than with businessmen or shop assistants could not be prototypically *bourgeois*. The purpose of the pages that follow will be to provide at least provisional answers to a number of overlapping questions: Who influenced the Queen's religious views and attitudes? What beliefs and assumptions came to constitute her personal faith? What was her attitude toward the clergy and towards church services? As formal head of the established Church of England, how did she react to the various conflicting forces within the Anglican world: Low Church Evangelicals, High Church Tractarians and Ritualists, and Broad Churchmen toying with heresy? What were her criteria in the selection of new bishops and archbishops, and how powerful was her influence on the selection process? How did the Queen respond to the other religious bodies that dwelt in her kingdom, her empire, and her world: the Presbyterians of Scotland; the Nonconformists of England; the Roman Catholics of Ireland, Great Britain and the continent; the Moslems and Hindus of India; the Jews; the Greek Orthodox; the professing rationalists and atheists? When laws affecting the place of religion became the focus of political controversy, how did Victoria react and, on occasion, help determine the end result?

Answers to these questions may suggest that, professing Christian as she always saw herself, the Queen could at times look upon the world in a notably 'un-Victorian' manner and (a fact her biographers have neglected to note) that a number of her views

altered over time. At the very least, such answers support the con-
clusions of Archbishop Davidson that the Queen's religious stand-
point was 'unusual' and Lady Longford's contention that it is non-
sensical to depict Victoria's nature as 'crystal clear, uncompromis-
ingly sensible and utterly lacking in imagination.'[9]

II

Since her father died before the young princess had reached the age
of one, it was to her mother, the Duchess of Kent, and her
governess, the Baroness Lehzen, that the youthful Victoria owed
her early religious upbringing. Both women were pious German
Lutherans, the baroness indeed the daughter of a Lutheran pastor
in a small village near the city of Hanover. They sought to mould
the princess into a comparably serious and pious girl who read
educational books rather than frivolous novels.[10] When her
mother's brother, Uncle Leopold, who in 1830 became the King of
Belgium, sent sage letters of advice to his royal niece, he repeatedly
urged her to emphasise her devotion to the Church of England:

> You know that in England the Sovereign is the head of the
> Church, and that the Church looks upon the Protestant religion
> as it is established as the *State* Religion . . . You will do well,
> whenever an occasion offers itself to do so without affectation,
> to express your sincere interest for the Church, and that you
> comprehend its position and count upon its good-will . . . I
> know you are averse to persecution, and you are right; miss,
> however, *no opportunity* to show your sincere feeling for the
> existing Church . . . You cannot, without *pledging* yourself to
> anything *particular, say too much on the subject.*[11]

The young Victoria's chief tutor from eight until eighteen was
the Rev. George Davys, a fellow of Christ's College, Cambridge,
and the author of numerous tracts published by the Society for
Promoting Christian Knowledge.[12] Davys was an evangelical; that
is, he sympathised with those who had reacted against the often
arid rationalism of the eighteenth-century Church of England.
They placed new stress upon the importance of individual salvation, upon the need to read and to know the Bible and to engage in
missionary work at home and abroad, and upon the desirability of

eradicating such blots on the face of Christendom as the slave trade and indeed slavery itself. Evangelicals felt a sense of kinship with the Wesleyan Methodists outside the Church, and they re-emphasised the *Protestant* nature of the Anglican community.

Whatever his personal inclinations, Davys sought to inculcate in his pupil a form of Christianity that would be tolerant of the divergent strands of belief to be found within the kingdom. By the age of eleven, Victoria was sufficiently versed in the principal doctrines of the Church of England to pass with flying colours an examination by the Bishops of London and Lincoln. 'In answering a great variety of questions proposed to her,' the bishops reported, 'the Princess displayed an accurate knowledge of the most important features of Scripture History, and of the leading truths and precepts of the Christian Religion as taught by the Church of England.'[13] Davys became much attached to his young charge, and in his later career as Bishop of Peterborough he would happily recall Victoria's penchant for strict truthfulness.

The Queen was to look back on Davys with less fondness than he did on her, but, whatever his limitations, his influence was considerable. In the summer of 1835 Victoria underwent confirmation by the Archbishop of Canterbury, William Howley. Two years later Howley was one of the two emissaries who conveyed to the princess the news that her uncle was dead and that she was now Queen. Victoria called upon Divine Providence for strength and assured the first meeting of her Privy Council that 'it will be my unceasing duty to maintain the Reformed Religion as by law established, securing at the same time to all the full enjoyment of religious liberty.'[14] At the opening of Parliament in November 1837 she read the required Royal Declaration against the Roman Catholic doctrines of transubstantiation, the sacrifice of the mass, and the invocation and adoration of saints. These practices were condemned as superstitious and idolatrous.[15] Half a year later, at her coronation, Archbishop Howley again presided: he anointed Victoria with holy oil; he administered the sacrament of communion; and he presented her with the crown and regalia of monarchy. The Queen solemnly promised to 'maintain the laws of God, the profession of the Gospel, and the Protestant Reformed Religion established by law', to 'preserve inviolably the settlement of the United Church of England and Ireland', and to uphold the rights and privileges of that church's bishops and clergy.[16]

By the time of her coronation the young queen had fallen under a new influence, that of her 58-year-old prime minister, the well-read and urbane Lord Melbourne who viewed most man-made institutions, including churches, with an air of cynical detachment and who was suspected of being an atheist at heart. When asked by an Archbishop of York to attend an evening as well as a morning worship service, he declined. 'No, my Lord, once is orthodox, twice is puritanical.' When implored by an emotional evangelical preacher to contemplate the dire consequences of sin, Melbourne exclaimed, 'Things are coming to a pretty pass when religion is allowed to invade private life.'[17]

As political and social as well as religious tutor to the young Queen, Melbourne had no desire to undermine either Victoria's piety or the regularity of her church attendance. He admitted that since his days at Eton he had rarely attended himself. 'People didn't use to go so much formerly', he explained. 'It wasn't the fashion; but it is a right thing to do.'[18] He encouraged the Queen to 'read the simple truths' rather than to trouble herself with theological conundrums. It was best not to puzzle over matters like the nature of Christ if only because 'the Trinity isn't comprehensible'.[19] She agreed with Melbourne that short sermons were best, that few preachers spoke well, and that there was little need to look up to the episcopal hierarchy with awe. 'Those clergymen, they are always poking themselves into everything,' he warned her. 'You bishops are sad dogs,' he told the Archbishop of York in her presence.[20] Melbourne cautioned her against both the Low Church evangelical enthusiasts and the High Church doctrinaires who were seeking to remodel the Church of England. In Melbourne's eyes, that church required no remodelling to speak of; its chief virtue among the world's religious bodies was that it was 'the least meddling'. For a time the young Queen came to look upon her prime minister's religious views as 'so *right, just,* and *enlightened*', and Owen Chadwick has persuasively argued that, although Melbourne's nonchalance was soon to be supplanted by Albert's earnestness, the former's influence did much to estrange the young Queen from the main religious movements that were stirring the church of which she was supreme head.[21]

Prince Albert, who married Victoria in 1840, came from the same German Lutheran background as did the Queen's mother. In drafting Victoria's announcement of the forthcoming marriage to the Privy Council in 1839, Melbourne had neglected to specify — in keeping with the Act of Settlement of 1701 — that Albert was a

'Protestant' prince. (Melbourne's apparent motive had been to appease Daniel O'Connell and the other Irish Roman Catholic MPs who provided his Whig government with its narrow majority in the House of Commons.) Associates of the ultra-Protestant Duke of Cumberland (Victoria's uncle and heir to the British throne until Victoria had children of her own) immediately spread rumours that Albert was a Roman Catholic, rumours given weight by the fact that a number of Coburg cousins had either converted to Roman Catholicism or had, like Victoria and Albert's Uncle Leopold, married a Roman Catholic wife.[22]

When the Foreign Secretary, Lord Palmerston, formally enquired of Albert's emissary, Baron Stockmar, whether Albert 'belonged to any special Protestant sect that will prevent him from taking the Sacrament with the Queen', Stockmar responded stiffly: 'There is no essential difference between the communion services of the Protestant German and the English Churches, except that perhaps the German is the more reverent.'[23] A few years later, on their first visit to Coburg, Albert and Victoria attended an impressive Lutheran service, and Albert was pleased to show Victoria the very castle room in which Luther had composed 'A Mighty Fortress is Our God'.[24] Prior to their taking the Anglican communion together for the first time, at the Easter following their wedding, Albert and Victoria followed the German custom of withdrawing completely from society for twenty-four hours. During that time, Albert played for her a piano version of Mozart's Requiem, read passages from a German devotional work, and walked with her quietly in the garden. They did not take communion again until Christmas, and Victoria remained convinced for the rest of her life that a twice-a-year pattern sufficed.[25]

Serious and devout as Albert was, and desirous as he clearly was to maintain and enhance the respectability of the British court, his religious attitudes had been moulded by forces other than simple Lutheran piety alone. As his most recent biographer has urged,[26] Albert was the product of that early nineteenth-century German cultural awakening in scholarship, literature and the arts epitomised by Goethe and Schiller, as well as that spirit of German nationalism unwittingly evoked by the armies of Napoleon. Albert's education included several months at Brussels and then a year at the University of Bonn, where he eagerly applied himself to the study of mathematics, the natural sciences and political economy, as well as music. The influence of Karl Gottlieb

Bietschneider, a highly controversial theological scholar at Bonn, helped confirm in Albert an attitude of amused detachment toward disputes over Biblical interpretation. He looked upon science and scholarly inquiry as buttresses rather than as enemies of religion. As Professor Emmanuel Herman Fichte had taught at Bonn: 'Through work and effort shall come salvation.' For Fichte the essence of true religion was the individual conscience, moral freedom, and strenuous activity.[27]

It is hardly astonishing therefore that when, during a tour of Switzerland in 1837, Albert secured a scrap of Voltaire's handwriting, he should send it off to Victoria as a gift. A few years later he was to alert his wife to Saint-Simon's advice to princes: they should promote religion by leading moral lives rather than by 'slavishly attending services in Church'.[28] Albert believed that the monarchy should serve as a moral agency in the land fully as much as the church, and Victoria in turn became convinced that Albert could provide religious instruction superior to that of any clergyman she knew.[29] As Dean Davidson was to note later in the century, 'the Prince Consort brought into her life a large religious element, but I should think it was, in his case, of a very nebulous sort so far as Christian dogma goes'.[30]

III

An examination of the religious predispositions of Victoria and Albert helps explain the manner in which the royal couple reacted towards the 'Low Church', 'High Church' and 'Broad Church' tendencies as they manifested themselves within the Church of England during the 1840s and 1850s and — in the case of Victoria — in the decades that followed Albert's death in 1861. Doubtless there are Victorian churchmen and laymen who fit poorly into any implicit framework of *Ecclesia Anglicana est omnis divisa in partes tres.* Some indeed sought to deny or to ignore the reality of those divisions in the seamless Christianity to which they aspired. Yet such an explanatory framework oversimplifies only a little; it was, in any case, one that Victoria and Albert came to accept without cavil.[31]

Albert and, to a lesser degree, Victoria found themselves most in sympathy with Low Church evangelicalism when it expressed itself in the form of 'good works'. The very first public speech that Albert ever gave in England was in June 1840 as newly appointed president of the Anti-Slavery Society.[32] In 1848 the Queen became a Life Governor of the Church Missionary Society, and in Windsor Castle she and the Prince interviewed Samuel Crowther, the Nigerian slave boy converted by the society who in 1851 was ordained as the first black bishop of the Church of England. When in 1848 the society forwarded to the Queen a petition from several West African chiefs in which they denounced slavery and expressed their appreciation for the work of Christian missionaries among them, Victoria formally replied:

> The commerce between nations in exchanging the fruits of the earth, and of each other's industry, is blessed by God. Not so the commerce in slaves, which makes poor and miserable the nation which sells them, and brings neither wealth nor the blessing of God to the nation who buys them, but the contrary. The Queen and people of England are very glad to know that Sagbua and the chiefs think as they do upon this subject of commerce. But commerce alone will not make a nation great and happy like England. England has become great and happy by the knowledge of the true God and Jesus Christ.[33]

Albert's interests were not limited to humanitarian efforts abroad, and having developed a high admiration for the pre-eminent evangelical social reformer of the day, Lord Ashley (after 1851, the 7th Earl of Shaftesbury), Albert hoped for a time to attach him to the royal household as social reform mentor.[34] Ashley preferred to remain in the House of Commons to continue his campaign to place legal limits upon the work of children and women in mines and factories. When Ashley's Commission reported in 1842, Albert felt overwhelmed: 'I have been horror stricken by the statements which you have brought before the country,' he wrote to Ashley. 'The nation must be with you, at all events I can assure you that the Queen is.'[35] As President of the Society for Improving the Condition of the Labouring Classes, Albert publicly urged in 1848 that the worker's lot would be improved if those with capital gave practical assistance by investing in model houses for working people and by providing loan funds and land allotments to those who sought self-improvement. 'The interests of classes, too often confronted, are identical,' declared Albert, 'and it is only ignorance which prevents their uniting for each other's advantage. To dispel that ignorance, to show how man can help man . . . ought to be the aim of every philanthropic person; but it is more peculiarly the duty of those who, under the blessing of Divine Providence, enjoy station, wealth, and education.'[36]

At Windsor Albert sought to practise what he preached, and he designed and oversaw the construction of neat small family houses on the royal estate — only to learn with surprise that some of the beneficiaries were unhappy to be uprooted from their old neighbourhood.[37] Albert had far greater success in 1844 in inducing the Duke of Wellington and Sir Robert Peel's cabinet to amend the Articles of War so as virtually to end the ancient custom of the duel — another of Ashley's *bêtes noires* — and in Albert's eyes an 'unChristian and barbarous custom'.[38] There was little doubt in Albert's mind that the clergy too had the function of combating such social evils. As he reminded Samuel Wilberforce, the new Bishop of Oxford, in 1845,

[a bishop] ought to be a guardian of public morality, not, like the Press, by tediously interfering with every man's private affairs, speaking for applause, or trampling on those which are fallen, but by watching over the morality of the State in acts which expedience or hope for profit may tempt it to commit, as well in Home and Colonial as in Foreign affairs.[39]

The evangelical concern for which Victoria showed greatest public sympathy was not factory legislation or lower-class housing but the Royal Society for the Prevention of Cruelty to Animals. As she wrote to that organisation in 1874, 'The Queen hears and reads with horror of the sufferings which the brute creation often undergo from the thoughtlessness of the ignorant, and she fears also sometimes from experiments in the pursuit of science.'[40] Victoria became a confirmed anti-vivisectionist, and in 1876 she was instrumental in securing a bill that subjected the practice to detailed government regulation.[41]

With other evangelical 'reforms' the royal couple found themselves much less in sympathy. When Gladstone first dined at Buckingham Palace in 1842, he was surprised to find that Grace was not said before the meal.[42] Victoria did not favour drunkenness, to be sure, and in 1846 she stopped the custom of giving tickets for ale as New Year's gifts to the poor at Windsor. She was also willing to become a patron first of the British and Foreign Temperance Society and later of the Church of England Temperance Society, but both organisations condoned a limited amount of beer and wine drinking. The Queen became neither a teetotaller nor a prohibitionist, and at Balmoral she readily tolerated occasional over-indulgence on the part of her Scottish servants.[43]

In her early years as Queen, Victoria defied evangelical precepts not only by reading novels but also by playing cards, by dancing far into the night, and by attending performances of Italian opera and French ballet. Albert preferred an 'early to bed, early to rise' regime, but he shared her devotion to the theatre. Victoria and Albert saw it as their duty 'to revive and elevate the English drama' and to purge the world of actors and actresses from the customary taint of immorality and rowdyism. A presentation of *The Merchant of Venice* at Windsor Castle in 1848 was the first of numerous command performances there, and late in her reign Victoria awarded a knighthood to Henry Irving, the first actor to be so honoured.[44] During the 1860s and 1870s the Queen would often condemn the frivolity, hedonism, and immorality of aristocratic high society in Britain, but she and Albert were quite willing to attend the races at Ascot for what Lord Ashley derisively termed 'the annual exhibition of the sovereign to the people', and on occasion she would bet a few shillings on the outcome of a horse race.[45]

The evangelical tenet to which the royal couple objected most strongly was that of sabbatarianism. Albert has often been credited (or debited) with endowing the Victorian ethos with much of its earnestness and prudery. Yet when it came to 'the English Sunday', he and Victoria found themselves fighting a rearguard battle. The ten thousand inhabitants of Albert's native Coburg could celebrate Sunday in thirty-two public gardens drinking beer and listening to band music. Why could not two million Londoners do the same? Yet a religious outcry forced the government to close Kew Gardens to military bands on Sundays, and the House of Commons refused to permit museums to open their doors.[46] When one Sunday the Queen entered the home of a poor Scottish woman living near Balmoral and presented her with a gift, the woman protested. 'Ye're violatin' the Sabbath,' she told the Queen. Assured that Christ himself had performed good deeds on the Sabbath, the woman agreed to take the present, but she got in the last word:

'Ah wiel, then I dinna think ony mair of him for it.'[47] The sabbatarians in due course succeeded in stopping Sunday postal
deliveries, but they failed to prevent the Queen from travelling by
train on that day when she saw fit — though the Queen sought to
mollify the objectors by calling as little attention to the custom as
was practicable.[48] Albert told the tutor of his eldest son that Sunday
was 'to be kept as a day of recreation & amusement', and Victoria
was to assure her granddaughters that they might play tennis on
Sundays so long as they did not ask servants to chase after the balls.
'Being Sunday, I do not think it right to make others work for your
amusement.'[49] As the Queen wrote to her eldest daughter in 1859,
'You know I am not at all an admirer or approver of our very dull
Sundays, for I think the absence of innocent amusement for the
poor people, a misfortune and an encouragement of vice.'[50]

IV

On one major issue the royal couple remained in strong sympathy
with the evangelicals, in their increasing fear — as the 1830s and
1840s unrolled — of what became known as the Oxford or Tractarian or Anglo-Catholic movement. Borrowing an evangelical
method, four fellows of Oriel College, Oxford, began in 1833 to
publish a series of *Tracts for the Times*, erudite essays appealing to
the Anglican clergy to turn away from accommodation with church
reform under secular auspices in order to return to a pre-Reforma-
tion doctrinal and liturgical ideal. Men like John Henry Newman,
John Keble, Hurrell Froude, and Edward Bouverie Pusey emphasised concepts such as obedience, holiness, devotion, sacrament,
fasting and mortification. For them it was not the statutes Parliament had passed in the days of Henry VIII but the doctrine of apostolic succession that constituted the foundation-stone of the
Church of England. That body had become in their eyes too little a
divine institution and too much a department of state.

Albert and Victoria opposed the Tractarians on grounds both of
doctrine and of form. In reproaching a kingdom that had granted
civic equality to Protestant Nonconformists and to Roman Catholics and that was revamping church finances by means of a state-
appointed Ecclesiastical Commission, the Tractarians seemed to be
in revolt against the monarchy that had formally sanctioned such
acts. When Tractarian divines publicly deplored the appointment

of Professor R. D. Hampden as Bishop of Hereford because he wanted to admit nonconformists to Oxford and regarded the Bible as more important than the traditions of the Church, Albert felt a sense of outrage. 'Perhaps the next suggestion will be that Hampden should be burned at the stake,' he wrote bitingly to his adviser Baron Stockmar.[51]

The Tractarian practices that troubled Victoria most involved the veneration of saints, the use of the sign of the cross, the chanting of the liturgy, the use of oral confession, and the administration of penance and absolution. All these tendencies seemed to prove that Puseyite clerics were 'snakes in the grass . . . in fact the hidden Jesuits of this country'. The so-called 'priests' of the 1840s were clearly not the clergymen of earlier times, 'and it is from this *priestly domination*', Victoria wrote privately to her uncle, 'that I recoil with horror & against them that I protest in the name of Protestantism'.[52] Conversion to Rome between 1845 and 1851 by several leading Tractarians like John Henry Newman led to the fear that the entire Anglo-Catholic movement would soon transfer its allegiance to a rapidly reviving Roman Catholic Church within England. Victoria shared with Prime Minister Lord John Russell deep suspicion of the Romanisers who remained within the Anglican fold. In response to a petition signed by 63 peers, 108 MPs, and more than 300,000 lay Anglicans, Victoria formally asked the Archbishop of Canterbury 'to maintain the purity of the doctrines taught by the clergy of the Established Church, and to discourage and prevent innovations in the mode of conducting the services of the Church not sanctioned by law or general usage'.[53]

Victoria repeatedly warned prime ministers not to recommend Tractarians to high clerical office. Thus, when the deanery of Winchester fell vacant in 1845, she wanted to fill it with 'a person decidedly averse to Puseyism'. When Lord Derby first took over the prime ministership in 1852, she asked for his assurance that he would not recommend '*Puseyites* or *Romanisers*' as bishops.[54]

Victoria's concern with 'Puseyism' had waned a little during the 1850s and 1860s, but when some ritualistic clergyman protested in 1863 against the wedding of the Prince of Wales and Princess Alexandra taking place during Lent, the Queen waxed indignant. 'The objections rest merely on fancy or prejudice and one in this case based on no very elevated view of one of God's holiest ordinances . . . Marriage is a solemn holy act *not* to be classed with amusements.'[55] During the early 1870s Victoria became absorbed anew by ritualism. By then Anglo-Catholicism had dispersed from Oxford to individual parishes all over the kingdom, and its emphasis had shifted from doctrine to worship. Utilising richly ornamented churches and colourful vestments and ceremonies, men like Charles Lowder had become successful 'priests' in slum parishes like those of London's East End. The Queen was unimpressed, and she remained as insistent as ever — if not totally successful — on keeping ritualists out of high church office. She remained far more sympathetic to Lutheran usages. As she wrote to her eldest daughter in 1873,

> In Germany you can afford not to dread these terrible High Church and ritualistic attempts and movements — which are mere aping of Catholic forms and an undermining of Protestantism, because your Church is really Protestant and all Catholic forms are expunged from it. But here flowers, crosses, vestments, all mean something most dangerous![56]

The problem, the Queen told one of her Liberal ministers, was that 'we are *in fact in form* NOT Protestants though we are in doctrine'.[57] Since the law courts had been unsuccessful in halting the ritualising process in numerous parish churches, the Queen, with the co-operation of Archbishop Archibald Tait, launched the campaign that led to the Public Worship Act of 1874. It was one of the most significant examples of royal legislative initiative of the second half of the nineteenth century, because it is clear that Prime Minister Disraeli pushed it through Parliament expressly at the Queen's desire. The measure drafted by Tait sought to simplify the process whereby extreme ritualists could be disciplined by church courts. The measure's bark was greater than its bite, and it ultimately passed through Parliament with relative ease. Although Disraeli's biographer was to conclude that 'it proved difficult to enforce and caused more harm than good', it delighted Queen Victoria.[58] His parliamentary success confirmed Disraeli's place as her favourite prime minister. At his next audience 'I really thought she was going to embrace me,' Disraeli reported afterwards. 'She was wreathed with smiles, and, as she talked, glided about the room like a bird.'[59] She remained hostile to ritualism to the end, and as late as 1889 she barred Prime Minister Salisbury from nominating Canon H. P. Liddon as Bishop of Oxford. 'He might ruin and taint all the young men as Pusey and others did before him,' she wrote.[60]

V

Since she believed, as she observed to Disraeli in 1874, 'that the extreme evangelical school do the established church as much harm as the high church,'[61] the Queen may most appropriately be described as Broad Church in sentiment. In her youth she had read, at Melbourne's suggestion, the sermons of Dr Thomas Arnold, the reforming headmaster of Rugby and Regius Professor of Modern History at Oxford. Arnold served as a kind of godfather to Victorian Broad Churchmen who sought to transform the Church of England into a truly national church, narrow neither in creed nor practice. Thus she and Albert very much approved of men like Edward Stanley, Bishop of Norwich (1837–49), who in his inaugural sermon declared conscientious dissent to be neither sinful nor schismatic and who approved of education even when not under religious auspices. The young Victoria was so delighted that she invited him to preach at Buckingham Palace. Stopford Brooke, who served as her personal chaplain from 1867 to 1880, held comparable views as did another royal favourite, Arthur Penrhyn Stanley, the biographer of Thomas Arnold and Dean of Westminster from 1864 until 1881.[62] That such clergymen constituted a select minority may be gathered from a royal memorandum concerning the religious education of her two oldest children: 'A good, moral, religious but *not bigoted* or narrowminded education is what I pray for,' the Queen wrote in 1846. 'But where to find exactly what one wants?'[63]

Victoria was untroubled by the fact that Frederick Temple, who became Bishop of Exeter in 1869, Bishop of London in 1885 and finally Archbishop of Canterbury in 1896, had as a young clergyman contributed to *Essays and Reviews* (1860), the notorious volume described by one critic as 'infidelity with a surplice on'. Its authors had stated bluntly that a gap had opened between Christian doctrine on the one hand and the everyday assumptions of educated Victorians on the other, and they went on to insist, among other things, that the truth of Christianity did *not* depend on accepting as literal fact every statement in the Bible.[64] Nor was Victoria troubled by J. W. Colenso, the Bishop of Natal from 1853 to 1883, who, while translating the Old Testament into the Zulu language, came to the quasi-heretical conclusion that the Bible partook of myth and legend as well as of history and that the Pentateuch had been compiled by more than one author.[65] It was to Bishop Colenso that Queen Victoria in 1874 addressed her strongest plea for inter-racial harmony. She praised him for

> his noble, disinterested conduct in favour of the natives who were so unjustly used, and [expressed] in general her very strong feeling (and she has few stronger) that the natives and coloured races should be treated with every kindness and affection, as brothers, not — as alas! Englishmen too often do — as totally different beings to ourselves, fit only to be crushed and shot down![66]

Prince Albert, who regarded the science of the day as fully compatible with his religious creed, served Cambridge University as a reforming Chancellor from 1847 on. There he was distressed to find what the geologist Charles Lyell called 'a vast theological seminary' whose students largely neglected the natural and physical sciences as well as history, economics and modern languages. Albert strongly supported a move to introduce degree courses in the Moral Sciences (philosophy, economics, history and law) and the Natural Sciences.[67] The importance that Albert attached to learning can similarly be discerned in the advice with regard to clerical appointments that the Queen sent to Lord Palmerston in 1860. She asked the prime minister 'to bear in mind that the Bench of Bishops should not be left devoid of some University men of acknowledged standing and theological learning . . . Lord Palmerston may now have an opportunity of selecting a stronger man of Liberal views from Cambridge.' Lord Palmerston was doubtful. He reminded the Queen that bishops were less involved with learning than with 'watching over the clergy of their diocese . . . preserving harmony between the clergy and the laity, and softening the asperities between the Established Church and the Dissenters . . . Much mischief has been done by theological bishops.'[68] As this exchange suggests, the Queen had less sense of the role of clergyman as pastor than as upright and learned man. Although she appreciated those who knew how to cater to her personal concerns, she found it difficult to understand 'why the clergy should go fussing about the poor or servants . . . The servants are very good people — why can't they be let alone?' She rather suspected that a parson who concentrated on visiting the sick or instructing the poor was unduly 'clerical' or 'sacerdotal'.[69]

The Queen played a highly significant role in the making of

church appointments. As Gladstone put the matter in 1881, four factors entered into every nomination: 'If I am one of them, so the particular diocese is another, the Queen a third, the Liberal party a fourth.'[70] Prime ministers, whatever their concern for the interests of religion, could not ignore the fact that bishops were members of the House of Lords and might vote on political issues. When bishoprics fell vacant the Queen generally left the initiative for making nominations to the prime minister as (in Dean Davidson's words) the 'representative of the English people', but the Queen was fully prepared to recommend particular clergymen who merited consideration for promotion, to specify the sort of individual needed for a particular post, and to exercise a veto. In her later years 'the veto was exercised a great many times'.[71]

Successive prime ministers cringed under the pressure the Queen placed on them. In 1864 Lord Palmerston complained: 'She fancies, poor woman, that she has special prerogatives about the Church because she is its Head, forgetting', he added ambiguously, 'that she is equally Head of all the Institutions of the Country'.[72] In the words of Dudley Bahlman, 'each prime minister thought he was being singled out for rough handling; but the Queen tried to have her way against her ministers' wishes from the time of Peel onwards'.[73] Victorian bishops, like the Supreme Court nominees of American presidents, did not always go on to play the roles predicted of them, but Owen Chadwick, for one, credits the Queen with gradually raising the calibre of Anglican bishops in wisdom, learning, and freedom from political entanglement.[74] Even as the Queen increasingly identified politically with the Conservatism of Disraeli and Salisbury rather than the Liberalism of Gladstone, she continued to favour Broad Church clerics likely to align themselves with political liberalism. As she wrote to Davidson in 1882, 'both extremes of High and Low Church are to be avoided', and as she insisted to Archbishop Benson in 1890, bishops were to be chosen 'for their real worth. We want people who can be firm and conciliating, else the Church cannot be maintained. We want large, broad views, or the difficulties will become insurmountable.'[75]

VI

Queen Victoria's personal faith in her later years revolved about the problem of death and of how to become reconciled to its all but overwhelming reality. As a young woman, she had matter-of-factly accepted the notion that religion provided comfort in the face of death. How unhappy must be those without faith at such a time, she had observed to Melbourne, 'when reliance on an all-merciful Redeemer is such a balm, and such a consolation!'[76] Yet, unlike most Victorians, Victoria did not encounter death at first hand for several decades. Her father had died before she was aware of the world around her; death had not struck any member of her Kensington Palace circle while she was growing up, and in defiance of the odds not one of her nine children died at birth or during childhood. Then in 1861 disaster struck. In March came the death of her mother, and the blow prostrated the Queen. It was the 'most dreadful day of my life,' she wrote to her eldest daughter, '. . . I feel as if my heart would break! You, my darling have seen a death bed — I never.'[77] Three weeks later she still felt 'stupified — stunned'. Indeed 'the more distant the dreadful event becomes, and the more others recover their spirits — the more trying it becomes to me!'[78] For hour after hour Prince Albert would walk with her up and down the terrace at Windsor while they talked about the after-life. They read *Heaven Our Home* and Bishop Joseph Butler's eighteenth-century treatise, *The Analogy of Religion*, in a search for solace.

Nine months later came the yet greater blow, the death of Albert. As one of her biographers has noted,

> In a sense, time stopped for Queen Victoria. For the rest of her life the hands of the clock would be pointing at 10:50 P.M., December 14, 1861, the hour when her beloved had passed away. The rest of her days would, in fact, be dedicated to preserving things exactly as they were at the moment that this most precious life was snuffed out.[79]

For a time the Queen thought that, like her grandfather King George III, she would go mad. She prayed that if God had taken Albert he should take her too, and she contemplated suicide. Her letters in the decades that followed often refer to the years of her widowhood as no more than a postlude. 'As my life is made up of work,' she wrote in 1867, 'I must live as I find I best can through that work. Mine is a weary, weary life.'[80] 'Pleasure has for ever died out of my life,' she noted in 1884. 'The sense of doing good to others is the only thing which still remains.' A year later, she added: 'Anxiety, trouble, and grief are all I have now — with nothing to cheer or brighten my sad life of constant and incessant labour!'[81]

In the short run she found comfort of sorts in decreeing the longest and strictest period of mourning in the history of the British court. Before being sealed, the room at Windsor in which the Prince had died was carefully photographed to guard against change. To the door was affixed a plaque with the words: 'Every article in this room my late lamented husband selected for me in the twenty-fourth year of my reign.' Above the empty pillow on the right side of every bed Victoria would afterwards sleep in, there would hang a photograph of Albert taken on his deathbed. Near by lay a plaster cast of the Prince's hand. Not only was Albert's room preserved as it had been at his death — the same held true for her mother's sitting-room at Frogmore and was to hold true for that of her beloved Scottish servant John Brown — but at Osborne, for the next forty years, Albert's clothes were laid out and hot water was brought to his dressing-room before dinnertime.[82] Dean Randall Davidson, who became the Queen's spiritual mentor during the 1880s, attributed this custom not to a belief on the part of the Queen that the spirit of the dear departed still haunted its old home but to the fact that Victoria had instructed her servants that nothing was to be moved or touched or changed until she gave orders to that effect. She *never* did, and none of her children or her spiritual advisers, including Davidson, ever found the courage to bring the matter up while talking to the Queen. The Prince of Wales did finally give such orders — but only after he had become King Edward VII.[83]

All the paraphernalia of mourning, such as the half-inch-wide black borders that framed her writing paper for the rest of her life and the church services marking each anniversary of the death and the innumerable memorials to Albert that she was to unveil, would have failed to suffice if she had not firmly believed in life after death.[84] As she wrote to the Duchess of Sutherland, who, in the name of the widows of the kingdom, had presented her with an address of condolence and a sumptuously bound Bible:

Pray express to all these kind sister-widows the deep and heart-felt gratitude of their widowed Queen, who can never feel grateful enough for the universal sympathy she has received . . . But what she values far more is their appreciation of her adored and perfect husband. To her, the only sort of consolation she experiences is in the constant sense of his unseen presence, and the blessed thought of the eternal union hereafter, which will make the bitter anguish of the present appear as naught.[85]

The Queen found special comfort in the decidedly unorthodox doctrine that the dear departed had gone on not to a Heaven far removed from earthly cares but to one in which, as the Reverend Charles Kingsley suggested to her, the deity had taken Albert to continue *working* above at all those tasks in which he had excelled on earth. 'Oh, surely that is so,' the Queen agreed.[86]

At rare intervals, it would seem, Victoria did experience '*flashes of doubtfulness*' as to the doctrine of immortality. 'And yet,' she told Dean Davidson, 'these feelings never last, for it is simply *impossible* to believe that the lives we have seen cut short in the full swing of activity can really have come then to an utter end, or that we shall not see and know them hereafter.'[87] Her views on the afterlife had a concreteness that her other doctrinal views lacked, and the church services of her widowhood that meant most to her were funerals and memorial services. They involved a form of 'prayer for the dead' that accorded far better with Roman Catholic theology than with the Protestantism the Queen continually professed.[88] Death came particularly near in the years 1878–84, during which she lost two of her children (Alice and Leopold), her favourite prime minister (Disraeli), her long-time spiritual mentor (Dean Wellesley) and her favourite servant (John Brown). The loss of Brown meant 'one of those shocks like in '61 when every link has been shaken torn'.[89] Such occasions tested the mettle of her spiritual guides. Thus for the memorial service at Frogmore on 14 December 1883, the twenty-second anniversary of the Prince Consort's death, the Queen asked Davidson to draw up a special prayer that would bracket Albert and John Brown and refer also to the death of Dean Wellesley and the hazards her son Prince Arthur currently faced while travelling in India. 'A very difficult task,' Davidson noted, 'but it must be done.'[90]

Queen Victoria was not the only Victorian to be absorbed by the subject of death, but her widowhood was not so much endured as flaunted, and with her attendants she created 'something like a sacred College of Vestal Widows' to tend the flame of her sorrow.[91] Her favourite poem was Tennyson's elegiac *In Memoriam*, and on occasion she would quote a verse in a letter to her daughter.[92] She loved to plan funerals and to put up monuments. In 1872 she erected one in St George's Chapel at Windsor in honour of her father. 'A recumbent figure on a tomb which is what I always like best,' she wrote, and what she chose for Albert and herself.[93] Her private secretary thought that on occasion the Queen's grief became excessive — as if to compensate for having paid too little attention to the deceased when alive, and late Victorian designers of women's clothing found that decrees of mourning depressed their business at all too frequent intervals. Since Queen Victoria was 'related to most of the reigning houses,' one journalist noted, 'this comes pretty hard on our fashion providers'.[94] Talk in the royal household was ever of coffins and of winding sheets, for the Queen took the keenest interest in the funeral of even the lowliest of her servants. Funerals and memorial services 'are very trying,' one of her ladies-in-waiting noted in 1900, 'but I think the Queen enjoys them, at any rate they are the only lodestones that draw her within the precincts of a church!'[95]

On subjects other than personal immortality, the Queen's views were far less definite, and she would often comment to Dean Davidson: 'I suppose the orthodox belief is so and so; do you think we have really ground for holding it firmly? Do you really and truly believe it yourself or is it only a pious opinion?'[96] At the same time Victoria had no desire to have sceptics destroy belief in a personal deity. As she reminded her eldest daughter in 1878,

A mere abstract idea of goodness which is very much what philosophers profess and advocate is not desirable, nor does it lead to the very perfection which it pretends to do. It is only by trusting in God's all merciful goodness and in following the precepts of His beloved Son, that one can go through the trials, sorrows, and difficulties of this life. Without this conviction sorrows and trials will lead to feelings of despair and bitterness, whereas if you can say 'Thy will not mine be done' and 'God's ways are not our ways' and you will feel a peace and contentment as well as courage far different to the courage and sense of duty of Socrates. It is this alone which makes life and our future hopes a reality.[97]

In the Queen's eyes, such an attitude did not represent fatalism. Back in 1846, she and Albert had objected to Lord Brougham's statement in the House of Lords that the Irish famine was God's way of keeping the population down. And she agreed with her eldest daughter in deploring 'that dreadful idea that whatever happens you are to do nothing to prevent it etc. That, in my opinion, is going against the laws of an all-wise all-merciful and all-loving God and Father.'[98]

Victoria was not a fundamentalist. She rejoiced that 'the belief in eternal punishment has almost entirely disappeared'. In its old form she found it 'perfectly absurd and monstrous'.[99] A Scottish preacher learned to his chagrin that his sermon on the devil had gone over badly with the Queen because — as one of her daughters gently explained to him — 'the Queen does not altogether believe in the devil'.[100] Lady Errol, one of Victoria's ladies-in-waiting and 'a hot Evangelical', amused the Queen by handing out tracts predicting the end of the world within twenty years. When she presented a tract on temperance to one of Prime Minister Salisbury's cabinet colleagues, the royal dinner table exploded with laughter.[101] When, shortly after Albert's death, one clergyman sought to give comfort by pointing out that, with Albert gone, 'henceforth you must remember that Christ himself will be your husband', Victoria's response was succinct: 'That is what I call twaddle.'[102]

Did Queen Victoria's personal faith include a significant element of superstition? Presumably her belief that animals had souls — at least 'the very intelligent and highly developed ones' — would be seen as an example of heterodoxy (with which many pet-owners might sympathise) rather than of superstition.[103] Although the Queen had, as we have seen, no objections to weddings during Lent, she readily accepted the old Scottish superstition that marriages in May turned out badly; she could cite the marriage of her parents and of her Uncle Leopold and Princess Charlotte as examples. 'I never let one of our family marry in that month,' she decreed.[104]

Like other Victorians, she was interested in pseudo-sciences like phrenology. She was also intrigued, in the 1850s, by the psychic claims of Daniel Dunglass Home, whose seances were attended by the novelist Edward Bulwer-Lytton and by Robert and Elizabeth Browning. On one occasion she and Albert tried their hands at table turning at Osborne, but the episode can be explained more as a parlour game than as a conversion to spiritualism.[105] The Queen apparently attributed the force that turned the table to some form of magnetism or electricity. It is true that when Disraeli lay on his deathbed and was asked whether he would like a visit from the

Queen, he replied: 'No, it is better not. She would only ask me to take a message to Albert.'[106] Affectionately ironic as the remark may have been, it also suggests that the retired prime minister had not heard the Queen speak of alternative media of communication with the next world.

One facet of the Queen's personal faith requires separate consideration. Persuaded as Victoria was that 'an Empire without religion is like a house built upon sand', and equally persuaded as she was that it was wrong for a government 'to try and increase the dislike of and contempt for the clergy, amongst the masses',[107] the Queen maintained throughout her life a predisposition that may fairly be called anti-clerical. During her childhood years Victoria developed 'a great horror of *Bishops* on account of their wigs and *aprons*'.[108] It was never altogether to disappear, and it was confirmed at her coronation service in 1838. The Bishop of Durham, complained the Queen, was 'remarkably maladroit and never could tell me what was to take place'. The Archbishop of Canterbury jammed the ring on the wrong finger so that she nearly screamed with pain, and the Bishop of Bath and Wells prematurely informed her that the service was over. A few minutes later the Queen had to be fetched back from the chapel of Edward the Confessor for the final Hallelujah Chorus.[109] Sixty-two years later, Victoria agreed to the appointment of Dean Davidson to the Bishopric of Rochester. She had no right to bar him from a higher church office, she told him, but she felt duty bound to warn him that she had 'never found people promoted to the Episcopate remain what they were before'. They preached more poorly. 'The whole atmosphere of a Cathedral and its surroundings — the very dignity itself which accompanies a Bishopric — seems to hamper their freedom of speech.'[110] Victoria's Diamond Jubilee celebrations in 1897 involved innumerable gatherings with dignitaries from home and abroad. After one exhausting reception of a group of black-gaitered and aproned divines, the Queen went for her customary afternoon drive. She broke the silence by declaring, 'A very ugly party.' 'I do not like bishops!' the Queen went on. Her companion, Lady Lytton, was horrified: 'Oh, but Your dear Majesty likes *some* bishops — for instance, the Bishop of Winchester and the Bishop of Ripon.' Victoria relented only a little: 'I like the man but *not* the Bishop!'[111]

The acme of clerical incompetence involved, it is true, not a bishop at all but the Dean of Windsor who, in 1841, upon the birth of the Prince of Wales, solemnly congratulated the Queen on 'saving us from the incredible curse of a female succession'.[112] The Queen's antipathy did indeed extend to the lesser clergy as well. Thus she and Albert were adamant that their eldest son's tutor — unlike Victoria's own — would not be a cleric. Some years later she explained that one of her younger sons, Prince Leopold, was to have a new teacher:

> Mr. Duckworth, his instructor and a really most talented and charming person, will become his tutor or governor. The only objection I have to him is that he is a clergyman. However he is enlightened and so free from the usual prejudices of his profession that I feel that I must get over my dislike to that.[113]

'There are not many good preachers to be found,' Queen Victoria had told Lord Melbourne when she was still a royal teenager.[114] The Queen found the solemn, slow-moving grandeur of Anglican cathedral worship tiring beyond all bearing — 'Two-and-three-quarter hours,' she noted, with exclamation marks, in her journal. Even at the age of forty she found the standard Anglican service 'so cold — such a repetition of the same prayers again and again, that it quite takes off the effect — added to which the mumbling of the clergyman to himself each time' — all in all 'very unpleasant'.[115] In 1859 the Queen, with the sanction of the Archbishop of Canterbury, caused an abridged liturgy to be used in her private chapels, a process given broader authorisation by a parliamentary statute of 1872.[116] Dean Davidson wondered in the 1880s if the Queen would not enjoy the services more if she permitted some of the colour and ceremony that the ritualist movement had added elsewhere in the country, but such alterations Victoria strictly forbade. Even the service at the local parish church near Osborne was thought by the Queen to be 'rather advanced' because the clergyman preached in a surplice rather than the plain black gown to which she was accustomed.[117]

As for the sermons themselves, the Queen liked them to be simple, to deal with everyday truths, to be expressed with feeling, and to make some reference to incidents connected with the royal household — such as a death or an illness or an anniversary. Most of all the Queen wished them to be short.[118] The story is told of a young curate who, in the 1890s, was unexpectedly asked to preach the Sunday sermon at Windsor. When he sought the advice of the

Queen's private secretary, Sir Henry Ponsonby responded: 'It doesn't much matter *what* you say, because Her Majesty is too deaf to hear, and will probably go to sleep, but on no account let it last for more than five minutes.'[119] Not only did the Queen like sermons to be brief — the thousand-word sermons of Canon Charles Kingsley suited her admirably[120] — but she also liked to have the text in front of her so that she could follow it word for word.

Many preachers must have found the experience chilling because, in the domestic chapel within Windsor Castle, a clergyman who had ascended a hidden staircase to the pulpit found himself looking down upon the congregation but level with Victoria. She sat in a gallery seat, and in the words of the observant son of her private secretary, her 'unflagging attention was more often accompanied by a look of disapproval than of appreciation'.[121] The gauntlet that preachers to the Queen were compelled to run is made clear by a surviving exchange of 1879:

A submission of a list of preachers for Osborne, suggested by the Dean of Windsor.

Name	*Queen's remarks*
The Dean of Westminister	*Too long*
The Dean of Christchurch	Sermons are like lectures
Dr. Bradley	Excellent man but tiresome preacher
Mr. Roberts	X
Mr. Birch	X
Mr. Tarver	X
Mr. Rowsell	

The Queen's Minute — The Queen likes none of these for the House. The last of all is the *only good* Preacher excepting Dean Stanley & he is too long. Mr. Rowsell unfortunately reads very disagreeably but those crossed are most disagreeable Preachers and the Queen *wonders* the Dean c[oul]d mention them.. . .[122]

Exceptions of course there were, and Queen Victoria occasionally found good things to say about Archbishops of Canterbury like A. C. Tait (1868–82) and his successor E. W. Benson (1883–96). The latter made an excellent first impression, 'so agreeable — so kindly — sensible — so humble and yet with such right views — and very large-minded and charitable; . . . a fine, intellectual benevolent face'.[123] Yet no sooner had the archbishop taken office than she was prepared to oppose him on a highly contentious religious issue — whether the law should be changed so as to permit men to marry the sisters of their deceased wives; the Queen was staunchly in favour, the archbishop opposed.[124] She had felt warmly about Gerald Wellesley, the Dean of Windsor (1854–82), who for more than twenty years provided a personal link with the life of the family before Albert's death. On his demise in 1882 she lamented him as the 'last of her valued *old* friends . . . was large minded c[oul]d understand anything so well — made allowances for everything & was such a wise, excellent adviser'.[125] His successor, after a brief interval, proved equally promising. Randall Davidson, a son-in-law of Archbishop Tait, was only thirty-four, but he appeared 'most sensible and agreeable, with excellent judgment, and singularly kind and sympathetic which is what I want so much'.[126] Not the least of Dean Davidson's virtues in Victoria's eyes was the fact that he was a Scot, born to Presbyterian parents in Edinburgh.

This link appropriately leads to a consideration of a final facet of the Queen's personal faith. The longer Victoria reigned, the fonder she became of Scotland — for as much as five months of the year she resided at Balmoral — and the fonder too of Scotland's established Presbyterian Kirk, its services and its ministers. It was in 1844, on her second visit to Scotland, that the Queen for the first time attended worship services in a Presbyterian Church — to the disgust of Tractarian critics south of the Tweed. The *English Churchman* complained that by so doing Victoria was 'forfeiting her character as a member' of the church into which she had been baptised.[127] The Queen was to attend innumerable Presbyterian services, however, in the course of the next half century. Some of her ministers in attendance deplored the poor hymn singing, the lack of kneeling, and the absence of the Lord's Prayer, but Victoria was more often delighted by the simplicity of the proceedings, the propriety and goodness of the humble worshippers, and the beauty of the sermons. The Queen was charmed rather than perturbed by the practice of one minister of taking his collie Towser into the pulpit with him. Whenever the sermon lasted a few minutes longer than customary, Towser would get up, stretch himself, and yawn.[128]

Her particular favourite among Scottish divines was Dr Norman Macleod. No clergyman turned out to be more helpful than he in comforting her after Albert's death. The bluff jovial Glaswegian ecclesiastic would read the poems of Robert Burns aloud to her while she found a therapeutic distraction in operating a spinning wheel. The very first time she had heard him preach he spoke so simply and eloquently as to give her a lump in the throat, and when he died in 1872, she remembered him warmly:

> He was so kind and encouraging to me in the early days and months of my great sorrow, and in all religious matters we agreed so well, and I always felt the better for all he said and preached. He was truly the religion of Love. He wished to impress all with the feeling that God was our loving father and not a hard judge.[129]

By 1867, Victoria admitted to her eldest daughter that in religion 'I am very nearly a Dissenter — or rather more a Presbyterian — in my feelings.'[130] It was not until 1873, however, that the Queen for the first time received communion at a Presbyterian church among the servants and tenants of her Balmoral estate. Her Anglican spiritual advisers were uncomfortable with the step, but dared not positively recommend against it, and several members of her immediate household were shocked. For a time the event was referred to euphemistically as 'The Event of Last Sunday'. The secret could not be kept for long, however, and one nonagenarian Anglican cleric publicly protested — 'The Church is in great peril from a Kirk-going Queen'[131] — but the innovation became an annual custom, and in *More Leaves from the Journal in the Highlands* (1883), Victoria wrote publicly about 'the grand simplicity' of the Presbyterian Communion Service.[132]

The Queen acquiesced reluctantly in the disestablishment of the Church of Ireland in 1869 by Gladstone's Liberal Ministry, but from then on she came to define a possible disestablishment of Scotland's Presbyterian Church as one of '*certain* things which I *never can* consent to'. The Presbyterian elders of the established Church of Scotland might not recognise her as head in the same fashion as the clergy of the Church of England did, but she had come to regard Presbyterianism as 'the real and true stronghold of Protestantism' in the British Isles, and late in her reign she gave instructions to the Court Chamberlain that, on future state occasions, the Moderator of the General Assembly of the Scottish Church should rank next after the Bishops of the Church of England and be given precedence over mere barons and privy councillors.[133] The Queen's personal faith partook of many elements, but the Scottish was by no means the least.

VII

The religious spectrum of Victorian Britain was not limited to Anglicans and Presbyterians. What was the Queen's attitude towards English Nonconformists, Jews, Roman Catholics, and, for that matter, agnostics and atheists? And what of the Hindus and Moslems over whom she reigned as Empress of India?

Non-Anglican Protestants — Wesleyans and other Methodists, Baptists, Independents, Presbyterians, Quakers, and Unitarians — played a significant role in the society of mid-Victorian England. Such people dominated the religious life of the burgeoning industrial cities of England as well as of urban and rural Wales, and they made up about half of all the Sunday worshippers counted during the unique Religious Census of 1851. Yet the Queen had remarkably little to do with them privately or politically. To the extent that some Nonconformists pushed for the disestablishment of the Church of England, the Queen would have opposed them, but such a proposal never became a matter of practical politics in Parliament, and Victoria did not oppose another major Nonconformist political objective, the commutation in 1868 of obligatory Church Rates (property taxes that non-Anglicans might have to pay for the upkeep of parish churches). Thus, when London's Nonconformist ministers presented a loyal address on the occasion of Victoria's Golden Jubilee in 1887, the Queen responded amiably:

It is most gratifying to me to receive from the general body of Protestant Dissenting ministers such warm declarations of continued loyalty and devotion on the attainment of the fiftieth year of my reign. I recall with satisfaction the assurances of respect for the rights of conscience which I gave to my subjects at the beginning of my reign, and I now repeat the like assurances with the full conviction, confirmed by experience, of the beneficial results which flow from a large and generous toleration extended to every form of earnest religious belief.[134]

For Britain's approximately 35,000 Jews, the early Victorian years constituted an era of legal emancipation climaxed by the admission to Parliament in 1858 of the first professing Jew, Lionel Rothschild. Victoria had helped the process along on her accession in 1837 when she became the first British monarch to confer a knighthood upon a Jew, Moses Montefiore. It was a step, she wrote, '*I* think quite right'.[135] Montefiore's knighthood was in due course followed by a baronetcy. In Victoria's eyes he was 'an excellent man, charitable to the highest degree & universally respected'.[136]

When Gladstone in 1869 wished to take the next step, to promote Lionel Rothschild's son Nathaniel to the peerage, Victoria was more reluctant. The Liberal Government wanted to honour Rothschild the banker as one of 'the great representatives of commerce of this country' as well as personally 'amiable and popular', but the Queen reminded Gladstone that bankers like the Rothschilds were often involved less with legitimate trade than with 'a species of gambling'.[137] By 1885 she had changed her mind, and Nathaniel Rothschild did not merely become a baron, but he and his wife were also honoured by an invitation to stay overnight at Windsor Castle. On that occasion Victoria asked the cooks to prepare a special hamless pie for their dinner — in order to display publicly her respect for the Jewish religion.[138]

Disraeli's Jewish origins constituted no barrier to the Queen's affections — even if one critic wrote of Victoria's visit to Disraeli's country estate as 'the Queen going ostentatiously to eat with Disraeli in his ghetto'.[139] One of the few subjects on which she agreed with Gladstone in the 1880s was distress at the persecution of Jews in Eastern Europe. She also admired her eldest daughter's criticism of anti-semitic disturbances in Berlin and elsewhere in Prussia in 1881. 'I own one is shocked and disgusted at this movement,' wrote the Crown Princess, considering that the Jews 'are so generous and charitable'.[140] Late in her life, when the Dreyfus Case stirred France, the Queen became a staunch Dreyfusard. In 1899 she cabled a British envoy in Paris: 'Thanks for your telegram with news of this monstrous verdict against this poor martyr. I trust he will appeal against this dreadful sentence.'[141] It is possible that Victoria's attitude toward Jews was affected by the theory, which apparently appealed to her,[142] that the English people were descended from the Ten Lost Tribes of Israel and that she herself was a direct descendant of King David — but her general sympathy for a policy of religious toleration may readily suffice as an explanation.

How to fit the claims and assumptions of Roman Catholics into a framework of religious toleration proved as puzzling for Queen Victoria as it did for many Victorian Liberals. The Queen had grown up in the era of Catholic Emancipation in England (1829), and initially she assumed that the ideological wars of the Reformation were past history. When at the age of sixteen the then princess was first exposed to the words of a professedly anti-Catholic preacher, she was deeply disturbed: 'In all my life,' she wrote in her journal, 'I never heard such a sermon . . . It was a most impious, unchristian-like and shocking affair. I was quite shocked and ashamed.'[143] A few years later the easy-going Melbourne alerted her to the fact that since the Pope 'was still a great man in Europe', it would be useful for Britain to establish diplomatic relations with him, but because of anti-Catholic feeling 'it wouldn't do to try in this country'.[144] When in 1845 Sir Robert Peel sought to ease the Irish Question by greatly enlarging and making permanent the annual government subsidy to Maynooth, the Roman Catholic seminary that educated a majority of Irish priests, Victoria and Albert stood firmly in his corner. As the Queen wrote privately to her uncle, 'I am sure that poor Peel ought to be *blessed* by all Catholics for the manly and noble way in which he stands forth to protect and do good to poor Ireland.' She was deeply troubled, however, by the anti-Catholic passions the measure inspired: 'the Protestants behave shockingly, and display a narrow-mindedness and want of sense on the subject of religion which is quite a disgrace to the nation.'[145]

The 'Papal Aggression' controversy of 1850 awakened the Queen's own suspicions of Roman Catholicism. It involved what she termed

> an extraordinary proceeding of the Pope, who has issued a Bull, savouring of the times of Henry VIII's reign, or even earlier — restoring the Roman Catholic 'Hierarchy', dividing this country publicly and openly into an Archbishopric and Bishoprics, saying that England was again restored to the number of Catholic Powers, & that her religious disgrace had been wiped out.

It seemed clear to the Queen that Pope Pius IX's actions were 'in the highest degree wrong' and that they constituted 'a *direct* infringement of my prerogative'.[146] In the aftermath, the Queen calmed down rather more quickly than did many of her countrymen. She did not oppose the Ecclesiastical Titles Act, with which the Prime Minister, Lord John Russell, sought ineffectually to counter the Catholic affront, but she did deplore the mass protest meetings 'and the great abuse of the Roman Catholic religion' which took place there; it was 'unchristian and unwise'.[147] As she wrote to her aunt, the controversy was 'so painful and so cruel towards many good and innocent Roman Catholics' — people like her Roman Catholic lord-in-waiting Lord Camoys, who deplored the 'inopportune' Papal Bull. 'Poor man,' the Queen noted, 'so sensible'.[148]

She and Albert found it possible even to extend a degree of sympathy to actual converts to Roman Catholicism like Newman and Manning, who seemed willing to sacrifice social position for religious principle, as opposed to pseudo-Catholics like the Puseyites who continued to claim their Anglican titles and privileges. Victoria was personally very fond of her Roman Catholic aunt-by-marriage, Queen Louise of Belgium, and of the Empress Eugénie of France, who was to spend much of her widowhood in England.[149] In 1858 the Queen used her influence to end the official Anglican service commemorating the foiling of the Gunpowder Plot of 1603. It had come to impress her as an unnecessary insult to her Roman Catholic subjects.[150]

In the course of the 1850s, however, and even more so during the 1860s and early 1870s, the Queen became increasingly censorious towards the Papacy, its claims, and its representatives. Thus when a public procession by the Roman Catholics of Stockport led to a riot in the summer of 1852, the Queen deplored the response but approved of the royal proclamation sought by the first Derby Ministry forbidding such processions.[151] She was generally sympathetic to the unification of Italy during the late 1850s under the auspices of the King of Sardinia, even if that meant the dismemberment and the ultimate disappearance of the Papal States. The alternate possibility of an Italian federation under the presidency of the Pope impressed her as impractical. 'How Italy is to prosper under the Pope's presidency the Queen is at a loss to conceive,' she wrote to Lord John Russell in 1859.[152] Although both her eldest son and her eldest daughter had paid courtesy visits to Pius IX — the latter had found him personally 'amiable, kind and friendly'[153] — the Queen was increasingly troubled by the mid-century drive in the direction of Roman Catholic 'triumphalism' as manifested in the Syllabus of Errors (1864) and the Vatican Council and its

Declaration of Papal Infallibility (1869–70). In England, she was willing in 1869 to go along with the new Liberal Party policy of ennobling Roman Catholics in rough proportion to their numbers in the general population, but, although she could not halt the statute, she looked upon Gladstone's policy of disestablishing the Church of Ireland (1869) as a form of appeasement that would not work. In due course Gladstone would see, she wrote to him, 'that it will not do . . . to give way to the Catholics in the hope of conciliating them. They will take everything & not be grateful for it. To treat them with perfect equality is an impossibility. Other Countries show this clearly.'[154]

Bismarck's response to the Vatican Council and to the rise of a new predominantly Roman Catholic Centre Party in the Reichstag of the new German Empire was the *Kulturkampf*, a series of measures designed to limit the educational and spiritual authority of the Roman Catholic clergy in Prussia. It led to the arrest of many. In their private correspondence, Queen Victoria proved far more sympathetic than did her eldest daughter, the German Crown Princess, to Bismarck's programme. 'I am sorry that the education measures have produced such excitement,' she told her daughter, 'but these Catholic priests must really be checked.' The actions of Roman Catholic priests in Prussia and in Ireland demonstrated, the Queen insisted a year later, that 'all over Europe there is an attempt made to resist authority and to defy it, by the Priesthood . . . wherefore we should all try and unite the Protestant Churches as much as possible together in order to make a strong front and protest against sacerdotal tyranny.'[155]

When the Crown Princess warmly recalled how, when she was a child, her mother had shown her spirit of religious tolerance by speaking out against 'vulgar prejudice and foolish violence against the Catholics', her mother responded somewhat testily: 'While I detest intolerance as much as you, I do not think they [the Roman Catholics] can be treated as people of other religions. They will not be conciliated and wish to persecute and, by foul means or fair, to obtain the upper hand.'[156] In 1874 the Queen deplored several notorious conversions to Rome, such as that of Lord Ripon (a member of Gladstone's cabinet) and the Queen of Bavaria: 'It is a complete surrender of your intellect — and individuality to another — and when one thinks of what the confession is . . . one can't understand anyone who has been a Protestant ever submitting to this.' The Roman Catholic religion was after all 'so aggressive, so full of every sort of falseness and uncharitableness and bigotry (unlike any other) that it must be resisted and opposed'.[157] During the 1870s the Queen made fun of a pilgrimage of English Roman Catholics to a French shrine, denounced the Jesuits as 'a fearful body — and I am doubtful whether any laws can be severe enough against them', and presumably agreed with her favourite servant John Brown when he characterised the Catholic clergy as 'nasty beggars!'[158] At that time Victoria truly was, as she called herself, 'very anti-Catholic'.[159]

Yet it is well to keep in mind that none of these private reflections were made public until a few years ago and that by the 1880s the Queen's attitude had changed once more — as, to a degree, had the Roman Catholic Church with its new Pope, Leo XIII. On her travels in Switzerland and France she paid cordial visits on several occasions to Roman Catholic churches and monasteries; she even observed Catholic religious services.[160] When the papacy quietly inquired in 1887 whether a papal representative would be welcome at the Golden Jubilee ceremonies, Victoria cordially agreed and sent the chief English Catholic layman, the Duke of Norfolk, to Rome to assure Leo XIII of the Queen's 'sincere friendship and unfeigned respect and esteem'. When a strong protest arrived at Windsor, the Queen noted that the Protestant objectors 'entirely forget how many 1000 Catholic subjects the Queen has who cannot be ignored — And it is grievous to think that what w[oul]d be good for the peace of Ireland will probably be prevented by these well meaning but fanatical Protestants.'[161] At the Jubilee reception, the papal envoy turned out to be the only foreign delegate whom the Queen received by rising from her chair. By then the Queen had placed Roman Catholic and Church of Ireland bishops on full equality of status at ceremonial occasions,[162] and when Victoria visited Ireland in the spring of 1900 she made a special point of visiting Roman Catholic institutions. On this remarkable occasion she was received in Dublin with immense enthusiasm. As she explained, 'I am their Queen, and I must look after them.'[163] On the subject of Roman Catholicism, the Queen's attitude in her last years appears to have come full circle.

The Queen had relatively few personal contacts with the Greek Orthodox branch of Christendom, and what she knew of it she did not much care for. 'Does not every true Protestant feel the errors of a superstitious religion,' she asked rhetorically, 'full of strange observances repugnant to all the simplicity of our Saviour's teaching?'[164] Under the circumstances, she was acquiescent rather than delighted when in 1873 her second son, Prince Alfred, married the Grand-Duchess Marie, the daughter of Russia's Tsar Alexander II. She was very much conscious of the fact that the occasion was the first since 1688 on which an immediate member of the British royal family had wed a non-Protestant.[165] During the mid-1870s, Victoria's memories of the Crimean War were stirred anew, and sympathy with the Turks went hand-in-hand with hostile reflections upon the religion of Russia. The Queen and her eldest daughter agreed that there was little to choose between Islam and the Christianity of Eastern Europe. 'If the Turks are no Christians,' the Queen pointed out in 1877, 'they at least believe most sincerely in a God — while the so-called Christians of the Principalities [modern Rumania] are said to be the most superstitious, horrible creatures possible.'[166] Late in her reign, Victoria felt happier about the Greek Orthodox Church, and when Tsar Nicholas II and the the Tsarina Alexandra (her granddaughter) visited her at Balmoral in 1896, she was delighted by their willingness to attend Scottish Presbyterian services with her. As she observed to her attendants, no Roman Catholic visitor would show such a spirit of tolerance.[167]

It was the Hindus and Moslems of the subcontinent of India who constituted the largest number of religious believers to be found in the British empire of Queen Victoria's day. In 1858, in the aftermath of the Great Mutiny of the previous year, India formally became a Crown Colony. From the first, Victoria and Albert counselled moderation rather than vengeance in dealings with the defeated mutineers. When the Viceroy reported that 'a vast number of the European community would hear with pleasure and approval that every Hindoo and Mohammedan had been proscribed', the Queen objected strongly. She insisted on the inclusion in the Royal Proclamation of this passage:

> Firmly relying ourselves on the truth of Christianity, and acknowledging with gratitude the solace of religion, we disclaim alike the right and desire to impose our convictions on any of our subjects. We declare it to be our royal will and pleasure that none be in anywise favoured, none molested or disquieted by reason of their religious faith or observances, but that all shall alike enjoy the equal and impartial protection of the law.[168]

Victoria believed that Britain could exercise a humanising and civilising influence in Asia but not by means of forcible Christianisation. A number of evangelically-minded Britons complained, indeed, in 1875–6, when the Prince of Wales on an official journey to India visited many more Hindu temples than Christian missions.[169] The Queen's closest personal associate in her last years turned out to be 'the Munshi', a young Moslem from Agra who was first brought to Balmoral in 1887 and who rose rapidly to become Victoria's 'Official Indian Secretary, Hafiz Abdul Karim'. The Queen persuaded herself that he was the son of a Surgeon-General in the Indian army rather than, as appears to have been the case, an apothecary at the Agra jail. Many members of her household and family found 'the Munshi' both arrogant and potentially dangerous, but he did teach the Queen the rudiments of the Hindi language, and his rise illustrates how seriously Victoria took her role as head of a multi-racial and multi-religious empire.[170]

Such benevolence did not extend to avowed atheists like Charles Bradlaugh, whose attempt in 1880 to take the parliamentary seat to which the voters of Northampton had elected him led to an imbroglio that lasted five and a half years. The Queen sympathised with Bradlaugh's opponents: 'It is not *only* his known atheism but it is other horrible principles wh[ich] make him a disgrace to an assembly like the House of Commons.' Bradlaugh had been the most militant of the leaders of Britain's republican campaign of the early 1870s, and more recently had given new life to the movement to disseminate information on birth control, a programme that the Queen, like other Victorians, equated alternately with 'free love' and prostitution.[171] The man who in 1878 wounded but failed in his attempt to assassinate the German emperor turned out to be a socialist, an atheist, and a Doctor of Philosophy to boot. 'So much for philosophy!' was the Queen's response, and in her later years Victoria became less certain than Albert had been — and her eldest daughter continued to be — that science and religion were readily reconcilable. 'Science is to be greatly admired and encouraged,' the Queen conceded, 'but if it is to take the place of our Creator, and if philosophers and students try to explain everything and to disbelieve whatever they cannot prove, I call it a great evil instead of a great blessing.'[172]

VIII

In her lifetime Queen Victoria sought and in part arrived at 'simple truths' in religion, but it appears more appropriate to conclude a survey of her place in the religious spectrum of Victorian Britain with a series of paradoxes.

She held a public office that, according to Walter Bagehot's *The English Constitution* (1867), had become predominantly cere-monial rather than 'efficient', and yet for most of her reign she scorned such a role. She saw her prime duty as exercising influence behind the scenes, and she played a greater role in determining Church appointments than Bagehot suspected.

She was eminently sympathetic to a Victorian religious revival that has almost universally been described as a middle-class phenomenon. Yet what she knew of middle-class society she derived solely from the occasional novel or newspaper article. In terms of personal experience, the day-to-day lives of her middle-class subjects were to Queen Victoria virtually a closed book.

She saw her primary public religious role as that of Head of the Church of England, and yet she much preferred Lutheran, and — even more — Presbyterian services to Anglican ones.

She was unsympathetic to most of the manifestations of the two great religious movements that stirred the nineteenth-century Church of England, evangelicism and ritualism. She sympathised most of all with the general approach (if not the reasoned theology) of the Broad Church rather than the Low Church or the High Church, even though Broad Churchmen made up less than one in twenty of the Anglican clerics of her day. She was far more tolerant than were most of her subjects in her attitude towards Protestant Dissenters, Roman Catholics (except for a time in the 1860s and 1870s), Jews, Moslems and Hindus.

She had no desire whatsoever to disestablish the hierarchical Church of England, but she was censorious of a majority of clerics as preachers, teachers and administrators, and she did not hesitate to wield a secular tool — Parliament with the Public Worship Act of 1874 — to keep recalcitrant clerics in line.

She professed a 'love for the very simplest, purest faith as near to our Saviour's precepts as possible',[173] and yet she 'celebrated' death in a manner far more elaborate and with a conviction far more intense than that of most fellow Victorians. Her love for the simple notwithstanding, she found herself drawn time and again to the exotic — in Disraeli's flowery oratory, in the traditions of continental Roman Catholic monasteries, in the customs and costumes of the exotic East.

Tom Cullen wrote some years ago that 'most of the misunderstandings concerning Queen Victoria have arisen from trying to judge her by ordinary standards when she was, by virtue both of her position and of her character, an extraordinary being.'[174] Not least of all does that judgement apply to the topic of the Queen and religion — both as private faith and as public policy. Four years before her death she drew up her final will:

> I die in peace with all fully aware of my many faults relying with confidence on the love, mercy and goodness of my Heavenly Father and His Blessed Son & earnestly trusting to be reunited to my beloved Husband, my dearest Mother, my loved Children and 3 dear sons-in-law. — And all who have been very near & dear to me on earth. Also I hope to meet those who have so faithfully & so devotedly served me especially good John Brown and good Annie Macdonald who I trusted would help to lay my remains in my coffin & to see me placed next to my dearly loved Husband in the mausoleum at Frogmore.[175]

It is at Frogmore that her remains lie today, the best-known woman of the nineteenth century, in a memorial completely inaccessible to the general public.

As Archbishop Davidson noted in 1926, Victoria's personality involved a remarkable disjunction between the woman — shy, humble, unprepossessing — and the Queen — immensely dignified, forceful, and proud,[176] looking down from a tall quasi-religious pedestal upon the vast Victorian empire and the yet wider Victorian world. In truth she was a most unusual Victorian.

Notes

1. G. Kitson Clark, *The Making of Victorian England* (Cambridge, Mass., 1962), p. 50.

I am grateful to my University of Illinois colleagues, Professors Paul P. Bernard and Caroline M. Hibbard, and to my wife, Charlotte Arnstein, for reading the manuscript and making numerous helpful suggestions.

2. R. C. K. Ensor, *England 1870–1914* (Oxford, 1936), p. 137.

3. Walter Walsh, *The Religious Life and Influence of Queen Victoria* (London, 1902), p. 264. In 'Queen Victoria's Religious Life', *The Wiseman Review*, 236

(Summer 1962), pp. 107–26, Elizabeth Longford, in sympathetic but undocumented fashion, anticipates the approach she was to take three years later in what remains the best one-volume biography of the Queen, *Victoria, R.I.* (London, 1965).

4. Much of the correspondence covering the years 1858–85 has been edited by the late Sir Roger Fulford in five volumes, *Dearest Child* [1858–61] (London, 1964); *Dearest Mama* [1861–4] (London, 1968); *Your Dear Letter* [1865–71] (London, 1971); *Darling Child* [1871–8] (London, 1976); *Beloved Mama* [1878–85] (London, 1981).

5. Most significantly the Reverend Randall Davidson, Dean of Windsor from 1883 to 1891. (He afterwards became Bishop of Rochester (1891–5), and of Winchester (1895–1903), and Archbishop of Canterbury (1903–28).) See G. K. A. Bell, *Randall Davidson, Archbishop of Canterbury*, 2 vols (New York, 1935).

6. See Philip Magnus, *King Edward the Seventh* (New York, 1964), pp. 461–2.

7. See, for example, 'The Religious Census of 1851' in G. M. Young and W. D. Hancock (eds), *English Historical Documents*, vol. XII, Pt. 1 [1833–74], pp. 383–94.

8. Cited in Lady Gwendolyn Cecil, *Life of Lord Salisbury*, 4 vols (London, 1921–32), III:186–7.

9. Cited in Bell, *Davidson*, I:81; Longford, *Victoria*, p. 54.

10. Cecil Woodham-Smith, *Queen Victoria* (London, 1972), pp. 78, 105.

11. *Letters of Queen Victoria*, 1st Series, 3 vols (London, 1907), I:51–2, 72, 79.

12. Woodham-Smith, *Queen Victoria*, p. 103.

13. *Letters*, 1st Series, I:16; Walsh, *Religious Life*, p. 3.

14. Bell, *Davidson*, I:83; cited in Walsh, *Religious Life*, p. 10; see also pp. 6–7.

15. Cited in Walsh, *Religious Life*, p. 11.

16. Cited in ibid., pp. 13–14.

17. Cited in David Cecil, *Melbourne* (London, 1955), p. 151.

18. Viscount Esher (ed.), *The Girlhood of Queen Victoria: A Selection from Her Majesty's Diaries Between the Years 1832 and 1840*, 2 vols (London, 1912), II:27.

19. Ibid., pp. 27, 56.

20. Owen Chadwick, *The Victorian Church*, 2 vols (London, 1966, 1970), I:160.

21. Ibid., pp. 161–2; Esher, *Girlhood*, II:18, 56.

22. See Woodham-Smith, *Queen Victoria*, pp. 173, 258–9; Robert Rhodes James, *Albert Prince Consort* (London, 1984, p. 87).

23. Cited in Daphne Bennett, *King Without a Crown: Albert, Prince Consort of England 1819–1861* (Philadelphia, 1977), p. 35.

24. Ibid., pp. 34, 36.

25. Bennett, *King Without a Crown*, p. 57; Victor Mallet (ed.), *Life With Queen Victoria: Marie Mallet's Letters from Court, 1887–1901* (Boston, 1968); p. 14.

26. James, *Albert*, p. 2.

27. Ibid., p. 34; Bennett, *King Without a Crown*, pp. 22, 160.

28. Bennett, *King Without a Crown*, p. 24; Longford, *Victoria*, p. 425.

29. Sir Charles Petrie, *The Victorians* (London, 1961), p. 58; Longford, *Victoria*, pp. 326–7.

30. Cited in Bell, *Davidson*, I:84.

31. Although as late as 1856 Palmerston assumed that the Low Church predominated 'among the middle and lower classes of our churchmen', an observer of 1877 estimated that the 23,000 clergymen of the Church of England might appropriately be classified as follows: 5,000 Low Church; 5,000 doubtful; 10,000 High Church; 2,000 Ultra-High Church Ritualists; 1,000 Broad Church. See Dudley W. R. Bahlman, 'Politics and Church Patronage in the Victorian Age', *Victorian Studies*, 22 (Spring 1979), pp. 266–7.

32. James, *Albert*, p. 109.

33. Cited in Walsh, *Religious Life*, p. 55.

34. Bennett, *King Without a Crown*, p. 101.

35. Cited in James, *Albert*, p. 153.

36. Cited in ibid., p. 191.

37. Bennett, *King Without a Crown*, p. 101.

38. James, *Albert*, p. 144.

39. Cited in Bennett, *King Without a Crown*, pp. 163–4.

40. Cited in Walsh, *Religious Life*, pp. 169–70.

41. Frank Hardie, *The Political Influence of the British Monarchy 1868–1952* (New York, 1970), p. 67.

42. Philip Magnus, *Gladstone* (London, 1954), p. 57.

43. Brian Harrison, *Drink and the Victorians* (London, 1971), pp. 340, 107, 157; Tom Cullen, *The Empress Brown: The True Story of a Victorian Scandal* (Boston, 1969), pp. 169–73.

44. Stella Margetson, *Leisure and Pleasure in the Nineteenth Century* (London, 1969), p. 73; see also Longford, *Victoria*, p. 53.

45. Ashley, cited in Bennett, *King Without a Crown*, p. 81; Alan Hardy, *Queen Victoria Was Amused* (London, 1976), p. 137. See also *Your Dear Letter*, p. 165.

46. Bennett, *King Without a Crown*, p. 162; James, *Albert*, pp. 259–60.

47. Cited in Hardy, *Queen Victoria*, p. 77.

48. Cf. Longford, *Victoria*, p. 267.

49. Cited in James, *Albert*, p. 236; Hardy, *Queen Victoria*, p. 136.

50. *Dearest Child*, p. 188.

51. Cited in Bennett, *King Without a Crown*, p. 165. See also *Letters*, 1st Series, II:139.

52. Cited in Woodham-Smith, *Queen Victoria*, p. 417.

53. Cited in Walsh, *Religious Life*, p. 84.

54. *Letters*, 1st Series, II:35, 376. The Queen's dislike of ritualism was linked to her hostility towards days of national prayer and supplication proclaimed in her name. Only reluctantly was she won over to the transformation of monarchical ceremonies into quasi-religious rituals like the Golden Jubilee of 1887 and the Diamond Jubilee of 1897. Cf. *Darling Child*, pp. 30–2; Chadwick, *Victorian Church*, I:490–1.

55. Cited in Battiscombe, *Queen Alexandra* (Boston, 1969), pp. 42–3. See also Walsh, *Religious Life*, pp. 133–4.

56. *Darling Child*, p. 104; see also Chadwick, *Victorian Church*, II:337–9; and Geoffrey Rowell, *The Vision Glorious* (London, 1984).

57. Cited in Arthur Ponsonby, *Henry Ponsonby, Queen Victoria's Private Secretary: His Life from His Letters* (New York, 1944), p. 178; see also Philip Guedalla, *The Queen and Mr. Gladstone* (Garden City, NY, 1934), pp. 434–5.

58. Robert Blake, *Disraeli* (London, 1966), pp. 528–9. Peter Marsh provides the most comprehensive account in *The Victorian Church in Decline* (London, 1969).

59. The Marquess of Zetland (ed.), *The Letters of Disraeli to Lady Bradford and Lady Chesterfield*, 2 vols (London, 1929), I:129.

60. *Letters of Queen Victoria*, 3rd Series, 3 vols (London, 1930–2), I:427.

61. *Letters of Queen Victoria*, 2nd Series, 3 vols (London, 1926–8), II:342.

62. Chadwick, *Victorian Church*, I:125–6; 166; 266; II:135–6; Longford, *Victoria*, p. 205.

63. Cited in Longford, 'Religious Life', pp. 116–17. In her journal, the Queen sought on behalf of her youthful eldest daughter 'the feeling of devotion and love which our Heavenly Father encourages . . . and not one of fear and trembling, and that the thoughts of death and an afterlife should not be represented in an alarming and forbidding view and that she should be made to know *as yet* no difference of creeds, and not think that she can pray *only* on her knees . . .' Cited in Nina

Epton, *Victoria and Her Daughters* (London, 1971), p. 42.

64. Chadwick, *Victorian Church*, 2:75–8.

65. Ibid., 2:90–2.

66. *Letters*, 2nd Series, II:361.

67. James, *Albert*, pp. 177–80.

68. *Letters*, 1st Series, III:416.

69. Victoria's comments to Dean Davidson are cited in Chadwick, *Victorian Church*, II:336.

70. Cited in Bahlman, 'Politics', p. 255. See also Dudley W. R. Bahlman, 'The Queen, Mr. Gladstone, and Church Patronage', *Victorian Studies*, III (1960), pp. 349–80.

71. Bell, *Davidson*, I:164–5, 176.

72. Cited in Bahlman, 'Politics', p. 293.

73. Ibid., p. 290.

74. Chadwick, II:340.

75. Cited in Bell, *Davidson*, I:61 and Walsh, *Religious Life*, p. 223.

76. Esher, *Girlhood*, II:35.

77. *Dearest Child*, pp. 317–18.

78. Ibid., p. 319; Longford, *Victoria*, pp. 426–7.

79. Cullen, *Empress Brown*, p. 59.

80. *Your Dear Letter*, p. 118; also Cullen, *Empress Brown*, pp. 57, 60; Longford, *Victoria*, p. 428.

81. *Beloved Mama*, pp. 168, 185.

82. Cullen, *Empress Brown*, p. 60; Bell, *Davidson*, I:84.

83. Bell, *Davidson*, I:84–5; Neville Williams, *The Royal Residences of Great Britain: A Social History* (London, 1960), p. 225.

84. A. Ponsonby, *Henry Ponsonby*, p. 79.

85. Cited in Walsh, *Religious Life*, p. 116.

86. The Queen's Journal, cited in Longford, *Victoria*, p. 427.

87. Cited in Bell, *Davidson*, I:82.

88. Cf. Longford, *Victoria*, pp. 428–9.

89. Victoria to Henry Ponsonby, cited in A. Ponsonby, *Henry Ponsonby*, p. 129.

90. Cited in Bell, *Davidson*, I:86.

91. Longford, *Victoria*, p. 387.

92. See, for example, *Beloved Mama*, p. 174.

93. *Darling Child*, p. 24; Longford, *Victoria*, p. 707.

94. A. Ponsonby, *Henry Ponsonby*, pp. 79–80; R. D. Blumenfeld, *R. D. B.'s Diary* (London, 1930), p. 120.

95. Mallet, *Life with Queen Victoria*, pp. 44, 179.

96. Cited in Bell, *Davidson*, I:83.

97. *Darling Child*, p. 293.

98. Bennett, *King Without a Crown*, p. 135; *Darling Child*, p. 52.

99. *Darling Child*, p. 293.

100. Cited in Mallet, *Life with Queen Victoria*, p. xxi.

101. Bell, *Davidson*, I:79; Mallet, *Life with Queen Victoria*, pp. 78, 83.

102. Cited in Bell, *Davidson*, I:83.

103. *Beloved Mama*, p. 87.

104. *Your Dearest Letter*, p. 123; Longford, *Victoria*, p. 424.

105. Cullen, *Empress Brown*, p. 87; Longford, *Victoria*, pp. 418–25. In the years of Victoria's widowhood, at least one mock household séance took place, but none of the Queen's immediate associates took spiritualism seriously. Elizabeth Longford has successfully disproved the oft-repeated story that, after Albert's death, the Queen sought regularly to communicate with her dead husband by using John Brown as a medium.

106. Cited in Blake, *Disraeli*, p. 210.

107. *Darling Child*, p. 293.

108. Cited in Woodham-Smith, *Queen Victoria*, p. 77.

109. Ibid., pp. 208–12. Another example of episcopal maladroitness that caused members of the court circle to shake their heads in the 1890s involved the Bishop of London, who was chatting amiably to a middle-aged man at the annual Buckingham Palace garden party. 'Well, and how is your father?' asked the bishop. 'Don't you remember, he died long ago', was the reply. Then 'How is your mother?' the bishop went on. 'Very well for her years', was the answer. Afterwards the bishop turned to his wife: 'Now who was that charming young man I was talking to just now?' It was one of Queen Victoria's younger sons, the Duke of Connaught. Cited in Mallet, *Life with Queen Victoria*, p. 93.

110. Cited in Bell, *Davidson*, I:197.

111. Princess Marie Louise, *My Memories of Six Reigns* (New York, 1957), pp. 115–16.

112. Cited in Chadwick, *Victorian Church*, I:160.

113. *Your Dear Letter*, p. 141.

114. Cited in Chadwick, *Victorian Church*, I:160. The Prime Minister's response was apropos: 'But there are not many very good anything.'

115. Cited in ibid.; *Dearest Child*, p. 186.

116. Walsh, *Religious Life*, p. 103.

117. Bell, *Davidson*, I:85.

118. Ibid., p. 86.

119. Cited in Christopher Hibbert, *The Court at Windsor* (New York 1964), pp. 224f.

120. Susan Chitty, *The Beast and the Monk: A Life of Charles Kingsley* (New York, 1975), p. 201.

121. A. Ponsonby, *Henry Ponsonby*, p. 401.

122. Ibid., p. 46.

123. *Beloved Mama*, p. 132.

124. Bell, *Davidson*, I:96.

125. Cited in A. Ponsonby, *Henry Ponsonby*, p. 62.

126. *Beloved Mama*, p. 139; Cullen, *Empress Brown*, p. 212.

127. Cited in Walsh, *Religious Life*, p. 29.

128. See, for example, Cullen, *Empress Brown*, pp. 43–4; Walsh, *Religious Life*, pp. 88–9.

129. *Darling Child*, p. 48: cf. Walsh, *Religious Life*, p. 87; Cullen, *Empress Brown*, p. 222. The Rev. John Tulloch, a fellow member of Scotland's Broad Church school of theology and Principal of St Mary's College of the University of St Andrews, came to serve as a partial replacement for Macleod. Victoria was to recall him as 'one of our most distinguished men, noble, brave, most intelligent, large-hearted and liberal-minded'. Cited in Bell, *Davidson*, I:86f.

130. *Your Dearest Letter*, p. 161.

131. *Beloved Mama*, pp. 102f. See also Cullen, *Empress Brown*, p. 162.

132. Cited in Walsh, *Religious Life*, p. 31.

133. *Letters*, 2nd Series, III:47; Longford, *Victoria*, p. 227; Walsh, *Religious Life*, p. 239. See also A. Ponsonby, *Henry Ponsonby*, pp. 277–8.

134. Cited in Walsh, *Religious Life*, p. 208.

135. Cited in Longford, *Victoria*, p. 91. See also Bennett, *King Without a Crown*, p. 161.

136. Guedalla, *Queen and Mr. Gladstone*, p. 633.

137. Ibid., pp. 253–4.

138. Miriam Rothschild, *Dear Lord Rothschild* (London, 1983), p. 29.

139. *Darling Child*, pp. 271f.

140. Guedalla, *Queen and Mr. Gladstone*, p. 585; *Beloved Mama*, pp. 93, 95.
141. Cited in Hardie, *Political Influence*, pp. 31f.
142. Michael MacDonagh, *The English King* (London, 1929), p. 69.
143. Cited in Woodham-Smith, *Queen Victoria*, p. 141.
144. Esher, *Girlhood*, II:36–7.
145. *Letters*, 1st Series, II:36–7. See also Longford, *Victoria*, p. 452; and Bennett, *King Without a Crown*, p. 131.
146. Victoria's journal cited in Woodham-Smith, *Queen Victoria*, p. 417.
147. *Letters*, 1st Series, II:279.
148. Ibid., II:281; Longford, *Victoria*, p. 254.
149. Bennett, *King Without a Crown*, pp. 161, 165; Woodham-Smith, *Queen Victoria*, p. 417; *Beloved Mama*, p. 48.
150. Chadwick, *Victorian Church*, I:491.
151. *Letters*, 1st Series, II:391; Walsh, *Religious Life*, p. 75.
152. Cited in C. T. McIntire, *England Against the Papacy, 1858–1861* (Cambridge, 1983), p. 125. See also Harry Hearndon, 'Queen Victoria and Foreign Policy: Royal Intervention in the Italian Question' in Kenneth Bourne and D. C. Watt (eds), *Studies in International History: Essays Presented to W. N. Medlicott* (London, 1967).
153. *Darling Child*, p. 280.
154. Guedalla, *Queen and Mr. Gladstone*, pp. 249, 252.
155. *Darling Child*, pp. 67. 34, 114.
156. Ibid., pp. 103, 115.
157. Ibid., pp. 151, 157, 158.
158. Ibid., pp. 111, 51; Cullen, *Empress Brown*, p. 88.
159. *Darling Child*, p. 178.
160. Cf. *Beloved Mama*, p. 186; Walsh, *Religious Life*, pp. 149, 194; A. Ponsonby, *Henry Ponsonby*, p. 283.
161. Chadwick, *Victorian Church*, II:406–7; A. Ponsonby, *Henry Ponsonby*, p. 50.
162. Walsh, *Religious Life*, pp. 245, 196.
163. Ibid., pp. 250, 261.
164. *Darling Child*, p. 104.
165. Ibid., p. 103.
166. Ibid., p. 256.
167. Mallet, *Life with Queen Victoria*, p. 94.
168. *Letters*, 1st Series, III:251, 304; Walsh, *Religious Life*, p. 101.
169. Bennett, *King Without a Crown*, p. 309; *Darling Child*, p. 101; Walsh, *Religious Life*, p. 173.
170. Mallet, *Life with Queen Victoria*, p. xxii; Cullen, *Empress Brown*, pp. 13, 76; Longford, *Victoria*, p. 639.
171. Guedalla, *Queen and Mr. Gladstone*, p. 466. The parliamentary struggle is recounted in Walter L. Arnstein, *The Bradlaugh Case*, new edn (Columbia, Mo., 1984).
172. Longford, *Victoria*, p. 526; *Darling Child*, p. 193. Such an attitude did not prevent the Queen from honouring distinguished scientists. The famous geologist, Charles Lyell, was knighted in 1848 at Prince Albert's personal request, and T. H. Huxley, the noted biologist, educator, and coiner of the word 'agnosticism', was made Privy Councillor in 1887 (after he had politely declined a peerage). See James, *Albert*, pp. 177f; Cyril Bibby, *T. H. Huxley: Scientist, Humanist, Educator* (London, 1959), p. 32.
173. *Darling Child*, p. 157.
174. Cullen, *Empress Brown*, p. 223.
175. Cited in Longford, *Victoria*, p. 417.
176. Bell, *Davidson*, II:1216.

Chapter 6

Virgin Vows: The Early Victorian Artists' Portrayal of Nuns and Novices*

Susan P. Casteras

One relatively unscrutinised dimension of 'women's work' during Victoria's reign is that of feminine religious commitment and its application in the real world. The early Victorian period of the 1840s and 1850s significantly expanded the opportunities for women to serve God and their communities, for it was within those decades that the concept of Anglican sisterhoods was revived. It is coincidentally these years that not only generated much public controversy on this subject but also witnessed the proliferation of certain types of imagery of the nun and nunneries. The often vacuous stereotypes of nuns found in paintings, art journals, Keepsake annuals and popular magazines all reinforced the partly sensationalised, partly sentimentalised attitudes towards this topic, and there was considerable repetition with little ingenuity or variation of the basic strands of this quasi-religious imagery from the 1840s to the end of the century. As provocative icons and as documents of opinion about contemporary religion and religious practitioners, this strand of semi-sacred, semi-profane imagery reveals much that has previously only been alluded to about the Victorian psyche.

It is no surprise, of course, that the nun might qualify as a perfect embodiment of the Victorian idealisation of womanhood, particularly with her qualities of virginity, docility, dedication, spirituality and modesty. Marriage was certainly the definitive career for women, with spinsterhood, one alternative to the wedded state, ungraciously denigrated as a half-life in which the female 'redundant' or 'superfluous' being was dependent for her subsistence upon the generosity of a father, brother, or other male relative.[1] As has been previously well researched by numerous scholars, the unattached woman in 1850 was essentially a social embarrassment. Instead of remaining burdens on their families, however, some single women chose the alternative of entering a

129

sisterhood, a relatively recent historical possibility in England created by the conventual revival which the Oxford Movement had fostered. It is the visual strand of imagery that parallels this development in religion which is the focus of the essay, for the myriad images of nuns produced by contemporary artists reflected a distinct attitude towards the subject as well as underscoring certain prevailing beliefs about female sexuality in general.

The major theme which unites paintings of this subject in the 1830s, 40s and 50s (as well as in later decades) was that of repressed sexuality. Although this element of a nun's life was in actuality not the sole inflammatory issue or objection cited by the public, it was none the less the aspect seized on by most male artists to exploit in their representations of novices as 'victims' of thwarted or disappointed love affairs. The majority of nuns depicted in this rather peculiar genre are quite pretty, being at the same time unattainable to all men except one 'secret' love (who could be mortal or even Christ himself). Such a simplistic approach seems to belong to the 'if only' school of emotionality, one in which several complex motives are reduced to one that seemed particularly congenial to male Protestantism. This attitude simultaneously satisfied the fantasies of male artists and viewers on the subject and also reinforced the Protestant belief that no woman could possibly prefer the life of a nun to that of a wife and mother.

Historically, the Oxford Movement was a phenomenon concentrated in the years from 1835 to the 1850s with religious leaders such as Edward Pusey, John Keble, John Henry Newman and others in the forefront. The aim was basically to restore High Church ideals to the Church of England, which had suffered a decided weakening of spiritual devotion and influence. These men and their followers believed that the Church of England was the direct heir (through the Anglican priesthood) to Christ's ministry and thus shared continuity with the medieval church as well as certain affinities with the Roman Catholic Church. In his famous sermon at Oxford in 1833 on 'National Apostasy', Keble asserted that the clergy derived its fundamental authority from the concept of Apostolic Succession and denounced Parliamentary infringement on matters he deemed the sole jurisdiction of the Church.

Although the Reverend Alexander Dallas in an 1826 pamphlet and Robert Southey in his book *Sir Thomas More: or, Colloquies on the Progress and Prospects of Society* (1829) had both advocated religious orders for women before J. H. Newman did so, it was the efforts of the Oxford Movement that rendered such an idea feasible.[2] In Newman's 1835 article on this subject in the *British Magazine*, he wrote that sisterhoods could 'give dignity and independence to the position of women in society'. Convent life could also provide a refuge for 'redundant' females, since,

> As matters stand, marriage is the sole shelter which a defenceless portion of the community has against the rude world; — whereas foundations for single females, under proper precautions, at once hold out protection to those who avail themselves of them, and give consideration to the single state itself, thus saving numbers from the temptation of throwing themselves rashly away upon unworthy objects, transgressing their sense of propriety, and embittering their future life.[3]

Yet while Newman endorsed this concept in a somewhat passive way, his colleague Pusey affirmed the value of a celibate religious life in an even more vigorous manner. He actively encouraged the revival of monasteries — colleges of unmarried priests and communities for sisters of charity as well — along with requirements of obedience to strict rules of discipline, devotion, and stated holy principles. He believed that sisterhoods should undertake useful work in hospitals, prisons, lunatic asylums and magdalen homes, and thought them 'desirable (1) in themselves as belonging to and fostering a high tone in the Church, (2) as giving a holy employment to many who yearn for something, (3) as directing zeal, which will otherwise go off in some irregular way, or go over to Rome'.[4]

For nearly two hundred years there had been monastic communities in England, and so the founding of Anglican sisterhoods in the early 1840s was a landmark occurrence. After 1845 'Protestant nunneries' or 'colleges of maids' increased in number, with six sisterhoods (apart from unsanctioned or informal parish versions) established between 1845 and 1951. Nine more of these communities were officially started between 1851 and 1858, and fifteen more added between 1870 and 1900.[5] Cities all over England — including London, Oxford, Leeds, Devonport and others — were affected by this widespread phenomenon, which interestingly both pre-dated and outnumbered the subsequent re-institution of religious communities for men.[6]

Middle- and upper-class ladies were perhaps the most vulnerable to the novelty and spiritual allure of sisterhoods, and it was this dimension that *Punch* occasionally lampooned. An anonymous satirical piece in the 18 October 1850 issue entitled 'Convent of the Belgravians' alleged that some women were known to have handed over their entire dowries to nunneries, in addition to paying a monthly 'rent' for services and lodgings. The author also claimed that vows and celibacy were rather lightly taken, that Roman Catholic practices of 'maceration' were being replaced by the use of stays (a stylish mortification of the flesh for Englishwomen), and that servants could be hired by occupants for the upkeep of individual cells, which were 'fitted up comfortably, combining the *boudoir* and oratory'. An illustration of the same title (Plate 1) captures the tongue-in-cheek tone of the article, with one young woman trying on a wimple and veil as if they were the newest millinery concoctions in order to gauge the effect of calculated simplicity and humility in the mirror. The article, moreover, commented facetiously that

> the costume of the sisterhood will consist of a judicious admixture of the conventual style with the fashion of the day. The Nun will not be obliged to sacrifice her hair, but only to wear it plain, *à la Madonna*.
>
> Absolute seclusion will by no means be enforced; indeed it will be incumbent on the Nuns to appear in society, in order to display the beauty of sanctity . . . At the same time, they will renounce the world, in the Belgravian sense . . . That the Anglican Convent, thus constituted, will lead to 'perversions' there is no fear. Alas! the hard multitude will rather say that the Puseyite sisters are only playing at Roman Catholics, and the vile punster will remark that their Convent is more a Monkey-ry than a Nunnery.[7]

This jab at Belgravians was undoubtedly a reference to the episcopal anxiety, the public censure and the ultimate riot that took place in 1850 at the church of St Barnabas in Pimlico.[8] The incumbent, the Rev. W. J. E. Bennett, was given to certain ritualistic practices that caused an outcry and his resignation (before he had a chance to start a sisterhood, one of his goals).

Such violent reactions were part of the larger, more encompassing Protestant fear of Roman Catholicism in general and of Papal Aggression in particular and were not, of course, simply due to a dislike of religious communities. *Punch* exemplified such an acerbic position in its 30 November 1850 issue, in which a cartoon entitled *Fashions for 1850; — or A Page for the Puseyites* ridiculed new 'Papist' or 'Romish' costumes which some clergy wore. It was certainly not mere coincidence that just two months earlier Pope Pius IX had issued a papal bull restoring the Roman Catholic hierarchy to England, an act of 'Papal Aggression' that unleashed anxious, even paranoid, responses from the contemporary press and other quarters. Negative reaction directed primarily against the threat of encroachment by Roman Catholicism, conflated with the concomitant dislike of Anglican sisterhoods, can be found in the cartoon entitled *The Kidnapper — A Case for the Police* (Plate 2) from the 29 March 1851 issue of *Punch*. This illustration followed a piece describing a young woman with a large dowry who had been educated at a convent at Taunton and was 'so charmed and edified by the conventual life, that it is said she feels inclined to adopt it altogether; and taking the church for her bridegroom, will possibly endow her mystic spouse with her eighty thousand pounds'.[9] The cartoon accordingly shows a monk holding up a nun's veil as bait for a childlike female 'victim'; he avariciously eyes the girl's dowry, which would soon, as 'ransom' (in the opinion of the author) become church property. (There was even a suggestion in a subsequent issue that a bill should be drawn up to protect young women against 'kidnap' by religious houses.)[10] The greediness of sisterhoods was also pointedly scorned in a mock-medieval poem entitled 'Taking the Veil' in an 1851 issue of *Punch*; in this tale, an heiress named Ladye Blanche (with a £90,000 estate) is deceptively beguiled by convent life and its abbess and priests, the latter portrayed as fortune hunters interested only in 'catchyng an Heiress'.[11]

Realisation of the goal of establishing Anglican sisterhoods began in 1841. Newman had taken steps to launch such a project by 1840, when he wrote that

> Pusey is at present very eager about setting up Sisters of Mercy. I feel sure that such institutions are the only means of saving some of our best members from turning Roman Catholics; and yet I despair of such societies being *made* externally. They must be the expression of an inward principle. All one can do is to offer the opportunity. I am sceptical, too, whether they can be set up without a quasi-vow.[12]

Within a year of this date a young woman named Marian Hughes (who stated that she had been profoundly influenced in her decision by reading Newman's *Church of the Fathers*) was the first to profess a personal vow of holy celibacy; in 1849 she became the Mother Superior of the Society of the Holy and Undivided Trinity in Oxford, which became known for its nursing work during the cholera epidemic of that year.[13] Pusey's own daughter, Lucy, had also dedicated herself to a religious career in 1841, but she died while still an adolescent and left the legacy of her spiritual involvement for other young women to fulfil.

In 1845 the Sisters of Mercy was founded at Park Village West; this community was begun by two friends, Jane Ellacombe and Mary Bruce, and was thereafter headed by a Miss Landsdon under the direction of the Rev. William Dodsworth of Christ Church, Albany Street. It was this sisterhood that had been broadly supported by a group of distinguished laymen, including W. E. Gladstone, Lord John Manners, and Lords Lyttleton, Campden and Clive, as a fitting memorial to Southey and his early advocacy of Anglican sisterhoods. In 1848 Priscilla Lydia Sellon, with the approval of the Bishop of Exeter, established a religious community to serve the poor in the three towns of Plymouth, Devonport and Stonehouse. She set up a ragged school for poor children, an orphanage for sailors' offspring, soup kitchens and temporary lodgings for the indigent, and an old-age home for sailors, often using her own private funds to finance these projects. She also was named the Superior of the Sisters of Mercy, donning the controversial habit of black and a black wooden cross. Her 'Sellonites' helped to take care of the afflicted in the cholera plague of 1849 and worked with Florence Nightingale's forces at Scutari, as did some of the Park Village sisters. Counterparts to these communities included Clewer House of Mercy, which was opened in 1849 as a penitentiary settlement to serve the fallen and the destitute and was headed first by a Mrs Tennant and later (in 1852) by Harriet Monsell, who was made the first Mother Superior of St John the Baptist, Clewer. Monsell's house successfully spawned numerous branches in England and India, all of these performing rescue, mission and parochial work along with service to schools, orphanages and hospitals. A related effort was made by William John Butler, the Vicar of Wantage, who designed a sisterhood especially devoted to female education and the training of sisters as teachers. The Wantage community, founded in 1849 and headed by Elizabeth Lockhart as the first Superior of St Mary the Virgin, expanded its influence through numerous branch missions. Nursing the poor was the chief aim of the sisterhood of St Margaret at East Grinstead, an order begun by Dr John Mason Neale in 1865; this community also grew in size and scope after its initial work among the impoverished.

The continual growth of sisterhoods, especially their rapid increase in the first ten years of existence, attested both to their limited successes and to the fact that they served a real social need by ministering to the poor, the homeless, the ill, the elderly and the unfortunate. Perhaps it was as Mrs Anna Jameson remarked in *Sisters of Charity* (1855): 'Why is it that we see so many women carefully educated going over to the Roman Catholic Church? For no other reason but that for the power it gives them to throw their energies into a sphere of definite utility under the control of a higher religious responsibility.'[14]

Having briefly examined the commitment to sisterhoods of certain individual Victorian women, it is timely to consider the motives that figured in the decision to enter a convent. In the cases of the women mentioned, undoubtedly genuine religious vocation was the primary impetus, with the desire to be of service to humanity a secondary and interdependent motive. As one historian has remarked, 'In all the early Anglican sisterhoods the desire to do good works was more prominent a motive than the desire to lead a particular kind of life.'[15] Yet in an article of 1840 one Protestant propagandist suggested less altruistic factors that could affect such a choice:

> The convent was too often the refuge of disappointed worldliness, the grave of blasted hopes, or the prison of involuntary victims . . . The sensitive entered upon life oppressed with fears and terrors; with a conscience morbid, not enlightened; bewildered by the impossibility of reconciling principles and duties. The ardent and sanguine, longing to escape from restraint, pictured to themselves in these unknown and untried regions, delights infinite and unvaried.[16]

In addition, Charles Kingsley, a strong opponent of High Church views who detested all forms of Roman Catholicism, wrote a novel entitled *Yeast, A Problem* in 1850 in which the subject of nuns is treated. A female character in this work similarly assessed her own reasons for contemplating the life of a nun, comparing her own motives with the purer ones of a colleague named Honoria:

> She had taken up the fancy of becoming a Sister of Charity not
> . . . from genuine love of the poor, but from 'a sense of duty'.
> Almsgiving and visiting the sick were one of the methods of
> earning heaven prescribed by her new creed. She was ashamed of
> her own laziness by the side of Honoria's simple benevolence;
> . . . she longed to outdo her by some signal act of self-sacrifice.
> She had looked to this nunnery, too, as an escape, once and for
> all, from her own luxury, just as people who have not strength to
> be temperate take refuge in teetotalism; and the thought of
> menial service towards the poor, however distasteful to her,
> came in quite prettily to fill up the little ideal of a life of romantic
> asceticism and mystic contemplation, which gave the true charm
> in her eyes to her wild project.[17]

As such admittedly prejudiced contemporary accounts suggest,
the sisterhoods apparently attracted a wide range of candidates in
addition to those motivated purely by religion: romantics who
envisioned sainthood in such a life, women who were unable or
unwilling to marry, and those who preferred dedication to nursing
or community service to a life of enforced idleness in a parlour. The
convent life thus could fulfil various needs on the part of its
aspirants: a spiritual vocation, a career in social work, and a
general retreat. It is provocative, however, that most artists of the
period capitalised on the less idealistic side of such a decision, pre-
ferring to imply that the pretty young women had forsworn the
external world because of a broken engagement or an unhappy love
affair and were thus immured behind high cloistered walls.

While there were clearly supporters of the idea of sisterhoods,
many Victorians were appalled by such a prospect, which to them
was an unnatural withdrawal from the world and an abdication of
family ties. In a society that idolised the sanctity of the family and
of motherhood, it was not readily conceded that holy celibacy
could be a more honourable spiritual state than matrimony or
maternity — or that women possessed any right to dedicate their
bodies and souls to God instead of to a husband. Kingsley
denounced clerical celibacy and its counterpart for religious
females, proclaiming in *Yeast, A Problem* that 'for true woman,
the mere fact of a man's being her husband, put it on the lowest
ground that you choose, is utterly sacred, divine, all-powerful'

(Chapter 11). Similarly Frederick Denison Maurice, the oracle of Christian Socialism, stated in his 1863 essay, 'On Sisterhoods', that 'there is a power committed to women, to all in different measures, of which they have no right to deprive the world; from the loss of which all society must suffer'.[18] Such female self-abnegation not only constituted a slur against marriage to some critics, but it also disrupted the order of the domestic structure. The danger of supplanting parental (especially paternal) authority with religious hierarchy (direction from a priest or Mother Superior) was a source of suspicion, and numerous clergymen and writers railed against this supposed threat to family stability and happiness. Even more moderate arguments against the claustration of women were tinged with disapproval, as when Mrs Jameson commented,

> I conceive that any large number of women shut up together in the locality, with no occupation connecting them actively and benevolently with the world or humanity outside, would not mend each other, and that such an atmosphere could not be perfectly healthy, spiritually, morally, or physically.[19]

In addition to the implied affront to wedded life, the Victorians often were suspicious of sisterhoods because they doubted the efficacious result of such a retreat or isolation from society. More than one author argued that the female members of a parish ministered to the needs of the poor or ill just as thoroughly and loyally as did cloistered nuns. Apart from objections to enclosure, another concern focused on a woman's control of her property and her freedom to depart the sisterhood at will.[20] The issue of 'Romish' vows of chastity, obedience and poverty was also volatile, a prickly topic even among leading clerics, like Bishops Archibald Tait, Charles Blomfield and Samuel Wilberforce, who supported other aspects of conventual life. A typical reaction among the critics was voiced by F. D. Maurice when he wrote, 'I hold the idea of the vow as the contract of an individual soul to the celestial Bridegroom is subversive of the Catholic Church, denying the dignity, annulling the obligations of other Christians.'[21] The issue of vows, the arbitrary authority of the Mother Superior and the possible confiscation of personal property were all troublesome matters. It is fascinating that personal liberty seemed at stake to some, since women were not otherwise accorded much freedom under the law; ironically, the decision to enter a convent was one of the rather few assertions of independence that a female might be able to demonstrate and as such might be considered a quasi-feminist statement.

Another target of hostility was the usage of the Thirty-Three Chapters of Rule, a form of spiritual discipline which Pusey had adapted from St Augustine's rule and Catholic tracts. The rule insisted on cultivating certain Christian virtues, implementing this through regulations prescribing specific modes of obedience, humility, silence, confession, meditation, mortification of the flesh, intercourse with strangers, etc., plus an hourly schedule (or horarium) by which sisters were to live. The Rules were considered perverse and immoderate by some Victorians, but in fact leaders of religious communities often tried to discourage the more bizarre behaviour inherent in penance, for example. None the less, Victorian readers were curious about these requirements and some rare or atypical penalties inflicted, and these aspects were sensationalised by lay writers with vivid imaginations and disgruntled ex-sisters with the proverbial axe to grind. Tales were told of young women being punished for misdeeds by having to eat off the floor, being blindfolded for looking at a lay person, wearing a piece of bread around the neck for two days for thinking of worldly matters, being confined to the cell for a week for going beyond the convent walls without permission, or having to make the sign of the cross on the floor with one's tongue for a breach deemed sufficiently serious by the Mother Superior. Reports of such penances deeply offended (and simultaneously intrigued) the critics.[22]

The more lurid aspects of convent life also proved of interest to contemporary literature. Some works purported to be non-fiction, as R. McCrindell's *The Convent: A Narrative, Founded on Fact*, which was described by the *Athenaeum* reviewer in 1848 as a 'protest by an "English Governess" against free will immured by papistical bigotry'.[23] Others endorsed the romantic reasons for entering a sisterhood; for example, in the anonymous *A Woman's Way; or, The Chelsea Sisterhood* (1865), a female embraces convent life because of a broken engagement but ultimately leaves years later when her ex-lover acquires a title and the two are reconciled. An even more popular mode was the confessional tract allegedly written by a former postulant or nun, such as a late-century work by Sister Mary Agnes entitled *Nunnery Life in the Church of England*. The novel combining these elements was typified by a work such as *Maude or The Anglican Sister of Mercy*, edited by Miss E. J. Whately and published in London in 1869.[24]

Among the many acid remarks in *Maude* about sisterhoods is the following passage describing the women attracted to this institution:

> Duties many of them might have found, in their own circles and homes had they sought for them; but it was too much trouble to look prayerfully and humbly for God's guidance, and simpler to break through all home ties, and then persuade themselves and others that the choice lay between a life of inaction and luxury's ease at home, and the unselfish devotedness of a Sister of Mercy. And how easily disappointed feeling, boredom, vain craving for excitment, and a thousand other tendencies of our own fallen nature, may assume the mask of devoteness to God's service, all who know something of their own sinful hearts can bear witness . . . Many of such erring and misguided ones are found to swell the ranks of those who are pressing into the sisterhoods and vainly hoping that the serge dress and black veil will shield them from all the dangers and temptations of the world.[25]

The theme of religious vows taken as a deliberate and repentant denial of earthly affections was also a leitmotif in contemporary poetry, best represented by the poems of Christina Rossetti, herself a convert to Catholicism as well as the sister of a woman who chose to enter a convent. Numerous poems such as 'The Novice' (1847), 'Three Nuns' (1849–50) and 'The Convent Threshold' (1858) contained such allusions, but a particularly explicit statement of this notion is found in the following excerpts from the 1858 work:

> . . . I choose the stairs that mount above,
> Stair after golden sky-ward stair,
> To city and to sea of glass.
> My lily feet are soiled with mud,
> With scarlet mud which tells a tale
> Of hope that was, of guilt that was,
> Of love that shall not yet avail.

> . . . You sinned with me a pleasant sin:
> Repent with me, for I repent.
> I turn from you my cheeks and eyes,
> My hair which you shall see no more —
> Alas for joy that went before,
> For joy that dies, for love that dies!

. . . If now you saw me you would say:
Where is the face I used to love?
And I would answer: Gone before;
It tarries veiled in Paradise.[26]

Clearly there was more to Victorian attitudes, both in life and literature, than revulsion or censure — there was curiosity as well, and this was also true of contemporary art depicting nuns or nunneries. Just as the bland prettiness of secular young ladies in Keepsake annuals found a ready audience, so too did pictures of lovely nuns eschewing society for a Heavenly Bridegroom. The piquancy of female charm always found a ready market, and this somewhat sensational subject was no exception. Previous depictions of nuns and nunneries certainly did exist, as in Henry Singleton's *A Nun's Going to Matins* (1802), Isaac Pocock's *The Nun (from Bowles' Sonnets)* (1805), William Havell's *Nuns at the Convent Door Near Torre del Greco* (1834), or Henry Willson's *The Capuchin Convent, Castle Vetrano* (1836). These and other earlier nineteenth-century paintings used literary or continental religious models for inspiration, and Victorian artists continued to utilise primarily Roman Catholic and foreign sources. As the appendix to this chapter indicates, an increased interest in this subject began in about 1839 (before the first sisterhoods were instituted but at the height of the Oxford Movement), after which time at least one depiction of a convent scene appeared nearly every year at the Royal Academy or the British Institution until the end of the century.[27] It is unlikely that this would have initially occurred without the impetus of the controversy about religious communities for women, and artists continued to exploit this topical theme in a variety of subtle and unsubtle ways.

The early 1840s witnessed a spate of such paintings and depictions, including those in the pages of Keepsake annuals. In a poem and illustration entitled 'The Novice' in *Friendship's Offering* (1841), for example, the poet asks the fair young female protagonist: 'Hast thou no closely clinging ties, / That bind thee down to earth? . . . Thou art too like the summer flower / That lives in light and gloom, / To lose the freshness of thy hours / Within the convent tomb.'[28] This and a kindred illustration of the same title by A. J. Woolmer from *Forget-Me-Not* (1844) signalled the beginning of the Victorian pictorial cult of the nun. In the engraving of Woolmer's canvas, a sweet maiden is shown braiding a crown of white roses and 'Thinking how, as these shall wither, / They shall image forth her fate, / All that once was bright and radiant, / Thorny now, and desolate.'[29]

Another classic approach which reiterated the biases of contemporary novels and journalism is found in William Collins's 1843 Royal Academy entry, *The World or the Cloister* (Plate 3). The contrast between young females in secular and religious dress which so piqued the interest of Victorian viewers is repeated here, emphasised by the presence on an old nun who physically exemplifies the loss of external beauty, the withering of the physical life, in the encloistered existence. Apparently the young lady on the right, who wears a crucifix, is being interviewed as a possible candidate by the Mother Superior, who gestures imploring while a younger nun (a postulant, judging from the lighter colour of her habit) assists by turning the pages of a book and perhaps listening to the recitation of requirements for admission to the sisterhood. The *Art-Union* critic added an extra fillip of meaning in his interpretation of the situation: 'The lady in blue has been disappointed in the fidelity of her lover, or been eclipsed at a ball: but, however annoyed for a moment, "she won't be a nun." '[30]

Given the controversy raging over this socio-religious issue in the 1840s and 50s the image was practically guaranteed notoriety. Even when no specific depictions of nuns were included at the Royal Academy in a particular year, there was a very good chance that an illustration would appear in an art journal or Keepsake annual. The beautiful virginity and inaccessibility of the woman were key components, and many artists chose to peep behind closed doors to envision their subject. It was as if the decision to renounce matrimony and the outside world — not to mension sex — merely enhanced the nun's desirability, creating an eroticism out of virginity itself.

Perhaps this religious prototype of the 'pin-up' was also fired by male fantasies about what actually took place in nunneries. A (lost) work in this category might be Thomas Uwin's *Making A Nun*, which appeared in the 1846 Royal Academy exhibition and was described as follows by the *Art-Union* critic that year:

She is, for the last time, attired in the richest habit which she was accustomed to wear 'in the world', as it is expressed, of which she is despoiled, and receives in its stead that of the sisterhood of her adoption. The moment chosen is that in which the abbess is about to cut off the hair — the jewels have already been removed from the person; and the hair is now being severed, and is about to be received upon a salver held by a young attendant for that purpose. Besides the abbess, a number of sisters are present, whose sombre dresses contrast strongly with the bridal attire of the new sister, who, dressed in the 'shroudlike habit' of the order, is again led forth in procession to the outer chapel, to receive the veil from the hands of the bishop, and the ring by which she says he marries her to Jesus Christ.[31]

A far more overtly voyeuristic view of convent life is found in an engraving of Alexander Johnston's *The Novice* (Plate 4), which hung as an oil painting in the 1850 exhibition at the British Institution and was accompanied by some of the following lines of verse: 'This vestal cloak shall fold my fading bloom, / Of virgin vows and purity the token; / This cell sepulchral-like shall be the tomb / Of withered hopes, Vows broken as soon as spoken, / Of Love despised, of peace destroyed, and of a heart quite broken.'[32] Here the decidedly romantic reasons expediting the girl's choice — a disappointed amorous experience — are made explicit in the poem, and in this voluntary prison an elegant young lady slowly removes her precious bracelet, as a skull on the window-sill balefully watches her. Replacing this wordly adornment will be the rosary beads beneath the skull; the woman's fading youth and soon-to-be-sacrificed beauty are similarly paralleled by the fallen rose on the floor, perhaps a final vestige of her renounced love in the external world.

A more sophisticated example that borrows at least part of its meaning from the idea of the abnormality of cloistered life for a woman can be found in Charles Allston Collins's 1851 canvas, *Convent Thoughts* (Plate 5). In its earliest stages, the painting started out as an illustration of Shelley's 'The Sensitive Plant', with two preliminary studies depicting the woman in dark, simple secular attire.[33] By the third sketch, however, the anglican Lady of the poem had been transformed into a postulant contemplating a passion flower and holding a Bible. In the final work, which was at first entitled *Sicut Lilium*,[34] the young woman wears the light grey habit and white wimple of a postulant, perhaps that of a Poor Clare; at any rate, her garb indicates that she has probably not yet taken her final vows.[35]

Convent Thoughts, an 1851 Royal Academy entry, was also

accompanied by several lines chosen by the artist from both *A Midsummer Night's Dream* and a passage from Psalm 113, 'I meditate on all thy work; I muse on the work of Thy hands.' Using this biblical allusion, Collins places a surrogate Mary figure amidst virginal lilies as she meditates on God's work — her physical surroundings — in this modern *hortus conclusus* or enclosed garden of chastity.[36] The rose with thorns growing in this garden contrasts implicitly with the thornless Virgin, who was exempt from the consequences of original sin. The sober-looking postulant marks two places in her missal with her fingers: one is an image of the crucified Christ, the Holy Bridegroom to whom she is now promised, and the other is a scene of an annunciation, perhaps an allusion to the role of mother and wife which she has spurned by electing to become a sister. As with other representations of this type, the young woman is isolated from the outside world in a religious inner sanctum bordered by a high brick wall that restricts her sphere of action and forcibly closes out all memories from the past. Several goldfish and tadpoles reside in the pool on this tiny island of chastity, contrasting their own procreative state with the nun's virginity. The beautiful blossoms — agapanthus, lobelia, fuschia and others — similarly confirm the luxuriant, colourful vitality of nature, thus reiterating the contrast between their bountiful lushness and the woman's austere garments and life.[37]

Similarly, the lines from Shakespeare which Collins selected — 'Thrice blessed they, that master so the blood / To undergo such maiden pilgrimage' — suggest a dilemma between actual death for the female protagonist in the play and a death-like, barren existence of 'withering on the virgin thorn' (*A Midsummer Night's Dream*, I.i.78). Collins, who was himself an Anglo-Catholic (and was teased by his close friend John Everett Millais and especially by Dante Gabriel Rossetti for his purported asceticism),[38] may none the less be concurring with the view of Theseus in *A Midsummer Night's Dream* that the young woman in question should carefully weigh the results of the sterile and inhibiting life of sequestered virtue which she has undertaken. Whether or not the novice is pondering her plight is, of course, ultimately a matter of conjecture.

The reactions of the press to *Convent Thoughts* was generally mixed, *The Athenaeum* hailing the 'earnestness in this work worth a thousand artistic hypocrisies'.[39] On the other hand, 'Punch among the Painters' in the 1851 volume of *Punch* applauded the visual truth of the picture but disliked the 'unattractiveness of the demure lady' and mocked the amorphous body under the robes and the oversized head. The familiar complaint about the unwomanliness of such a choice also recurs:

> Whether by the passion-flower he has put into her hand, he meant to symbolise the passion with which Messrs. Lacey, Drummond, and Spooner are inspired against the conventual life, or the passion the young lady is in with herself, at having shut up a heart and life capable of love and charity, and good works, and wifely and motherly affections and duties, within that brick wall at her back — whether the flower regarded, and the book turned aside from are meant to imply that the life of nature is a better study than the legend of a saint, and that, therefore, the nun makes a mistake when she shuts herself up in her cloister, we are not sufficiently acquainted with Mr. Collins's ways of thinking to say.[40]

Interestingly, John Ruskin at first castigated this painting for its supposedly 'Romanist and Tractarian tendencies',[41] but afterwards revised his initial estimation, having apparently been convinced by Collins in a letter of May 1851 that such overtones were not intentional. Collins's attitude toward sisterhoods in *Convent Thoughts* is perhaps ambivalent; it is unresolved whether some degree of censure of this mode of life was expressed by the artist. Collins submitted another canvas on this subject to the Royal Academy in the following year, 1852. Significantly, this lost work drew its title, *Lyra Innocentium* from some 1846 writings by Keble, perhaps another sign that the artist's Anglo-Catholicism found conscious or unconscious expression in his paintings. *The Athenaeum* described the subject as 'a young girl who — we are to imagine — preserves her "chrysom" purity by wearing a sort of white, flannelly nun-robe; but her cherry-ripe lip and plump cheek are hardly in keeping with the sentiment of the downcast eye and ascetic costume'.[42] Here, as in *Convent Thoughts*, Collins may have used actual Anglican sisterhoods (perhaps from Oxford) as his model, rather than foreign sources.

The thought of spurning real suitors for a mystical union with Christ and an austere life on earth stimulated many artists to produce pictures in the 1840s and 50s. One work, Charles Eastlake's *A Visit to the Nun* (Plate 6) from the 1846 Royal Academy exhibition, elicited different responses from reviewers discussing the painting a decade apart. In 1846 *The Art-Union* merely described the scene as a recently veiled nun visited by a married sister in the monastery: 'The one is wedded to the humanities of the world: and the other is, in the language of the Church, "the bride of Heaven", whose story is at once legible in the exquisitely delicate characters in which it is written.'[43] This neutral editorial commentary changed drastically ten years later when the picture was published as a full-page engraving in *The Art-Journal* and was accompanied by the following interpretation:

Now, whatever the purpose of Sir Charles Eastlake may have been in this touching and most beautiful composition, we have no idea he had any intention of putting it forth as an argument in favour of monastic life — a life, we are so heterodox as to believe, altogether opposed to the doctrines of the Divine Founder of the Christian faith and his immediate followers, who taught us 'to USE the world without abusing it', and to 'let our light so shine before all men, that they may see our good works'. But we are not about to preach a homily on the conventual system, and perhaps should not have referred to it at all if the picture did not seem to invite the observation. We read it, however, in a way far from favourable to monasticism. The visitors to the Nun, we presume to be a married sister and her two children. The married sister is evidently urging upon the attention of the recluse some topic to which she listens with emotion, though her head half-turned away, and her downcast eyes, show but little inclination to yield to the argument, whatever that may be. The elder of the children is, in the expression of her look, a silent pleader in the same cause, while the younger child holds up a small nosegay of wild flowers, as if to indicate how much there is in a world beyond the dreary walls of the convent from the enjoyment of which, no less than from the sacred lessons all the works of nature teach us, the Nun has voluntarily excluded herself. These are the principal characters in the story: but there are others bearing a part in it. The old nun to the right is closing the door against some unseen individual — certainly not the father confessor; possibly — though not with much probability, considering that such a visitor could scarcely have penetrated so far into the convent, unless by the influence of bribery — one who feels especial interest in the young recluse who has 'put lover, friend, and acquaintance out of her sight.'[44]

As such a review suggests, the furore about sisterhoods was only gaining momentum in the 1850s.

Moreover, the contrast between the fate of most women and the disavowal of 'natural' instincts conveyed in Eastlake's and Collins's paintings was played up in other canvases which extend the setting and story-line slightly. This obsession with feminine abnormality — coupled with a hint of thwarted romantic love — as symbolised by such a choice is clearly reflected, for example, in the response of *The Athenaeum*'s critic to Alfred Elmore's 1852 painting *The Novice* (Plate 7):

> A fair maiden, in the blossom of youth and beauty, sits pensively in a lonely cell on a wretched pallet . . . Her dimpled cheeks — are those on which neither time nor sorrow have yet set their mark, and contrast with the hard, cold and stony prison in which so much promise, so much capability in giving and sharing delight, is immured alive . . . All the creature comforts that sweeten and humanize existence are banished, and give place to the forms and appliances of self-sacrifice and mortification. While within all is sadness, without the tide of the gay world is at its height . . . The novice has laid down her mass book, and casts a wistful glance at what she has given up. Seemingly she muses on the hopes and possible affections of wife and mother, all of which she has exchanged, ere she knew their value, for a cheerless, unnatural celibacy from which death is the only release.[45]

Perhaps even more compellingly, when a foreign critic, Théophile Gautier, saw Elmore's canvas in 1855 and described it in *Les Beaux-Arts en Europe* that year, he confirmed these readings of the painting and added a few new points of interpretation. Gautier saw her as a prisoner held in by bars and stone walls that became her tomb, this claustration in contrast with the sounds and smells that floated freely past her window. Furthermore, the austere presence of the old abbess was heightened by the fatal overtones of the melancholy cemetery in the background.[46]

The allusion to noisy carnival life outside the window that diverts the attention of the novice from her devotions in Elmore's canvas suggests a continental setting (perhaps French or Italian) for the scenario, which may similarly be the case in John Calcott Horsley's

1856 Royal Academy entry, also called *The Novice* (Plate 8). There is a decidedly less pensive or mournful look to the sweet, almost angelically pretty young nun here, thus making this seem more like a fancy-dress or frothy costume piece; but this lighter tone did not exempt it from equally vehement condemnations from the press about the subject's 'unnaturalness'. *The Art-Journal* basically echoed the objections to the theme that had been voiced earlier about Elmore's painting (and similar works), once again heightening the contrast between a life of youthful vigour and fulfilment in the outside world and one of desiccated sterility among aged nuns in the convent.

And Mr. Horsley's Novice seems not to have forgotten altogether that external life from which she is about to separate, should resolution hold out the requisite term of probation. The dove she caresses so gently is, or may be accepted as, a messenger from the world beyond the convent-walls, bringing to her, unlike the dove of Noah, thoughts that breathe not of the subsiding of the waters, but of the social enjoyments of her girlhood's home and its tenderest endearments; perhaps, thoughts of one dearer than all the world beside. The book of devotion is laid aside, the chaplet of flowers she is weaving for some holy rite has fallen from her hands, as the winged emblem of innocence flew into her bosom, breaking in upon her devotion and her labours. Those aged nuns, who have become habituated to the austerities of the community, regard her, as they saunter up the burial-ground of the sisterhood — recognized by the turf-mound's on the left — with looks of suspicion, as if they would connect the act with something sinful, or, at least savouring more of worldliness than is consistent with strict conventual life, which would shut out all the finer feelings of our nature and every source of pleasure God has placed bountifully within the reach of all.[47]

There is an unspoken hope by the author of this passage that the novice, who is still only a probationary nun, may change her mind and re-enter the world outside the monastery, flying back home like the messenger bird, perhaps to join the company of one 'dearer than all the world beside'.

One of the variations on the theme of sexual sublimation and denial can be found in Millais' *The Vale of Rest* (Plate 9), which failed to fulfil the essential Victorian expectations of the 'nun-picture'. Millais' painting was too unhappy — with its explicit references to death, not mere claustration — as well as being too de-sexualised. These factors, along with the generally hostile reactions to the idea by critics like Ruskin, help to explain why this painting did not receive very enthusiastic reviews when it was exhibited at the Royal Academy in 1859. Although the artist had intended to create a painting with nuns in it as early as 1855 (when he was on his honeymoon trip), he waited a few years before utilising the background wall and trees he had studied at Bowerswell or the freshly dug grave he had sketched in a churchyard at Kinnoull. While the technique was praised by numerous critics, the morbid subject-matter was often singled out for reproach. *The Athenaeum* sensitively described Millais' consummate painterly skills before commenting on what was perceived as *The Vale of Rest*'s more grisly aspects:

There is poetry in the clear, calm twilight sky and the chapel-tower and bell cutting dark against it. How finely, too, the tall columns of the poplar trees fret against the opalline dimness of the evening. Mr. Millais has caught admirably the awkwardness and weakness of the woman using the unaccustomed spade, and has thrown a fine ascetic meditativeness over the face of the seated nun, — not that her red skull of a face and staring, coarse black eyes are pleasing, — far from it, they are as hard and painful as those of some of Hogarth's viragoes. . . . He has expressed, too, with rare force, the rank growth of the burial ground grass, thick and dank from its horrible nurture, and the way the dying light is carried among the leaves of the bushes, the spotted laurels and rather clotted ivy is most daring and masterly. An air of ascetic meditations and self-immolation is kept up through this powerful, though not very pleasing, picture.[48]

The young nun with the 'unaccustomed spade' may be a postulant: knee-deep in a grave, she uses a sexton's shovel to heave up earth, which is intermingled with some human bones. Her older colleague grimly supervises the labour and sits atop some tombstones that mark the lives of deceased nuns. On the rosary beads hanging from the waist of this seated figure is an ominous skull. Even the array of trees in the garden — poplars, ashes and elms — was viewed as melancholy, as was the early evening hour. A coffin-shaped cloud in the sky may foreshadow an early demise for both women; this was certainly the reading of the picture given in *The National Magazine*, which noted: 'According to ancient Scottish superstition, whenever a cloud of evening assumes, to the excited fancy of the beholder, the shape of a coffin, that is the signal of death.' The elder nun, with 'wreaths of immortelles' by her feet, comprehends this premonition, 'deems death's approach as near, and, turning therefrom, looks to the opposite quarter of the sky, longing for a peace the world has not given her'. Thus it was not only the incongruity of this hard physical task being performed by the gentler sex which would have alarmed the public — it was also the thought that one or both figures were metaphorically at least digging their own graves. Others, however, might have seen the painting as a representation of the vale of rest, 'where the weary find repose', combining religious love with death, an interpretation supported by an excerpt such as the following from Pusey's writings:

As this hidden life is obtained by deadness to the world — 'ye are dead and your life is hid with Christ in God' — so, by that deadness, is it to be cherished, maintained, perfected . . . Seek only to be 'buried with Christ' from this world and its vanities, hidden in His Tomb, so that the show and pomps of this world may but flit around us as unreal things, but not catch our gaze, nor draw our hearts, which have been 'buried with Him' and are now 'risen with Him'.[49]

Thus the vale of rest, 'where the weary find repose', combines religious love with death, for as Pusey's lecture reveals, digging one's own grave as Millais depicts it may be a form of achieving spiritual union with Christ.

Kindred undertones of moroseness and potentially fatal consequences can be detected in Harriet Martineau's seven-part novelette, *Sister Anna's Probation*, which was serialised in *Once a Week* in 1861–2 and illustrated by Millais. The story exemplifies what might be called the 'rescued nun syndrome', a popular fictional theme which commonly featured secret communications with a former lover outside the high walls and a last-minute reprieve (with his aid) from the monastic surroundings. The happy ending predictably included marriage to the deliverer, or at least a return to the domestic confines of home and family.

Martineau's tale focused on the plight of the winsome Anna, who, compelled by family circumstances, enters the cloister (so that her sister can marry with the benefit of a dowry) for a one-year provisional term. She leaves behind her the unrequited love of Captain Henry Fletcher, who in the opening chapter reveals that he is enamoured of Anna partly because she has forsworn men to become the bride-elect of Christ. It is he who predicts the investigations and the break-up of the 'Romish' convent at the close of the novel; it is also he who sends messages to her over the wall, arranges forbidden rendezvous, and ultimately elopes with her. Although this novice is at first enthralled by the prospect of the life she has selected, she soon becomes disillusioned by the partiality, the inflexibility and the pettiness of the sisterhood. Two of the several moments that Millais illustrates are revealing: in one Sister Anna and a fellow postulant are ruminating about the outside world in the garden when a noise startles them: it is the arrival of commissioners with a royal warrant to investigate conditions at the monastery. The other scene reunites Anna with her lover in Ireland, where the two are depicted as a married couple locked in a typical 'courtship' embrace. The story is replete with anti-Catholic sentiments, the main objection to nunneries being the standard one of their unnaturalness. As Captain Fletcher neatly summarises in his speech to Anna, 'Let those bear the blame . . . who shut you up before you could know what the act of obedience imported. I respect you more for rebelling against your bonds than I could for submitting to them.'[50]

There continually seemed to be the hint of an absent suitor, the whisper of a broken love affair, or the innuendo of a denial of womanhood hovering in the background meaning of these paintings, at least in the minds of the reviewers. There were myriad images of picturesque postulants contemplating their fates as they read the Bible, toyed with sprigs of flowers or prayed behind monastery walls, including close-up 'portraits' of this type by Charles W. Cope (*Maiden Thoughts*), James Sant (*The Novice*), William Powell Frith (*Devotions*), and Frank W. W. Topham (*Taking Her Vows*). Gustave Pope's *Reflections* (1863) is typical of this genre, with its rather mawkish depictions of a comely young female in nun's garb and with a prettily (often insipidly) soulful expression. There is a covert delight in the almost delectable, girlish unavailability and chastity of this pseudo-religious subject, a quality that becomes more pronounced in the 1880s and 90s. The very title of some of these depictions of one or two nuns, for instance William Quiller Orchardson's *Resignation*, underscores the different levels of worldly negation — sexual, material and maternal — perceived in such a choice. A late-century painting such as Marie Spartali Stillman's *The Convent Lily* (1890) (Plate 10) simultaneously complies with the rather vacuous images of nun-worship in Keepsake sources and retains an affinity with the notion of walled virtue. Much as Charles Collins's *Convent Thoughts* and Millais' *The Vale of Rest* had dramatised moments of contemplation about the transience of life and the nature of feminine self-sacrifice, this painting is similarly imbued with an elgiac mood and uses the shared mystique of the garden setting, albeit here with rather saccharine results. Clutching a bouquet of virginal Madonna lilies and holding rosary beads and a Bible with illuminated pages, this adolescent novice, like her more commanding counterpart in Collins's icon, presides in a walled garden whose very perimeters are reminders of the physical and other restrictions imposed by conventual vows and life. Yet this blandly pretty figure wears no postulant's robes, allowing the viewer to indulge in the fantasy that she may only be a visitor, not a member of this religious community. Such tableaux of girlish innocence, replete with looks of unspoken anticipation and solitary confinement, could thus generate multiple meanings to the viewer in a way that was no longer controversial.

In the last quarter of the century the juxtaposition of two feminine options — a worldly life or renunciation of it — recycled the notion used much earlier in William Collins's 1843 painting, *The World or the Cloister*. In Francis S. Walker's *The Convent Garden* (1878) (Plate 11), for example, the secular and sacred alternatives merge in one world. A novice with white wimple is being promenaded by an older nun in the foreground, perhaps being instructed about the life she has chosen. Behind them a group of nuns sit in the shade of a tree, while in the background a few ladies in normal attire stroll in the sunlight or loll in the grass, their picturesque leisure a contrast with the dark sobriety of the nuns.

The choice between a sacred or 'profane' life was also reflected in a rather mawkish strand of late-century imagery typified by works that qualify more as a bizarre type of quasi-religious, almost 'courtship' imagery, with a covert rivalry set up between the Spirit and the Flesh, Christ or a mortal lover as the contenders for a woman's love. This tendency, highly charged with melodrama, is evident in works like George Hall Neale's *Christ or the World?* (1892) and Arthur Hacker's *The Cloister or the World?* (1896) (Plate 12), both of which exploit with histrionic visual results the inherent tension between romance and religion in this period. In Neale's version, a youthful swain has proposed in a parlour just as his sweetheart experiences a vision of Christ, a handsome Holy Spouse, and she is overcome with emotion and indecision. In Hacker's painting the temptations of the flesh and spirit vie for possession of the tormented nun in an updated drama of Poussin's (and other artists') *The Choice of Hercules*. As the pretty nun swoons with indecisiveness a white-robed, soulful angel personifying purity brings an emblematic lily, as if to re-enact an annunciation. She regards ruefully, almost apprehensively, the embodiment of pleasure gaudily bedecked in feathers and flowers and beckoning with a smile from her swirl of rainbow colours. The formula for such pictures was at this stage rather hackneyed and the melodrama so obviously overwrought that even a conservative critic commented, 'It is possible to raise against it the objection that it has a certain falseness of sentiment.'[51]

In a striking turn-of-the-century example of the 'rescued nun syndrome', Edmund Blair Leighton's *Vows* (1906) (Plate 13), salvation from the stereotyped evils of convential life quite literally materialises over the high brick wall at which the novice has been waiting. The young woman's anguished countenance expresses the mingling of fear and intense emotions evoked by the young man on the ladder, as he holds her hand and urges her to escape with him. The viewer's fantasy of 'saving' the woman from the abnormal life she has made for herself is thus manifested in an extravagantly theatrical piece.

There is the implication throughout this selection of characteristic images of nuns that the Victorians projected a lot of wishful thinking about the loss to the world of cloistered feminine beauty and purity. Most artists portrayed the nun as rather young, in spite of the fact that women were technically supposed to be of legal age or to have obtained parental permission before they could enter into convent life. Similarly, the central female figure is invariably a novice or a postulant in status, an indication perhaps that male artists wanted to depict the subject *before* she had totally relinquished the outside world, leaving open a chance that she could change her mind or, better yet, that she could be snatched back. This emotional predicament allowed the artist to concentrate on an amorous conflict which presumably had to be repressed or even forgotten by the young woman after (and if) she took her final vows. The dangling possibility of a reprieve constantly lingered, since the Victorians did not seem otherwise able to accept this situation in a straightforward way. The element of renouncing earthly love or beaux enhanced the woman's appeal and added a degree of martyrdom as well, thereby heightening her Madonna-like qualities at the same time that it made her perversely inaccessible.

It is difficult to determine whether the specific topics represented here were Anglican or Roman Catholic, British or Continental. Perhaps it was ultimately 'safer' to choose a non-Anglican subject, since such a desicion would be less controversial and less likely to brand the artist as displaying 'Popish' inclinations. The settings are thus only vaguely medievalising, and the women are fundamentally neutral or nondescript as to nationality or precise era. But the conventual revival was clearly the major impetus as well as a burning — sometimes lurid — issue in the 1850s, one which might need to be cloaked in foreign or indeterminate pictorial terms in order to remain respectable enough for Royal Academy walls.

Curiosity, anxiety and notoriety seem to have motivated the popularity of these pictures, which responded to the latent need of the public for such contemporary icons to loathe or to admire. At times this fascination bordered on the prurient, with artists and their audiences voyeuristically peering behind convent walls to imagine the life, the devotions, the excesses and the sacrifices of the inhabitants. Protestant fear of Catholicism often had an impact on the interpretation of this imagery, and the mixture of repulsion and attraction which the artistic subject could elicit mirrored the alloy of emotions that the religious issue evoked on its own.

Thus the re-establishment of Anglican sisterhoods in the Victorian era created a genre or sub-genre of painting which conveyed degrees both of reality and of fiction in its stereotypes of sequestered innocence. The aura of hothouse but holy virtue undoubtedly made the nun-picture a somewhat sensational, perhaps even a saleable, commodity after 1850, bringing with it accrued anxieties and criticism of things 'Romish'. Yet this genre also cheapened the subject in some respects, making pretty pin-ups and picturesque intrigues out of the often noble sacrifices and serious commitment of women like Harriet Monsell, Lydia Sellon, Marian Hughes and other 'sisters of mercy'. This trivialising or sentimentalising of the theme produced what amounted to an entire iconographic vocabulary that sustained a sense of awe, beauty, innocence and sexual repression all in one pictorial component, the traditional subject in art of a lovely young woman. The range of convent scenes outlined in this essay and in the appendix that follows attest to the fact that from the 1850s onward the nun and her moments of religious conscience were far from private or even sacred matters, at least in art; for this symbolic lily of virginity and spirituality, much like her secular sister in real life, was enshrined in an atmosphere of mystery and unattainability that made her simultaneously innocuous to some Victorians, repugnant to others, and generally titillating in her modern *hortus conclusus* of femininity and chastity.

Appendix: Selected Nun and Convent Imagery

The numbers following each title indicate its entry number in an exhibition. Unless otherwise noted, the numbers refer to the Royal Academy annual exhibitions. Works shown at the British Institution are denoted by BI, and those shown at the Society of British Artists by SBA.

Year	Title and Artist
1780	*Portrait of a Nun*, Mrs Vernon (90)
1802	*A Nun Going to Matins*, Henry Singleton (287)
1805	*The Nun (from Bowles' Sonnets)*, Isaac Pocock (400)
	A Nun at the Altar, W. Rennell (590)
1808	*A Nun*, Eliza Jones (BI 77)
	The Convent, Rev. W. Horner (671)
1809	*The Novice*, Isaac Pocock (BI 14)
	The Nun, I. Pocock (BI 15)
1811	*The Abbess and Nuns of St Hilda*, Mrs Elizabeth Carmichael (BI 84)
1819	*A Nun Reading in an Oratory*, Henry J. Fradelle (BI 125)
	Interior of a Convent, Henry J. Fradelle (BI 129)
1827	*The Nunnery, Isle of Man, the Seat of General Goldie*, Henry Gastineau (498)
1829	*A Nun at Her Devotions*, Thomas H. Illidge (BI 382)
1833	*Taking the Veil*, Thomas Uwins (336)
1834	*A Nun at her Devotions*, Josiah Squire (BI 192)

Year	Title and Artist
1834	*A Procession of Nuns*, J. Miles (BI 334)
	Nuns at the Convent Door near Torre del Greco, William Havell (324)
	The Novice, H. S. Smith (357)
1835	*A Portrait of a Young Lady in the Habit of a Nun*, Mrs Briane (633)
1836	*The Capuchin Convent, Castle Vetrano, Sicily*, Henry Willson (BI 250)
	A Capuchin, Convent Door at Noon, Charles W. Cope (BI 410)
1839	*Capuchin Convent at Amalfi*, James Uwins (BI 394)
1841	*The Novice*, Thomas H. Illidge (BI 96)
1842	*Convent of St Cosimato, near Rome*, William Havell (113)
1843	*The World or the Cloister*, William Collins (94)
1844	*The Franciscan Convent, Cintra*, James Holland (BI 4)
	A Wounded Soldier Returned to His Family Visited by a Sister of Charity, Frederick Goodall (472)
1846	*A Visit to the Nun*, Charles Eastlake (111)
	Making a Nun, Thomas Uwins (300)
	Convent Porch, Amalfi, Joshua E. A. Dolby (309)
	The Visitation and Surrender of Syon Nunnery, Paul F. Poole (575)
1847	*Maiden Meditation*, Charles W. Cope (43)
1848	*The Entrance to a Roman Convent*, W. Cowen (BI 320)
	A Nun at the Order of the Good Shepherd with Three Penitents, Miss Raimbach (748)
1849	*A Sister of Charity of Ravenna*, Solomon A. Hart (93)
1850	*The Novice*, Alexander Johnston (BI 138)
	Holy Maiden, Frank Williams (515)
1851	*Convent Thoughts*, Charles Allston Collins (493)
	Convent near Nice, George E. Hering (793)
1852	*'So keep thou by calm prayer and searching thought'*, Charles Allston Collins (493)
	The Novice, Alfred Elmore (353)
1853	*Claudio and Isabella*, W. H. Hunt (44)
1856	*A Sister of Mercy*, Anna E. Blunden (125)
	The Novice, John Calcott Horsley (311)
	A Sister of Mercy, E. Havell, Jr (BI 831)
1857	*Buried in a Cloister*, James Hayllar (46)

Year	Title and Artist
	The Novice, Gustav Pope (110)
1858	*Love and the Novice*, Alexander Rowan (407)
	In a Convent, William S. Burton (437)
1859	*The Vale of Rest*, John Everett Millais (15)
1860	*Matins*, James D. Wingfield (BI 221)
	The Novice, T. Earle (BI 638)
1861	*The Nun's Smile*, Charles Martin (513)
	Consolation, Abraham Solomon (180)
	Fasting Day at the Convent, George D. Leslie (SBA 334)
1862	*The Convent Shrine*, Francis Wyburd (BI 616)
	The Sisters of Charity, Robert Hannah (495)
1863	*Within the Convent Walls*, Alfred Elmore (216)
	In the Cloister of Arles, Philip Calderon (264)
1864	*The Nun*, Alfred Elmore (324)
1865	*The Sister of Charity*, John A. Fitzgerald (BI 381)
1867	*'Her thoughts on holy things are bent'*, Emma Brownlow (BI 381)
	The Old Convent Garden, J. J. Lee (570)
1869	*Sisters of Charity Teaching Blind Girls to Sing*, James Collinson (364)
1870	*The Nun*, A. F. Payne (28)
	The Nun, E. Dudley, (386)
	Lost, Emily Mary Osborn (458)
1871	*Memories of the Past*, Charles Rossiter (340)
	Sisters of Charity, Charles B. Barber (530)
1872	*A Sister of Mercy*, Frederick B. Barwell (370)
1874	*The Convent Boat*, Arthur Hughes (584)
	At the Convent of San Francesco d'Assisi, Frank W. W. Topham (1382)
1875	*Convent Life*, Sophie Anderson (199)
1876	*An Old Convent, Venice*, John P. McDonald (130)
1877	*The Sister of Charity*, Alphonse Neumans (384)
1878	*The Convent Garden*, Francis S. Walker (345)
1879	*The Convent Garden*, John B. Burgess (453)
1883	*The Convent*, S. A. Forbes (1467)
1888	*The World Renounced*, Francis S. Walker (644)
1892	*Christ or the World?* George Hall Neale (907)
1896	*The Cloister or the World?* Arthur Hacker (478)
1900	*The Convent's Chronicler*, Philip Connard (1650)
1901	*The Cloister and the World*, George S. Knowles (392)
	The Blind Abbess, Talbot Hughes (735)

Notes

*An earlier version of this essay was published in *Victorian Studies*, XXIV (1981), pp. 157–84.

1. These pejorative epithets appeared in articles such as W. R. Greg, 'Why are Women Redundant?', in *Literary and Social Judgments* (Boston, 1868), and Jessie Boucherett, 'How to Provide for Superfluous Women', in Josephine Butler (ed.), *Woman's Work and Woman's Culture* (London, 1869).

2. A fuller examination of these examples of early advocacy of sisterhoods in the nineteenth century can be found in Michael Hill, *The Religious Order: A Study of Virtuoso Religion and its Legitimation in the Nineteenth-Century Church of England* (London, 1973), pp. 168–70.

3. [J. H. Newman], 'Letters on the Church of The Fathers', *British Magazine*, VI (June 1835), p. 667.

4. Cited in Henry Parry Liddon, *The Life of Edward Bouverie Pusey* (London, 1894), III:6.

5. These figures are based on extensive consideration of this development in Peter F. Anson, *The Call of the Cloister: Religious Communities and Kindred Bodies in the Anglican Church* (London, 1956), Chs 2, 3 and *passim*. See also Vernon F. Storr, *The Development of English Theology in the Nineteenth Century 1800–1860* (London, 1913).

6. On Anglican brotherhoods, see Hill, *The Religious Order*, pp. 204–8 and 304–7. It is worth noting parenthetically that although representations of nuns are fairly common, those of their male counterparts are less numerous. Paintings specifically alluding to the theme of sexual or material renunciation by monks include Alfred Elmore's *The Novice* (1843) (a male novice in this case), R. Little's *Renunciation* (1887) and Frank Dicksee's *Vows* (1888).

7. 'Convent of the Belgravians', *Punch*, XIX (19 October 1850), p. 163.

8. Parishioners complained of some of Bennett's ritualist practices. In July 1850 Bennett threatened to resign and convert to Roman Catholicism; allegations in the press and among the church hierarchy triggered a near-riot that autumn by some discontented members of the congregation and others. See Owen Chadwick, *The Victorian Church*, 2 vols (London, 1966, 1970), I:301–3.

9. 'No Business of Ours', *Punch*, XX (29 March 1851), p. 20.

10. A visual variation on the entrapment motif, probably in the context of Romanism, appeared in *Punch*, XX (5 April 1851), p. 139, in a cartoon entitled *Little Red Riding Hood*, which portrayed a clerical wolf preying upon a susceptible young female.

11. 'Taking the Veil', *Punch*, XX (5 March 1851), p. 133. The drawings to illustrate the mock-epic tale were done by John Tenniel; one scene, for example, shows the heiress's hair being clipped by a nun in the presence of no less than Cardinal Wiseman himself.

12. Newman's thoughts on the subject were contained in a letter of 21 February 1840 to his friend Bowden; J. H. Newman, *Letters and Correspondence*, ed. A. Mozley (London, 1891), II:299.

The general details of the founding of specific female communities are available in, for example, Hill, *The Religious Order*, Anson, *Call of the Cloister*, and especially A. M. Allchin, *The Silent Rebellion: The Anglican Religious Communities, 1845–1900* (London, 1958). See also Thomas Jay Williams and Allan Walter Campbell, *The Park Village Sisterhood* (London, 1965).

13. Some of the rather poignant text of Hughes's diary entry acknowledging Pusey's impact can be found in Hill, *The Religious Order*, pp. 151–2.

14. Mrs Anna Jameson, *Sisters of Charity: Catholic and Protestant, Abroad and at Home* (London, 1855), pp. 101–2.

15. Charles Philip S. Clarke, *The Oxford Movement and After* (London, 1932), pp. 253–4.

16. [Sarah Lewis], *Woman's Mission* (Boston, 1840; orig. publ. London, 1839), p. 70.

17. Charles Kingsley, *Yeast, A Problem* (London, 1860), Ch. 10.

18. Frederick D. Maurice, 'On Sisterhoods', *The Victoria Magazine*, I (August 1863), p. 300. Maurice drew a clear distinction between Catholicism and catholicity in his often abstruse writings and was claimed by various religious factions, although his philosophical system ultimately seemed uniquely of his making. For more information, see Frances Warre Cornish, *The English Church in the Nineteenth Century*, (London, 1910), I:193–6; or the more recent Allchin, *Silent Rebellion*, esp. pp. 348–63.

19. Jameson, *Sisters of Charity*, p. 51.

20. Policies on the issue of property varied among sisterhoods; at Clewer, for example, sisters were supposed to contribute £50 yearly if they could afford it, and could not take away any property they had originally brought in with them. Complete surrender meant in this case that 'a Sister should have no longer any property whatever at her own disposal, for purposes of personal use or enjoyment. She may be possessed of capital, but the annual proceeds must be given either to the Community Fund or to objects external to the Community, according to the agreement made with the Warden and Superior at the time of her Profession'; cited in Ralph W. Sockman, *The Revival of the Conventual Life in the Church of England in the Nineteenth Century* (New York, 1917), p. 139.

21. Maurice, 'On Sisterhoods', p. 301. In contrast, the point that there could be an element of incipient feminism in such a decision, as in the concept of the sisterhood itself, is made in, for example, Hill, *The Religious Order*, p. 271; Allchin, *The Silent Rebellion*, p. 116 and Ch. 7; and Raymond Chapman, *Faith and Revolt, Studies in the Literary Influence of the Oxford Movement* (London, 1970), p. 171.

22. Such sensational information was often conveyed in tracts supposedly written by ex-postulants or ex-nuns.

23. 'Our Library Table. *The Convent: A Narrative. Founded on Fact*', *The Athenaeum*, XXI (29 January 1848), p. 110.

24. The general consensus of popular literature was that entering a nunnery was an irresponsible, even wasteful act, an attitude conveyed even in humorous sources; see, for example, The Hon. Hugh Rowley, *Gamosagammon; or Hints on Hymen* (London, 1870), p. 179: 'As for Nunneries, Ladies' Convents, etc., they may or they may not be all "hotbeds of untempted sin": "as we never tempted them we can't say" but we can and do most distinctly say we consider them — collectively and singly — an immense and most disgraceful waste of the Raw Material!'

25. Miss E. J. Whately (ed.), *Maude or The Anglican Sister of Mercy* (London, 1869), p. 218.

26. Excerpts from stanzas 1, 6, and 7. W. M. Rossetti (ed.), *The Poetical Works of Christina Rossetti* (London, 1906), pp. 340–2. The poet's elder sister Maria entered an Anglican sisterhood, St Mary Magdalene's Home at Highgate, in 1873 to work with fallen women; she died three years later. Dante Gabriel Rossetti wrote of his sister Maria's decision, 'I simply could not exist on such terms — it would be a novitiate for another world; and I view the matter as most serious for her.' See O. Doughty and J. R. Wahl (eds), *The Letters of Dante Gabriel Rossetti* (London, 1967), III:1216.

27. The appendix includes only a selection of exhibited works from major institutions; in addition to this tally, however, myriad other images (paintings, engravings, and otherwise) appeared on the contemporary art market. These include such works as William Q. Orchardson's *The Story of a Life* (1866) and James Smetham's *The Nun Prioress* (1864).

28. Catherine H. Waterman, 'The Novice', *Friendship's Offering* (Boston, 1841), p. 34.

29. Miss Skelton, 'The Novice', *Forget-Me-Not* (London, 1844), p. 89.

30. 'The Royal Academy', *The Art-Union*, V (1843), p. 161.

31. *The Art-Union*, VIII (June 1846), p. 174.

32. Algernon Graves, *The British Institution: A Complete Dictionary of Contributors and Their Work from the Foundation of the Institution, 1806–1867* (London, 1908; special Anderdon annotated copy in the Royal Academy Library), unnumbered 1837–52 volume, p. 12.

33. The two early studies are in the British Museum; the third and fourth stages of the design are at the Ashmolean Museum and the Tate Gallery respectively.

34. The alternative title was the one under which Collins's patron apparently bought the work. According to a label on the back of the painting, as cited in the files of the Ashmolean Museum, there was a note affixed by the purchaser, Thomas Combe: 'For this "Silicut Lilium" I gave only 150 pounds and it was the largest sum Charles Collins ever made from a picture.'

35. Regarding the latter point it is not possible to identify the robe of the postulant with a specific sisterhood. But letters from the artist to a colleague do indicate that he had borrowed a nun's garment in order to depict accurately the arrangement of the chasuble and scapulum. The relevant correspondence is in the Ashmolean Museum.

The novice in Collins's painting may have been a member of the Society of the Holy and Undivided Trinity at Oxford, which was where the artist created the work and might have seen or known of the sisterhood. Grey robes were worn in other Anglican nunneries (e.g. at the Nursing Sisters of the Community of St Margaret or St John the Divine), but light grey seems to have been reserved for probationary stages at Oxford and elsewhere. The sister who had taken final vows was more likely to wear a habit of a darker grey or even black hue.

36. According to a label on the back of the painting written by Thomas Combe, 'It was done with great labour and perseverance. He worked very slowly and I know that a flower of one of the lilies occupied a whole day — the flowers were all painted from nature in the Clarendon Press Quadrangle.'

37. It is not clear whether the flowers are intended to be symbolic, although the passion flower she contemplates was in contemporary floral lexicons often associated with religious superstition.

38. Collins's Anglo-Catholicism was the butt of considerable teasing by his Pre-Raphaelite cronies. Millais supposedly said. 'He is as good a little chap as ever lived, with no nonsense about him, except perhaps his new inclination to confession and fasting, and he does not let strangers see his asceticism, which is only the result of his being hipped in love.' William Holman Hunt, *Pre-Raphaelitism and the Pre-Raphaelite Brotherhood* (London, 1905), I:190. In another anecdote reported by Hunt, Millais' joking was more pointed, almost sarcastic in tone; he allegedly commented to Collins, 'You know you like blackberry pudding as much as I do, and it is this preposterous rule of supererogation which you have adopted in your high-churchism which made you go without it. I have no doubt you will think it necessary to have a scourge and take the discipline for having had dinner at all.' Ibid., p. 207.

39. 'The Royal Academy', *The Athenaeum*, XXIV (7 June 1851), p. 609.

40. 'Punch Among the Painters', *Punch*, XX (1851), p. 219.

41. In a letter to *The Times* (13 May 1851), Ruskin wrote, 'No one who has met with any of my writings will suspect me of desiring to encourage them [the Pre-Raphaelites] in their Romanist and Tractarian tendencies . . . I have no particular respect for Mr. Collins' lady in white, because her sympathies are limited by a dead wall, or divided between some gold fish and a tadpole'; E. T. Cook and Alexander Wedderburn (eds.), *The Works of John Ruskin* (London, 1904), XII:320–1.

Eighteen days later his revised opinion appeared in *The Times*; see ibid., p. 327.

42. 'The Royal Academy', *The Athenaeum*, XXV (22 May 1852), p. 582.

43. 'The Royal Academy', *The Art-Union*, VIII (June 1846), p. 174.

44. 'The Royal Pictures', *The Art-Journal*, XVIII (1856), p. 174.

45. 'The Royal Academy', *The Athenaeum*, XXV (29 May 1852), p. 607; see also 'Selected Pictures', *The Art-Journal*, XXVII (1865), p. 68.

46. Théophile Gautier, *Les Beaux-Arts en Europe* (Paris, 1855), I:80–1.

47. 'Selected Pictures', *The Art-Journal*, XXIX (1867), p. 184. As in Eastlake's case earlier, both Elmore's and Horsley's paintings were given full-page engravings when illustrations of them were published in *The Art-Journal*.

48. 'The Royal Academy', *The Athenaeum*, XXXII (30 April 1859), p. 586.

49. Cited in Owen Chadwick, *The Mind of the Oxford Movement* (Stanford, 1960), pp. 211–13.

50. Harriet Martineau, 'Sister Anna's Probation', *Once A Week*, VI (1861–2), p. 372.

51. 'The Royal Academy', *The Athenaeum*, LXIX (6 June 1896), p. 752.

Plate 2 John Leech, *The Kidnapper — A Case for the Police,* wood engraving, *Punch,* 29 March 1851

Plate 1 *Convent of the Belgravians,* wood engraving, *Punch,* 18 October 1850

Plate 3 William Collins, *The World or the Cloister*, oil on canvas, 1843, Art Gallery and Temple Newsam House, Leeds

Plate 4 Alexander Johnston, *The Novice*, engraving with etching, 1850, private collection

Plate 5 Charles Allston Collins, *Convent Thoughts*, oil on canvas, 1851,
Ashmolean Museum

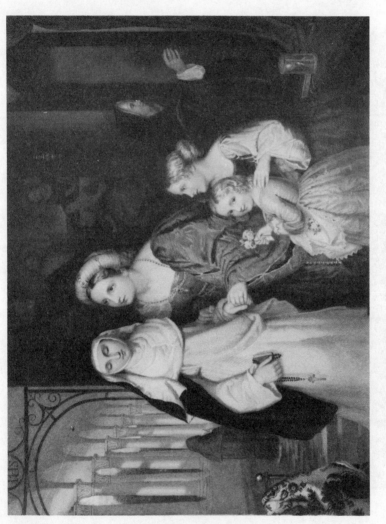

Plate 6 Charles Eastlake, *A Visit to the Nun*, engraving with etching, 1846, from *The Art-Journal*, 1856

Plate 7 Alfred Elmore, *The Novice*, engraving with etching, 1852, from *The Art-Journal*, 1865

Plate 8 John Calcott Horsley, *The Novice*, engraving with etching, 1856, from *The Art-Journal*, 1860

Plate 9 John Everett Millais, *The Vale of Rest*, oil on canvas, 1859, Tate Gallery

Plate 10 Marie Spartali Stillman, *The Convent Lily*, oil on canvas, 1890, Ashmolean Museum

Plate 11 Francis S. Walker, *The Convent Garden*, oil on canvas, 1878, Leeds City Art Gallery

Plate 12 Arthur Hacker, *The Cloister or the World?*, oil on canvas, 1896,
from *The Royal Academy Pictures of 1896* (London, 1896)

Plate 13 Edmund Blair Leighton, *Vows*, oil on canvas, 1906, photo courtesy of Sotheby's Belgravia files

Chapter 7

The Female Diaconate in the Anglican Church: What Kind of Ministry for Women

Catherine M. Prelinger

The nineteenth-century deaconess movement in the Anglican communion represented the most comprehensive effort to address the relationship of women to the church since the Reformation. To institute a female diaconate meant not only to provide women with opportunities for Christian service; it signified the installation of an office for women within the ecclesiastical hierarchy itself. By way of definition, the diaconate provided a consecrated office for single women while it supported, trained, placed and supervised them in various occupations important to the church and society, occupations like nursing, settlement-house work, and education both at home and abroad. It was customary in the nineteenth century to speak of the 'restored female diaconate', by implication referring both to scriptural and early church precedent as well as to the centuries-long lapse of the office. The extent and intensity of controversy surrounding the deaconess issue in popular literature and in the official assemblies of the church strain modern credulity; the number of participants in the controversy far exceeded the number of women ever interested in the Anglican diaconate, which remained relatively small. The institution of deaconess was none the less an important one. First of all, for those who chose it, the diaconate uniquely empowered women in terms of personal calling and conscience as well as with respect to the scope and definition of their service to the church. Secondly, because the office provoked such impassioned discussion, it provides the modern scholar with a valuable prism within which to analyse gender and class issues in nineteenth-century British society. At the turn of the century, as gender became an increasingly apparent means of determining occupational hierarchy in the professions, the female diaconate played a part in shaping the structure of the clerical profession. This essay will examine the deaconess movement from these perspectives.

I

The deaconess institution in its modern form originated in Germany in 1833 when Theodor Fliedner, pastor of the local Evangelical church in Kaiserswerth, and his wife converted their garden house into a refuge for women recently discharged from prison. The deaconess mother-house was founded three years later. Fliedner's tombstone reads: 'Restorer of the Apostolic Office of Deaconess', as indeed he was. From the very beginning, the female diaconate in England was a conscious adaptation of the German precedent; conversely, Fliedner was indebted to England for his own conversion to the advocacy of female philanthropy. Until Fliedner's experiment, Protestant charity in Germany was a male preserve. As a young cleric, Fliedner had travelled to England to solicit funds for his struggling congregation, a Protestant diaspora in the overwhelmingly Roman Catholic province of the Rhine. There he became familiar with the reform work of Elizabeth Fry (1780–1845) among the women prisoners incarcerated at Newgate. On his return, he founded the Rhine-Westphalia Society for Prison Relief, the association which served as the immediate antecedent of the Rhine-Westphalia Society for the Education and Employment of Evangelical Deaconesses. Antagonism to Roman Catholicism acted as a powerful reinforcement to Fliedner's evangelical zeal. He undertook the restoration of the scriptural office of deaconess as a calculated response to the Sisters of Charity, but consciously rejected the convent as an institutional model. What he did instead was to pattern the deaconess institution after the contemporary patriarchal family, *das ganze Haus* or household, which in Germany was still the basic unit of production. The hospital, the nursery school, the several hostels — all the components of the original diaconal institution — were additions to the Fliedner household. The deaconess candidates themselves, like other family dependents, were household members. The authority structure, but also the emotional and productive reciprocity of the patriarchal family, were thus embedded into the very essence of the deaconess institution.

The family structure of the diaconate was apparently a major inducement to the early recruits, young single women to whom the traditional family economy no longer offered a secure existence. Their applications for admission to the deaconessate testify to the material impoverishment which accompanied their spiritual longings. The familial rhetoric of the diaconate appealed to unsatisfied yearnings for a family surrogate. The mother-house system as it developed at Kaiserswerth promoted intense female bonding and *esprit de corps* within this otherwise vulnerable sector of German womanhood. This, I think, is the key to the spectacular success of the German diaconate. At the turn of the century there were nearly fifteen thousand deaconesses stationed all over the world bound to the Kaiserswerth rule; in the same decade, fewer than two hundred women counted themselves members of the Anglican diaconate.[1]

Florence Nightingale herself introduced the British public to the experiment at Kaiserswerth. Nightingale's acquaintance with the institution derived from two protracted sojourns there, one in 1850, the other in 1851. Although she subsequently denied that she had been 'trained' at the Kaiserswerth hospital, she served what amounted to an apprenticeship in contemporary nursing practice there, and she also engaged as a full participant in the religious life of the community. She publicised her observations in a promotional brochure entitled *The Institution on the Rhine for the Practical Training of Deaconesses*, a concise but comprehensive survey of the institution. Nightingale became Fliedner's principal liaison for promotion and fund-raising in England. Single British women like herself were the intended target of Nightingale's brochure:

> The want of *necessary* occupation among English girls must have struck every one . . . In the middle classes, how many there are who feel themselves burdensome to their fathers or brothers but who, not finding husbands, and not having the education to be governesses, do not know what to do with themselves.

> More labourers are wanted [as deaconesses], and more will come. If this be their future, the fear of becoming 'old maids' will disappear; . . . Let those women who sit in busy idleness, look at Germany.[2]

The British context within which Nightingale wrote her brochure was, of course, different from that of Germany, particularly in so far as options for women were concerned. When the notion of a diaconate for women entered the British consciousness, English-women were already engaged in various forms of Christian service on a massive scale. The Anglican evangelical Hannah More (1745–1833) has set a rigorous standard. A social and intellectual celebrity, she generated Sunday schools in the midst of squalor and pressed her friends to agitate for the abolition of slavery.[3] The network from More to Fry embraced hundreds of women; the work they did proliferated and diversified to include virtually every form of contemporary philanthropy. As Nightingale knew so well, however, their efforts were limited by voluntaryism and lack of professional status, and there was often a desultory quality to their commitment.[4]

Nightingale was not alone in alerting the British to the virtues of the female diaconate. Clergy of Low Church persuasion had motives of their own for applauding the institution at Kaiserswerth. They were sensitive to any experiment which seemed to offer the model for a viable alternative to the convents patronised with such enthusiasm by their High Church peers. The Anglican revival represented by Tractarianism in the 1840s had stimulated the appearance and rapid proliferation of women's religious orders modelled on historic Catholic sisterhoods, a development fostered by the High Church and deplored as Romish by the Low.[5] On the surface the issue of sisterhoods functioned as a dimension of the High Church/Low Church controversy; beneath the surface, however, often quite explicitly, the debate concerned the place of women in the family and the authority of the family within society at large. In fact, sisterhoods not only anticipated the Anglican female diaconate chronologically; they generated virtually all of the arguments which were subsequently marshalled, although often transposed, in the debate over deaconesses.

The issue of women's communities in the church became the subject of a pamphlet war. Aligned on one side were, among other, vocal fathers and mothers of women who had entered sisterhoods in apparent defiance of parental authority. In one widely publicised correspondence a father, himself a parson, accused the director of St Margaret's, East Grinstead of luring his daughter to the convent behind his back.

> I beg to ask by what light or authority — upon what principle of honour or religion — is my household broken into — my family peace invaded — my parental authority contemned. I shall be glad to have these touching questions replied to, and to be assured whether there is or is not any segment of the Church of

England whose system it is to sap the unity of families, to creep into houses by person or by letter, unknown to fathers. . .[6]

By contrast, High Church clergymen in the dispute were able to present the authority issue in very different terms. The Rev. Cecil Wray of St Martin's Church, Liverpool, in a sermon called *Sisterhoods on their Trial* could ask with great conviction: 'Are mothers of England quite sure that there is not in the hearts of their children a longing for something higher than the empty life which they are condemned to lead amid the shackles of fashionable society, and the world-vows under which many a soul is groaning for liberty?'[7] Edward Pusey, who commanded a unique authority in High Church circles, not only allied himself unequivocally with the conventual movement; he felt strongly that women should govern their own communities. As he wrote in 1865: 'I think it a wrong ambition of men to wish to have the direction of the work of women. I should fear that it would be for the injury of both.'[8] Yet the administration exercised by Mothers Superior, such as the notorious Priscilla Lydia Sellon, over women in the sisterhoods could be capricious and arbitrary, as women who had themselves been sisters sometimes testified.[9]

The issue of leadership in the sisterhoods simply cannot be considered under the rubric of gender alone, as the British sociologist Michael Hill does when he speaks of incipient feminism in connection with conventual patterns. Class was involved as well. Here Anne Summers's analysis in her 'Pride and Prejudice: Ladies and Nurses in the Crimean War'[10] can be instructive. Like the lady-nurses, the lady-sisters had had no previous leadership experience except in the role of mistress over servant. The rule of obedience practised in communities not only gave scope to arbitrariness; the hierarchy of class divisions in society at large were reflected by ranks within the sisterhoods themselves which dictated that the lowliest tasks be performed by sisters of second rank. (In contrast, when the Anglican female diaconate finally organised, class distinctions among deaconesses were seldom incorporated into the institution.) Negative impressions of the sisterhoods were, however, significantly mitigated by their reputation as nurses in the Crimean War and in the several cholera epidemics which plagued nineteenth-century English cities. Furthermore, and in this they paved the way for the deaconess movement, the sisterhoods demonstrated, as Janet Grierson argues, 'that women of gentle birth could work safely in the roughest districts, and, moreover, achieve a full and satisfying life beyond the protection of the parental roof and without husband or children of their own.'[11] This was no small accomplishment, since at first there was fear 'lest such close intercourse with the fallen should injure the pure',[12] and it had been thought 'ludicrous and lamentable' that 'these young ladies, brought up in all the refinement of polite life, [were known] to be carrying at half-past five o'clock in the morning a large dust-barrel to the top of the Court'.[13] Links between the two movements or forms of ministry, the ministry of sisterhood and the ministry of deaconess, were complex, far more so than the issue of gentility suggests, and a closer look at the female diaconate documents the complexity.

The deaconess movement gained full momentum in England during the decade of the 1860s. This was the consequence of a number of concurrent developments, three of them of particular importance. First was the appearance of a vast literature — and the consciousness it produced — about what came to be known as 'the problem of redundant women': the disparity between the female and male population established by the 1851 census. The census revealed that in the age group over twenty, the numbers of women exceeded those of men by something over 400,000. The perception of the issue, though not in fact the reality, was that the 'excess' was concentrated among 'ladies' — women of the upper and middle classes.[14] Many people of distinction addressed this issue in the press; commonly there was a marked difference according to gender in the way they approached it. Men characteristically analysed the census figures almost entirely in terms of marriage and the maintenance of existing social relations. Women used the occasion to plead for greater educational and occupational opportunities. The signal article of the debate, W. R. Greg's 'Why are Women Redundant?' in the *National Review*, argued for a straightforward, misogynist, and mechanical solution: the export — or, more politely, the emigration — of 500,000 women from England each year to other regions of the empire. Domestic servants were not, however, to be considered among those eligible for export, since '*they do not constitute any part of the problem we are endeavouring to solve. They are in no sense redundant; . . . they fulfil the essentials of woman's being; they are supported by, and they minister to, men.*'[15] Women spoke in a different voice. Feminist writers such as Anna Brownell Jameson argued very cogently in her *Sisters of Charity, Catholic and Protestant*:

The education given to our women is merely calculated to render them ornamental and well-informed: but it does not train them, even those who are so inclined and fitted by nature, to be effective instruments of social improvement. . . . an intelligent and amiable man will say: — 'It is all very well; but I should not like my daughter to do so-and-so.' But the question is not what this or that individual would choose his daughter to do. It remains with him to settle this within the precincts of his family; only it is most unjust to make his particular feelings and opinions the rule of life for others, without once approaching the question as one of social morals, as one of justice and humanity; without once reflecting that all the unemployed and superfluous women in England cannot be semptresses, governesses, and artists.[16]

L. F. M. Phillips vigorously supported Jameson's stance, arguing that 'all women should be helpers'.[17] Jessie Boucherette added, 'The plan, then, which I advocate for superfluous women is that of allowing them to engage freely in all occupations suited to their strength.'[18]

Second among the reasons for an intensified interest in the prospects for a female diaconate in the Anglican Church was the actual establishment of an English training centre for deaconesses in August 1860. An Anglican clergyman in the village of Barnet, William Pennefather, and his wife, consciously following the Kaiserwerth example, recruited eleven young women in the first six months for spiritual and practical training in the fields of domestic and foreign missions. This was the origin of the Mildmay Deaconess Home which took its name from Mildmay Park in London, where the Pennefathers and their mission moved in 1864.[19]Mildmay accepted women of 'Christian character . . . educated . . . [and] not fully occupied by home duties', for 'as long or as short a time as you please. Some ladies whose home ties prevent their giving up much time to out-door labour, come here for a month or two in the year in order to be able to devote a small portion of their time to systematic work for the Lord'; others devoted a lifetime. There were no vows, but the women wore a distinctive garb, and the training and work was structured, with an emphasis on a *'definite and systematic course of active ministry'*.[20] Essentially they performed the work of an inner-city mission, but as time went on and with the addition of new facilities at the institution, it assumed great diversity. Home visits, nursing, and the preparation of special dishes for invalids were part of the original programme; literacy classes for men, sewing classes for women, Scripture lessons, mothers' meetings and a variety of similar services followed. Much, though not all, of the work was done away from the deaconess home, but the deaconesses themselves habitually returned to Mildmay at night, partly for reasons of the 'purer air',[21] partly for the importance that the Pennefathers, like the Fliedners, attached to a communal domestic and spiritual life. As one woman wrote, 'No one can live in this home without feeling the power of a Christian life, the stir of a mission spirit, and without being brought to a deeper study of God's Word. This house is humming all day long with the song of happy toil.'[22]

Mildmay was an early venture in practical ecumenism. Both the Deaconess Superintendent and the Treasurer were Presbyterians.[23] Pennefather, a Low Church Anglican, had a world reputation for ecumenism even before the introduction of his deaconess experiment, by virtue of the enormous conferences he convened embracing peoples of all Christian denominations at home and abroad.[24] For twenty years after his death in 1873, his widow maintained and expanded the deaconess programme.[25] The Mildmay Institution had a more direct role in modelling the Methodist than the Anglican deaconess movement, though it acted as a powerful catalyst to the Anglicans and was ultimately incorporated into their network in 1917.[26]

The third and probably most important event to focus British attention on the possibility of a female diaconate in the Anglican Church was the publication in 1862 of the book entitled *Deaconesses: The Official Help of Women in Parochial Work and in Charitable Institutions* by the Rev. John Saul Howson (1816–85). 'Official' was the key word here. What Howson envisaged was a female ministry of the church, and accordingly he defined the ideal of the English deaconess as 'something between the desultory Lady Visitor and the member of a strictly conventual Sisterhood. . . . the great and essential feature of the deaconess . . . is, that she should be *professionally* set apart for her work.'[27]

In Howson's work one captures the true flavour of gender, denominational and class needs which had to be satisfied if the female diaconate was to win acceptance among Anglicans. Howson displayed his conservatism in the definition he chose for woman's work: 'helping work', the virtual equivalent of the term 'deaconess' in Greek: 'helpful service'. Howson was not unaffected by the findings of the 1851 census; what he focused on was not the evidence of 'redundant women' but rather the evidence of remuneratively employed women. He rejected what he called 'the theory of men', that all employed women should be in domestically oriented labour, and that men should hold themselves responsible for women's support.[28]

Howson constructed his confessional — or denominational — argument for the introduction of an Anglican diaconate on what he called 'Primitive and . . . Protestant fact'. Thereby, as he boasted, 'we separate it off at once from what is distinctively Roman Catholic'.[29] An eloquent description of Kaiserswerth followed the rather pedantic analysis of scriptural and early church precedent. Howson had visited the Fliedner Mother House and continental deaconess establishments before he himself took up the cause. At Kaiserswerth, the emphasis on training and the centrality given to the ritual of consecration impressed him, but what he found most appealing was the distinctively Protestant character of the German diaconate. 'If we were to single out one religious peculiarity of Kaiserswerth as conspicuous above the rest, it would be the close and discriminating study of the Bible'. He even contrasted the blue gown of the Kaiserswerth deaconesses 'representing their cheerful and serene spirit of Protestantism', with the Roman Catholic of black.[30] The familial atmosphere of Kaiserswerth evoked paeans from Howson: 'the corporate feeling in a happy and cheerful allegiance to the "Mother-House" ', maintained through the practice of frequent home visits for those sisters scattered over the world. Although he was impressed with the parental authority built into the patriarchal model of the institution, he also recognised the intense intimacy and sisterhood 'maintaining a loyal and affectionate feeling among the members of the community'.[31]

It is consequently the more striking that when Howson turned to the application of the Kaiserswerth precedent to English practice, he insisted on discarding all elements of communal life. He seriously questioned the desirability of surrogate family living any longer than was minimally required for training, for he believed that in England:

The most encouraging prospect is afforded by detached parochial efforts . . . The parochial most nearly resembles the primitive Diaconate, and . . . it is least likely to produce that jar of social distinctions which is always to be apprehended in the

midst of an artificial civilization; when those who belong to different grades of society are brought into close and almost equal
cooperation, this danger is considerable; but not so when the
efforts are detached and independent, and each under the super-
intendence of a parochial clergyman.[32]

At the church congress of the same year he reiterated his thesis:
'our system should be parochial and diocesan'.[33] All the continuing
connections of the familial structure which sustained the German
deaconesses Howson wanted abolished, particularly the female
centred ones such as maternal oversight and protracted sisterhood.

The pattern finally adopted in England generally followed the
Howson prescription: first, training in an institution modelled,
rather like Kaiserswerth, on the patriarchal family; second, consecration or setting apart at the hands of a bishop; third, parochial
assignment in which the deaconess served as an assistant to the
priest of the parish, totally isolated from the contact of peers.
There is reason to believe, however, that the ultimate prevalence of
Howson's formula in England contributed to the relatively small
numbers of women attracted to the diaconate. Nor did the parochial scheme succeed without strong resistance in a number of
quarters. The diaconal community, St Andrew's Deaconess
Community, which achieved the greatest measure of historical continuity and coherence was, and is, one which violated the diocesan-
parochial model in favour of sisterhood.

Elizabeth Catherine Ferard was the first woman 'duly set apart
as the first episcopally ordained deaconess in the English Church
since the Reformation.'[34] Ferard, who came from an old Huguenot
family, decided after the death of her mother to go to the institution at Kaiserswerth. Her stay, from 28 August to 13 December
1858, is chronicled in her handwritten journal. Ferard was profoundly moved by the spirituality and sisterly climate of Kaiserswerth, but otherwise rather overwhelmed. Since the town itself was
predominantly Roman Catholic, probationers and resident
deaconesses had virtually no opportunity to practise benevolent
visiting. Ferard's German was inadequate to the option of
penetentiary work among the former sexual 'offenders' who came
to the institution after they were released from prison. She soon
discovered that deaconesses and administration alike at Kaiserswerth 'do not seem to understand anyone going [to work in the
hospital] who does not like to do everything, however disagreeable

. . . Sister Hedwig says that unless you have the entire charge of some sick you would feel no interest.' Her 30 August entry goes on to say, 'Pastor Fliedner's opinion is that an Institution for Deaconesses will not answer in England until English ladies give up the expectation of having everything disagreeable done by servants.'[35]

While at Kaiserswerth she had met some English Sisters of Mercy from Suffolk who 'were anxious to avoid extremes', so on her return she worked briefly in their community of All Hallows, Ditchingham. In 1861 she ' "offered herself" to revive the Deaconess Order of England'. With the help of the Rev. Pelham Dale, a relative by marriage, and two other women she settled in a house in Burton Crescent near Kings Cross. She attended the Jubilee Conference of Deaconesses at Kaiserswerth the same year and there raised the question of accepting only educated women from the upper classes into the Anglican order. Strongly reproached, she nevertheless held her ground, arguing that social conditions in England were different from those in Germany. Nevertheless, the first rules of what became formally the North London Deaconesses Institution explicitly state that the association was to be modelled after Kaiserswerth, and Fliedner sent a 'highly gifted and thoroughly skilled deaconess' to train the English sisters.[36] There was a small ward set aside in the institution itself to care for 'females of respectability': domestic servants, shop assistants and similarly situated women who required nursing. Soon the deaconesses took over the nursing department of the Great Northern Hospital; in the cholera epidemic of 1866 they established three mission stations in Bethnal Green. Infant-school teaching and night classes for adults also became part of the programme. Probation, which usually consisted in working alongside experienced women of the community, lasted two years.[37]

In 1862, Ferard was 'set apart' by the Bishop of London, Archibald Tait. Tait himself had assumed an active role in the sisterhood controversy. Perpetual vows and auricular confession he explicitly opposed, and on these grounds he had declined to serve as Visitor to a number of religious communities. At the same time he enthusiastically welcomed the formal re-institution of women's work in the church 'to act amongst the sick', 'alleviate the sufferings of the poor', and 'resist the barbarism which, in the overflowing population of a vast people, is apt to spring up side by side with the highest refinement'. Hence he fully endorsed the restoration of the female diaconate which would satisfy these goals and at the same time acknowledge that

> family ties are imposed direct by God. If family duties are over-looked, God's blessing can never be expected . . . all who enter such communities must be at full liberty to leave them as the readings of God's providence point to another sphere of Christian duty . . . There must be no encouragement to a self-righteous estimate of the life embraced, as if it were more perfect than that of the family.[38]

Ferard, 'a manager of decision and power', according to the Rev. Dale's daughter,[39] differed from the archbishop. Her experience at Ditchingham as well as at Kaiserswerth, and the loss of some of her better deaconesses to the Anglican sisterhoods, reinforced her decision to move in the direction of a richer conventual life. The institution had relocated in 1873; in 1887, the title of Head Sister was changed to Mother Superior, and the Offices of the Church rather than the Book of Common Prayer became the devotional guide of the community.[40] The training function continued; deaconesses were prepared for both parochial work and overseas missions but the women who remained resident at St Andrew's House lived as a community of sisters. They do today; those — and they are the majority — who are engaged in parochial or diocesan work come and go, much as the Mildmay deaconesses did in the nineteenth century, returning in the evening to participate in the common spiritual and domestic life of the sisterhood. They are allowed by the rule under which they live, with the assent of the Mother Superior, to miss the observation of one of the Offices of the Church each day. This pattern of ministry, while the exception, was adopted by a few of the other English deaconess institutions.

Isabella Gilmore (1847–1923), who became Head of the Rochester Deaconess Institution, moved in an entirely different direction, one more in keeping with Howson's original intention. At Rochester the deaconess was first trained, then ordained by the bishop, and finally sent to serve essentially as a curate to a parish vicar, often with no regular contact with her peers. By 1907 Rochester had trained forty-one deaconesses; they received £75 a year for their services, and returned once a month to their institu-tion for worship.[41] Gilmore had been serving as a nursing sister at Guy's Hospital in 1886 when Bishop Thorold approached her to initiate and direct a deaconess programme in his diocese of Rochester. A recent widow, Gilmore came from a wealthy family; her brother was the artist and utopian socialist William Morris. Hestitant at first, she finally agreed on conditions that she and Bishop Thorold mutually determined.

> We felt that though the Sisterhoods had their great work in the Church, it was not ours; and I can remember how firmly Bishop Thorold said, 'a quasi-sisterhood I will not have'. We then planned out together our future: the women were to be as nearly as possible in the same position as the Deacons; and they were to work solely under their Parish Priest; they were to be free of the institution except so far as it was to be a house of rest and refreshment: they were to live in their parish, and if a near rela- tive could live with them, so much the better; in any difficulty the matter was to be referred to the bishop. According to the 'Rochester Lines', a Deaconess is an official of the Church under the Authority of the bishop and must not be confused with a Sister.[42]

The parishes in Battersea were Gilmore's first undertaking. She loved the people she visited: 'it was agony to find how terrible was their condition'. They were 'heathen' whom the Education Act and the Sanitary Laws did not reach.[43] To her surprise, recruits were slow in coming, but finally in the third year her house was full and the diocese sought larger quarters. Originally most of the training was practical, in the field, though ultimately Gilmore came to believe that more rigorous training in theology would be desirable.[44] Women stayed the first three months as visitors, then advanced through probation which normally lasted another two years. They were then ordained by the bishop, and given a letter of orders and a license. Gilmore insisted, 'We were sending out women and not children: if our training was worth anything they ought at the end of their two years to do well, working entirely under their parish priest, to receive their own stipend, live in their own house or rooms, and order their own lives.'[45] On one further issue Gilmore was equally insistent: the deaconess should receive twenty-four hours off each week, and a month's holiday each year: 'she is not a cast-iron machine'.[46]

Unquestionably a woman of Gilmore's personal confidence and ability could find personal autonomy and challenge within the parochial-diocesan arrangement. For others, however, the system was lonely and threatening. This is the clear implication of a memoir by Deaconess Charlotte Ransford, ironically one used to promote and publicise the opportunities of the female diaconate.[47] Ransford started her professional career as a Mildmay deaconess, but, as she said, 'felt the want of true Church principles and the absence of Church privileges in their fullest extent . . . I felt the need of a legitimate title to the name of deaconess, a commission from the bishop of the diocese.'[48] In order to legitimate her sense of vocation, Ransford entered the Salisbury Diocesan Deaconess Home where she completed three months of postulancy and eight months of probation. The description of her sojourn there is replete with images of domesticity and familial support. Ransford describes the ordination which admitted her to the Anglican Deaconess Order and the attainment of vocational status with anxiety rather than anticipation. For her it was a conclusion rather than a beginning:

> Then came the sad going forth from that sweet home of rest, to fight the devil in the world of sin. I seemed to have left a part of myself behind when the door closed upon me, and I parted from her whose loving training had brought me on to the fulfilment of my desires, from the saintly prelate who had been to each of us a very father in God, from the devoted chaplain whose advice had ever been so cheerfully afforded in our difficulties, and from that devoted band of consecrated women, my sisters in the bond of the spirit . . . My heart has never ceased to turn back to the fond memories of my Salisbury home.[49]

Ransford, like most of her peers among the Anglican deaconesses, entered on a career of city mission work, first in East London and then in a number of other urban centres and seaports: a life of responsibility, stress and isolation.

In her tribute to the training at Salisbury, Ransford ascribed to the curriculum not so much the acquisition of skills but rather the capacity for self-discipline. The Anglican system appropriated the German patriarchal family model for the training phase of the female diaconate: its utility was recognised as a means of internalising the values of obedience and subordination. '[Deaconess] training', she wrote, 'enables her to begin quietly and calmly while the habit of obedience makes her useful to her parish priest.'[50] The deaconess normally appeared at the vicarage on Monday mornings to receive the assignment for the week, her duties varying with the 'wishes of those under whom she serves,' as Dss Cecilia Robinson put it.[51] Or, as Ransford wrote, 'She comes and goes as he orders; she doesn't wait about the vestry doors, dictate to him and ask endless questions. She takes her orders as to the district appointed and diligently goes about the house to house visitation, recording in her book the names of families, unbaptized children or adults, candidates for confirmation, GFS girls, sick, poor, erring ones.' Then she reports to her parish priest any special cases requiring his attention. 'Of course,' Ransford continued, 'it may occasionally be necessary to go to the rectory but as much as possible the rector's time of quiet will be respected by the trained worker.'[52] *Her* time and space, by contrast, were not respected, particularly if she had rooms in the church house: her living habits were supposed to provide an example to the parish. She was ever accessible to the priest and his parishioners. The deaconess who worked in a diocesan hospital or centre on a daily basis experienced some degree of freedom from the parochial clergy. The extended paternal protection in the mother-house system through which Theodor Fliedner interposed himself between the deaconess and the local German bureaucracy did not exist in the British system. It was replaced by what purported to be a professional relationship, however vulnerable, between the deaconess and the priest. Writing a decade later than Ransford, Dss Cecilia Robinson, whose *Ministry of Deaconesses* became the textbook of the order,[53] suggested that an occasional return visit to the Deaconess Institution to chat with the Head Deaconess could be both a comfort and a 'moral tonic'. Herself a great admirer of Gilmore, Robinson nevertheless had recourse to the kind of maternal imagery which was anathema to Gilmore: 'For hard worked and weary as the Head Deaconess may be, she is never too tired to welcome her children.'[54] Even Isabella Gilmore in her later comments acknowledged the necessity of some form of continuing bond for the deaconess with her institution and came to share Robinson's conviction that a scheduled monthly return could mitigate a sense of isolation. Neither Gilmore nor Robinson worried about the gender hierarchy which the subservience of the deaconess to the priest institutionalised in the system. Gilmore's age and class situation may well have inured her both to the sense of powerlessness and to the yearning for female companionship which appear to have been inevitable components of the parochial female diaconate. She was over forty when she entered the deaconess order with a full married life behind her; her brother and her mother were still alive and at hand.

Whether the gentility of Anglican deaconesses protected them against loneliness is problematic. What is certain is that many were either the daughters or the sisters of clergymen. Some entered the order with their natural sisters. Cecilia Robinson herself is an example: her sister Elizabeth was a deaconess; her brother, a clergyman and Dean of Wells. Mary Hepburn-Lyall, a widow, founded the Church Deaconess Home at Maidstone in 1874 with her daughter as her assistant.[55] To those from clerical families, the disciplined spiritual life was familiar and perhaps sufficient satisfaction. Certainly the situation of the Anglican deaconesses was dramatically different from that of the economically and emotionally deprived candidates for Kaiserswerth. At St Andrew's, where Ferard's unique place in the order gave the institution some leverage with the ecclesiastical hierarchy, women were not confined to the life of a rule or community; many of the deaconesses were socially well positioned to maintain continuing contacts in both society and the church.[56]

Whichever pattern the spiritual and domestic lives of the Anglican deaconesses might follow, parochial or communal, their occupations in the secular world were identical. The well-born Anglican deaconesses entered a 'helping profession' whereby they served the clergy in necessary if subordinate capacities, performing the essential pastoral ministry of the church. A novice at St Andrew's summarised what she had done in the course of her three-year novitiate for the newsletter of the community, *Ancilla Domini*. On her very first night she was assigned to supervise the preparation of dinner at St Gabriel's, an 'industrial home' for girls run by the institution, although she 'had never so much as boiled a potato' in her earlier life. Beginning in January 1897, she held a Sunday morning class for girls at Christ Church, North Kensington; in the afternoon, a similar class for a much tougher group of girls at St Agnes's Mission. Two nights a week she helped with a children's club of one hundred members; one night a week, with a Mothers' Meeting in the slums of Notting Hill. Another night each week she set aside to inaugurate a meeting for those too poor to attend church: 'All they learned of God was from me.' In August she did housekeeping for St Andrew's. By the end of the year, she had charge of a Sunday class of Big Boys — very difficult. The following year she devoted to more extended periods of training: three months at St Mary's, then two months residence at St Agnes's where she was in charge of the Big Girls, conducted evening classes, gave an address to forty men, and on Saturdays taught the gospels to infant boys from pictures. She was responsible for regular visitation on one side of St Ann's Road, where the laundresses lived, a neighbourhood she considered 'superior', and two houses in Bangor Street, reputed to be one of the worst slums in London. For a year she served as sacristan in the home chapel, followed by eleven weeks at St Michael's, Westgate.[57] The daily life of the parochial deaconess was similar: a round of Girls Friendly Societies, Mothers' Meetings, Industrials, temperance meetings, visitations and, by the end of the century, co-ordination with the Charity Organization Society and the District Visitor.[58]

Brian Harrison has suggested how organisations like the Girls Friendly Society tried to protect against what turn-of-the-century traditionalists viewed as imminent societal chaos, and acted to cement conflicting classes into a conservative social alliance.[59] Deaconesses performed a similar function, but the girls with whom the deaconesses worked, for instance at St Agnes's Mission, were too 'rough' to be eligible for the GFS. The anonymous deaconess who described her association with them displayed extraordinary insight — a sense of sisterhood surpassing class, one which in general came to characterise the accounts deaconesses gave of their own work. She said she called them 'rough girls' only because 'it is how laundry and factory girls are known', but she dissented from the term because it deprived them of self-respect and forced them to 'live up to the name'. Sensitivity to the severity of their domestic and occupational lives informed her account of their patterns of amusement and courtship. 'I don't know', she wrote, 'that sitting on doorsteps or low walls is much worse than sitting on staircases or in conservatories at dances, and yet such things are done and not considered very wrong.'

If they *do* dance to street organs, or skip and play games in the streets, where else can they do it? Other girls have their tennis, cricket, golf, cycling, but these girls who begin a 'working woman's' life at *fourteen*, who work from early in the morning 'till late at night, have nowhere to let off their spirits after work, except for the street; it is their garden, tennis ground, dancing room, everything; and this goes on all year round, without any 'outing' to the seaside or elsewhere.[60]

The writer hoped to recruit a woman to open a club for these girls, someone whose principal qualification should not be piety or reforming zeal but 'a sense of fun'.

In their passionate sense of mission to the poor, Anglican deaconesses were acutely aware of the competition from other groups. They started Saturday schools in addition to Sunday schools in order to attract the children of Dissenters, who had to accompany their parents to chapel on Sundays; the parents were delighted to have them 'out of the way'. The Salvation Army was a habitual rival: one woman served by St Agnes's Mission tried to extract more assistance from the deaconess home by playing off her prospects with the Army.[61] 'The Dissenters do their work with faithful zeal, the Salvation Army may be heard, Sundays and week-days, striving earnestly, however mistakenly, to raise souls out of misery and degradation; while work of the Church Catholic is represented by the efforts of some two or, at most, three workers.'[62]

II

While Anglican deaconesses grew more adept at their work, sensitive in their perceptions, sophisticated in their social judgements and universal in their vision, the clergy who controlled their fate were virtually unchanging. To read the institutional debates about the female diaconate is to enter another realm, so alien were the concerns of ecclesiastical officialdom to those of consecrated women. Particularly apparent is the time warp. The Anglican deaconesses — and conventual sisters as well — had evolved since the 1860s, or in the case of sisters even earlier, by refining their recruiting practices, their communal life and their approach to public service, but the ecclesiastical debate remained almost exactly where it was when the Tractarians originally launched their campaign.

In 1871 the Archbishops of Canterbury and York and eighteen bishops endorsed a statement of general principles and rules which gave formal recognition and direction to the order of deaconesses. The deaconess was defined as a woman set apart by the bishop: her work was under his authority and her activity in a parish was subject to the authority of the incumbent clergy. Only in the absence of parochial instruction could she act under the rules of her deaconess institution. A deaconess might resign her commission or be deprived of it by the bishop. The rules mentioned the necessity of probation, appropriate dress, religious knowledge and title, without designating specifics. Since Elizabeth Ferard herself as well as a number of male clergy active in deaconess institutions composed the guidelines to this document, it was generally well received by deaconess communities.[63]

Subsequent debates at the Convocations of Canterbury and York and those of the Church Congresses reveal the obstinacy of spirit which governed male decisions about female participation in the church. The prime concern of the Establishment continued to be one of authority, whether expressed in ecclesiastical terms as the right of episcopal discipline, or in familial terms as the right of parental control over the daughter who wanted to join an institution requiring obedience to someone other than a parent or guardian. The issue of vows impinged upon both ecclesiastical and familial sensibilities; so did the spectre of communal life entered by women for emotional and domestic reasons as well as spiritual necessity. The question of property sharpened the debate, as did that of permanence. Originally the deaconess option had appealed to Low Church circles who were attracted by the assurance of episcopal surveillance which the sisterhoods seemed to escape. Ostensibly within the order of deaconesses the donation of property and the exaction of perpetual vows posed no problem, hence familial authority was secure. As the Rev. Arthur Gore declared at the Church Congress at Stoke-upon-Trent in 1875:

> It must ever be carefully borne in mind that the deaconess pledges herself by no new vows, relinquishes no personal rights, remains possessor of her own property, violates no domestic ties and is, even, ready to resume her place among her kindred if at any time it shall appear to be the will of the great Head of the Church that she should do so.[64]

For, as the Rev. G. W. Werdon, Vicar at St Saviour's, pointed out at the Sheffield Congress three years later: it is 'not right that a daughter should "scorn a father's care", and be instructed by a certain class of ecclesiastics that she should eliminate the best instincts of her nature'.[65] The Bishop of St Asaph alleged that sisters and deaconesses should contribute to their own support but not be permitted to assign over property to their religious houses, because 'they might do very serious injury to their families and so bring discredit to the church'.[66] Even Low Churchmen, however, modified their opposition to deaconesses living some manner of communal life. As Howson declared in 1884 at the Convocation of York, reversing the position expressed in his book:

> It seems to be thought enough to plant such workers for the poor in solitary lodgings in gloomy streets. Now this appears to me to be cruelty. Work of this sort is conducted under the most depressing circumstances . . . and to condemn a woman of sensitive nature, who has worked in this way through the day, and perhaps through the night, to so dreary a home, is a bad policy, and implies a lack of sympathy.[67]

Significantly, another speaker at the same meeting asked why a deaconess should not 'be a member of a community', since men who became deacons, after all, had enjoyed 'the advantages of corporate life' either in their colleges, the University, or as members of the clergy.[68]

To mention male and female ministries as though they were comparable was, for the time, a radical departure from current practice, one which foreshadowed the debate of the twentieth century. A few clerics went so far as to question the practice of demanding celibacy of women when it was not required of men.[69] Canon Trevor, speaking with reference to the ritual of 'setting apart' at the Convocation of York in 1884, posed the question: 'Why should the marriage of a deaconess bring her ministry to an end, more than a deacon's?'[70] But clerics who did consider parallels between deacons and deaconesses usually confined themselves to primitive times, though this too could be dangerous. Howson took the tack at the Church Congress of Reading in 1883 that further study of the primitive female diaconate might indicate that it differed very little from the diaconate for men. He also made the bold if obvious recommendation that contemporary women, some with deaconess experience, be included in deliberations on the future of the order: 'they may know much that we do not know'.[71] The consensus, however, was that decisions affecting the female ministry should be made by men and that women's biological nature required governance. One clergyman credited the opinion that women would flock to the diaconate if only they were given strong direction:

> This House [the Lower House of the Convocation of Canterbury] ought to assist the Bishop to take these valuable institutions into their care, . . . I deny that Deaconesses are less devoted to the work of God than Sisters, or less inclined to give their whole time and energies to that work. The difference is rather to be explained by the nature of woman. In Sisterhoods, there are distinct rules of life laid down, while Deaconesses are left more at liberty, and woman's nature really requires direction. This is pretty evident, because you can always get Sisters — you cannot get Deaconesses; and if you get Deaconesses, unless you call them Sisters, they are ready to run away. I have come to the positive conclusion that when a woman desires to devote her life to the work of God she likes to be put under distinct direction.[72]

In the end, even Howson allied himself with the forces of convention and returned to the argument of his book.[73]

The 1891 resolutions, ultimately formulated by a joint committee of the Convocation of Canterbury, were distinctive by virtue of their emphasis on the responsibility of the deaconess to the bishop. To reinforce the non-clerical status of the deaconess, in contrast to that of the deacon, the act of consecration conducted by the bishop was referred to not as 'the laying on of hands' of tradition, but rather as 'laying on of hands', without the specificity of the definite article. The resolutions were also distinctive for what they evaded. The issue of permanent vows was dealt with by implication only: the bishop might release a deaconess 'from her obligations' if 'he think fit'. The issue of communal living, central to the debates, was absent altogether; so was the corrolary: the continuing relationship of the deaconess to her institution. A clarifying resolution from the Lambeth Conference of 1897, a bishops' conference, recommended the recognition of both community and parochial deaconesses; it urged the careful restriction of the term 'deaconess' to those women 'set apart' by a bishop and argued for greater uniformity in that ritual procedure.[74]

In numerical terms, the Anglican deaconess order did not flourish. Dss Cecilia Robinson in her *Ministry of Deaconesses* spoke of the 'discouragingly small' numbers — scarcely 200 — and she compared this figure to the 'several thousands' of deaconesses representing the Protestant churches of the continent.[75] Her figure is confirmed by Grierson's more recent study, which mentions the figure 180 at the turn of the century and 350 at the time of the First World War.[76] Strong and sustained support from prominent secular spokeswomen for a ministry structured along lines of gender did not alter the situation. Louisa Twining, for instance, one of the first women elected to the office of Poor Law Guardian, was an early advocate of a female diaconate in the Church of England: 'Multiply the clergy, Scripture readers, and missionaries, . . . there must still be want of *women* to do that work in the world which God has by many indications of His providence assigned to them as their province and their sphere.'[77] Anna Jameson concurred, recognizing that it was masculine opposition which reduced the ranks of the Anglican diaconate:

> How many women, widows, and unmarried of a certain age, would have gladly responded to the appeal . . . [to participate in an English institution like the one at Kaiserswerth] if ignorance, timidity, a defective education, and a terror of the vulgar, stupid prejudices around them — chiefly, I am ashamed to say, masculine prejudices, — had not stifled their natural feelings and trammeled their natural energies . . . There was an absurd horror of all innovation; want of confidence in the material to be employed, want of talent and influence to organize it.

Nursing and education belonged to the sphere of women, according to Jameson, supplying them with the means and training to assist 'our pastors and masters'.[78]

Ironically, as the Anglican female diaconate languished, diaconates in other denominations flourished. The ecumenical Mildmay Institution alone supported 220 deaconesses in the 1890s. Nonconformists organised by Michael Laseron, a converted Jewish physician and his wife, joined by Samuel and John Morley, organised a deaconess institution in 1867 which by 1889 oversaw the work of sixty-three women.[79] The English Wesleyans also launched a deaconess movement under the leadership of two of the most prominent evangelical ministers, the Rev. Hugh Price Hughes and the Rev. Mark Guy Pearce, organised along Mildmay lines.[80] Beginning in 1887 twelve Methodist 'Sisters of the People' lived in Katherine House near the British Museum; each conducted

benevolent evangelising visits and offered classes for various desig-
nated groups such as mothers and factory girls. This movement
rapidly expanded both numerically and in geographic range. By
1903 the Wesleyan Deaconess Institution had 15 probationers and
70 consecrated deaconesses in the field.[81] The enormous enthusiasm
which Sister Emmeline, better known perhaps as the suffragist
Emmeline Pethick-Lawrence, brought to her life as a deaconess she
herself believed was the result of the consistent support by clergy
such as Hughes and Pearce — this, of course, in dramatic contrast
to the uncertain commitment of Anglican clergyman to their
deaconesses. In her autobiography, Pethick-Lawrence wrote:

> It was a wonderful thing at that period to be young among young
> comrades, for the ninth decade of the last century was a time of
> expansion and vision. In spite of sordidness and insecurity in the
> lives of the poor, everything was on the upgrade . . . [It] was an
> era of religion and faith, and a time of intellectual challenge. We
> read, discussed, debated and experimented, and felt that all life
> lay before us to be changed and reordered by our vision and
> desire.[82]

Anglican deaconesses were certainly aware of what was going on
in other denominations; they knew the deaconess movement elsewhere was able to recruit large numbers and enjoyed strong clerical
support. Occasionally a Mildmay deaconess was pirated to fill a
position of Anglican leadership, and ultimately the Church of
England formally recognised the Mildmay Institution.[83] There is no
evidence to suggest that deaconesses themselves supported the
charge voiced by at least one clergyman to explain the scarcity of
Anglican recruits: 'Why do Sisterhoods flourish and Deaconess
Institutions flag? . . . The title of Deaconess has been dragged in
the mud. It is assumed by all sorts of people. Sometimes we find an
ordinary trained nurse, sometimes a mere Biblewoman, calling
themselves Deaconesses.'[84]

There is no way of knowing to what extent alternative opportunities either in the occupational world or in the Church of
England itself diverted women from the Anglican deaconess
option. At the turn of the century there were innumerable articles
in magazines like *The Young Woman* documenting the growth of
training and professional possibilities for women in medicine,
teaching, local government and business.[85] While these professions

may not have been compelling options for the devout Anglican woman, the newer occupations in the Church surely were. Overseas missionary activity in the empire became a particularly strong magnet. Increasingly, deaconess institutions found themselves training women who did not go on to become deaconesses. It is tempting to speculate that women with a strong religious vocation were driven into foreign missions by the intrusion of secular workers into the domestic arena. In 'A Look Back and A Look Forward' for *Ancilla Domini*, a deaconess defended the work of her sisters in the face of County Council lecturers and Charity Organisation officials. Theirs, she argued, was a distinctively spiritual task and it was important to disabuse critics of the Church of England of the view that the Church of England addressed only respectable people and left the 'outcast sinners' to the Roman church and the Salvation Army.[86]

What was truly galling to supporters of the diaconate, whether deaconesses themselves or their mentors, was the relative success of the Anglican sisterhoods which, after all, drew on precisely the same constituency. At a Mansion House meeting in 1887, presided over by the Bishop of London and directed to the subject of deaconesses, the Rev. Berdmore Compton allowed that he 'did not wish to say anything against the sisterhoods, but I think that why they are more attractive is that there is this independence; and ladies like independence as much as men do. But after all they are private institutions, and not part of the regular framework of the Church.'[87] Deaconesses themselves sought to enhance the distinctiveness and worth of their own office.[88] As Dss Cecilia Robinson wrote, the life of sisters 'does not depend upon their official recognition by the Church. But the Deaconess cannot live without episcopal sanction'.[89] Hence the failure of the church to clarify the status of the female diaconate was particularly cruel. Individual bishops formally institutionalised the female diaconate in their several dioceses; the Anglican Church as a corporate body did not.

The paralysing indecision of the clerical bureaucracy on the deaconess issue invites explanation and requires us to look beyond its immediate ecclesiastical context. The deaconess phenomenon belongs to the larger historical evolution of professions. Professionalism as it emerged at the turn of the century gradually usurped the role of other expressions of personal identity and other means of establishing social loyalty. Until recently, however, critical analyses of this societal process have failed to include gender as a crucial factor in the structuring of professional and occupational hierarchies. As historians Joan Brumberg and Nancy Tomes have recently pointed out, prestige in the contemporary professional world has been increasingly associated with theory and abstraction and with the practitioner removed from direct or extensive human contact, as in the case of the research physician or the theoretical physicist. '[T]he development of subordinate female professions greatly accelerated this process. Only by recruiting a vast workforce of helpers, regarded as intellectually inferior but altruistically superior, could male-dominated professions pursue their course of abstraction and isolation.'[90] The Anglican clergy was caught up in a particularly complicated version of this process. To maintain its traditional image and social status, the Church of England continued to recruit largely among gentlemen, and social position remained important for preferment and promotion. At the same time, in order to compete in the modern world where professions were defined by occupational standards rather than social status, concessions were necessary.[91] Some non-gentlemen were permitted to enter the ministry, certain standards of pastoral and theological training were advocated, and to some degree, the nature of professional expertise was identified and developed. This was the goal of the pastoral handbook which prospered as a nineteenth-century genre. There was a wholesale rejection of the 'dismal apathy' associated with the past century; residency was more strictly enforced, and identification with the life-style of the country squire spurned.[92]

High Churchmen accepted, even courted, professionalisation. They were able to identify the attributes they valued in the priesthood with professional-occupational expertise: the administration of the sacraments, the reinstatement of auricular confession and the daily celebration of communion, as well as the special ecclesiastical ornamentation and vestments associated with ritualism. Pastoral work was less important or at least less prestigious to High Churchmen; it was ideal women's work. By promoting the sisterhoods, the High Church was able to satisfy its thirst for tradition on the one hand, and restructure the profession in terms of gender on the other.

For some Low Churchmen, in this respect not unlike Dissenters, the new professionalism recommended itself as a move in the direction of talent rather than class, but these men tended to equate professional expertise with the ability to preach and to perform pastoral functions. Some of them, if not altogether free of gender distinctions, acknowledged traditions which embraced women preachers and prophets and proselytisers.[93] Many welcomed deaconesses and women's ministry in all its dimensions. As the vicar of St Saviour's, Chelsea, said at the Sheffield Congress:

> The Church wants nursing sisters for the sick, not nuns. It wants Bible women and mission women to visit the poor and ignorant. It wants preaching women. It wants Christian women who have the power given them by God to proclaim the glad tidings of salvation to those of their own sex who have not heard it, — yes, in their own sphere; and all I can say to those who object to women preaching is, that if all the clergy who fill our pulpits could only preach half as wisely or half as well as some women whom I have heard preach, there would be good times for the Church of England.[94]

For the Anglican clergy at large, however, the appearance of deaconesses, women who were apparent competitors in the clerical profession, constituted a potential threat. On the one hand, the location and nature of prestige in the clerical profession was not self-evident. The function of the clergy lay neither exclusively at the altar, nor in the pulpit, nor out in the parish. The Victorian clergyman no longer took on the multiple functions of untrained magistrate, almoner, teacher, doctor and civil servant like his eighteenth-century predecessor; his role nevertheless remained diffuse by contemporary occupational-professional standards.[95] A highly-regarded vicar might be recognised not by his expertise in a single area but rather for his talents as a generalist, his mastery of social skills and insights as well as his rhetorical gifts and moral fibre: in short, occupational traits with no theoretical foundation. The absence of theory, of discrete expertise and autonomy have been the qualities used to differentiate the professions from the semi-professions, occupations often associated with women.[96] Thus it is not surprising that the male clergy were deeply and persistently ambivalent about defining the female diaconal ministry. As Archbishop Davidson indicated in 1908 at the inaugural meeting of the Head Deaconess Association, 'the time ha[s] not yet come when it would be wise to work for legal enactments. The Deaconesses must prove their usefulness to the Church by quiet work, for some years to come, and wait until by this means their work and position [shall] be better known and recognized.' He said virtually the same thing in 1912 and again in 1926.[97] Male deacons have always been considered clergy in the Anglican church, yet at Lambeth Conferences in 1920, 1930, and again in 1968 the clergy still could not make up its mind whether deaconesses were or were not 'within the diaconate'.[98]

While indecision characterised clerical debates on deaconesses, women themselves struck a new note. The change was manifest at the Pan-Anglican Congress of 1908. Deaconesses and their allies no longer asked for privileges; they demanded rights. Most important, they set in motion the preliminaries for a network which has increasingly distinguished their efforts in the twentieth century. By collaborating with overseas representatives as well as deaconesses and lay churchwomen at home, they tried to surmount the isolation and quiescence which their indeterminate status in the church imposed. Their new posture took a variety of forms. The organisation of an entire day's programme devoted to the ministry of women preliminary to the Pan-Anglican Congress was one. The founding of the Head Deaconess Association was another; so was the creation of the Central Committee for Women's Church Work. Many deaconesses offered and found support in the Church League for Woman Suffrage, one of the first organisations to give voice to the demand not only for suffrage within both state and church, but also for the full ordination of women as priests.[99]

An examination of how this dialogue has evolved goes beyond the limits of this essay. The female diaconate itself experienced a growth spurt at the time of the First World War. Today the order is once again attracting probationers. But numbers have never been an accurate measure of the importance of the Anglican female diaconate: as an institution it has consistently represented the formal presence of women in the ministry since its inception and a force in defining the shape of the Anglican clergy. Today full female ordination is the issue challenging that hierarchy; it is increasingly clear that women will soon be priests in the Anglican Church. Within the deaconess community, some women have promoted the ordination movement; others have lent their efforts to the implementation of a permanent diaconate for women and men, an option fully compatible with a genderless priesthood, but one which would permit a continuity with the historic diaconate which its members cherish.[100] Whatever the outcome of the contemporary debate, deaconesses today are participants in an international network of lay and ordained women, a network the male hierarchy cannot afford to ignore.

Notes

1. C. M. Prelinger, 'The Nineteenth Century Deaconessate in Germany: The Efficacy of a Family Model', in Ruth Ellen-Joeres and Mary Jo Maynes (eds), *Condition and Consciousness: German Women in the 18th and 19th Centuries* (Bloomington, Ind., forthcoming [1985]); and, with Rosemary S. Keller, 'The Function of Female Bonding: The Restored Deaconessate of the Nineteenth Century', in *Women in New Worlds: Historical Perspectives in the Wesleyan Tradition* (Nashville, Tenn., 1982), II:260–315; for membership figures, Christian Golder, *History of the Deaconess Movement in the Christian Church* (Cincinnati, Ohio, 1903), p. 604, and notes 75 and 76 below.

2. [Florence Nightingale], *The Institution of Kaiserswerth on the Rhine* (London, 1851), pp. 7–8, 32.

3. Katharine M. Rogers, *Feminism in Eighteenth Century England* (Urbana, Ill., 1982), p. 273 and *passim*.

4. See, however, F. K. Prochaska, *Women and Philanthropy in 19th Century England* (Oxford, 1980), esp. p. 29 and appendices, suggesting the substantial financial involvement of women in philanthropy; also Anne Summers's excellent study, 'A Home from Home: Women's Philanthropic Work in the Nineteenth Century', in Sandra Burman (ed.), *Fit Work for Women* (London, 1979), pp. 33–63.

5. Thomas J. Williams, 'The Beginnings of the Anglican Sisterhoods', *Historical Magazine of the Protestant Episcopal Church*, XVI (1947), pp. 350–61, a High Church interpretation; Arthur A. Allchin, *The Silent Rebellion: Anglican Religious Communities 1845–1900* (London, 1958), a more balanced account.

6. *Statement of the Rev. J. Scobell . . .* (London, 1857), p. 7. This tract belongs to the large collection at Pusey House, Oxford.

7. *Sisterhoods on their Trial or Protestantism, Which?* (London, 1864), p. 14.

8. Quoted in Alan Deacon and Michael Hill, 'The Problem of "Surplus Women" in the Nineteenth Century: Secular and Religious Alternatives', *The Sociological Yearbook of Religion in Britain*, 5 (1972), p. 96. In his book, *The Religious Order: A Study of Virtuoso Religion and its Legitimation in the Nineteenth-Century Church of England* (London, 1973), Michael Hill makes the point that the High Church support of sisterhoods was an 'incipiently feminist conception of the role of women.' Concomitantly he believes 'those who favoured deaconesses . . . were far more likely to accept the prevailing role-definition of women and to regard them as in need of men's control and direction (p. 271). This is a provocative argument and one with considerable merit, but I find it unconvincing so far as sisterhoods are concerned. There were many nuances to the High Church position: the constraints of space do not permit a full elaboration of them here. Certainly one item in Pusey's agenda was an implicit critique of episcopal authority common to the High Church stance generally.

9. Margaret Goodman, *Sisterhoods in the Church of England* (London, 1863), p. 3 especially; Margaret Anna Cusack, *The Story of My Life* (London, 1891); Diana A. G. Campbell, *Miss Sellon and the Sisters of Mercy* (London, 1852); Sr Mary Agnes OSB [Miss J. M. Povey], *Nunnery Life in the Church of England* (London, 1890), pp. 1–7; also Thomas J. Williams, *Priscilla Lydia Sellon: The Restorer after Three Centuries of the Religious Life in the Church of England* (London, 1950).

10. Anne Summers, 'Pride and Prejudice: Ladies and Nurses in the Crimean War', *History Workshop. A Journal of Socialist and Feminist Historians*, 16 (Autumn 1983), pp. 33–55.

11. Janet Grierson, *The Deaconess* (London, 1981), p. 18.

12. Rev. Thomas T. Carter, *Is It Well to Institute Sisterhoods in the Church of England . . . ?* (London, [1852]), p. 3.

13. Rev. James Spurrell, *A Rejoinder to the Reply of the Superior of the Society of the Sisters of Mercy* (London, 1852), p. 52.

14. There is a fine discussion of this topic in Deacon and Hill, 'The Problem', pp. 90–1. These authors point out that emigration of men in greater numbers than of women and the higher infant mortality rate of boys, facts primarily accountable for the 'surplus', were lower-class phenomena. Probably 30% of all British women between 20 and 44 years old in 1851 were unmarried; of those in this category who were 'ladies', the most pressing cause of their spinsterhood lay in the late marriage pattern of upper- and middle-class men.

15. *National Review*, XIV (1862), pp. 459–60, 451.

16. *Sisters of Charity, Catholic and Protestant* (Boston, 1855), pp. 60–1, 118–19.

17. *My Life and What Shall I Do With It?* (London, 1860), p. 54.

18. Quoted in Deacon and Hill, 'The Problem', p. 94.

19. Harriet J. Cooke, citing Mrs Pennefather, says that not much is known of the early history of Mildmay. Cooke quotes from a brief account written from memory by Mrs Pennefather herself. Harriet J. Cooke, *Mildmay, or The Story of the First Deaconess Institution* (London, 1892), pp. 38–50.

20. Quoted from Cooke, *Mildmay*, p. 45; and from a visitor to Mildmay quoted in Henry C. Potter, *Sisterhoods and Deaconesses at Home and Abroad* (New York, 1873), p. 293; Rev. Robert Braithwaite (ed.), *The Life and Letters of Rev. William Pennefather* (New York, [1878]), p. 336.

21. Jane Bancroft [Robinson], *Deaconesses in Europe and their Lessons for America* (New York, 1889), p. 175.

22. Quoted in *Service for the King*, XIII (1893), p. 10. This was the Mildmay newsletter.

23. Mrs C. M. Mead, 'European Deaconesses', *Andover Review*, IX (1888), p. 586.

24. Braithwaite (ed.), *Life and Letters*, pp. 535, 531.

25. See her obituary in *Service for the King*, XIII (1893), p. 29.

26. Grierson, *The Deaconess*, p. 19.

27. J. S. Howson, *Deaconesses: The Official Help of Women in Parochial Work and in Charitable Institutions* (London, 1862), pp. 2, 142. See also Howson's article, 'Deaconesses', *Quarterly Review*, CVIII (1860), pp. 342–87. After his death his son put together a posthumous book of his essays called *The Diaconate of Women in the Anglican Church* (London, 1886).

28. See Deacon and Hill, 'The Problem', pp. 95–6; Howson, *Deaconesses*, pp. xix–xxiii, 17–21; and 'Deaconesses', pp. 345–6. See also, on Jameson, Eleanor S. Reimers and John C. Fout, *European Women, A Documentary History, 1789–1945* (New York, 1980), pp. 50–2.

29. Howson, *Deaconesses*, p. 32.

30. Ibid., pp. 80–1, 78–9.

31. Ibid., pp. 83, 82.

32. Ibid., p. 145.

33. *Report of the Proceedings of the Church Congress of 1862 . . . Sheldonian Theatre . . . Oxford* (London, 1862), p. 121.

34. Grierson, *The Deaconess*, p. 21.

35. St Andrew's Community Archives, Elizabeth Ferard, 'Journal of a Residence at Kaiserswerth on the Rhine', entry for 30 August 1858.

36. Sister Joanna, Dss, CSA, 'The Deaconess Community of St. Andrew', *Journal of Ecclesiastical History*, XII (1961), pp. 220, 220−1.

37. Grierson, *The Deaconess*, pp. 21−2; this is also the source for Ferard's familial relationship to the Reverend Dale, but Grierson, contrary to Sr Joanna — and I believe erroneously — gives Dale rather than Ferard the benefit of initiative in founding the North London Deaconess Institution. The community became generally known as St Andrew's after it moved to its present location in Tavistock Crescent, Westbourne Park, where the new quarters were named St Andrew's House in recognition that the institution had formally opened on that saint's day, 1861. Sr Joanna, 'Deaconess Community', pp. 220, 224.

38. See Randall Thomas Davidson and William Benham, *Life of Archbishop Campbell Tait, Archbishop of Canterbury* (London, 1891), I:449−69; quotations from 468−9, 468.

39. Quoted in Grierson, *The Deaconess*, p. 22.

40. Grierson, *The Deaconess*, p. 22; Sr Joanna, 'Deaconess Community', pp. 226−7. In the archives of the St Andrew's Community, London, is a manuscript dated 1874 and entitled 'House Rules', in the hand of Dale, in which one can witness his fruitless effort to preserve a Low Church quality to the life of the community. There is also a typescript called 'An Account of the History of the London Diocesan Deaconess Institution and St. Andrew's Community from its foundation in 1861 to the year 1900', which is particularly good as an account of the growth of the institution's services in response to changes in the neighbourhood it served.

41. Rev. Lawson Carter Rich, 'The Deaconesses of the Church in Modern Times', *The Churchman*, XCV (1907), p. 657.

42. Quoted in ibid., p. 656.

43. Dss Elizabeth Robinson (ed.), *Deaconess Gilmore, Memories* (London, 1924), p. 14.

44. Ibid., pp. 32−3; see also Dss Cecilia Robinson, *Ministry of Deaconesses* (London, 1898), p. 198, who applauds the greater intellectual rigour of deaconess training among Episcopalians in the United States.

45. Robinson (ed.), *Gilmore*, p. 19.

46. Ibid., p. 2.

47. Dss Charlotte Ransford, 'Life and Work of a Deaconess in England', *The Churchman*, LVII (1888), pp. 583−5, 612−13, 744−5. Reprinted in *Church Work*, IV (1889), pp. 200−6; 234−7, 258−61, 289−300.

48. Ransford, 'Life and Work', p. 584.

49. Ibid., p. 612.

50. Ibid., p. 744.

51. Robinson, *Ministry of Deaconesses*, p. 156.

52. Ransford, 'Life and Work', pp. 744−5.

53. See Dss Isabella Gilmore, 'Deaconesses: Their Qualifications and Status', *The Church and Its Ministry*. Pan-Anglican Papers (London, 1908), p. 1.

54. Robinson, *Ministry of Deaconesses*, p. 165.

55. Robinson (ed.), *Gilmore*, title page and p. 29; Gilmore, 'Deaconesses: Their Qualifications', p. 1; Grierson, *The Deaconess*, p. 26.

56. Ferard, as mentioned earlier, was related to the Rev. Pelham Dale, chaplain of the North London Deaconess Institution, by marriage; Grierson, *The Deaconess*, p. 21. From a typewritten notebook in the archives of St Andrew's entitled 'Portraits of Departed Sisters', one learns that Sr Anne Field (d. 1889) was the sister of Head Sister Mary Field (d. 1878). Sr Anne Norman was the stepsister of Sr Ada Norman of the Bedford Deaconess Home. The father of Sr Anna Sarah Lamb (ordained 1866) was a 'country clergyman'. Sr Aline, who wrote the Portraits, was a member of the family of the Earl of Lisbourne. A kind of necrology, the Portraits do not include all the women who were ever deaconesses at St Andrew's, nor is it

clear what basis of selection Sr Aline used. St Andrew's was not unique among deaconess institutions in its social composition.

57. A Novice of Genteel Background, 'My Experience', *Ancilla Domini*, 38 (1897), pp. 291–4.

58. Robinson, *Ministry of Deaconesses*, pp. 153–67.

59. Brian Harrison, 'For Church, Queen and Family: The Girls Friendly Society, 1874–1920', *Past and Present*, 61 (November, 1973), pp. 107–38.

60. *Ancilla Domini*, 52 (1902), pp. 41–2.

61. *Ancilla Domini*, 82 (1908), pp. 29–31.

62. *Ancilla Domini*, 9 (1889), 'A Plea for Help from Christ Church North Kensington', pp. 131–2.

63. Grierson, *The Deaconess*, p. 25.

64. *Authorized Report of the Proceedings of the Church Congress . . . Stoke upon Trent 1875* (London, 1875), p. 59.

65. *Offical Report of the 18th Annual Church Congress . . . at Sheffield 1878* (London, 1879), p. 362.

66. *Chronicle of Convocation . . . of the Convocation of Canterbury 1885* (London, 1885), p. 279.

67. *The York Journal of Convocation Containing the Acts . . . of the Convocation of York 1884* (London, 1885), p. 115.

68. Ibid., p. 126.

69. The Archdeacon of East Riding at the Convocation of York 1885, *The York Journal of the Acts and Debates . . . of York 1885* (London, 1885), p. 105; see also Canon Trevor, ibid., p. 95; and the Lord Bishop of Winchester at the Church Congress of Reading, *The Official Report . . . 1883* (London, 1884), p. 160.

70. *The York Journal of Convocation . . . 1884*, p. 129.

71. *The Official Report of the Church Congress held at Reading . . . 1883*, p. 144.

72. Archdeacon Kempe, *The Chronicle of Convocation . . . of Canterbury 1878*, p. 243.

73. *The Official Report of the Church Congress held at Reading . . . 1883*, p. 144.

74. Grierson, *The Deaconess*, pp. 33–5; no person representing a deaconess institution served on the committee which drew up the 1891 resolutions.

75. Robinson, *Ministry of Deaconesses*, p. 134.

76. Grierson, *The Deaconess*, p. 36.

77. Louisa Twining, *Deaconesses for the Church of England* (London, 1860), pp. 2–3.

78. Anna Jameson, *Sisters of Charity, Catholic and Protestant, and The Community of Labor* (Boston, 1857), pp. 101–9, quotations from 108–9.

79. *Service for the King*, XIV (February 1893), p. 29; Henry Wheeler, *Deaconesses Ancient and Modern* (New York, 1889), p. 226.

80. Ibid., p. 229.

81. Ibid., p. 233; Golder, *History of the Deaconess Movement*, p. 199; E. J., 'What it Means to be a Sister of the People: A Talk with Sister Lily', *The Young Woman*, X (Oct. 1901–Sept. 1902), pp. 406–8, the best of all the articles on the subject, speaks of twenty-seven sisters living together (p. 407), apparently after they had acquired new quarters for St Katherine's, in Viceroy Square, London. Sr Emmeline, 'The Life of a Sister of the People', *The Young Woman*, II (1893–4), pp. 129–31, mentions thirty.

82. Emmeline Pethick-Lawrence, *My Part in a Changing World* (London, 1938), p. 88. She believed zealously in a distinctive mission of women. See Sr Emmeline, 'The Life of a Sister of the People', p. 130.

83. Grierson, *The Deaconess*, pp. 19, 36, 41, 86.

84. The Rev. Berdmore Campton quoted at the Mansion House meeting of 31 October 1887, *Ancilla Domini*, 2 (November 1887), p. 22. See also, Mrs C. M. Mead, 'European Deaconesses', *Andover Review*, IX (June 1888), p. 582.

85. For example, A. Amy Bulley, 'How to Become a School Mistress', *The Young Woman*, I (Oct. 1892–Sept. 1893), pp. 383–5; Miss Billington, 'How Can I Earn My Living?': 1. As A Doctor, 2. As a Nurse or Teacher, 3. In the Civil Service, 4. Journalism, Art or Photography, 5. As a Waitress, in a Shop, or as a Clerk, 6. Conclusion: Some Miscellaneous Callings, *The Young Woman*, II (Oct. 1893–Sept. 1894), pp. 61–3, 166–9, 228–30, 307–10, 379–82, 412–15. See also, Albert Dawson, 'A Noble Woman and Her Work: A Talk with Mrs. Josephine Butler', *The Young Woman*, I (Oct. 1892–Sept. 1893), pp. 363–7.

86. See, for instance, 'Women's Work: . . . (c.) District Visitors, (d.) Mission Women', in the *Official Report of the Church Congress held at Reading . . . 1883*, pp. 146–61 and Appendix; *The York Journal of Convocation . . . 1885*, pp. xxv–xxxi. Grierson, *The Deaconess*, pp. 36, 39, 23. *Ancilla Domini*, 104 (October 1913), p. 58; see also Sr Margaret, *The Deaconess* (London, 1919), p. 39.

87. Quoted in *Ancilla Domini*, 2 (November 1887), p. 22.

88. Grierson, *The Deaconess*, p. 28.

89. Robinson, *Ministry of Deaconesses*, p. 135.

90. Joan Jacobs Brumberg and Nancy Tomes, 'Women in the Professions: A Research Agenda for American Historians', *Reviews in American History* (June 1982), p. 288.

91. Anthony Russell, *The Clerical Profession* (London, 1980), pp. 1–49; Brian Heeney, *A Different Kind of Gentleman: Parish Clergy as Professional Men in Early and Mid-Victorian England* (Hamden, Conn., 1976), pp. 1–10, and *passim*.

92. Heeney, *A Different Kind of Gentleman*, pp. 9, 13, 94–5; Russell, *Clerical Profession*, pp. 36–7, 253–7.

93. For traditions in which women had access to most functions of the clergy, see Deborah Valenze, 'Women Preachers in 19th Century England' (PhD thesis, Brandeis University, 1981); and Olive Anderson, 'Women Preachers in Mid-Victorian Britain. Some Reflexions on Feminism, Popular Religion and Social Change', *The Historical Journal*, XII (1969), pp. 467–84.

94. *Report of the Church Congress . . . Sheffield 1878*, p. 362.

95. Russell, *Clerical Profession*, pp. 40, 247–8.

96. Peter Jarvis, 'The Parish Ministry as a Semi-Profession', *The Sociological Review*, XXIII (1975), pp. 911–22. Jarvis does not, however, make the connection between the semi-professions and gender.

97. Quoted in Grierson, *The Deaconess*, p. 38.

98. Jackson W. Carroll, *Women of the Cloth* (San Francisco, 1983), p. 35.

99. *The Church and its Ministry: The Ministry of Women*, Pan-Anglican Papers (London, 1908); *The Church Times*, LIX (19 June 1908), p. 834; Grierson, *The Deaconess*, pp. 36–46; Brian Heeney, 'The Beginnings of Church Feminism: Women and the Councils of the Church of England 1897–1919', *Journal of Ecclesiastical History*, XXXIII (1982). (This essay is reprinted in the present volume.)

100. *Distinctive Diaconate*, a newsletter edited by Sr Teresa, Dss, of the Community of St Andrew, London.

Chapter 8

'Changes Are Dangerous':[1] Women and Temperance in Victorian England

Lilian Lewis Shiman

'Would you wish to vote like a man?' crossly demanded a big lord of creation of a sweet little lady who dared to say she would like to vote.

'No, like a woman', modestly replied the little lady.[2]

A woman's behaviour in early nineteenth-century English society was expected to conform to the teachings of St Paul, who would 'permit no woman to teach or to have authority over men: she is to keep silent'.[3] Her role was strictly circumscribed, especially in the middle and upper classes.

There is something unfeminine in independence. It is contrary to Nature, and therefore it offends. A really sensible woman feels her dependence; she does what she can, but she is conscious of inferiority, and therefore grateful for support . . . They should remember that by them influence is to be obtained, not by assumption, but by a delicate appeal to affection or principle. Women in this respect are something like children — the more they show their need of support the more engaging they are.[4]

Her position was defined according to her relationship to others: she was a wife or a mother and must act only according to this relationship. Well-bred ladies did not put themselves forward nor did they take any active role in public affairs. Their education was directed to minimal intellectual development and maximal domestic competence. The whole focus of female instruction was on achieving a 'good' marriage with a rich or well connected male. Most men wanted a pliable, docile wife who would not jeopardise her husband's position through unorthodox behaviour. (After marriage, a woman's duty was to raise and care for her children and support her husband in all matters.) Among the less prosperous families, of course, women had to work to help the family finances, but this situation was not regarded as desirable. Working women were blamed for drinking husbands, among other things; husbands, it was agreed, went to the public houses because their homes were 'without comfort'.[5] Home and children were the only approved objects of a woman's attention in the early decades of the nineteenth century.

But English society was in the process of change at this time. A developing technology and its economic repercussions were transforming English life. A new urban-based way of life was emerging which was to modify the social and religious structures of England and bring into question many traditional values. Women no less than men were caught up in the turmoil of change. By the end of the century there would be a rising crescendo of women's voices demanding equality, both political and economic. A few pathfinders showed the way and the multitude followed. By the end of the Victorian era the position of women was irrevocably altered.

This essay will trace these changes as they related to women in the temperance movement. We shall examine what happened when attempts were made to join the conservative temperance crusade with the radical women's cause. The progression of temperance women from a state 'something like children' to demonstrating for political equality came in three stages. In the first period they were segregated in their own Ladies Committees, and rarely were full members of a major temperance society. Eventually a few individual women emerged from obscurity and, willingly or unwillingly, showed the way to participation in public activities. The third period began when large numbers of women, following the few, were drawn into public life by their desire to work for the gospel temperance crusade. They did not achieve full equality in the period covered by this paper, but by the end of the Victorian era they were well on the way to reaching political parity with males of similar social standing.

'The Negro Pew',[6] 1829–1860

When the temperance movement was first introduced into England in 1829 it condemned only the drinking of spirits and supported the consumption of beer and wines in moderation. In these early days the churches played a prominent role in the movement; the Established Church as well as Nonconformist denominations were active in this anti-spirit work.

Although the early temperance movement made many people aware of the problems of intemperance, it did not seem to be effective in stemming the rising tide of drunkenness. In the mid-1830s some concerned Lancashire workingmen organised a new, more stringent form of the reformation, called teetotalism, which demanded total abstinence from all alcoholic drinks. Quickly teetotalism took over the old temperance reform, and temperance became synonymous with total abstinence. The churches were mostly hostile to this new doctrine; Wesleyans as well as Anglicans, Baptists along with Congregationalists, viewed it with suspicion and fear, concerned that the teetotal pledge would lead to religious 'infidelity'.[7]

From the beginning women were to be found among the ranks of the temperance reformers, both moderationist and teetotal. But before the 1860s their role was generally a supporting one and few were to be found as leaders in any branch of the movement. Many of the temperance societies that had sprung up throughout England (both in the anti-spirit period and the later teetotal times), had separate women's branches, the Ladies Committees. The Blackburn Temperance Society, for example, was reported in 1831 to have a large and active Ladies Committee which circulated tracts and collected signatures to support temperance.[8] The Leeds Temperance Society likewise had a Female Branch which claimed in 1839 to have a membership of 402, 'including reformed characters'.[9] But the women in their Committees did not make policy; nor did they speak at public meetings. They visited working-class families to talk to wives and mothers and warn them against the evils of drink. Working with men was a job for the male reformers.

In the early teetotal period, the 1830s and 40s, the English reformers organised 'experience meetings' where men and women gathered to hear about the conversion of some male member.[10] (The events leading up to the change and the subsequent benefits of it were often described in exaggerated style and lurid language.) These meetings were very popular among the working class and quickly spread across the Atlantic. In America they became transformed into the Washingtonian movement, which was devoted to reclaiming drunkards. American women, perceiving the possibilities in this new direction for temperance, set up their own organisation which they called the 'Martha Washingtonians'. These working-class women spoke on public platforms, made policy and otherwise played roles formerly reserved for men.[11] When the Washingtonian movement came to Britain, adding American polish to the old experience meetings, it soon became popular among the lower classes. But the Martha Washingtonians never took hold in England. English women, even working-class women, were not ready to take such a bold step.

Contrary to the general trend, however, there were a few independent women's groups organised. It is difficult to get any reliable information about them. A Women's Temperance Society was formed in Stockport in 1835 and was reported to have 140 members in its early days, but nothing more appears to be known about them.[12] Other women's groups no doubt arose and declined without much fanfare, few of them lasting long enough to make an impression on the movement or its historians. In 1849 the northern-based British Temperance League, concerned with the lack of women active in the movement, recommended the formation of ladies temperance societies at its Fifteenth Conference.[13] Nothing further was done.

A conference organised by the London-based National Temperance Society for women on 27 May 1853 did have some results and led to the organisation of the Birmingham Ladies Temperance Association; but the work of this group was no different from that of the Ladies Committees attached to the regular temperance societies.[14]

If there were no groups of women in this period doing notable work in the temperance reformation, there were a few individual women who could never be overlooked in a temperance history. The Band of Hope, a juvenile temperance organisation, was founded by a woman, Anne Jane Carlile, along with a male Baptist minister Jabez Tunnicliffe in 1847. Although women were the majority of volunteer workers in the local bands they played a very minor role in policy-making and in the larger unions; all the county and national offices were filled by men.[15]

Less important nationally but not locally was the work done by a handful of women in their own communities. Mrs Hawkins of Royal Mint Street, London, for example, laboured alongside her husband to save men and women from intemperance. When she died in 1858 more than 3,000 people attended her funeral procession, many of them 'reclaimed drunkards who had been rescued from intemperance through her exertions'.[16] Mrs Susan Theobald started her temperance work in 1854 and two years later led a temperance crusade among the miners of Northumberland. Active in the reform throughout her lifetime, in 1866 she set up the first retreat for inebriate ladies in England; it was still running in the 1890s.[17]

Many temperance books, tracts, pamphlets and articles were penned by women, who found their work fully accepted by temperance readers, male and female alike, perhaps because what they wrote was supportive of existing social patterns. None of these writings broke any 'sex barriers' or advocated greater independence for women. In fact, the typical heroine of a temperance tale reinforced the female stereotype. Mrs Henry Wood wrote a temperance novel, *Danesbury House*, which not only won the Scottish Temperance Society prize in 1860, but was a best-seller in non-temperance as well as temperance circles. (By 1892 over 304,000 copies had been sold in England alone.)[18]

One well-known writer of temperance stories who broke barriers in her actions but not in her writings was Mrs Clara Lucas Balfour. A prolific writer of temperance stories, conference papers and journal articles, Mrs Balfour was drawn to temperance after having married a drunkard. After signing the pledge in 1837 she became one of the very few women who would mount a public platform and address a mixed audience on the evils of drink. Her work generated much hostility because she was active 'beyond the sphere allotted to women . . . outraging the feelings — stepping over the bounds of her sex'.[19] Many lesser-known women contributed to the flood of temperance writings that gushed forth in the mid-nineteenth century. Overall, however, the work of women for temperance in this early period was very limited.[20]

'The Pathfinders', 1860–1875

In July 1861 the National Temperance League sponsored the first annual meeting of the Ladies National Association for the Promotion of Temperance. Despite the impressive title nothing permanent emerged, and no new ground was broken for women in temperance work.[21] The following year at an International Temperance and Prohibition Convention held in London only one paper on women's work was given and only one woman delegate seated. 'Woman's Work for the Temperance Reformation' by Charlotte H. Ferguson told the convention that a woman 'may use her influence in countless ways, and without the slightest outrage to the natural retiringness of her disposition; but chiefly her work lies with the young'.[22] No changes here. But developments were already taking place that were soon to have an impact on the work of women for temperance. An expansion of women's traditional missionary work was creating a new mood among women that was more demanding and more dynamic than in the past.

A good example of this is to be found in the career of Mrs Julia Wightman. Mrs Wightman had spent her early life in a very protected environment and married an Anglican curate. She looked forward to being a traditional clergyman's wife. But she was childless, though not by choice, and needed something to fill her time. Her husband suggested that she go and work among the parish poor. This was the beginning of a remarkable career. Other women were active in similar work but none were to have the impact Mrs Wightman had. By chance and circumstance, she progressed from organising cottage prayer meetings to leading evening public discussion groups, eventually running a temperance hall for workingmen in her town of Shrewsbury. At first she was very hostile to total abstinence and the pledge, believing the 'pledge an absurdity and total abstinence utterly unnecessary, if not fanatical'.[23] Her ultimate aim was not to eliminate drink from society but to save souls for Christ. She maintained close ties with the religious establishment.

In 1860 Mrs Wightman wrote a book about her experiences which she called *Haste to the Rescue*. Over ten thousand copies of this work were bought by the National Temperance Society and distributed to Anglican clergymen.[24] This book was later cited as being of major importance in the founding of the Church of England Temperance Society and in bringing many influential men, both inside and outside the Established Church, into the anti-drink crusade.[25] Numerous women were also influenced by her work. At a meeting called by the National Temperance Society in 1868 to discuss women's work for temperance, many of the speakers acknowledged the importance of Mrs Wightman's experiences in encouraging them to go into temperance work. The most popular activity of these women was running local mission halls as this clergyman's wife was doing.[26]

Another woman motivated by religious sentiments to work for temperance was Agnes Weston, a daughter of a well-to-do barrister living in Bristol. Her parents were pious and attended a church led by a cleric who was to become well known in temperance circles, the Reverend James Fleming. It was this Church of England evangelical who drew Agnes Weston into missionary work in 1856 when she was sixteen years old.[27] She signed the total abstinence pledge to encourage others,[28] and after working in Bath moved to Devonport where she went to work among the young boys training in the Royal Navy. There, in the early 1870s, she organised Sunday afternoon meetings which became so popular that the crowded assemblies attracted men as well as boys. The National Temperance League, hearing about her work and wanting to extend their temperance efforts to the Royal Navy, invited Miss Weston to work with the League.[29] In 1873 they joined forces and established a centre, an 'Institute', for their work in Devonport. This Institute, drink free, had rooms for the men to stay in when they were ashore as well as a special 'Hall' for Miss Weston's evangelistic work. Another house was soon rented, which was the start of the soon to be famous 'Sailors' Rests'.[30]

Much of the success of Miss Weston was due to her good relationship with the naval hierarchy with whom she came into contact. She was officially invited to visit the Royal Navy ships in the harbour and talk to the ships' companies.[31] The Royal Navy temperance work eventually expanded and spread to the Royal Marines.

Dame Agnes Weston had her counterpart in the British Army, Sarah Robinson. In the military town of Aldershot a Mrs Daniell had established and was running the Aldershot Mission Hall and Soldiers' Home, but, according to the famous teetotal military man, Sir Henry Havelock, her work was 'too religious and too sectarian to be widely appreciated by the soldiers'.[32] Miss Sarah Robinson came to Aldershot in the late 1860s to work with the soldiers and there joined forces with Mrs Daniell. When the latter died in 1871, Miss Robinson took over the mission and, with the support of the National Temperance Society, was able to extend her temperance work by outfitting and running a mobile coffee canteen for the soldiers on manoeuvres. Vans and tents were set up on Dartmoor Common and Cannock Chase, Staffordshire, where these manoeuvres took place. Though in poor health Miss Robinson was an energetic worker and quickly became an important link between the soldiers and the hierarchy of the army, trusted by both sides. Official recognition came when the Secretary of State for War visited one of her canteens and her work was publicised in the major newspapers, including *The Times*.[33]

There was nothing revolutionary about the work of Mrs Wightman, Dame Weston or Miss Robinson; all operated within the accepted bounds of traditional mission work. None challenged any authority. In fact it was reported that Miss Robinson, and without doubt the other two as well, encouraged their 'clients' to be content and accepting of their position in life.[34] The work they did was important to the Establishment, and so they met with very little opposition from any of the authorities. But they became role models for many future temperance workers. Their work was discussed extensively in the temperance journals, and they addressed many gatherings of women.

Mission work by women could lead to quite different paths. For Lady Henry Somerset, who started her mission to aid the local poor, it was to lead to radical political action in support of women's suffrage. For Catherine Mumford Booth, daughter of pledged teetotallers, it led to the founding of the Salvation Army.

Catherine Mumford came into contact with the evils of intemperance when her father broke his pledge and died a drunkard.[35] She worked for her local juvenile temperance society as its secretary. When she met the Methodist evangelist William Booth in 1851 she was a pledged teetotaller and he was not. She influenced him to become a total abstainer, and when the Salvation Army was established by the Booths total abstinence was a condition of membership. This work of Mrs Booth was not unusual except in that it lasted and spread; the 'army' she helped to found became a worldwide institution.

'The Multitude: Educate, Organise and Agitate',[36] 1875–1914

Throughout the nineteenth century the temperance movement in England owed a great deal of its impetus to American influence.[37] The close ties between the reformers of both countries were fostered by a common cause as well as a shared culture. In the United States the women reformers were far more active than their English sisters, who were for a long time reluctant to venture forth and challenge accepted behaviour patterns for women.

In the last quarter of the nineteenth century a new doctrine, developed in the United States, crossed the Atlantic and forever changed the role of women in the English temperance reformation. A new religious momentum arose that was to create a different temperance spirit from that of former times. Evangelical religion combined with temperance teachings to become 'Gospel Temperance', for which saving souls was the goal and signing the teetotal pledge only the means. Gospel Temperance missions sprang up all over the United States throughout the 1870s and 1880s and soon reached England where they were enthusiastically welcomed. American temperance evangelists united with their English brethren to organise the Blue Ribbon movement, a new crusade which led to a great upsurge in temperance activity throughout the British Isles.[38]

When gospel temperance arrived in England it was embraced not only by the old-established teetotallers but also by the churches of all denominations, who were developing a concern over the condition of the poorer classes. The new temperance reform, unlike the old, took root in and gave a new direction to numerous Protestant churches and sects. It drew into the anti-drink fold adherents of evangelical religion, including women of the middle and upper classes, many of whom were trying to give meaning to their 'empty' lives by working among those 'less fortunate'.[39] Some of these women came from temperance or evangelical families, but others chose this work against the wishes of their kin.

Elizabeth Ann Lewis was one of those who came from a temperance family and found suport for her work from both her parents and her husband. Her father had been an active worker for the early temperance reform, holding outdoor meetings to which he brought his young daughter. But it was not until 1882, when Mrs Lewis was thirty-nine years old, that she became active in the temperance reform, joining a Blue Ribbon mission in Blackburn. When this mission ended she wanted to continue the work, and with funds supplied by her husband rented a hall, hired an assistant, and set up her own permanent mission.[40] She organised a programme of house-to-house visitation and also set up activities in the hall to promote gospel temperance. At first not many people attended her mission, so she held old-fashioned experience meetings where reformed characters paraded in front of a fascinated audience telling of their fall into intemperance and their subsequent redemption. This 'entertainment', combined with the message that teetotalism leads to material benefits (new suits of clothing on redeemed drunkards and other signs of their prosperity), soon brought in the crowds and Mrs Lewis's mission prospered.[41]

At the time when gospel temperance arrived in England there was a widespread mood of militancy throughout the country affecting evangelistic work as well as other social movements. The heroes of the late Victorian decades were the soldiers of the Empire who were spreading British control and influence throughout the world; it is not surprising that 'armies' were popular. Armies saving souls for Christianity would be the spiritual counterpart of the armies defending British power abroad. 'Blue Ribbon Army' was a name often loosely applied to gospel temperance workers. Mrs Terrett started a White Ribbon Army in 1878 with its headquarters at her Mission Hall in Bristol. She was its 'General' and her husband its 'Lt General'. Companies were established throughout the south of England led by 'colonels', 'majors' and 'captains', and total abstinence was required of all her 'soldiers'.[42] Other armies appeared in various parts of the country but most were locally based and eventually faded away when the initial excitement created by gospel temeperance died down.

While some of the women involved in aggressive temperance missions were criticised for this work, they could not be accused of being social radicals. Their work was an offshoot of evangelical Christianity which had been endorsed, albeit sometimes reluctantly, by the religious denominations, many of whom ran their own gospel temperance missions. No one could fault the Christian charity that motivated these women temperance reformers, and their work did not openly challenge the authority of hierarchies that dominated Victorian society. This situation was to change, however, when yet another new movement arrived on British shores, a movement that intensified the female commitment to reform and broadened its scope. This movement, joined with another American import, the Independent Order of Good Templars, showed the way to greater independence for the women.

The Independent Order of Good Templars (IOGT) was a temperance fraternal order organised in the United States with a mixed membership. Women members could hold offices and positions of importance on an equal basis with men, and were encouraged to participate in policy-making decisions and to be active in all phases of the Order's work, public and private. When the Order was introduced into England in the 1860s it recruited both men and women.

For the first time in England women were permitted to participate in a mixed organisation on more than a token basis. The effect of the training and experience received by women in the IOGT was not to be felt immediately, but eventually women from the Order were to be the prime movers for a national women's temperance organisation in Britain in the late 1870s. When these women came into contact with the women of the American Christian Temperance Union a new cause was born. Whereas gospel temperance had given many upper- and middle-class women a justification for leaving their homes and taking up work outside the family, the new cause was to show them a way to enter public life.

In 1873 a group of Ohio women led by 'Mother' Eliza D. Stewart became very angry at intemperance in their town of Hillsboro. In protest they held prayer meetings and demonstrations outside the most notorious taverns, thus calling public attention to the evil. The women were successful and consequently able to get a number of the worst saloons closed down. These successes motivated women in other areas in the United States to organise and act in a similar fashion.[43] In August 1874, a number of these women crusaders attended a National Sunday School Assembly where they got together and agreed to hold a national convention to discuss the drink problem. Held in Cleveland, 18–20 November 1874, this convention gave birth to the Woman's Christian Temperance Union. A key figure in the formation of this union, and a heroine to many, was Mother Stewart.[44]

Simultaneously, across the Atlantic, a number of attempts were being made, some successfully, to set up temperance organisations solely for women. In Belfast a Ladies Temperance Union, originally established in 1863, was reorganised in 1874 and renamed the Belfast Women's Temperance Association.[45] In London in 1875 a Christian Workers Temperance Union was inaugurated for female abstainers, but it does not appear to have lasted past its first decade.[46] In the following year, 1876, a Women's Temperance Association was established in Manchester, and it flourished. Not to be seen dragging its feet, the Church of England Temperance Society organised a Women's Union in June 1876.[47] Though the number of these new societies is impressive, none of them broke new ground in the role of women in the temperance reformation. They were still concentrating on women as mothers and wives trying to eliminate drink from the home, and also deal with female intemperance. It was not these women's groups that were to give impetus to the formation of a national women's temperance organisation, though most of them affiliated with it when it was established.

One of the initiators of a national organisation was an English-woman, living in Scotland, who had been converted to temperance by James B. Gough, a famous Anglo-American temperance orator without religious connections. Mrs Margaret Parker had joined the IOGT on her conversion to the anti-drink cause and became a pro-minent and active worker in the Order. Her interest in temperance was motivated not by religion but by compassion for her fellow men.[48] In 1875 she was a delegate to an international convention of the Good Templars held in the United States, where she met Eliza Stewart and other women actively working for temperance. So impressed was Mrs Parker by the work of her American sisters that she persuaded Mother Stewart to come to Britain and talk to the women there about temperance work. Thus, in 1876 Stewart toured the British Isles holding meetings and speaking to women wherever she could.[49]

Another Englishwoman with a growing interest in a women's temperance organisation was Margaret Bright Lucas, the sister of John Bright. Mrs Lucas had become an abstainer early in her life but it was not until she was widowed that she became an active public worker for temperance and other women's causes. She became involved in women's suffrage, the Women's Peace and Arbitration Society, the Women's Liberal Federation, and many others. She was anxious for all women to have a larger share in the running of the country and her voice carried considerable weight because of her connection to the Bright family.[50]

In April 1876 the British Independent Order of the Good Templars held their national convention at Newcastle, and there the three women, Mother Stewart, Mrs Parker and Mrs Lucas, called a meeting of all interested in setting up a national women's temperance organisation. The meeting, with 150 women in attend-ance, was a great success, and the British Women's Temperance Association (BWTA) was established with Mrs Parker as president. The association's goal was to unite all the women's temperance groups already in existence in the United Kingdom and also to organise new groups where none existed.[51]

This early Association contained a mixed group of women from all over the British Isles. It had a president from Scotland along with twenty-two vice-presidents from the North of England,

Scotland, Dublin and London. The north country was perhaps most strongly represented, but temperance was generally stronger there. It was proposed that the Association hold semi-annual membership meetings, and an Executive Committee would meet more often, increasingly in London and usually at the home of Mrs Lucas, who was appointed treasurer. The autumn meeting of the general membership was held in different towns throughout the country, and the spring meeting became permanently fixed in London. After Mrs Parker had served one year as president, Mrs C. L. Balfour, the veteran lecturer and writer on temperance, became the BWTA's second president. At the end of her term, one year later, Mrs Lucas was again elected president and remained in that office until her death in 1890. The constitution of the Association stated:

> The object of this association is to form a union or federation of women's temperance societies existing in various districts within the United Kingdom and to promote the formation of others in the belief that by combined effort and united forces and funds, much greater work can be effected in the extension of the cause of Temperance in the control and ultimate suppression of the Liquor Traffic and thus the moral and religious elevation of the people.[52]

Thus the Association supported the prohibition movement as well as the moral suasion temperance reform, and this was to lead it into active political work which would have important consequences for the organisation and its members.

In its first decade the BWTA and its own local branches grew very slowly. Membership expansion occurred primarily in the affiliated regional societies, established independently of the national association and sometimes ante-dating it. Of 195 branches claimed by the BWTA in 1882,[53] more than 21 actually belonged to the affiliated Scottish Christian Union, centred in Edinburgh,[54] and more than 39 to the Belfast Women's Temperance Association, which had grown rapidly since its affiliation in 1877.[55] Still others belonged to the Yorkshire Union, organised with the help of the northern-based British Temperance League, and in 1880 it accounted for 26 BWTA affiliates.[56] Thus by 1892, when the national body claimed 570 branches with a total membership of 50,000, it must be understood that more than half the branches

(304) were affiliates with primary loyalty to their regional union.[57]

Despite the novelty of a national single-sex organisation, the work of the British Women (as the BWTA was often called) in the first decades was quite similar to that of many other female groups working within the accepted limits of their society. Although the Association claimed to be classless,[58] potential members were advised to see that the president of their branch was a 'lady of influence'.[59] It strongly emphasised the member's role as wife and mother.[60] The meetings of local chapters were truly gospel temperance with a strong leaning toward evangelical Christianity; at these meetings 'hymns [were] sung and portions of the Scriptures read'. 'Drunken women', one writer stated, 'could be drawn to meetings, not by mere human influence, but by the Spirit of God.'[61] Many BWTA branches supported gospel temperance meetings in their local villages. (One suspects that the women would have met with great opposition if they had tried to organise such meetings themselves in a more urban environment.)

But all these activities of the British Women's Temperance Association were also carried out by women outside the Association. In fact most BWTA activities were modelled on projects started by other temperance or reform organisations. The petitions it sponsored for Sunday Closing were drawn up and supplied by the Sabbatarians, who gave the women much advice on how to win support for this particular demand. Another project of the British Women was the sending of letters to headmasters asking them to support temperance instruction in elementary schools, a tactic which was already a part of Band of Hope efforts. Likewise, the public demonstrations for prohibition and the drawing-room meetings to encourage upper-class women to come into the anti-drink ranks originated in other temperance organisations. Even the BWTA periodical, the *British Women's Temperance Journal*, was published and edited by a man, a temperance supporter but also a professional in the publishing field. Only a small section of the *Journal* was set aside for use by the Association, which also had no control over the editorial page or its policy, as it discovered when controversial topics were aired.[62]

Most of the Association's meetings were chaired by men, usually prominent in evangelical or temperance circles; women were frequently in subsidiary positions in its public activities. Because it was difficult for many members to stand up in public and make speeches the Association preferred to rely on a few experienced spokeswomen to take an active role at meetings, instead of recruiting and training more women to spread the work. When other temperance organisations asked to have a woman come and address them, all too often there was no one to send and so valuable opportunities to put forth the women's position and provide exposure for new women speakers were lost.[63]

Thus the BWTA failed to take a leadership role in either the broader temperance movement or the developing women's movement. If it had been dissolved before the 1890s it probably would not have been missed by more than a handful of reformers. It can be readily understood why the Australian Women's Christian Temperance Union, the Canadian Women's Christian Temperance Association and other Empire branches looked to the United States and not to the 'Mother Country' for inspiration.[64]

Outside criticism of the work of the British women came in 1889 when the honorary secretary of the World's Women's Christian Temperance Union, the international women's temperance umbrella organisation, came to England for a few months to study the English situation. Mrs M. C. Leavitt, an American, addressed the Executive Committee of the BWTA before she left England and her remarks were recorded in their minutes. She told them that she was most disappointed with their progress, or the lack of it. Starting her analysis of their problems with the organisation itself, she recommended several changes: the energies of the Association should be focused more narrowly, on a few definite objectives, and then the work persevered in until success was attained. The organisation, she felt, was spreading itself too thin, moving from project to project without attaining anything concrete. The level of support the Association received from both its members and sympathisers also came in for criticism. Members should collect more money from among themselves and be more aggressive in raising funds from well-wishers of both sexes. A campaign should be launched, she said, to get upper-class women enrolled, and she suggested a house-to-house visitation as a fruitful way to increase membership. Finally the *Journal* came under her scrutiny. Mrs Leavitt suggested that it be converted to a weekly magazine with ownership and control in the hands of the women's organisation; shares in a publication company should be sold among the members themselves to finance the journal, and the Association itself should edit and publish it without outside interference.[65]

Although these criticisms were noted carefully in the minutes, they appear to have had little effect on the BWTA. Probably this was because the president of the Association, Margaret Bright Lucas, was by now very ill and her duties had been taken over by Mary E. Dowcra, a dedicated but conservative life-long tee-totaller.[66] She ran the Association until a new president was elected in May 1890. Before this presidential election took place, however, a reorganisation of the administration of the Association was proposed and passed; it divided the control of the BWTA between two presidents, the president of the Executive Committee and the president of the Association itself. The exact authority of each was never clearly defined, and this was to cause a great deal of grief in the next few years, especially as two women of dissimilar characters held the two positions.

Mary Dowcra was elected president of the Executive Committee, while Lady Henry Somerset, an aggressive pioneer in all kinds of women's activities and close friend of Frances Willard of the American WCTU, became the fourth president of the Association. Isabel Somerset was an active worker in temperance and other charitable causes, having run her own mission in Ledbury, near her home, and had scandalised her family and friends by her association with this kind of activity. Besides temperance she supported a broad range of causes including the 'do everything' policy of the American WCTU.[67] Women's suffrage, social purity, and opium control were other issues in which she was involved. The clash between the two presidents was inevitable and quickly erupted into a civil war within the Association. Lady Henry Somerset, leading the progressive wing, worked to bring the Association fully into the women's movement, while Miss Dowcra maintained her conservative stance, fighting to keep the Association from embracing any issue except temperance. Miss Dowcra took the position that Lady Henry Somerset was simply a figurehead who presided at the annual meeting but who was to leave the running of the organisation to the Executive Committee.[68]

Along with the personality differences and the political disagreements, the relationship between the two presidents was further exacerbated by a disparity in their attitudes towards their American sisters. The long-standing American connection and its role in the origins of the BWTA were ignored, and Lady Henry Somerset was accused of bringing American ways into a purely British organisation.[69] Miss Dowcra and her allies on the Executive Committee asserted that the Association was only an anti-drink organisation, and if members wanted to support women's suffrage or the peace movement there were other organisations devoted to those issues. The dispute between a 'do everything' policy and a limited 'one issue' programme was one that affected many in the temperance movement who were not members of the BWTA; temperance journals editorialised according to their own biases.[70]

Conflict between these two presidents came to a head at the annual meeting of the Association in 1893. Both sides stated their positions before an audience of delegates from member societies and affiliates. A limit of eight hours was imposed on the debate which raged for the full time. Finally, after much talk and politicking, a vote was taken on the evening of the second day. The members gave their approval to Lady Henry Somerset and the 'do everything' policy by a vote of 262 to 192.[71] Dowcra and her conservative supporters immediately resigned from the Association and withdrew from the meeting. Eventually they set up their own Women's Total Abstinence Union which was to make temperance its sole cause.[72]

The British Women, renamed the National British Women's Temperance Association, having shed its conservative element and at the same time encouraged by the loyalty of its branches and affiliates, forged ahead with its mission and became active in many causes. We do not know how effective their support was, but, as one history of the suffrage movement asserted: 'In terms of numbers the National British Women's Temperance Association was one of the most influential suffrage supporters.'[73] Some women belonged to the British Women as well as some other women's suffrage organisation, so it can be argued that without the adoption of a women's suffrage platform by the NBWTA these women would still have been active in the suffrage movement. But for the vast majority of women who saw their temperance association as the focus of their own activities and who belonged to no other women's groups, the work of the NBWTA was important in drawing them into political action; public demonstrations, the signing of petitions, and canvassing for support — activities they had traditionally engaged in for anti-drink reform — were now being focused on franchise reform.[74] Temperance and feminism were closely allied, especially in the north of England, and often worked together to get the same reform candidates sent to Parliament.[75]

Lady Henry Somerset continued as President of the Association until 1903 when she resigned because of ill health. She was succeeded by Rosalind Howard, Countess of Carlisle, a woman thoroughly committed to the cause of women's suffrage.[76] Mary Dowcra eventually became president of the Women's Total Abstinence Union which she had been instrumental in founding. The two women's organisations continued in their separate ways until 1926, when there was no longer the issue of women's suffrage and other 'do everything' matters to separate them.[77]

Although the British Women and the Women's Total Abstinence Union continued to be involved in the great temperance demonstrations of the 1890s, their work was mostly initiated by their male anti-drink colleagues. While there continued to be a few individual women who had leadership positions in the broader temperance movement, such figures were unusual. The British temperance movement as a whole was a male-dominated reform, and where a woman president was to be found in a mixed society (apart from the Good Templars and similar fraternal orders that treated their female members as equal to the males) the presidency was usually a purely honorific office.[78]

The temperance movement in England was a conservative reform effort which saw nothing wrong in the existing society that the elimination of drink could not solve. It was a narrowly based movement, as many of its critics pointed out, but it was that very narrowness that allowed it to spread into all branches of English society. Temperance societies were to be found in all the churches, Established and Nonconformist, in all political arenas and parties. Although the Liberal Party was the most thoroughly infiltrated by anti-drink ideas, Conservative Party teetotallers were not unknown.

In England there was no great Woman's Christian Temperance Union to bring thousands and even tens of thousands of women out of the kitchens and drawing-rooms into the council chambers and political halls, as happened in the United States. Consequently the temperance movement in England did not play the central role in the 'women's movement' that it did across the Atlantic. Unlike their American sisters, the English women had to contend with a rigid social structure where divisions were made according to gender as well as to class, and the whole weight of society during the Victorian era was against females having any independent role in public affairs. What little contribution was made by temperance women to the cause of social reform in the nineteenth century was motivated and sanctioned by an evangelical religious spirit that was widespread in England during the later decades of the century.

But Miss Tod was right, 'changes are dangerous': the role of women in the Victorian era was being irrevocably transformed. As one sympathetic observer wrote in 1888, observing the changes over the previous fifty years:

> the example of the women who speak, who write, who belong to professions, and are, generally, aggressive, threatens to change the manners of all women: they have already become more assured, more self-reliant, less deferent to men's opinions . . . They no longer dread the necessity of working for themselves; they plunge boldly into the arena prepared to meet with no consideration on the score of sex.[79]

Notes

1. When radical changes were proposed in the work and role of the British Women's Temperance Association at their annual conference in 1892, one of the leading conservative members, Miss Isabella Tod of Belfast, declared 'Changes are dangerous.' BWTA, Annual Conference, *Minutes* (London, 1892).

2. Story told at the National Prohibition Convention, Newcastle, 1897.

3. 1 Timothy 2.

4. Elizabeth Sandford, *Woman in her Social and Domestic Character* (1831), quoted in Walter Besant, *Fifty Years Ago* (New York, 1888), p. 119.

5. See, for example, James Kay-Shuttleworth, *Public Education, Four Periods of Public Education* (London, 1853), I:130.

6. The feeling against women participating in public affairs in England surfaced at an international anti-slavery convention held in Freemasons' Hall, London, in June 1840, when American lady delegates were not admitted as participants and could not address the convention. Instead a special section was railed off for them and other females. This area was nicknamed 'The Negro Pew'; 'Profile of Mrs. Stewart', *Wings*, XII (January 1894).

7. Charges of infidelity were often levied against the teetotallers. According to some religious leaders they emphasised man's ability to change himself in opposition to the Christian doctrine that God's grace was necessary. The teetotal pledge was said to replace the Baptismal vow in the lives of teetotallers. Their condemnation of alcoholic wine in the scriptures and at the communion table also made the abstainers unpopular in some religious circles. Finally, in the 1840s and 50s particularly, the teetotallers, many of whom were workingmen, were linked with socialists, atheists and others of non- or anti-religious views. At its June 1847 meeting in Edinburgh, the Evangelical Alliance proposed an investigation be made 'to ascertain the connection between teetotalism and infidelity'. After much publicity and hostility from temperance supporters the Alliance dropped this issue, but charges of infidelity continued. See the report of a Leeds Temperance Society delegation that visited all the religious ministers and clergy in Leeds in 1848 (inserted in the manuscript Minutes of the Society, Leeds Public Library Archives). On the Alliance proposal, see *The Teetotal Times*, October 1847, and Dawson Burns, *Temperance History* (London, 1889), I:285. On the temperance movement in general, see Brian Harrison, *Drink*

and the Victorians (London, 1971), and L. L. Shiman, 'Crusade Against Drink in Victorian England' (PhD thesis, University of Wisconsin, 1970).

8. Burns, Temperance History, I:54.

9. British Temperance Advocate, 15 January 1839.

10. These experience meetings originated in the evangelical revival of the eighteenth century and proved to be so popular that many secular reform groups adopted them.

11. The ultimate aim of the Martha Washingtonians was not to reform drunken women, of whom, it was thought, there were not many, but to reform the men and thus protect their children and homes from male drunkenness. Ian R. Tyrrell, Sobering Up: From Temperance to Prohibition in Ante-Bellum America, 1800–1860 (Westport, Conn., 1979), p. 181.

12. M. E. Dowcra, 'A Glimpse at Women's Work for Temperance During the Victorian Era', paper presented to the Women's Total Abstinence Union, Bristol, October 1897 (published as a leaflet by the Women's Total Abstinence Union).

13. Peter Winskill, The Temperance Movement (London, 1892), II:252.

14. Samuel Couling, History of the Temperance Movement (London, 1862), pp. 222–3. See also Women's Work in the Temperance Reformation, papers prepared for a Ladies Conference, 26 May 1868, and published by the National Temperance League (London, 1868), especially Mrs Joseph Sturges's paper.

15. L. L. Shiman, 'Band of Hope Movement: Respectable Recreation for Working Class Children', Victorian Studies, XVII (1973), p. 53.

16. Couling, History, p. 305.

17. Winskill, Temperance Movement, III:89.

18. Mrs Wood was not herself a total abstainer, a fact that upset many tee-totallers. Alliance News, 26 March 1887, p. 204.

19. Gospel Temperance Herald, 12 July 1882, p. 1.

20. In Brian Harrison's Dictionary of British Temperance Biography, Society for the Study of Labour History, Bulletin Supplement, Aids to Research no. 1 (Coventry, 1973), there are listed 387 persons important in the temperance reform from 1829 to 1872, and only 9 are women.

21. Temperance Advocate, I (27 July 1861).

22. Charlotte H. Ferguson, 'Woman's Work in the Temperance Reformation', in J. C. Street, F. R. Lees and D. Burns (eds), International Temperance and Prohibition Convention (London, 1862). There were three other papers by women: C. L. Balfour on children and temperance, Mrs William Fison on sanitation and temperance, and Miss Florence Hill on the liquor trade. Only one delegate to this conference was a woman, a Miss Chapman who represented the Band of Hope and Abstainers Union of Frome.

23. Rev. J. M. J. Fletcher, Mrs. Wightman of Shrewsbury (London, 1906), p. 66. See also Julia Wightman, Haste to the Rescue (London, 1860).

24. William Gourlay, 'National Temperance': A Jubilee Biograph of the National Temperance League (London, 1906), pp. 120–1.

25. Ibid.; see also H. J. Ellison, The Temperance Reformation in the Church of England, 3rd edn (London, 1878), p. 10. For the Church of England Temperance Society, see L. L. Shiman, 'The Church of England Temperance Society in the Nineteenth Century', The Historical Magazine of the Protestant Episcopal Church, XLI (June 1972), pp. 179–95; also Gerald Wayne Olsen, 'Pub and Parish, the Beginnings of Temperance Reform in the Church of England, 1835–1875' (PhD thesis, University of Western Ontario, 1971).

26. Of twelve contributions to Woman's Work in the Temperance Reformation, four directly acknowledge Mrs Wightman's influence (Miss Hartford-Battersby, Mrs Lucas-Shadwell, Mrs Lumb and Mrs Gass). Miss Robinson, Mrs Wightman and Mrs Balfour also gave papers at this conference. Of the rest, Mrs Ellis, a

a veteran of the movement mostly in temperance literature, talked on 'care of the young'; Mrs Sewell organised a rural temperance mission; Mrs Sturges, as we have seen (note 14), talked about the Birmingham Ladies Temperance Association; Miss Deacon discussed the Christian Temperance mission she was working with in Barton-under-Needwood (started in 1861); and finally Mrs Naish described non-alcoholic drinks that could be substituted for alcoholic ones.

27. *The Temperance Record*, 1 April 1886, p. 215.

28. Many women signed the pledge to encourage others to do so. In an article entitled ' "Why I Signed the Pledge" by Eminent Temperance Women', *Wings* (January 1895), most gave this as their reason for signing.

29. Gourlay, *'National Temperance'*, p. 183.

30. By 1905 there were three Sailors' Rests, in Devonport, Portsmouth and Keyham. To honour her for this work Weston was made a Dame of the British Empire. For a personal account, see Agnes Weston, *My Life Among the Bluejackets* (London, 1912). By the twentieth century the Royal Navy Temperance Society had the Lords of the Admiralty and the Prince of Wales as patrons.

31. Gourlay, *'National Temperance'*, p. 192.

32. Reported in *The Temperance Record*, 21 June 1877.

33. Winskill, *Temperance Movement*, III:82.

34. E. M. Tomkinson, *Sarah Robinson, Agnes Weston, Mrs. Meredith: 'The World's Workers'* (London, 1887), p. 17.

35. St John Ervine, *God's Soldier* (New York, 1935), p. 27; also Ernest Cherrington (ed.), *Standard Encyclopedia of the Alcohol Problem* (Waterville, Me., 1928), I:367.

36. Lady Henry Somerset proposed these words as the watchword for women 'in these anxious days' in a telegram sent to the National Prohibition Convention, Newcastle, 1897; Guy Hayler (ed.), *The Prohibition Movement* (Newcastle-upon-Tyne, 1897), p. 287.

37. For the history of women's temperance work in America, see Ruth Bordin, *Women and Temperance: The Quest for Power and Liberty, 1873–1900* (Philadelphia, 1980); and Barbara Leslie Epstein, *The Politics of Domesticity: Women, Evangelism, and Temperance in Nineteenth-Century America* (Middletown, Conn., 1980).

38. On this movement, see L. L. Shiman, 'The Blue Ribbon Army: Gospel Temperance in England', *The Historical Magazine of the Protestant Episcopal Church*, I (December 1981), pp. 391–408.

39. See the remarks of Mrs Sewell in *Gospel Temperance Herald*, 13 September 1882.

40. On Mrs Lewis's work, see W. H. Burnett, *Sunlight in the Slums* (Manchester, 1888); and W. E. Moss, *Book of Memories* (Blackburn, 1951). Moss was Mrs Lewis's assistant.

41. Burnett, *Sunlight*, p. 22.

42. *Alliance News*, 24 February 1883.

43. When the Salvation Army in England tried to imitate the Americans they got different results. An article headed ' "Whisky War" in South London', *Alliance News*, 8 October 1881, reported that when the Army held meetings on Sundays in front of public houses, instead of closing them down it 'raised the ire' of many citizens who objected to this kind of activity. The *Gospel Temperance Herald*, 26 April 1882, commented, 'we are getting accustomed, unhappily, to riots in connection with the Salvation Army'.

44. For further information about this work, see Eliza Daniel Stewart, *Memories of the Crusade* (Columbus, Ohio, 1888); Bordin, *Women and Temperance*, Ch. 2; and Epstein, *Politics of Domesticity*, pp. 95ff.

45. Dawson Burns, *Temperance in the Victorian Age* (London, 1897), p. 121.

46. M. E. Dowcra, 'Women's Work for Temperance During the Victorian Era', paper published by the Women's Total Abstinence Union (London, 1897).

47. Olsen, 'Pub and Parish', p. 365; Burns, *Temperance in the Victorian Age*, p. 126.

48. Winskill, *Temperance Movement*, III:258.

49. Burns, *Temperance History*, II:261–2. See also Eliza Stewart, *The Crusader in Great Britain* (1893).

50. Margaret Bright Lucas (1818–90) signed the pledge when sixteen years old and was active in temperance work from the 1840s. She became a member of the Good Templars in 1872 and was also a supporter of the social purity and women's suffrage movements; see obituary in *Women's Suffrage Journal*, 1 March 1890, p. 33. Also Louisa Stewart, *Memoirs of Margaret Bright Lucas* (London, 1890); and H. Heath, *Margaret Bright Lucas: The Life Story of a 'British Woman'* (London, 1890). Mrs. Lucas's niece, Helen Bright Clark, was president of the Western Temperance League in 1891–2.

51. Winskill, *Temperance Movement*, p. 258.

52. Minutes of Executive Committee meeting, 3 December 1879. There are fourteen volumes of manuscript minutes, most of them of the Executive Committee, at the headquarters of the British Women's Total Abstinence Union in London. After the split in 1893 the books of the NBWTA appear to have disappeared, and only the WTAU minutes for the years 1894–1910 have survived.

54. Cherrington (ed.), *Standard Encyclopedia*, IV:1853.

55. There was a continuing problem over the affiliation with the Scottish women, who wanted the word 'Christian' in the name of the organisation (Minutes, 3 December 1879); but more important, they wanted their own national organisation. At a meeting of the Executive Committee of the Edinburgh Centre of the BWTA on 31 October 1879, they claimed to be 'a nationally distinct organization', willing to 'work in perfect harmony and sympathy with the London Executive'. So the Scottish Christian Union came into being as the women's temperance organisation in Scotland and maintained only a very loose connection with the British Women's Temperance Association. (See note on Minute Book of the London Executive Committee, November 1879.)

55. Cherrington (ed.), *Standard Encyclopedia*, IV:1853.

56. Yorkshire Women's Christian Temperance Union, *Eleventh Annual Report* (n.p., 1888).

57. Cherrington (ed.), *Standard Encyclopedia*, IV:1853; *A Century of Service, 1876–1976* (London, 1976), p. 11. The latter is the official history of the National British Total Abstinence Union (as it is now called).

58. M. E. Dowcra, 'The British Women's Temperance Association: What it is, What it has done and What it still has to do', paper published by the BWTA (n.p., n.d.).

59. Miss Forsaith, 'The Work Done by our Association', paper given in 1886 and printed as a leaflet (n.p., n.d.).

60. A popular item for sale through BWTA branches was a non-alcoholic cookery-book by M. E. Dowcra, published in 1879.

61. Forsaith, 'The Work Done'.

62. On 4 January 1888 the Executive Committee of the BWTA notified the editor of their *Journal* of their 'deep regret' that he had allowed Mrs Zadel B. Gustafson to air her views in an article 'containing an unjustifiable attack on kindred societies' (i.e. the United Kingdom Alliance and the IOGT) and sent an apology to these two organisations. (See Executive Committee minutes, 4 January 1888.) Later the editor, through his support of women's suffrage and other controversial issues, angered the conservatives of the Association to the point of buying up all copies of one offending issue; BWTA, *Annual Report* (1893).

63. Requests for speakers appear throughout the minutes of the Executive Committee. At the meeting of 12 September 1878 the Committee did ask for more women speakers, but nothing further seems to have been done.

64. For the Australian Women's Christian Temperance Union, see Ian R. Tyrrell, 'International Aspects of the Women's Temperance Movement in Australia: The Influence of the American WCTU, 1882–1914', *Journal of Religious History*, XII (1983), pp. 284–304. Also Anthea Hyslop, 'Temperance, Christianity and Feminism: The W.C.T.U. of Victoria, 1887–1897', *Historical Studies*, 17 (April 1976), pp. 27–49. After attending a meeting in the United States in August 1874, Mrs Letitia Youman returned home to Picton, Ontario, and started a WCTA branch there; she then expanded the organisation to the rest of Canada; Anna A. Gordon, *The Beautiful Life of Frances E. Willard* (Chicago, 1898), p. 196.

65. Minutes, Executive Committee, 30 October 1889.

66. Mary Elizabeth Dowcra came from a Quaker family, many of whose members were active in the anti-drink cause. She joined the Band of Hope in her teens and then became a leader in the IOGT.

67. On the American 'Do Everything' policy, see Mary Earhart, *Frances Willard: From Prayer to Politics* (Chicago, 1889).

68. British BWTA, *Annual Report*, May 1893. Remarks of Miss Atkinson.

69. Kathleen Fitzpatrick, *Lady Henry Somerset* (Boston, 1923), p. 186; Constance Battersea, *Reminiscences* (London, 1923), p. 432.

70. *The Temperance World*, June 1892, and *The Temperance Record*, 15 December 1892, condemned the broadening of the work of the women's organisation. Edward T. Bennett, editor of the *British Women's Temperance Journal*, supported the changes in the *Journal*, and this upset many of the Association's conservatives (see *Journal*, March 1892). *The Temperance Record*'s editorial was reprinted and circulated to BWTA branches by conservative members of the Executive Committee who opposed these changes; BWTA, *Annual Report*, 1893.

71. For a detailed account of the Annual Meeting of 1893, see BWTA, *Annual Report*, 1893. Also Fitzpatrick, *Lady Henry Somerset*.

72. In 1896 this Union had 970 members; Dowcra, 'Women's Work for Temperance'.

73. Jill Liddington and Jill Norris, *One Hand Tied Behind Us: The Rise of the Women's Suffrage Movement* (London, 1978), p. 240.

74. The Association joined a deputation to the Prime Minister in support of women's suffrage, 19 May 1904 (ibid., p. 202).

75. Ibid., p. 240. One issue that split the allies temporarily was the temperance movement's strong opposition to the employment of women in licensed premises. Some suffragists, especially the radical wing, saw barmaids as exploited women and wanted to see their working conditions improved. They would not support any move to discriminate against women by forbidding them to work in pubs. The relationship between suffragists and the temperance movement can be traced in the pages of the *Englishwoman's Review*.

76. Lady Carlisle played a leading role in getting the Women's Liberal Federation actively to support women's suffrage, a move that split the Federation as it has the BWTA. David M. Fahey, 'Rosalind (Stanley) Howard, Countess of Carlisle' (unpublished paper), p. 9; also C. Roberts, *The Radical Countess* (Carlisle, 1962).

77. At a joint meeting in 1924 the two women's temperance societies found their policies to be in agreement and determined that the official reunification would take place in May 1926, at the Jubilee Council meeting.

78. Fahey, 'Rosalind Howard', p. 7.

79. Besant, *Fifty Years Ago*, p. 264.

Chapter 9

Respectable Sinners: Salvation Army Rescue Work with Unmarried Mothers, 1884–1914

Ann R. Higginbotham

In February of 1879, the citizens of Nottingham's slums must have been startled by the appearance of a young woman running up and down the back alleys, streamers flowing from her unbound hair. On her back she bore a large placard that proclaimed, 'I am Happy Eliza.' While she ran, she exhorted the unsaved to attend a prayer meeting that evening. Happy Eliza was the vanguard of the Salvation Army's assault on Nottingham, chosen as an early target for the expansion of the Army outside of London because it was the birthplace of General William Booth. Attendance at the first meetings held in Nottingham had been sparse, and Lieutenant Eliza Haynes had decided to attract some attention to the Army's fledgling mission.[1] Neither Happy Eliza's unconventional behaviour nor her presence as co-leader, with Captain Carrie Reynolds, of the Salvation Army's efforts in Nottingham was unusual. Women played an important role in Army activities from the beginning. Catherine Booth, the wife of the founder of the Salvation Army, ardently supported the right of women to preach and herself began a public ministry while her husband was still associated with the Methodist New Connexion.[2] When William Booth established an independent ministry in East London in the 1860s and 70s, he used his female supporters to meet the expanding need for evangelists, and, when he reorganised his East London Christian Mission into an Army to combat sin, 41 of his 91 officers were women. The young women evangelists, the 'Hallelujah Lassies' with their black bonnets and tambourines attracted attention to Salvation Army meetings in much the same way as the brass bands, the Hallelujah giant, the converted chimney sweep, the Salvationist prize-fighter and the other novelties that the Army used to entice the unchurched masses; but women also played important roles in leading Salvationist missionary efforts and

216

administering Salvationist programmes.[3] Salvationist women could attain the same ranks as men, and their importance was demonstrated in the Army's decision to exclude the Lord's Supper from Salvationist meetings in part to avoid any obstacle to women leading the services.[4]

Although female street-corner evangelists remained the most enduring image of Salvationist women, their work for the Army had another, more conventional side. The Women's Social Services, begun nearly seven years before General Booth published his scheme for social regeneration, *In Darkest England, And the Way Out* (1890), became one of the largest rescue organisations in Victorian and Edwardian Britain.[5] It had responsibility for the Army's work with children and with fallen, homeless, or alcoholic women, but by the end of the nineteenth century the Women's Social Services were particularly noted for their work with a special class of fallen women — unmarried mothers. Salvationist women raised and administered the necessary funds for the Women's Social Services, which operated independently from other branches of the Army. One observer described the Army's rescue workers as 'ladies by birth and instinct'.[6] Rescue work may well have appealed to Salvationist women who would have hesitated to lead a brass band or harangue a crowd in the slums of Whitechapel. Vicars' wives and squires' daughters participated in work to reclaim fallen women throughout the Victorian period without any loss of respectability.[7] The more respectable, or less adventurous, of the Salvation Army's female converts could have found an acceptable outlet for their energies in the homes and missions established by the Women's Social Services.

Salvation Army interest in saving fallen women was usually credited to Catherine Booth. She had participated in the Midnight Meeting movement in the 1860s, and in 1868 attempted to begin a rescue mission in connection with her husband's evangelical work in the East End, but the mission failed for lack of funds.[8] Until the 1880s the Booths offered the promise of salvation to prostitutes who came to the penitent form at their meetings, but did not operate rescue homes or engage in formal rescue work. Some Salvationists would take repentant fallen women into their homes, however, and the Women's Social Services evolved out of this practice. According to Army tradition, the first rescue home was opened by Mrs Cottrill, a Whitechapel soldier. She provided temporary shelter for prostitutes in her home and found them respectable jobs. Her husband, who was not a Salvationist, objected to the continual presence of streetwalkers at his breakfast table, and in 1883 Mrs Cottrill removed her work to a Whitechapel lodging house. A year later, General Booth proclaimed 'A New National Scheme for the Deliverance of Unprotected Girls and the Rescue of the Fallen'.[9]

General Booth chose his daughter-in-law, Florence Soper Booth, to head the Army's new venture. Florence Booth was the daughter of a Welsh physician and had joined the Army in 1880. Two years later she married the General's eldest son, William Bramwell Booth. She was only twenty-two in 1884, but youth was not unusual among Salvationist leaders; her husband was only twenty-four when he was selcted as chief of staff. The General's biographer described Florence Booth as 'typical of the well-educated, rather shrinking and self-conscious girl of the English professional classes', and the General apparently had some reservations about her ability to manage the new rescue home.[10] Despite her youth and retiring nature, however, Florence Booth succeeded in establishing and expanding Salvationist rescue work. During the nearly thirty years that she headed the Women's Social Services, its operations grew from one rescue home in Whitechapel to 117 homes for women in Britain and around the world.[11] Under the direction of Florence Booth and her assistant Adelaide Cox, a vicar's daughter who joined the Salvation Army in 1881, the Women's Social Services earned a reputation as one of the largest, most effective, and, to some extent, most innovative rescue organisations in Britain.[12] Florence Booth was probably responsible for the Army's entrance into a relatively new area of rescue work, caring for pregnant single women and women with illegitimate infants. She certainly retained an interest in and enthusiasm for this branch of Army rescue work. In 1906, she noted that unmarried mothers were 'the class I most love to help'.[13] The Salvation Army's success in what came to be called maternity work moved one Anglican rescue worker to urge that the 'Church ought to do its own work and not leave it to the Salvation Army'.[14] The Army's work with unmarried mothers presented certain practical and moral difficulties that traditional rescue work with prostitutes did not raise. A woman with an illegitimate child posed, as Florence Booth noted, a 'double problem'.[15] She was both a fallen woman and a mother, and her dual, seemingly contradictory nature shaped the direction of the Army's work with this particular class of sinners.

Although early Salvationist rescue work concentrated on saving prostitutes, the Women's Social Services began work with unmarried mothers quite early in its existence. The scheme for rescue work outlined by General Booth in 1884 included three target classes: prostitutes, young girls in danger of falling into sin, and 'girls who have been ruined and forsaken but who are opposed to leading an immoral life'.[16] This last class undoubtedly included unmarried mothers, who were often described as having taken only the first step on the 'downward path'.[17] The early records of Salvation Army rescue homes show that, by 1886, the Women's Social Services was receiving frequent requests for aid from both pregnant single women and women with illegitimate children.[18] By 1890 the Women's Social Services had two separate homes for women with infants, and, in that year, they opened Ivy House, a small maternity hospital. Before the opening of Ivy House, pregnant women who came to the attention of the Women's Social Services were sent to the workhouse, to lodgings, or, after 1888, to the home of Mrs Walker, a Chelsea midwife who undertook to care for Salvationist cases during their confinement.[19] The newly confined women and their infants then returned to a Women's Social Services home. Once the Salvation Army began offering facilities for childbirth, the demand was high. By 1894, one-third of the letters received at the Women's Social Services headquarters contained requests for help for maternity cases. In 1909 the Army responded to the need for maternity care and opened a maternity hospital in Hackney that provided accommodation for several hundred unmarried mothers a year.[20]

The Salvation Army was not the first rescue group to recognise the special needs of the unmarried mother or to provide separate homes for women with illegitimate children. In the 1860s and 70s a number of London charities, loosely or formally connected with the Church of England, began offering help to unmarried mothers. Homes such as Mrs Main's Refuge for Deserted Mothers and Their Infants and the Homes of Hope were opened to receive women with illegitimate infants. By the last decades of the nineteenth century, large rescue organisations, including the Female Mission to the Fallen and the Rescue Society, became increasingly involved with caring for maternity cases. They either opened their homes or directed unmarried mothers to homes and refuges operated by other organisations, including the Salvation Army. By the early twentieth century London had at least two dozen homes intended solely for unmarried mothers, and parish rescue and preventive associations claimed to have contact with as many as half of the approximately five thousand unmarried mothers who gave birth in London each year.[21] But few other organisations worked on the scale of the Salvation Army.

The need for special homes for unmarried mothers arose from the experience of rescue workers who came into contact with fallen women who were pregnant or responsible for young children, and the identification of the unmarried mother as a special case deserving special assistance. Unmarried mothers presented problems for most rescue homes, which did not have the facilities for handling childbirth or caring for young children. The Women's Social Services justified its maternity work in part on the grounds that unmarried mothers were often turned away from rescue homes designed for prostitutes.[22] Women's Social Services rescue workers saw the need to separate unmarried mothers from the ordinary rescue cases because of their special circumstances. Ivy House was intended for 'girls who previous to their fall, have led respectable lives, and who have been betrayed by the so-called men to whom they have been engaged and whom they have loved not wisely, but too well'.[23] Rescue workers frequently described unmarried mothers as the victims of male lust rather than active participants in sin, and emphasised the women's prior respectability rather than their present fallen condition. These women had more potential for reform than prostitutes because of their inherent respectability and their limited experience of sin. They argued that a young, almost innocent unmarried mother did not belong in a home with prostitutes. Nor should she be sent to the workhouse where 'she might be compelled to associate with hardened and habitual inmates, and her sense of shame dulled and almost obliterated'.[24] Victorian rescue workers, whether Salvationists or Anglicans, saw the workhouse as a source of moral contamination from which the potentially respectable must be saved before they succumbed to the infection carried by more disreputable inmates.

Unmarried mothers were seen as the most hopeful of all rescue cases. Florence Booth stated that 'no class of women for whom we have worked has yielded such uniformly encouraging results'.[25] Certainly the Army did claim a high success rate for its maternity work. In 1894 rescue workers reported that they had maintained contact with 85 per cent of their maternity cases for three years after they left the homes. All were doing well. In later years, the

Army boasted that their success rate with unmarried mothers was as high as 92 per cent.[26] The records of the Salvation Army's maternity homes reveal that, indeed, very few pregnant women or women with young children were dismissed for bad conduct or left without permission. The behaviour of almost all the unmarried mothers was described as satisfactory, good, or very good. This view of the tractability of unmarried mothers is not surprising; they were, to some extent, a captive group. Their pregnancy or responsibility for an infant limited their options and may have made them more dependent on charitable assistance than other fallen women. In addition, unmarried mothers were recognised as occupying a higher position in the hierarchy of the fallen and so were not subjected to the rigorous discipline and restrictions of the penitentiaries for prostitutes.[27] This leniency may have prevented the restlessness and disobedience that was often attributed to fallen women who found themselves in more strictly-run rescue homes.

The bleak prospect facing an unmarried woman attempting to support a child as well as herself may have accounted for the ease with which the Salvation Army — and other such charities — filled their homes. More than a quarter of the unmarried mothers who came to the Salvation Army, whether pregnant or with illegitimate children, had applied themselves, either by letter or in person (see Table 9.1). Another 19 per cent were referred by a relative, usually a parent. The remainder were sent by Salvationists or other individuals outside the family. A few women in this group were referred by neighbours, landladies, or fellow servants — members of their own class and community; but most were sent by middle-class individuals, including members of rescue committees, district and workhouse visitors, clergymen's wives, or employers.[28] Women referred by Salvation Army officers may have applied directly to their neighbourhood Salvationist barracks or may have been

Table 9.1: Referrals to Salvation Army Homes, 1886–1906

Who referred	Per cent	Number of cases
Self	26.8	147
Family member	18.8	103
Neighbour or friend	1.3	7
Salvation Army member	20.1	110
Other individual	33.0	181

Source: Casebooks of the London Rescue Homes, 1886–1906, Salvation Army.

found by Salvationist rescue workers. Salvationists from outside the metropolitan area undoubtedly passed maternity cases to London where they could receive more specialised attention than could be provided by rescue agencies in their own towns or villages.

The Salvation Army could attract women to its homes easily because its mission was widely advertised and because it had evangelists and slum officers who visited working-class neighbourhoods and sought out rescue cases. The *War Cry* and other Salvationist publications carried advertisements urging any fallen woman to contact Catherine Booth directly.[29] The Women's Social Services served both a national and a local clientele. Unmarried mothers applied for help from as far away as Scotland, indicating the national appeal of a large rescue organisation, but they often came from the immediate neighbourhood of the homes as well. In the late nineteenth century more women entered the London maternity homes from Hackney, where both the homes and the Women's Social Services headquarters were located, than from any other part of the city.[30]

Women in Salvationist homes were expected to work during their stay. Unmarried mothers usually performed light household tasks, cared for infants, or did needlework that could later be sold by Salvationists for the benefit of the home. Florence Booth rejected laundry work — the usual task required of fallen women in rescue homes — because the inmates found it distasteful and because it was not so conducive to the repentance of past sins as quiet sewing.[31] In addition to work, the women in the homes participated in singing and prayers and sometimes attended classes. Unmarried mothers spent relatively little time under the discipline of Salvationist homes. Their average stay was about three and a half months, but a few women stayed for only a week or two and nearly 20 per cent stayed for less than two months (see Table 9.2). At the time of their confinements, unmarried mothers spent about three weeks in Ivy House or, later, in the maternity hospital, further shortening the period of exposure to the rescue home. The length of time an unmarried mother stayed in a Salvationist home was apparently determined by the timing of her entrance. Few women remained more than four to six weeks after giving birth, regardless of the time they had spent in the home before their confinements. Those women who entered in an early stage of pregnancy might spend six or seven months in the home while women who entered immediately before giving birth remained only a few weeks. The

Table 9.2: Average Stay in Women's Social Services Maternity
Homes, 1897–1906

Length of stay	Per cent	Number of cases
Less than 1 week	0.2	1
1 week to 1.9 months	18.9	97
2 to 3.9 months	50.6	260
4 to 5.9 months	23.4	120
6 to 7.9 months	6.1	31
8 months or longer	0.8	4

Source: Casebooks of the London Rescue Homes, 1897–1906.

Women's Social Services apparently viewed the speedy return of
the unmarried mother to a productive life as more important than a
prolonged period of penance.[32]

Nearly one-third of the women who entered a Salvation Army
maternity home returned to family and friends at the completion of
their stay. About half, however, went to positions as domestic
servants found by the Women's Social Services.[33] The Army
operated small workshops for women in London, including a knit-
ting factory, laundry and bookbindery, but only one or two unmarried mothers a year were sent to these facilities. The Army's
reliance on service is not surprising since 80 per cent of the
unmarried mothers in the maternity homes had been servants
before the birth of their children.[34] But the decision to send women
to situations was not based entirely on their former employment.
Mill girls and seamstresses were also sent out as servants after a few
weeks of training. This extensive use of domestic service may have
reflected the demand for servants in late Victorian London. The
Women's Social Services apparently had little difficulty in placing
their rescue cases, perhaps because a fallen woman could not
demand the same wages as a servant of unblemished reputation.[35]
More important, however, was the conviction that service was the
only possible option for a fallen woman. Like many other moral
welfare organisations, the Women's Social Services viewed service
with 'a good Christian lady' as the best and safest place for a fallen
woman. Here she would be removed from temptations and placed
under the watchful eye of a careful mistress. Only those women
who were too old or too 'simple' to make acceptable servants were
directed to alternative employment.[36]

In the case of unmarried mothers, a policy of placing rescue cases in service created some complications. Domestic servants living in their employers' homes could not care for their infants, and alternative homes had to be found. In the 1880s, the Women's Social Services made an effort to find adoptive parents for illegitimate children by advertising for Christian couples willing to provide a home for such a child. In 1887 twelve children were placed out in this way.[37] Adoption also posed some problems because, until 1927, English law made no provision for legal adoption of a child whose mother was alive.[38] In addition, most Victorian rescue workers opposed adoption of illegitimate children since it removed the burden of the child's support, which served as a constant reminder to the unmarried mother of the consequences of her sin. Without this reminder, she might be careless enough to fall again.[39] By the 1890s, the Women's Social Services had apparently accepted this view and stopped using adoption except in cases where the mother had died, married a man unwilling to accept the child, or proved herself incapable of supporting herself and the child. Instead, their policy emphasised the mother's duty to her child: 'We endeavour, in every case, to throw the responsibility upon the mother, feeling she is much more likely to persevere in doing right if she carries, in this sense, her own burden.'[40]

The unmarried mother was expected to bear the burden of support rather than the responsibility of care. An infant born or brought into a Women's Social Services maternity home remained with its mother only a few weeks. If the woman was sent to a situation, her infant was placed with a 'nurse mother', unless a relative could be found to care for it. Nurse mothers were usually older working-class women, married or widowed, who took one or two children for a weekly fee of 4s or 5s. They took complete responsibility for feeding and caring for the children left with them. While under the care of a nurse mother, infants, regardless of their age, were bottle fed. Nineteenth-century medical men estimated that 60 per cent or more of nursed-out infants died in the first year. These charges were based on less than precise information about either the number of infants at risk or the numbers dying, but they were widely reported and accepted as true.[41] Given the absence of secure supplies of sterile milk and the high cost of suitable baby food, hand-feeding undoubtedly did lessen an infant's chances of survival. The Women's Social Services asserted that they selected their nurses with great care, and many of their nurse mothers lived in northeast London where they could have been closely supervised from the Social Services headquarters in Hackney.

The Army may have felt some concern over the dangers facing children at nurse, however, for by the 1890s they had opened a baby home where illegitimate children could be cared for at 5s a week under the direct supervision of Women's Social Services staff.[42] Even after the opening of this home, close to 50 per cent of the infants who left the maternity homes were placed out to nurse.[43] This continued use of a system reputedly so threatening to infant life was the result of the accepted philosophy of rescue work with unmarried mothers. The rescue worker's first concern was the restoration of the woman to a moral life, not the welfare of her child. Maternity work, whether by the Salvation Army or some other group, was motivated by the strong conviction that the woman, however innocent and respectable before her fall, had taken the first step on a long road that led ultimately to prostitution, disease and death. Intervention in this downward progress and restoration of the mother to respectability and economic self-sufficiency constituted an important part of her rescue. The use of nurse mothers was dictated by the choice of service as the preferred position for the unmarried mother rather than office, shop, or mill work that might have left her free to care for her child in the evenings. Work of this sort was felt to be morally dangerous and threatening to the woman's character, perhaps because it allowed her more freedom and took her out of a 'home environment'. Such a policy must have had a devastating impact on relations between mother and child. The early separation of mothers and infants and the restrictions of a servant's life would inhibit the formation of a strong bond between mother and child. Although Salvationist rescue workers stated, and probably sincerely believed, that they encouraged the affection of a mother for her child, they also, paradoxically, taught her to regard her child primarily as a financial drain.

The stated goal of all Salvation Army rescue work was the spiritual redemption of the sinning woman. 'We think our labour is useless', one Salvationist worker explained, 'unless the girls become really converted to God.'[44] The Army's success in bringing unmarried mothers to a sense of sin was difficult to assess. Reports maintained an optimistic tone: 'there certainly have been some wonderful stories of real conversion'.[45] But much of the justification for maternity work emphasised economic reintegration of the woman rather than the state of her soul. Daily life in Salvationist homes included periods for prayer and singing, but the homes admitted women of all faiths, and, apparently, no one was forced to attend Salvationist services.[46] Despite Salvationist concern with the conversion of sinners, rescue workers may have contented themselves with good conduct even if unaccompanied by religious enthusiasm. The behaviour of unmarried mothers was almost invariably described as 'good' or 'satisfactory', but very few were actually listed as 'well and soundly saved'. In the case of one young unmarried mother, the worker noted that she 'felt no remorse or penance' despite her good conduct in the home, while another 'professed to be grateful but her great aim was to be helped'.[47] It is tempting to suggest that the women who entered Salvation Army homes felt less in need of a thorough change of heart than rescue workers hoped.

Information about the unmarried mothers assisted by the Women's Social Services was disseminated primarily through case histories and descriptions included in Salvationist journals and annual reports. One typical case, which appeared in a number of different publications, concerned 'May', a 15-year-old, motherless girl who was seduced by the local squire's son. One version of her story explained that 'some villain in Norfolk ruined a simple, trusting, country lass, who, mad with despair, flung herself before a racing locomotive.' May did not die as a result of her suicide attempt, but she lost both feet. She had her baby in the workhouse, and then, cast off by her father, she sought refuge in a Salvationist home where she devoted the rest of her life to assisting other young women.[48]

The story of May revealed the qualities most often associated with unmarried mothers described in rescue literature. These accounts emphasised the youth, innocence, friendlessness and despair of the pregnant unmarried woman. She was often portrayed as an orphan or, at the least, motherless. Unmarried mothers were almost always characterised as younger than nineteen. One account of Salvationist maternity work described two 'child mothers' of thirteen and fourteen who had come to the Army: 'both children bore out with them tokens of their shame their arms were hardly strong enough to carry far'.[49] Florence Booth spoke of girls as young as twelve entering Salvation Army homes to deliver their babies. Like May, some of the unmarried mothers were described as having been seduced by men from a class above them, men they could not have married. Above all these girls and women were described as having little choice except sin, death, or the Salvation Army, all as the result of the callous behaviour of the men who had seduced them. They were 'storm tossed and broken, nearly all by the sin, selfishness and deception of others'.[50]

A sample of cases taken from the records of the Women's Social Services discloses a rather more complex picture of the unmarried mothers who entered their rescue homes. They included not only young women having their first child but also women who had cohabited outside of marriage and had several illegitimate children. The Women's Social Services also took in women who had given birth to an illegitimate child several years earlier but had not made the transition back to an ordinary life. Very few, if any, of the women helped by the Women's Social Services resembled the heroines of Salvation Army rescue stories. The 'typical' unmarried mother was a servant in her early twenties who had both parents, or at least her mother, living, and she was not the victim of an upper-class seducer. Although the Army's stated policy was to take only 'first fall' cases, that is women who had had no sexual experience before they became pregnant, only about half the pregnant women who came to the Salvation Army were unambiguously classified as 'seduced'.[51] Nearly 20 per cent had either been prostitutes or had more than one illegitimate child. Others admitted having relationships with several men. Almost all of the 'first fall' cases indicated that the father of their child was their 'young man' or the man they intended to marry. Their pregnancies, in other words, represented failed courtships with men of their own class rather than seductions across class lines. The putative fathers of their children were labourers, carpenters, butchers and policemen, not idle aristocrats or even lecherous middle-class householders.[52] Fewer than 7 per cent claimed to have been seduced by their masters or by gentlemen. The average age of pregnant single women who came to the Women's Social Services maternity homes was twenty-two, an age at which a working-class woman might well expect to marry. Only a handful of the rescue cases were seventeen or younger, and none was younger than fifteen.

It is not surprising that the real women in maternity homes should have differed markedly from those who inhabited rescue journals and annual reports. The rescue stories were intended to attract support and justify rescue work. The story of 15-year-old May, seduced and abandoned by an irresponsible country gentleman, was certainly more acceptable to Victorian sympathies and

Victorian pocketbooks than the story of 23-year-old Nelly who did not know which of the two soldiers she had 'walked out with' was the father of her child. Women's Social Services rescue workers clearly adopted a more pragmatic approach to both the type of women they would assist and the results they might expect than was possible for the policy-makers and apologists, who emphasised the melodramatic tales of those 'who have been deceived and deserted'.[53] The needs of individual unmarried mothers who applied to the Army for help and the obvious problems facing any pregnant single woman undoubtedly influenced the admission policies of Salvationist homes as much as the expectations of the public determined the image they presented in published accounts of their work.

Inherent in the contradiction between the ideal unmarried mother and her less romantic, real-life counterpart was the nature of what Florence Booth called the 'double problem'. The unmarried mother was clearly a fallen woman in Victorian terms. She carried visible proof of her fall and could therefore be more clearly identified as fallen than many prostitutes. She was also, however, a mother and a woman who had fallen through seeking to marry. She had often, though not always, led a blameless life as a respectable servant before her fall. In the Army's eyes, she had already suffered some punishment for her sins while her equally, or more, guilty partner went free.[54] This dual nature influenced both the practice and justification of Salvation Army rescue work. The unmarried mother could not be locked up in a penitentiary — as homes for prostitutes were usually called — for two years while she did laundry work and prayed. Neither her condition nor her background made that advisable. But neither could she simply be assisted to have her child and return to a normal life as though nothing had happened. Even the Salvation Army, which was known for its pragmatic approach to welfare problems, could not condone sin. Besides, having fallen once, she was in a dangerous position and might fall again if her life was made too easy. The Salvation Army's solution was to house the woman, however briefly, in a home under the direct supervision of rescue workers, to find her a position as a servant and make her responsible for paying as much as 5s a week, which often represented 80 per cent of her wages, for someone else to care for her child. This gave her a permanent economic bond to the child but not the nurturing role that would be permitted to an unfallen mother. The relative

leniency with which she was treated was justified by her circumstances and background. They were sinners but still somehow
respectable, 'children brought up in sheltered homes, sinned
against, very often, more than sinning .[55]

In the late nineteenth and early twentieth centuries, the care of
unmarried mothers and their children interested a variety of individuals and organisations from medical men to rescue and social
purity organisations. The difficulties facing fallen women with
infants were cited to explain infanticide, infant mortality and
female poverty. The Salvation Army offered little in the way of
radical solutions, but it did manage a certain pragmatic balance
between practical assistance and attempted moral reform. The
Women's Social Services emphasised the need for repentance and
sometimes appeared to regard illegitimate infants as little more
than instruments to that end, but they relied on the unmarried
mother's inherent respectability and her ties to her child to effect
her reformation, rather than a lengthy period of penance and discipline. Their homes provided an alternative for women who might
otherwise have given birth in the workhouse and may well have
eased the return of at least some unmarried mothers to the labour
force. Florence Booth wrote in 1890 that 'our very success in
dealing with this . . . problem will naturally attract to us more than
the due proportion of these sufferers. I have in my own mind
settled it, that to help a mother to provide for her little one is the
wise and right method . . . It is a prudent and profitable expenditure.'[56] Her words proved prophetic. Salvation Army work with
unmarried mothers prefigured developments in social work during
the inter-war years when the provision of maternity care replaced
brothel visiting and Piccadilly patrols as the chief occupation of
church-connected moral welfare workers.

Notes

1. Frederick de Latour Booth-Tucker, *The Life of Catherine Booth, Mother of
the Salvation Army*, 2 vols (New York, 1892), II:215–17; Robert Sandall, *History
of the Salvation Army*, 4 vols (London, 1947–66), II:15–16.

2. Harold Begbie, *The Life of General William Booth, the Founder of the
Salvation Army*, 2 vols (New York, 1920), I:245–50; Booth-Tucker, *Catherine
Booth*, I:116–17, 343–9, 357–63; and Norman H. Murdoch, 'Female Ministry in
the Thought and Work of Catherine Booth', *Church History*, LIII (1984),
pp. 348–62.

3. Sandall, *History of the Salvation Army*, II:6–13. For an account of the
reasons for the appeal of the Salvation Army, see K. S. Inglis, *Churches and the*

Working Classes (London, 1963), pp. 185–8.

4. Bernard Watson, *A Hundred Years War: The Salvation Army, 1865–1965* (London, 1965), p. 22. Women officers were not, however, paid at the same level as male officers until the mid-twentieth century.

5. F. K. Prochaska, *Women and Philanthropy in Nineteenth-Century England* (Oxford, 1980), pp. 190–1.

6. F. A. McKenzie, *Waste Humanity: Being a Review of Part of the Social Operations of the Salvation Army in Great Britain, 1908–09* (London, 1909), pp. 53–4; C.S.R., 'Our Rescue Work', *All the World*, III (1887), p. 162; W. B. Booth, *Work in Darkest England in 1894* (London, 1894), p. 57.

7. For a description of mid- and late-nineteenth-century rescue work, see Prochaska, *Women and Philanthropy*, pp. 182–221; Edward J. Bristow, *Vice and Vigilance: Purity Movements in Britain since 1700* (Dublin, 1977), esp. pp. 69–71, 156–9; Ian Bradley, *The Call to Seriousness: The Evangelical Impact on the Victorians* (New York, 1976), pp. 121–5.

8. Madge Unsworth, *Maiden Tribute: A Study in Voluntary Social Service* (London, 1949), pp. 2–4; Sandall, *History of the Salvation Army*, I:100.

9. Unsworth, *Maiden Tribute*, pp. 5–9; Sandall, *History of the Salvation Army*, III:14–16; *All the World*, I (1884–5), pp. 212–14; *The Salvation Army, 1884* (London, 1884), p. 143; *War Cry*, 15 August 1884.

10. Begbie, *William Booth*, II:38, 46; W. B. Booth, *These Fifty Years* (London, 1929), pp. 89–90; Sandall, *History of the Salvation Army*, II:59–60.

11. Salvation Army, *Yearbook*, 1914, p. 22. This included twenty-four homes for unmarried mothers.

12. Sandall, *History of the Salvation Army*, II:61. For some contemporary views of the Women's Social Services, see F. B. Meyer, 'The Nurture of the Home', in James Marchant (ed.), *Public Morals* (London, 1902), p. 82; National Union of Women Workers of Great Britain and Ireland, *Report of the Conference of Rescue Workers* (London, 1897), p. 26; Church of England Report, 1919, quoted in M. Penelope Hall and Ismene V. Howes, *The Church in Social Work: A Study of the Moral Welfare Work Undertaken by the Church of England* (London, 1965), p. 38. For a less enthusiastic assessment, see *The Times*, 27 December 1890, p. 5, and 2 January 1891, p. 5.

13. *Women's Social Work Anniversary in the Silver Wedding Year* (London, 1907), pp. 14–15; 'Mrs Bramwell Booth and Her Work', *All the World*, IV (1888), pp. 19–20.

14. Minutes, Willesden and Kensal Green Ladies Association for the Care of Friendless Girls, June 1908, A/LWC/52, Records of the London Diocesan Council for Penitentiary, Rescue, and Preventive Work, Greater London Record Office.

15. Florence Booth, 'Progress', *Deliverer* (March 1890), p. 117.

16. *All the World*, I (1884–5), pp. 212–14.

17. *Quenched: Report of Rescue and Women's Social Work* (London, 1895), p. 8; 'In the Beginning', *All the World*, XVIII (1897), p. 216; Annie S. Swan, *The Outsiders* (London, 1905–6), p. 97; *The 'Darkest England' Social Scheme: A Brief Review of the First Year's Work* (London, 1891), p. 115.

18. Casebooks of London Rescue Homes, Book I, 1886–8, Social Services Headquarters, Salvation Army, London. Much of the information for this study was obtained from a random sample of approximately 600 unmarried mothers who entered Women's Social Services homes from 1886 to 1888 and from 1896 to 1906. I would like to thank the Salvation Army for their permission to use this material and the staff of the Social Services Headquarters in Hackney for their kind assistance.

19. Ellen Steinmetz, 'Nursery Home', *Deliverer* (January 1890), pp. 88–9; Unsworth, *Maiden Tribute*, pp. 55–6; Sandall, *History of the Salvation Army*, III:53; Casebooks of the London Rescue Homes, Book I, 1886–8.

20. Susie F. Swift, 'Mrs Bramwell Booth's Rescue Homes', *All the World*, IV (1888), p. 19; *Broken Fetters: Report of Women's Rescue and Social Work* (London, 1894), p. 7; F. Booth, 'Progress', p. 117.

21. The development of charities to assist unmarried mothers was traced in the annual volumes of Herbert Fry, *The Royal Guide to London Charities* and W. R. Howe (ed.), *Annual Edition of the Classified Directory to the Metropolitan Charities*, as well as the Charity Organisation Society, *Charities Register*, 1890, and charity journals and annual reports. See also Mrs Robert Peel Wethered and Mrs Henniker, 'Infant Life Protection Act', *Poor Law District Conference Reports* (1901–2), pp. 646–7.

22. Susie F. Swift, 'Jottings from the Rescue Work', *All the World*, IV (1888), pp. 64–8; Swan, *Outsiders*, pp. 95–7; *Salvation War*, p. 136. The Magdalen Hospital, the oldest rescue home for prostitutes in London, excluded pregnant women as did the homes of the Rescue Society, at least until 1890.

23. *Saved in Time: Annual Report of the Women's Social Work for 1892–93* (London, 1893), p. 11.

24. G. S. Railton, *Forward against Misery, 1912–13* (London, 1913), p. 70; 'In the Beginning', p. 215. For the views of other rescue societies and workers, see Female Mission to the Fallen Women of London, *Annual Report*, XLII (1900), p. 19; *Seeking and Saving*, XIX (1890), p. 479; Beatrice Allen, 'Notes on Rescue Work', *Threefold Chord*, II (1893), p. 5; Arthur J. S. Maddison, *Hints on Rescue Work: A Handbook for Missionaries, Committees, Clergy, and Others* (London, 1898), p. 133.

25. Florence Booth quoted in Sandall, *History of the Salvation Army*, III:201; see also Ethel Salmon, 'A Visit to the Bristol Rescue Home', *All the World*, XIV (1894), p. 111.

26. Railton, *Forward against Misery*, p. 69; Salmon, 'Bristol Rescue Home', pp. 110–14; *Snapshots: Women's Social Work, 1914–15* (London, 1915), p. 9; W. B. Booth, *Work in Darkest England*, pp. 13–14; W. B. Booth, *Light in Darkest England in 1895* (London, 1895), p. 74.

27. Swift, 'Rescue Homes', p. 262; Steinmetz, 'Nursery Home', p. 89.

28. Individuals listed as referring unmarried mothers to the Women's Social Services were sometimes identified, but often only their name was given or the note 'a lady' or 'gentleman'.

29. *Saved in Time*, p. 15; the Casebooks of the London Rescue Homes listed women who had responded to Catherine Booth's advertisements.

30. Between 1886 and 1906, 18.2% of the women who entered the maternity homes came from Hackney, Edmonton or West Ham, districts close to the Women's Social Services homes in northeast London.

31. Florence Booth, 'Principles of Rescue Work — I', *All the World*, VII (1891), p. 35; 'Many Excursions to Our Maternity Home', *Deliverer* (February 1900), p. 115; *Jewels for the King: A Brief Report of the Rescue Work of the Salvation Army* (London, 1887), p. 9.

32. The data from the casebooks on the length of the average stay in a maternity home tallied with the Army's own estimates, see W. B. Booth, *Work in Darkest England*, p. 59; *Quenched*, p. 14; *The Babe and the Veteran: Being a Report of the Women's Social Work of the Salvation Army* (London, 1916), p. 6.

33. Out of 538 cases, 31.1% returned to their homes, 56.4% were sent to service, 2.5% were sent to other types of work, and 9% either died in the home or left for the workhouse, hospital or lodgings.

34. Out of 191 unmarried mothers who entered between 1886 and 1896, the only period for which data on occupation was given in the casebooks, 80.6% were servants; the remaining women were needleworkers, factory hands, laundresses, shopgirls, etc. For a discussion of the relationship between service and illegitimacy,

see John R. Gillis, 'Servants, Sexual Relations, and the Risks of Illegitimacy in London, 1801–1900', *Feminist Studies*, V (1979), pp. 142–67.

35. Mrs Col. Pepper, 'Our Servants', *All the World*, XV (1895), p. 448; W. B. Booth, *Light in Darkest England*, p. 73. The casebooks indicated that almost all unmarried mothers were placed within a month to six weeks of having given birth.

36. Swift, 'Rescue Homes', p. 260; 'Through the Women's Social Buildings', *All the World*, XI (1893), pp. 179–80.

37. Florence Booth, *Rescue Notes* (London, 1887); Swift, 'Rescue Homes', p. 261; Swift, 'Jottings', p. 66.

38. T. E. James, 'The Illegitimate and Deprived Child: Legitimation and Adoption', in R. H. Graveson and F. R. Crane (eds), *A Century of Family Law* (London, 1957), pp. 39, 46.

39. For the views of rescue workers on the importance of maintaining a bond between mother and child, see Caritas, 'The Main Memorial Home', *Humanitarian*, XVII (1900), pp. 116–18; E. C. Tait, 'Homes for Mothers and Children', *Seeking and Saving*, XX (1890), p. 491; 'Home of Compassion', *Seeking and Saving*, II (1882), p. 73; Maddison, *Hints on Rescue Work*, pp. 60–1; Mary Jeune, 'Helping the Fallen', *Fortnightly Review*, XLIV (1895), p. 680.

40. *Talks with Rescuers: Review of Women's Social Work for 1898* (London, 1899), p. 25; 'The Children's Aid Department', *Deliverer* (July 1900), p. 5. See also Adelaide Cox's remarks quoted in Associated Societies for the Care and Maintenance of Infants, *Report of the Select Committee Appointed to Examine the Principle and Practice of Child Adoption* (London, 1920), pp. 12–13.

41. The dangers of nursing-out were dealt with by several parliamentary commissions; for examples of the most serious charges, see the testimony of Ernest Hart and J. B. Curgenven in 'Report from the Select Committee on the Protection of Infant Life', pp, 1871, VII. See also George Behlmer, *Child Abuse and Moral Reform in England, 1870–1908* (Stanford, 1982), pp. 17–38.

42. McKenzie, *Waste Humanity*, p. 61; Charles Ray, *People of the Abyss: Essays and Sketches, the Salvation Army* (London, 1906), p. 244; 'In the Beginning', p. 216; the casebooks for 1896 to 1906 indicate where babies were placed, whether at nurse, with their mothers, or in the baby home, but they do not, unfortunately, provide information on the mortality of nursed out infants.

43. Approximately 51% of the infants who survived their stay in the maternity home were sent to nurse, 42% either left with their mothers or were placed with relatives, and the remainder were adopted or sent to the baby home. Over 17% of the infants born in the maternity homes died soon after birth, in part perhaps because of the effects of venereal disease. On this, see 'In the Beginning', p. 215.

44. *Talks with Rescuers*, p. 19; F. Booth, 'Principles of Rescue Work', p. 149.

45. *Quenched*, p. 14; Railton, *Forward against Misery*, p. 69.

46. Inglis, *Churches and the Working Classes*, p. 200; Staff Captain Marshall, 'Our Rescue Work', *All the World*, I (1884–5), p. 237.

47. Cases 113 and 102, Book II, Casebooks of the London Rescue Homes. See also Arthur Brinckman, *Notes on Rescue Work*, 2nd edn (London, 1894), p. 114.

48. 'Women — of All Sorts and Conditions', *All the World*, XVIII (1897), p. 305; Railton, *Forward against Misery*, pp. 58–9. For examples of similar stories, see 'London over the Border', *All the World*, I (1884–5), p. 86; W. B. Booth, *Work in Darkest England*, pp. 62–3.

49. *Saved in Time*, p. 11.

50. Marianne Asdell, 'Maternal Home', *Deliverer* (January 1890), p. 88; Salmon, 'Bristol Rescue Home', pp. 110–11; Railton, *Forward Against Misery*, p. 68; F. B. Meyer, 'The Nurture of the Home', pp. 82, 84; Salvation Army, *Yearbook*, 1914, p. 51; *Salvation War*, p. 138; Swift, 'Jottings', p. 66; 'Grove House', *Deliverer* (November 1894), p. 66; *Wounded in the Warfare of Life:*

Report of the Women's Social Work (London, 1900), pp. 15–16; Swift, 'Rescue Homes', p. 261. This image of unmarried mothers was common among rescue workers; see Judith R. Walkowitz, *Prostitution and Victorian Society: Women, Class, and the State* (Cambridge, 1980), pp. 16–17, 34, 246–7.

51. Information on the unmarried mothers' backgrounds was available only for the first few years of the maternity home records and distinctions between first-fall cases and others were difficult to make.

52. Information on the occupation of the putative fathers was only available for 1886 to 1888. See also Gillis, 'The Risks of Illegitimacy', pp. 158–9.

53. Ray, *People of the Abyss*, p. 244.

54. 'Grove House', p. 66; W. B. Booth, *Social Reparation, or Personal Glimpses of Work for Darkest England* (London, 1899), pp. 26–9; Salvation Army, *Yearbook*, 1914, p. 45; 'A Flying Visit to the North Country', *All the World*, XI (1893), pp. 41–44.

55. Railton, *Forward against Misery*, p. 68.

56. F. Booth, 'Progress', p. 117.

Chapter 10

'She Looketh Well to the Ways of Her Household'[1]: The Changing Role of Jewish Women in Religious Life, c. 1880–1930

Rickie Burman

'Eshet chayil' ('a woman of worth') affords the clearest and most sustained ideal of womanhood in Judaism. The title of a passage from Proverbs traditionally recited on the eve of the Sabbath, it evokes the attributes of the virtuous woman, who rises before dawn and works tirelessly into the night, to provide for her household and assist the needy. The constancy of the declared paragon belies, however, some remarkable shifts in the actual significance of Jewish women's domestic religious practices. This study will explore one such transformation: the shift of a consistent set of female practices from a situation where they were viewed as relatively peripheral to the fundamental concerns of Jewish religion, to one where they emerged as core reference-points in the form and maintenance of Jewish identity.

The context for this transformation is provided by the experiences of immigrant women who came to England in the late nineteenth and early twentieth centuries, and in particular those who settled in the provincial city of Manchester. It is these immigrants and their children who formed the subject of a major research project, conducted in Manchester between 1976 and 1984,[2] in which some 300 Jewish people, born mainly between 1890 and 1910, were interviewed about their early life.[3]

It is estimated that in the years between 1881 and 1905, when immigration from Eastern Europe reached its height, over 100,000 Jewish immigrants settled in England.[4] Of these, some 15,000 settled in Manchester, bringing the city's Jewish population to an approximate total of 30,000 by 1910. The interviews indicate that the majority of immigrants left Eastern Europe to avoid the poverty and oppressive conditions of life under the Tsarist regime. In Manchester they settled in the working-class districts of Strangeways and Red Bank, only half a mile from the city centre, and

234

many entered the workshop trades of tailoring, waterproofing, cap-making and cabinet-making.[5] For the most part they had little personal contact with members of the Anglo-Jewish community, merchants, professional men and their families who lived in the suburbs, several miles out of the city, although the latter wielded considerable authority as the managers or philanthropic supporters of institutions, such as the Jews' School and Jewish Board of Guardians, which played a prominent role in immigrant life.

This study will consider the significance of women's religious practices in three related contexts. Brief discussions of women's situation in the *shtetls* of Eastern Europe, from which many of the immigrants came, and in the long-established Anglo-Jewish community, will provide a comparative context for a more detailed examination of the changes that took place within the Manchester immigrant community.

I

A recent discussion of women's experiences of Judaism emphasises the distinction between *halacha*, the detailed code of Jewish law, representing for the Orthodox a divinely prescribed guide to life, and 'custom', the actual social realities existing at a particular moment in historical time.[6] Whereas for many Jews in modern, secularised society, a wide gap exists between *halachic* theory and practical observance, in Jewish society in Eastern Europe there was a marked congruence between law and custom, and this was reflected in the position of women within religious life. The following account therefore provides a summary description both of Jewish laws relating to women's religious observance and of their actual practice within the Eastern European context.

Jewish settlement in Eastern Europe was characterised by a distinctive pattern of social and cultural life centred upon the *shtetl* communities, which began to emerge in sixteenth-century Poland-Lithuania and crystallised following the partitións of the eighteenth century. Whilst in areas under Habsburg rule communities were more dispersed, Jewish residence within the Russian Empire was largely restricted to the 'Pale of Settlement', which extended from the Black Sea to the Baltic.[7] In this context, *shtetl* culture developed partly in isolation, partly in opposition to the wider society. While our interviews suggest that many of the immigrants to England came from this background, it should be noted that the nineteenth century saw an increasing trend towards urbanisation and industrialisation in Russia,[8] with possible ramifying effects also on the smaller *shtetl* communities.

Within the *shtetl*, the major arenas of religious practice, the synagogue and study-house, were essentially the preserve of men. Male status was closely bound up with religious scholarship, which represented a primary avenue to social recognition and an important source of political influence.[9] Where wealth had been acquired but religious legitimation was lacking, the daughter of a wealthy man would often be married to a promising scholar, who would bring *yichus*, prestige and status, to his father-in-law and descendants.[10]

Although women could serve as a channel through which male status could be attained, they had little religious status in their own right. According to traditional Jewish law,[11] they were excluded from the obligation of observing 'time-bound' religious commandments (which tended to relate to public worship), so as to be free to fulfil their 'primary domestic functions'. They were therefore not counted in a *minyan*, the quorum of ten adult men required for a religious service to take place. They were not allowed to lead or play any public role in communal prayer and were often actively discouraged, and even prevented, from learning the sacred language of Hebrew and studying religious texts.[12]

Women's domestic activities were often extended to include breadwinning, women attending to the material concerns while their husbands engaged in more spiritual pursuits. Thus an interviewee born in Manchester in 1910 notes that her grandmother ran a little grocery shop in Lithuania, which 'more or less kept the family going' while her husband 'prayed all day' in synagogue.[13] In other cases the material/spiritual division was maintained even when a woman's work required her to travel away from home on business.[14] A woman could assume an active economic role, but she remained dependent on her husband for religious status.

To underline their responsibilities within the domestic sphere, three specific *mizvot* (religious duties) were assigned to women: the lighting of the Sabbath candles, the setting apart of a small portion of dough when baking bread, as a gift to God, and the observance of the laws of *niddah*, which entailed abstinence from sexual intercourse for at least twelve days during and after menstruation, and purification in the ritual bath, or *mikveh*, at the conclusion of this period. In addition, as a routine part of their housekeeping role, women were responsible for the maintenance of *kashrut*, the Jewish dietary laws, and for the housework and cooking necessary to celebrate Sabbaths and Festivals in the appropriate spirit. These activities were taken for granted as part of the very rhythm of domestic life, and were not seen in themselves as essentially religious acts.

The marginalisation of women from spiritual life was increased by the accentuated demarcation of gender divisions, which was legitimated by an emphasis on their sexuality. Women were seen as a constant source of temptation and distraction to men. To limit their attractiveness to men other than their husbands, women were expected to cut their hair on marriage and wear a *sheitel* or wig.[15]

Although by the late nineteenth century the *shtetl* was undergoing considerable socio-economic change, our interviews suggest that for the majority of the immigrants the sexual demarcation in religious life had remained substantially unchanged.

II

The Anglo-Jewish community was already well integrated into English society by the time the influx of Eastern European immigrants reached its height. Strongly middle-class in composition, it was dominated by a small number of interrelated families, who combined an attachment to Jewish affairs with an equal dedication to English life and institutions.[16] In contrast to the *shtetl*, which had developed its social values partly in opposition to those of the wider society, Anglo-Jewry was strongly influenced by the mores of the English middle classes.[17] As in Eastern Europe, however, a major distinction was drawn between the natural qualities and appropriate spheres of activities for men and women, and women's essential domesticity was stressed. But whereas in the *shtetl* a primary division was drawn between the spheres of the sacred and the profane, with women relegated to the latter, among Anglicised Jews, as in gentile society, the major separation was between public and private spheres, the workplace and the home.[18] Occupational status and prestige in the eyes of the wider society, rather than religious scholarship, represented the primary avenues to social recognition.

Following the precepts of the domestic ideology current in

Victorian Britain, Anglicised Jews tended to see breadwinning as a male prerogative and responsibility; a woman's involvement in paid work would have cast a dark shadow on her husband's integrity and social standing.[19] Furthermore, in prosperous families the wife's direct involvement in practical domestic activities was out of the question, the employment of domestic servants being another indicator of social status. This resulted in a striking inversion of the gender roles tradition in the *shtetl*. Women were seen not as material providers but as spiritual helpmeets, and the home was envisioned as a secure and sacred haven rather than a source of worldly distraction.

Earlier in the century Grace Aguilar had written eloquently on the vocation of the Jewish woman in England:

> The ordinances and commands of our holy faith interfere much less with woman's retired path of domestic pursuits and pleasures than with the more public and more ambitious career of man. Her duty is to make home happy; her mission, to *influence* man, alike in her relative duties of mother to her son, wife to her husband, sister to her brother, and, in her own person, to upraise the holy cause of religion . . . To obtain this superiority is to become more spiritual; for in that single word every feminine grace and Jewish requisite is comprised.[20]

She argues that spirituality is 'so peculiarly woman's attribute, that without it her loveliest charms, her highest intellect, appears imperfect. By many it is unattainable . . . unless infused by the influence of woman'.[21]

This view of woman's innate spirituality is still evident at the turn of the century. By this time an increasing number of middle-class women were turning to philanthropic work, a branch of public life perceived as a natural extension of their domestic role and in keeping with their spiritual vocation.[22] In 1902 a Conference of Jewish Women was held with the aim of enabling women philanthropic workers from all parts of the country to meet and 'interchange information as to various methods of communal work'.[23] A *Jewish Chronicle* report of the event speaks of a 'tremendous revelation to the community of its latent spiritual forces', and contrasts the women's conference with a Conference of British Congregations held at the same time and regarded as a 'similar movement in the purely masculine sphere':

The activities of the Ladies' conference will centre round the religious and educational needs of our people; the efforts of the 'Conference of British Congregations' will be addressed to matters of more secular concern. The division of labour is not unnatural.[24]

Despite this emphasis on their spirituality and benevolent work, women continued to be excluded from active participation in communal worship and synagogue affairs. These limitations were underlined by the Rev. A. A. Green in a paper read before the fashionable Hampstead Synagogue Guild in 1899:

It must be confessed that looking around the community the opportunity and the influences of the Jewish woman cannot be said to present entirely satisfactory features . . . Still the daily prayer provides for the Jewish man the words which make him bless and praise the Almighty who has not made him a woman. Still the authority of the Jewish Synagogue system recognises as a congregant a boy of thirteen, while it ignores the contribution to the formation of *minyan* of that child's mother, though she may be a saintly woman. Still the Barmitzvah is reserved for the boy for whom the doors of the congregation are opened wide, while his sisters pass unnoticed as though it were of more consequence how a boy should grow into a man than how a girl should approach the dawning duties of womanhood. Still the women sit unnoticed in the gallery, while the so-called honours of the synagogue go one and all to men; and still the laws of the United Synagogue give a voice in the synagogue management to 'male persons above the age of 21 years occupying seats in the body of the synagogue'. We might perhaps have less to regret today if in the constitution and management of our synagogue affairs there was less said about that 'body of the synagogue' and a little more thought about its soul.[25]

Most women accepted their indirect role in religion, seeking to achieve a sense of self-worth within the limits imposed. Thus Miss Raphael, headmistress of the Manchester Jews' School, speaking at the 1902 conference, records the ideals held out by a local minister to working girls in weekly addresses at their Sabbath services:

They learnt that the future of our race will depend on the

goodness of the woman, and that while all cannot be clever and beautiful, each one can improve the world by cultivating gentleness, piety, firmness and graciousness. Women may not take an active part in the public functions of our religion, but it is the mother, sister or wife of the man who helps him in some way to produce each religious observance.[26]

She reinforces the minister's message of cheerful compliance:

He taught them that there need be no question of 'Women's Rights', a girl and woman would always have them so long as she does her duty well, and remembers that she was created as the helper of man . . . The true woman should be the soul of her home, and if she wants to be happy, should cultivate cheerfulness and make the best of her surroundings.[27]

A decade later, however, it became evident that a number of influential women were growing dissatisfied with the contradiction between the spiritual role assigned to them and their exclusion from communal religious life.[28] These were well-educated women, who had gained confidence and experience through their involvement in philanthropy. At a time when declining church attendance figures had become a matter of general concern, it was apparent that, whereas women provided the main support of the Church of England, the proportion of women attending synagogue services was markedly lower.[29] It was feared that some anglicised women were drifting away from a religion from which they felt excluded.[30] As early as 1899, attempts were made to secure for at least widows and single women the vote in synagogue elections.[31] However, although not oblivious to feminist demands, the United Synagogue (the association of Ashkenazi congregations under the religious authority of the Chief Rabbi) remained obdurate.[32]

The failure of the institutions of Orthodox Judaism to accommodate to the needs of women was an important contributory factor in the development of Liberal Judaism. Lily Montagu, a distinguished communal worker and founder of the Jewish Religious Union (1902), which developed into the movement of Liberal Judaism (c. 1911), drew a direct connection between her rejection of the traditional role of women in religion and her interest in reform.[33] From the inception of the movement it was determined that men and women should be equal in their congregational privileges, boys and girls both receiving 'confirmation', men and women sitting together, and women holding seats and voting rights on the synagogue council as a matter of course, although the privileges of leading a service and delivering sermons were not granted to women until after the First World War.[34]

The emergence of the Liberal Movement may, however, have strengthened the conservatism of mainstream Judaism, opposed to this schism.[35] In 1912 further efforts were made to improve the position of women with the establishment of the Jewish League for Women's Suffrage.[36] Although a concerted campaign by the League for the 'enfranchisement of women seat-holders' met with some success in individual synagogues, it was not until 1954 that female members of the United Synagogue were finally granted voting rights.[37]

III

The immigrants arriving in England from Eastern Europe in the late nineteenth and early twentieth centuries differed from the established Anglo-Jewish community in class, culture and religious values. They settled in different areas and established their own patterns of communal life, founding the *chevras*, *cheders* and other institutions which had characterised religious life in the *shtetl*.[38] While the established community took an active interest in the development of immigrant life, seeking to discourage the continuance of 'alien' customs and institutions in England, there was little interaction between the two groups at an individual level.

Within the immigrant community, the change in the centrality of women's religious observances resulted more from a shift in the relative importance of their activities than a change in their aspirations or practices. The evidence from the 150 Manchester interviews analysed suggests that most immigrant women continued to play a minimal role in formal religious life, even in the most orthodox families, generally attending synagogue only on the High Holydays.

Thus an interviewee, born in 1900 to immigrant parents, recalled how, although her father went regularly to synagogue on the Sabbath and prayed at home during the week, she and her mother only attended synagogue on Festivals. Their duties were of a different kind. 'Father went to *shul* (synagogue). Mother would have the table all laid with all the things he liked, you know. The usual fried fish for *Shabbos* after *shul*, a schnapps and home-made cake and that.'[39]

This pattern of synagogue attendance by women only on Festivals, is noted by many different respondents, even in a case where the interviewee's father himself prayed in synagogue three times a day.[40] The son of the unofficial rabbi and cantor of one of the larger immigrant synagogues estimated that in the 1920s about fifty people would attend Sabbath services, including only a half-dozen women. But on Festivals the synagogue would be 'packed' with some ninety men and sixty women.[42]

Many of the smaller immigrant congregations met in the attics or upper storeys of private houses, and those few women who did attend the Sabbath services often had to listen from a separate room, or, in the case of the Solela Chevra in Manchester, from the bedroom of the house next door.[42]

Many immigrant women were illiterate in Hebrew, and where a woman could '*daven* (pray) like a man', she was seen as quite exceptional.[43] This was the case with Mrs Singer, who was descended from a 'high rabbinical family' in Austrian Galicia and was widowed soon after her arrival in Manchester in 1904. Her daughter related:

My mother was a very proud woman, and she went to *shul* (synagogue) every Saturday. On Purim . . . about ten women used to come in and they used to sit around my mother and she used to say the book of Esther in Hebrew, and they all used to say it after her, because none of them had been taught anything . . . she was a very well learned woman.[44]

This woman seems to have continued a tradition known from the *shtetl*, where a more learned woman would act as a *zogerin* ('sayer'), leading others in prayer.[45]

The same pattern was evident in the field of religious education, in particular prior to the 1920s. A historical survey of the Manchester Talmud Torah Schools, which provided tuition for thousands of Jewish children in the late nineteenth and early twentieth centuries, emphasises the important role played by the 'pious mothers of the Talmud Torah movement'. It records that the movement for the establishment of the institution in Manchester started 'in 1879 in the humble home of Mrs Rose Fineberg, who hailed from Kalvaria in Poland'.[46] Mrs Fineberg had been an active worker for the Talmud Torah in her native town and continued to support it from Manchester, enlisting the aid of her friends as regular contributors. Then:

> One day the idea occurred to her that there must be many Jewish children in Manchester whose poor parents could not afford to pay for their Hebrew and religious instruction, and, being a woman of action, she made a tour of the streets of Cheetham, picked up half a dozen boys and placed them in the charge of a Hebrew teacher, whom she persuaded to give his services gratis.[47]

Mrs Fineberg was joined by Mrs Joseph Taylor and Mrs Leah Berman, who suggested that funds might be raised by collecting weekly penny subscriptions from Jews living in the immigrant areas: 'Fitting the action to the word, she forthwith placed on the table the first penny', and so became the first contributor to the fund.[48]

This account presents a vivid illustration of the responsibility which immigrant women often assumed for the religious instruction of their sons. Yet only rarely did this concern extend to the religious education of their daughters. Although immigrant parents were prepared to make considerable sacrifices to send their sons to the Talmud Torah or to a religious *cheder* (class) run by a private *rebbe* (teacher), there was a strong resistance to the provision of religious education for girls, based on the 'erroneous belief that girls are not allowed to study our Torah (law)'.[49]

Among the Manchester interviewees, 88 per cent of men from an immigrant background mentioned receiving a formal religious education, but this was true for only 28 per cent of the women. One man, born into a very religious family in 1916, contrasted his own education with the more practical training received by his sisters:

> Religion, learning, *chumash* (the Pentateuch), and things like that wasn't for girls. In fact, it was looked upon almost a little askance. Well, a girl doesn't need to learn . . . a girl needs to know her *dinim* (laws), whatever she needs to know, *dinim shabbos* (laws pertaining to the Sabbath), and so on, but it was left to the male members of the family to learn.[50]

There were exceptions to this pattern, however, as was shown by the daughter of Mrs Singer: 'Me and me sister went to *cheder* like a boy . . . not many girls went in those days . . . We went four days a week . . . I had to go and give the sixpence which my mother could ill-afford, but she was determined that we had to learn Hebrew.'[51] Occasionally a girl managed to obtain a Hebrew education without parental encouragement. One woman, born to Lithuanian parents in 1907, said her mother insisted that her brothers not only attend *cheder* in the evenings, but also receive extra tuition at home during school dinner-hours. This gave the daughter the opportunity to sit and learn with them: 'Until my mother found out, I learned Rashi with the boys. Then one day mother walked in and she found I was learning with them — needless to say I found it very interesting . . . And so she says, "Oh, that's not for a girl!" So she puts me onto Yiddish.'[52]

For the majority of girls, the only formal religious tuition received was that provided by the Anglo-Jewish community in the Manchester Jews' School and by two Board Schools with substantial Jewish populations. This instruction seems to have had little impact, and many girls reached the top class of the Jews' School without having learnt any Hebrew.[53]

If the restrictions imposed on women's participation in public religious life continued to operate in England, a similar continuity is apparent in the domestic sphere of activities with which women were more positively associated in the *shtetl*. The majority of immigrant women in Manchester remained conscientious in their domestic observances, at pains to follow the dietary laws, and to consult a rabbi if questions arose about the laws governing *kashrut*. One man, whose family lived several miles outside the immigrant area, remembers as a 10-year-old being made to travel into the area and back by tram three times on a Friday, until he had found a rabbi to look at a hen in which his mother had seen 'something which she did not like'.[54] Another recalled the anxiety of her mother on asking a *sheilah* (religious question) of the rabbi:

Oh, what a nightmare! What a nightmare! God forbid if we found a pin inside the fowl. If we found anything inside, we had to run to the *rov* (rabbi) . . . And we used to have to stand, and he'd come back and he'd say it was quite all right. But the trouble of going was awful, and the fear every time a fowl was opened — in case . . . in case there was anything wrong inside and it would have to go back, and then it would be made *treife* (not *kosher*), and you couldn't get another one in time. It was an awful worry.[55]

The domestic preparations for the Sabbath and Festivals required a considerable amount of work in cooking and baking, and a careful management of the household economy to make possible the purchase of the customary extra luxuries. Considerable physical effort also had to be expended in cleaning and other household chores. The following extract gives a vivid impression of the work entailed in the annual changeover of foods and utensils for the festival of Passover.

> Everything had to be changed . . . We had big cellars and all your pots had to be changed, and we had two big chests, that had all the Passover pots inside, that you only used for Passover. All the pots we had in the back kitchen . . . had to be taken down and washed and put away in a box and taken into the cellar, and all the tables and cupboards had to be washed down, fresh white paper put inside . . . We had a red rug in the back kitchen that had to be red raggled and the yard had to be whitewashed . . . The oven had to be whitewashed inside, because we'd cooked ordinary food during the year.[56]

Less extensive, but still time-consuming, preparations were made on a weekly basis for the Sabbath, which was ushered in as women lit the Sabbath candles on the Friday evening:

> On a Friday afternoon, before the Sabbath, my mother had done all the baking, fried all the fish and she had her white apron on . . . There was always linoleum, a rug. Every Thursday night, it was known in all the Jewish houses, if the daughters were respectable or not, they all stayed in and used to rub up the fenders with emery paper to make them shine. And then there used to be a black oven, and they used to polish it, and it was done in every household.[57]

Two other aspects of women's traditional observances, the covering of the head with a *sheitel*, or wig, and the immersion in the ritual bath, or *mikveh*, were not so extensively carried over from Eastern Europe. Only 27 per cent of the Manchester interviewees questioned on this subject recalled their mother wearing a *sheitel*, and, even in these cases, several noted that she had subsequently discarded it or worn it only on ritual occasions. In England the *sheitel* was seen as old-fashioned and ugly, attracting hostile attention, and the pressure exerted on women to relinquish it soon outweighed that of custom, as in the case of this interviewee's mother, who emigrated from Lithuania in 1907: 'It's a funny thing but my mother said when she first came over, she wore a *sheitel*. As soon as she walked in, [one of my aunties] said to Mammy, . . . "That goes off, you don't wear it here".'[58] Still more extreme was the reaction of Mrs Singer's wealthy London relatives, who visited Manchester to attend her daughter's wedding: they burnt her wig the night before the wedding, telling her, 'Mimi, you've got such nice hair. What do you want to cover it with that for? A black *sheitel*, you haven't even got black hair.'[59]

Among the children of immigrants, the wearing of a *sheitel* did not inspire respect. Asked if his mother wore one, a male interviewee replied, 'No! No! She wasn't that barmy . . . Those were the barmy ones. There were one or two in the neighbourhood that wore sheitels.'[60] Few women held out against such negative reactions. A woman born in 1890 related how the children prevailed on her mother to remove her *sheitel*, 'We didn't like it . . . She looked so much nicer without. She cried when we made her take it off.'[61]

In contrast to the practical activities which women carried out within the privacy of the home, the wearing of the *sheitel* in England assumed the role of a public act. The observance of laws regarding 'family purity' and immersion in the ritual bath or *mikveh* was a more personal matter, and information is consequently less readily available. Propriety demanded discretion on visiting a *mikveh*, as the following extract suggests:

> I couldn't understand, as a youngster, that at night she used to close the shop at eight o'clock and she would get on the bus. 'Where're you going, Ma?' 'I'm going out.' And she'd come back about half past nine and her hair would be wet with a little scarf on it. 'Your hair's wet, Ma.' 'It's no business of yours.' But I didn't know till later on that she used to go to the ritual bath.[62]

The limited evidence available from Manchester suggests that a substantial majority of married immigrant women continued to attend the *mikveh* on a regular basis.[63] The son of a *mikveh* attendant, born in 1894, remembered that

> there were three classes of *mikveh*, first class, second class, and third class. It depended on how rich you were, how much you gave my mother. The first class had a tallboy . . . and chairs and you would get a nice cup of tea and biscuits and things like that . . . I can remember the third class was just like our wash-house . . . and not as posh as the other ones.[64]

Some of the daughters of immigrants attended the *mikveh* before their wedding, but generally they did not go thereafter, seeing the practice as anachronistic and rather distasteful in the 'dusty, dingy and horrible conditions'.[65] In the rare cases where the daughters of immigrants continued to visit the *mikveh*, it was often the result of pressure from older relatives. Thus one interviewee related that her grandmother took her to the *mikveh* before her wedding-night, in 1927, and that, at her grandmother's insistence, she continued to go regularly for four years, until her son was born. The fact that she then ceased to attend may perhaps be related to a belief in an association between fertility and *mikveh* attendance.[66] By 1921 the decline in attendance was so great that two *mikvehs* in the Manchester area were on the verge of closing, and a local immigrant rabbi was moved to write to the *Jewish Chronicle*, urging more support for what he regarded as a basic principle of traditional Judaism.[67]

Despite the rapid relinquishing of the *sheitel* and the more gradual decline in *mikveh* attendance, the domestic religious practices of immigrant women in England were characterised by a strong continuity. The maintenance of a *kosher* home and the preparations for Sabbaths and Festivals were seen as private acts, which were not incompatible with modernity or acceptance into English society. While among the women of the Anglo-Jewish community these practical activities had become of less direct importance, being observed with less rigour or carried out through the agency of domestic servants,[68] for the immigrant women they constituted an integral part of daily household labours. Their concern was directed not to an abstract 'spiritual sphere', which the more anglicised women now saw as their province, but to the practical management of the material world. They accepted as their lot the sexual division of labour familiar from the *shtetl*.

Despite this continuity in role expectations, a major disjuncture was evident in the sphere of male observance. In the new, urban environment, religious scholarship and piety no longer provided major avenues to status and respect. The son of an immigrant tailor expressed contempt, rather than admiration, for a pious uncle who prayed three times a day and refused to work on the Sabbath. 'To me, he didn't bring his children up right. All that he worried was *davening* [praying], *davening*, *davening*. There was other principles in life, . . . which he didn't uphold.'[69] The uncle's scrupulous observance left him little time to provide for his wife and children, who consequently 'had a poor life'.

The erosion of traditional values, consequent upon the immigrants' more open interaction with the wider society in England, was reinforced by the policies of anglicisation adopted by the Anglo-Jewish establishment. The negative view which the latter took of the immigrant religious institutions has been well documented for Manchester.[70] In 1881 an English-born rabbi explained to an immigrant audience that

> England was not famous for its *Yeshibot* [religious colleges] because Hebrew learning did not pay in this commercial country, and therefore it was incumbent upon them to do something more than educate their children solely in Hebrew and Rabbinical teachings.[71]

On a more practical level, synogogue attendance and religious study did not combine well with the economic demands and opportunities in England. An 'ethical sermon delivered to the working classes' by a London *dayan* (religious judge) observed that, back in Eastern Europe, 'it [was] easy to be pious and it [was] no great matter to uphold the Divine Commandments. But here, in this country, it is a great thing and a very great test.'[72] It was estimated that more than half the Jews of London went to work on the Sabbath, although the observance of Festivals was more general.[73]

These observations are borne out by respondents in Manchester. Here an immigrant recalls his sadness on first going to work on the Sabbath, 'I just put up with it, but . . . I hated it . . . I remember the first day, it's a *shabbos* . . . I was broken-hearted . . . Yes, they used to work *shabbos* them days, tailors.'[74] An immigrant draper explained succinctly, 'We thought, "It's a necessity." That's how it was. You couldn't make a living if you didn't work on a Saturday in England.'[75]

In some cases, liberation from the restrictions of orthodox observance was welcomed by the immigrants,[76] but even those who retained an active interest in religious prayer and study had little success in communicating that enthusiasm to their children.[77] Although most Jews retained a nominal affiliation to a synagogue and attended on High Holydays, in general the synagogue and its related institutions lost their dominance in communal life, remaining the core preoccupation only for an attenuated minority.[78]

In this context women's traditional domestic practices acquired a new significance. What had previously been merely an accepted part of daily life, the observance of Jewish dietary laws and the preparation for Sabbaths and Festivals, now assumed a greater prominence as religious acts which served to define the Jewish identity of the household, and to distinguish the homes of Jewish families from those of their gentile neighbours. Many interviewees described how, although their fathers worked on the Sabbath, their mothers continued to follow tradition and create a special Sabbath atmosphere. The child of a credit draper in Stockport recalled,

> We were told what dad had to do for the business. That was our living and our bread and butter, it couldn't be helped, but we weren't allowed to do anything. We had a fire goy [gentile] who came in to do the fires and my mother didn't do any cooking on the Sabbath.[79]

Although Jewish children often mixed freely with their non-Jewish neighbours in the street, and sometimes visited their homes, the warning not to eat non-*kosher* foods, as well as the different dishes cooked in gentile homes, gave them an early consciousness of their Jewishness. This was expressed well by an interviewee, who related that the neighbours

> used to come in — not a lot, because we couldn't go back to their house and have a cup of tea with them, you see . . . They'd have bacon in the house, and my mother said, 'Well, you can't go in and have a cup of tea out of pots that have been washed in soap and water. We don't use soap and water for washing cups.' So we didn't go. There was no bar, but we just didn't go.[80]

Thus for many of the immigrants' children, a sense of identity as

Jews was closely linked to early memories of their home environment. The most vivid recollections, related with enthusiasm, are often of mothers preparing for the Sabbath, cooking traditional dishes and scrubbing the house clean; or of the Friday night meal with the family assembled before the glowing candles in their newly washed and pressed clothes.[81] Here the son of a *rebbe* (Hebrew teacher) describes his mother lighting the Sabbath candles after completing her household preparations:

> Soon it was time for me to get washed and to change into my Sabbath suit. My mother spread a white cloth on the table and transferred the two old brass candlesticks from the dresser to the table . . . They came from the homeland, from 'der heim'. In honour of the Sabbath, my mother had rubbed them bright and shiny with Brasso . . . Our mother looked beautiful and mysterious as she covered her head with a lace shawl, made ritual gestures over the candles in the shiny candlesticks, covered her face with her hands and murmured the prescribed blessing, praising God for his gift to mankind of a day of rest and spiritual refreshment. She appeared to me like a priestess, the guardian of the sacred fire, a ritual older than Judaism.[82]

In a major study of patterns of acculturation among the children of immigrant Jews, Rosalyn Livshin has shown that, although many of these children drifted away from regular synagogue worship and Sabbath observance, and although many went dancing or courting with non-Jews, very few took what was seen as the ultimate step towards assimilation — that of marrying a non-Jew.[83] It was not the dictates of formal, public religion which held them back, but, rather, concern for their parents and the association of Jewishness with their early life in the home.

A respondent who, from an early age, had begun to question the relevance of religion and who called himself an atheist, noted that, although many of his friends kept away from formal religion, 'The funny thing is, every one of us married Jewish girls . . . of my particular crowd, there was one, three, nine, ten, there was twelve children of my age in the street and not one of them married a non-Jewish girl.'[84] Another stressed that, although he went out with a non-Jewish girl, for him, intermarriage 'was impossible. I would never have dreamt of it . . . because you've been brought up in a Jewish atmosphere . . . fancy sitting down on a Friday night without *lockshen* soup . . . the candles not lit, things like that.'[85]

Such homely details should not be dismissed as mere nostalgia. They clearly had the power to create a strong impact on children, constituting part of the fabric of their lives, and at the same time something special which set them apart.

Although an affective identification with Judaism was maintained in the second generation, by the 1920s it was becoming recognised that many of the children of immigrants had only a shallow knowledge of their own religious laws and history. A new impetus developed to improve teaching methods and establish study circles at a higher level.[86] At the same time there was a growing awareness of women's importance in the transmission of religion. In 1922 a *Jewish Chronicle* report of a meeting of the Union of Jewish women noted that 'the well-being of the community depended just as much — more, perhaps — on the religious education of those future mothers, as it did on the religious education of the future fathers'.[87] In keeping with these developments, and with the general interest in improving girls' education, girls were included in these efforts. In Manchester this was marked in 1930 by the inauguration of the Ivriah School for Girls, the first of several measures taken to increase the availability of Jewish education for girls.[88]

The patterns developed in the turn-of-the-century immigrant community can still be discerned. A recent survey of the London borough of Redbridge, one of the densest areas of Jewish settlement in Britain, revealed a low participation in the predominantly male sphere of public worship, but a strikingly high level of home observance.[89] Whereas in 70.2 per cent of households women lit the Sabbath candles, only 9.7 per cent of the adult population attended synagogue on a regular basis, the majority of these being male.[90] Men's observance of home rituals was also more lax than women's: the high proportion of women lighting candles contrasts with the lower proportion (26.4 per cent) of men reciting *kiddush* (the customary blessings over wine and bread) on Friday evenings. Associated with this pattern of strong domestic observance was a low rate of intermarriage, and a high degree of commitment among women to the transmission and preservation of Judaism.[91] While women in every age group had received a lower average Jewish education than men, a consistent improvement in their access to education had occurred since the Second World War.

It thus appears that, among the descendants of the immigrants, the gender-based division of labour within religious practice has been maintained: public religion has remained a predominantly male arena and domestic observances the responsibility of women. And while the actual practices of women have undergone relatively little alteration, the significance of these activities has changed. Once regarded as mere adjuncts to the major sphere of male religion, in twentieth century Britain they have assumed a greater importance.

In the three situations compared in this paper, Jewish women have been subject to the same formal religious laws. Yet, in effect, both the content and the significance of their role in religious life have differed markedly in important ways. In all three situations women's domesticity was stressed, but with differing results. In the *shtetl*, the profane associations of the domestic sphere strengthened the barriers excluding women from the recognised arenas of religious endeavour, but gave some scope for their involvement in independent economic activities. In contrast, the association of domesticity and spirituality in the Anglo-Jewish community, although providing a justification for women to engage in philanthropic work, excluded them from the economic sphere and gave them little effective power in mainstream religious life. In the immigrant community, formal religion and spiritual endeavours continued to be seen as more properly the preserve of men, but their declining relevance to daily life, combined with economic pressures and opportunities, gave women's domestic practices a new centrality. Formerly regarded as peripheral, they now developed as key components in the transmission of a sense of Jewish identification and attachment.

The shift in the centrality of women's domestic observances was thus closely related to a major change in the nature of Jewish identification. For many Jews, the migration from East to West marked a transition from a society where Jewish status was primary, automatic and non-negotiable, defined according to external structural constraints and a cohesive internal ideology, to one in which the status of individuals was no longer necessarily subsumed by their Jewishness.[92] Active identification with the group became more open to personal choice, and, as Gartner has noted, it became possible to retain a stake in 'Jewishness', a consciousness of being Jewish, without fulfilling the formal dictates of 'Judaism'.[93] With the development of this more optional ethnicity, the significance of women's religious practices moved from periphery to core.

Ironically, the limitations imposed on women's religious role in Eastern Europe, in a new context, became a source of strength. The very fact that they were rooted in the material world and integrated with the routine, practical tasks of the domestic environment, gave to women's observances their power of continuity and affective valency. Yet in Britain, despite some improvements in women's status, the increased centrality of their role in religion did not result in a corresponding increase in communal stature or authority. For religion no longer represented a major avenue to social status, and the focus of male aspirations had changed.

Interviews Cited

Numbers in parentheses indicate tape reference numbers within the Manchester Studies archive. A — Immigrant; B — English-born interviewee.

A1   Born Przemysl, Galicia. Came to Manchester 1904 with parents. Father died shortly after migration; mother a credit draper (J104).

A2   Born 1883, Kalvariya, Russian Poland. Father an innkeeper. Arrived 1898 to join his brother. Tailor (J29).

A3   Born 1895, Vitebsk, Belorussia. Father a tea-traveller. Arrived Manchester, 1910. Wholesale draper (J218).

B1   Born 1910, Manchester, to Belorussian father and Lithuanian mother. Father a cap-maker, mother a dressmaker (J219).

B2   Born 1907, Cheetham, Manchester, to Russian father and Romanian mother. Father worked initially as Hebrew teacher in Manchester, then opened a drapery business (J87).

B3   Born 1908, Wigan, to Lithuanian father and Russian mother. Father a credit draper (J192).

B4   Born 1897, Cheetham, Manchester. Parents from Lithuania c.1890. Father had been a scholar in Eastern Europe; in Manchester opened a wine shop (J98).

B5   Born 1916, Salford, to Galician father and English-born mother. Father the founder of an Orthodox religious movement in Manchester.

B6 Born 1907, Lower Broughton, Manchester, to immigrant parents from Lithuania. Father a rag merchant (J49).

B7 Born 1917, Hightown, Manchester, to Romanian father and English-born mother. Parents ran second-hand clothes shop (J228).

B8 Born 1909, Southport, to Lithuanian father and English-born mother. Father a furniture manufacturer (J229).

B9 Born 1905, Hightown, Manchester, to Latvian father and Lithuanian mother. Father a tailor (J142).

B10 Born 1904, Strangeways, Manchester, to Galician parents. Father a synagogue official and dealer in ritual objects (J242).

B11 Born 1908, Stockport. Father an immigrant of 1906. Father a credit draper (J202).

B12 Born 1918, Cheetham, Manchester, to Austrian father and Romanian mother. Father a cap-maker, mother ran grocery and sweet shop (J254).

B13 Born 1909, Strangeways, Manchester, to Galician parents, who ran a grocery shop in Manchester (J273).

B14 Born 1893, Strangeways, Manchester, to Lithuanian parents. Father a slipper-maker (J71).

B15 Born 1890, Strangeways, Manchester, to Russian parents. Father worked as a glazier in Russia, became a credit draper in England. Mother worked as a cook prior to marriage (J27).

B16 Born 1900, Cheetham, Manchester, to Russian father and German mother. Father a tailor (J53).

B17 Born 1908, Hightown, Manchester, to Lithuanian parents. Father a Hebrew teacher, mother a cap-maker prior to marriage (J216).

B18 Born 1912, Lower Broughton, Manchester, to Latvian parents. Father a decorator, mother worked as a house-keeper prior to marriage (J272).

B19 Born 1904, Lower Broughton, Manchester, to Lithuanian parents. Father worked as a religious official abroad; in Manchester became a waste dealer. Mother a cap-maker prior to marriage (J243).

B20 Born 1909, Strangeways, Manchester, to Lithuanian father and English-born mother. Father a tailor (J232).

B21 Born 1902, Strangeways, Manchester, to Galician father and Romanian mother. Father a tailor's presser (J214).

B22   Born 1915, Strangeways, Manchester, to Galician father
       and mother from Russian Poland. Father a tailor and
       mother a cap-maker (J94).

B23   Born 1894, Strangeways, Manchester, to English-born
       father and Galician mother. Father a synagogue caretaker
       and mother a *mikveh* (ritual bath) attendant (J92).

B24   Born 1907, Lower Broughton, Manchester, to father from
       Russian Poland and Dutch-born mother. Father a tailor
       (J222).

Notes

1. *Proverbs* 31:27. This quotation is taken from the passage, 'a woman of worth',
traditionally read in the home on the eve of the Sabbath.

An earlier version of this paper was presented at the History Workshop Conference on Religion and Society, in July 1983, and has been included in the
conference volume. The research on which it is based was conducted while I was
working as a Research Fellow at the Manchester Studies Unit, Manchester
Polytechnic. I would like to thank Judith Emanuel, Wendy Flanagan, Riva Krut,
Rosalyn Livshin, Daniel Miller, Sheila Saunders and Bill Williams for their help and
comments.

2. The interviews were recorded by Bill Williams, Rosalyn Livshin and myself as
part of a wider research project on the history of Manchester's Jewish community,
based at the Manchester Studies Unit. This essay is based on a detailed analysis of
150 of these interviews. Of the interviewees included in the sample, 44% were male
and 56% female; 14% were themselves immigrants and 80%, though British-born,
had at least one parent of immigrant origin.

3. The fact that the majority of our interviewees were the children of immigrants
reflects the relatively restricted period of Jewish migration to Britain, which was
curtailed by the Aliens Act of 1905. It is important to note this difference in
periodisation when comparing the experience of immigrant Jewish women in Britain
and America. For the latter, see S. Weinberg, 'The World of our Mothers: Family,
Work and Education in the Lives of Jewish Immigrant Women', *Frontiers*, VII
(1983), pp. 71–9. Weinberg's account is based on interviews with forty women who
arrived in the United States between 1901 and 1924.

4. V. D. Lipman, *Social History of the Jews in England, 1850–1950* (London,
1954), p. 90.

5. For the early development of the immigrant community in Manchester, see B.
Williams, *The Making of Manchester Jewry 1740–1875* (Manchester, 1976),
pp. 268–97.

6. J. Webber, 'Between Law and Custom: Women's Experience of Judaism', in
P. Holden (ed.), *Women's Religious Experience* (London, 1983), pp. 144–5.

7. For general historical accounts of Jewish life in Eastern Europe, see R.
Mahler, *A History of Modern Jewry 1780–1815* (London, 1971); and S. Baron, *The
Russian Jew under Tsars and Soviets* (London, 1964). A useful compilation of
source material is given in D. K. Roskies and D. G. Roskies, *The Shtetl Book* (New
York, 1979); and a more idealised view of *shtetl* life in M. Zborowski and E.
Herzog, *Life is with People* (New York, 1952). For an account with particular
reference to women, see P. Baum, P. Hyman and S. Michel, *The Jewish Woman in
America* (New York, 1977), pp. 55–89.

8. See E. Mendelsohn, *Class Struggle in the Pale: The Formative Years of the Jewish Workers' Movement in Tsarist Russia* (London, 1970).

9. The importance of religious learning for male status is more fully discussed in R. Burman, 'The Jewish woman as breadwinner: the changing value of women's work in a Manchester immigrant community', *Oral History*, X (1982), pp. 27–39.

10. A lively account of such match-making is given in N. Marsden (ed.), *A Jewish Life under the Tsars: the Autobiography of Chaim Aronson, 1825–1888* (Totowa, NJ, 1983), p. 28. See R. Burman, 'The Jewish woman', p. 34, for reference to an 'examiner of prospective bridegrooms', employed by wealthy but unlearned men eager for a scholarly son-in-law.

11. A detailed survey of women's status in Jewish law is provided in M. Meiselman, *Jewish Woman in Jewish Law* (New York, 1978). See also P. Hyman, 'The Other Half: Women in the Jewish Tradition', in E. Koltun (ed.), *The Jewish Woman* (New York, 1976), pp. 105–113.

12. See, for example, Esther Kreitman's autobiographical novel, *Deborah* (London, 1983; first published 1946). Women were generally literate only in Yiddish; in some cases, however, their exclusion from formal religious instruction and more open interaction with the wider society gave them more opportunity to learn the local vernacular. See R. Burman, 'The Jewish Woman', p. 30.

13. Interview B1.

14. Burman, 'The Jewish Woman', p. 35.

15. I. Abrahams, *Jewish Life in the Middle Ages* (London, 1932), pp. 303–4.

16. It has been estimated that, by 1880, 14.6% of London's Jewish population was upper or upper-middle class, with incomes over £1,000 per annum, and 42.2% were middle class, with incomes between £200 and £1,000. See Joseph Jacobs's statistical study of 1883, cited by V. D. Lipman, 'The development of London Jewry', in S. Levin (ed.), *A Century of Anglo-Jewish Life* (London, 1970), p. 47.

See C. Bermant, *The Cousinhood: the Anglo-Jewish Gentry* (London, 1971); and L. Gartner, *The Jewish Immigrant in England 1870–1914* (London, 1960), p. 21.

17. For the integration of these families into English life, see Bermant, *The Cousinhood*; V. D. Lipman, 'The Age of Emancipation 1815–1880', in V. D. Lipman (ed.), *Three Centuries of Anglo-Jewish History* (Cambridge, 1961), pp. 76–7; and, for Manchester, Williams, *Manchester Jewry*, pp. 335–7.

18. L. Davidoff, J. L'Esperance and H. Newby, 'Landscape with Figures: Home and Community in English Society', in A. Oakley and J. Mitchell (eds), *The Rights and Wrongs of Women* (Harmondsworth, 1976), pp. 139–75; and L. Davidoff, 'The Separation of Home and Work? Landladies and Lodgers in Nineteenth and Twentieth Century England', in S. Burman (ed.), *Fit Work for Women* (London, 1979), pp. 64–97.

19. C. Hall, 'The Early Formation of the Victorian Domestic Ideology', in S. Burman (ed.), *Fit Work*, pp. 15–32.

20. G. Aguilar, *The Women of Israel* (London, 1886), pp. 570–1. Aguilar (1816–47) wrote a number of novels directed to women, such as *Home Influence*, *The Mother's Recompense*, and *Women's Friendship*. See Sondra Henry and Emily Taitz, *Written Out of History: Our Jewish Foremothers* (Fresh Meadows, NY, 1983), pp. 283–8.

21. Ibid., pp. 573–4.

22. See F. K. Prochaska, *Women and Philanthropy in 19th Century England* (Oxford, 1980), pp. 5–8, for a discussion of the relation of philanthropy to women's perceived 'nature' and 'mission'.

23. *Jewish Chronicle*, 21 February 1902.

24. *Jewish Chronicle*, 25 April 1902.

25. *Jewish Chronicle*, 20 October 1899.

26. 'Occupation and Recreation of our Work Girls', *Jewish Chronicle*, 25 July 1902.

27. Ibid.

28. See E. de Bruin, 'Judaism and womanhood', *Westminster Review*, CLXXX (1913), pp. 124–30; and G. Spielmann, 'Woman's place in the synagogue', *Jewish Review*, IV (1913), pp. 24–35.

29. 'The Empty Benches and How to Fill Them' represented a theme of some concern in the *Jewish Chronicle* (e.g. I. Spielmann, 3 May 1899). The 1903 survey of church attendance showed the proportion of women attending London churches to be higher than that of men, except in the borough of Stepney, where synagogues were largely attended by men; H. McLeod, *Class and Religion in the Late Victorian City* (London, 1974), p. 30.

30. L. Montague, *The Faith of a Jewish Woman* (London, 1943), p. 13.

31. S. Oppenheim, 'Women's suffrage in the United Synagogue', *Jewish Chronicle*, 17 November 1899; 'An open letter to the members of the United Synagogue', *Jewish Chronicle*, 26 April 1901.

32. S. Bayme, 'Claude Montefiore, Lily Montagu and the Origins of the Jewish Religious Union', *Transactions of the Jewish Historical Society of England*, XXVII (1982), p. 63.

33. Ibid., p. 65.

34. Montagu, *The Faith*, pp. 38–42.

35. Bayme ('Claude Montefiore', p. 67) notes that as long as the Jewish Religious Union remained an ideological unit, holding private services, it incited little communal concern. But in breaking institutional ranks and establishing its own synagogue, it challenged influential prerogatives and evoked intense opposition.

36. *Jewish Chronicle*, 8 November 1912.

37. *Jewish League for Women's Suffrage, 1st Annual Report, 1913–1914*, pp. 12–13 (Fawcett Library, London). A. Newman, *The United Synagogue 1870–1970* (London, 1977), p. 197.

38. See Gartner, *Jewish Immigrant*, for an account of immigrant life in London, and Williams, *Manchester Jewry*, pp. 268–97, for the development of the immigrant community in Manchester.

39. Interview B16.

40. See interviews B13, B17, B18, and B15.

41. Interview B19.

42. Interview B2.

43. Interview B3.

44. Interview A1. 'Singer' is a pseudonym. Purim is the 'Feast of Lots', when the Book of Esther is read.

45. See J. Kugelmass and J. Boyarin, *From a Ruined Garden: The Memorial Books of Polish Jewry* (New York, 1983), pp. 76–8.

46. I. W. Slotki, *Seventy Years of Hebrew Education, 1880–1950* (Manchester, 1950), pp. 9–10.

47. Ibid.

48. Ibid.

49. Ibid., p. 71.

50. Interview B5. See also interview B4.

51. Interview A1.

52. Interview B6. Solomon Ben Isaac Rashi (1040–1105) was a leading commentator on the Bible and Talmud.

Although Yiddish declined with remarkable rapidity in England, this particular woman did learn to read and write Yiddish, and later used it in correspondence with her parents.

53. Interview B6.

54. Interview B7. Rabbi Shlosberg, a well-known figure of the immigrant area in Manchester, who was nicknamed 'The Penny Rov', as he would not charge more than a penny to housewives who came to ask a *sheilah*, is mentioned in interviews

B10 and B13.

55. Interview B16.

56. Interview B7.

57. Interview B21.

58. Interview B20.

59. Interview A1.

60. Interview B22.

61. Interview B15.

62. Interview B7.

63. It should be noted that in only 22 cases was information available regarding *mikveh* attendance.

64. Interview B23.

65. Interview B8.

66. Interview B27.

67. *Jewish Chronicle*, 1 April 1921, p. 17.

68. The daughter of a third generation English mother and a prosperous Lithuanian father notes that her family had separate pantries for meat and dairy produce; the kitchen was the province of the cook and housemaid and she had to knock before entering. She recalls that her family ate roast beef and Yorkshire pudding on a Sunday, and describes her mother's religion as 'a sort of anglicised *Yiddishkeit* [Jewishness] which . . . doesn't happen any more'. Interview B8.

69. Interview B9.

70. A detailed examination of the attitudes of the members of the Anglo-Jewish establishment and the impact of the institutions which they provided in Manchester for the immigrants' children is given in R. Livshin, 'Aspects of the Acculturation of the Children of Immigrant Jews in Manchester 1890–1930' (M.Ed. thesis, Manchester University, 1982).

71. Rev. A. L. Green, reported in the *Jewish Chronicle*, 1 April 1881.

72. B. Spiers, *Dibrey Debrash. Part 1. Eighteen Ethical Sermons Delivered to the Working Classes* (London, 1901), p. 11. Spiers was a member of the London *Beth Din*, the principal Jewish ecclesiastical court in England.

73. Gartner, *Jewish Immigrant*, p. 195, citing a paper delivered by Harry S. Lewis to the West End Synagogue Society and quoted in the *Jewish Chronicle*, 20 February 1903.

74. Interview A2.

75. Interview A3. For a further discussion of Sabbath work among Jewish immigrants, see B. Williams, 'The Jewish Immigrant in Manchester: The Contribution of Oral History', *Oral History*, VII (1979), pp. 44–7.

76. See Gartner, *Jewish Immigrant*, p. 195.

77. See, for example, the account of a man who was sent as a boy to a *Yeshiva* (religious college) by his father, a synagogue official, who wanted him to become a rabbi; he left, however, to work as a waterproof-garment maker. Interview B10.

78. Gartner, *Jewish Immigrant*, p. 268.

79. Interview B11.

80. Interview B7.

81. Good examples are interviews A2, B12 and B16. A similar point is made by Marion Kaplan in 'Priestess and Hausfrau: Women and tradition in the German-Jewish Family', in S. Cohen and P. Hyman (eds), *The Evolving Jewish Family* (New York, 1984).

82. J. Eker, 'Good-bye, Cheetham Hill', unpublished memoir (written 1976), in archives of the Manchester Jewish Museum. This memoir covers the period from the turn of the century to 1930. Eker was born in 1902 in Cheetham, Manchester, to Russian parents who had emigrated to England in 1890. The special Sabbath atmosphere is also evoked in J. White, *Rothschild Buildings: Life in an East End Tower Block 1887–1920* (London, 1980), pp. 90–1.

83. Livshin, 'Aspects', pp. 277–84.

84. Interview B22.

85. Interview B14.

86. Livshin, 'Aspects', pp. 208–20.

87. *Jewish Chronicle*, 24 February 1922.

88. Slotki, *Seventy Years*, p. 71.

89. B. Kosmin and C. Levy, *Jewish Identity in an Anglo-Jewish Community* (London, 1983). The survey was carried out in 1978.

90. These low figures for synagogue attendance contrasted with a high level of synagogue affiliation; ibid., p. 7, shows only 8.8% of households or 10.7% of individuals to be unaffiliated.

91. Ibid., pp. 16, 39. The survey indicated 3.4% cases of mixed marriages, with 88.8% of parents opposed to any potential out-marriage. This contrasted with a survey in Los Angeles, California. Here Sabbath candles were lit in only 18% of the households surveyed, and 74% of the sample indicated they would accept their children's marriage to a non-Jew. N. C. Sandberg and G. N. Levine, *The Changing Character of the Los Angeles Jewish Community* (Los Angeles, 1980), cited in Kosmin and Levy, *Jewish Identity*, p. 39.

92. See A. L. Epstein, *Ethos and Identity* (London, 1978), pp. 101–2; and S. Wallman, 'The Boundaries of "Race": Processes of Ethnicity in England', *Man*, XIII (1978), pp. 200–17.

93. Gartner, *Jewish Immigrant*, p. 273.

Chapter 11

The Beginnings of Church Feminism: Women and the Councils of the Church of England, 1897–1919*

Brian Heeney

Historians of the Church of England have paid little attention to the women's movement. There have been several serious studies of religious communities for women, and there is increasing interest in churchwomen's part in Victorian philanthropy and moral reform. Studies of Victorian marriage and family life have an important religious dimension. Alan Wilkinson's recent book on *The Church of England and the First World War* makes a number of references to women's work and aspirations, subjects virtually excluded from Roger Lloyd's standard history of the twentieth-century church.[1] The history of women's place in the management and recognised ministry of the Church of England, in its institutional life at local, regional and national levels, has not been touched.

Among historians whose professional interest does not extend beyond Victoria's death this neglect is not surprising; for until the twentieth century women occupied virtually no positions of leadership or responsibility in the official life of the Church at any level.[2] They served neither in the ordained ministry not on the consultative bodies which were somewhat tentatively established during the latter half of the nineteenth century to give laymen a voice in church policy in parishes, dioceses and in the national Church as a whole. They were excluded both from spiritual leadership and from secular management. Women's sphere in the late Victorian Church was decidedly subordinate, limited and controlled everywhere by the authority of men. In the words of a *Guardian* editorial (6 March 1919) women were 'no more than hewers of wood and drawers of water for the Church'.

Nevertheless, an enormous amount of work was done by Victorian women as Church agents (to say nothing of the large and varied philanthropic and educational activity undertaken from Christian motives, but organised independently of the Church system).[3] Looking back over seventy years in 1919, a committee appointed by the archbishop of Canterbury to study *The Ministry of Women* attributed much of 'the immense expansion of activity and of efficiency in ministry to the religious needs of the people' to 'the wonderful work accomplished by the mainly voluntary efforts of women'. Voluntary effort was supplemented by the labours of paid workers of various types and by the growing number of women committed to the religious life. The archbishop's committee wondered at the 'extraordinary amount of good work . . . achieved by women' since 1850 'under the different heads of district visiting, Sunday-school teaching, Church music, parochial clubs, missionary societies, study circles, rescue and preventive agencies, besides the larger organisations represented by the Sisterhoods and the Deaconess Institutions, by the Girls' Friendly Society and the Mothers' Union'. Added to all these were the accomplishments of 'hundreds . . . of wives, widows and daughters of clergymen, and of single women, who in obscurity have dedicated their lives and their substance to the promotion of the Kingdom of God in our own country and in heathen lands'. The standard response of bishops and other Church Congress speakers to this record of devotion and activity was a combination of condescending gratitude and tedious warnings about the danger of women abandoning home and family in favour of outside work, even work universally accepted as within their proper sphere. The Church was very reluctant to encourage initiative and independence among its female adherents; even after the first World War women church workers, according to the Archbishop's Committee, had 'no defined status' and received 'no official recognition' or 'authorisation' from the leaders of the Church.[4]

The quantity and variety of women's work was matched by a very high level of female participation in the worship of the late Victorian and Edwardian Church. Anxiety about the high proportion of women at religious services was evident from about 1880. It was intensified by Charles Booth's discovery that, in London, 'the female sex forms the mainstay of every religious assembly of whatever class', and by the statistics in Richard Mudie-Smith's survey of *The Religious Life of London* at the beginning of the new century which showed that nearly twice as many women attended Church of England services as men.[5]

In the same years that women became increasingly prominent in the day-to-day work and the worship of the Church in these ways, two related developments emerged on the English scene: the feminist cause and the movement to provide the Church of England with machinery for self-government including lay participation.

Feminists devoted themselves to raising women from subordination to equal status with men, to elevating them from legal and customary inferiority, to liberating them from stereotyped roles. Feminists were committed to expanding women's place in public life. Theirs was a cause with many sides, and much was achieved between 1850 and 1900. Institutions for the education of women at secondary and university levels were established and developed. Women's opportunities for independent careers grew, and included clerical and secretarial work as well as the rapidly expanding professions of teaching and nursing, and the traditionally male domain of medicine. Legislation was passed providing protection for wives and security for their property against exploitation by their husbands. Women participated vigorously in the National Association for the Promotion of Social Science from the late 1850s and, a decade later, led the campaign against the state regulation of prostitution and the double standard of morality that system implied. From 1869 women voted in borough elections; in the following year they gained the rights to vote for, and to serve on, school boards set up by the Education Act of 1870. From 1875 women were Poor Law guardians, and after 1888 they were chosen as county councillors although their right to sit on such councils was not secure until 1907. Just before the Second Reform Act, John Stuart Mill presented a petition to the House of Commons, signed by 1,499 women, demanding that franchise reform include votes for women. From that point the organised suffragist movement existed, although it was not until the National Union of Women's Suffrage Societies was established in 1897 that an effective and vigorous campaign was really launched.[6]

Late Victorian feminism was stimulated by the expansion of the male franchise in successive reform acts, and by the growing participation of adult males in national politics. There is no evidence that this trend in the direction of a democratic system of representation had any more influence in hastening ecclesiastical change than did the widening of women's place in public life or the development of feminist theory. Nevertheless, Church democracy matured more rapidly than did Church feminism. Whereas women's exclusion from the government and ministry of the Church continued and was little challenged before 1900, by the beginning of the new century laymen increasingly participated in ecclesiastical discussion and decision-making. The Church did not develop representative institutions before 1900, and the constitutional Church Assembly appeared only after World War I; yet the way was prepared in the previous years as laymen took a growing part in discussions at Church Congresses, diocesan conferences, voluntary parochial councils and the houses of laymen attached to the two Convocations.

In mid-Victorian times the Church felt threatened by militant dissenters committed to the Disestablishment cause, a threat which Gladstone himself seemed to emphasise as late as 1885 in his address to the electors of Midlothian.[7] Safeguarding the Establishment meant rallying the Church's defenders, encouraging faithful laymen to co-operate with bishops and clergy to ward off the evil day. From the early 1860s, annual Church Congresses provided regular national occasions for such co-operation for discussion of Church defence and reform. The Congresses were not representative or authoritative bodies; votes were not taken at any of their sessions, nor were decisions made. Anyone interested in Church affairs could attend a Church Congress, and women were admitted at an early stage although their contributions to discussion were expressed through male proxies until 1885 when Miss Agnes Weston read her own paper, a practice which was customary from then on.[8]

At the local level, the abolition of compulsory Church rates in 1868, and the establishment of secular parish councils twenty-eight years later, stripped the vestries of their general political interest and civil power. From the 1860s bishops encouraged the formation of voluntary parish councils for ecclesiastical purposes. As interest in these gained momentum in the 1890s they became an important means by which laymen were included in Church affairs at the parochial level. Beginning at Ely in 1866, diocesan conferences extended this form of lay participation; by the early 1880s nearly all dioceses held such conferences regularly.[9] In some places laymen shared in discussions at rural deanery meetings as well. Under the leadership of Archbishop Benson, a lay house of the Canterbury Convocation was created in 1885. Although it had no power and met only to be consulted by the bishops and clergy, its regular gathering from 1886 (1892 in York) marked yet another advance in lay-co-operation.

The early involvement of laymen in Church councils was a

response to external threat, an aspect of Church defence against dissenters and Disestablishment. From the 1890s the advocates of Church self-government, and of lay co-operation, often took a more positive line. In 1896 the Church Reform League was founded; a year later it published a pamphlet entitled *Reform of the Church* in which the cause of self-government within the framework of Establishment was linked to sweeping reform of Church patronage, discipline and finance. The reform movement was joined to social responsibility and even radicalism, especially in the minds of liberal Anglo-Catholics, Charles Gore and Henry Scott Holland and, later on, in the person of William Temple, the leading spirit in the Life and Liberty movement of 1917. Just as the feminist cause blossomed in Edwardian England and during the Great War, so the movement for self-government in the Church, and for the participation of laymen in that government, matured in the twenty years before the Treaty of Versailles.[10]

I

On 13 May 1897 the bishops in the Upper House of Canterbury Convocation adopted six resolutions designed to 'quicken the life and strengthen the work of the Church' by encouraging the formation of parochial church councils. The fourth proposal stipulated that 'elected councillors be male communicants of the Church of England of full age'. The bishops hesitated before accepting the word 'male'; a move to delete it was defeated, in fact, by only two votes. Their evident reluctance to rule out the election of women was caused by the bishop of Salisbury's revelation that he had two female churchwardens in his diocese and by the bishop of Chichester's assertion that there was 'an appreciable number' of women wardens.[11] As all churchwardens were to be put on the proposed councils as *ex officio* members, some bishops could see no reason to exclude women who might achieve the same position by election.

It was this very close vote by the bishops that provoked the first clear expression of Church feminism. In February 1898 a petition, signed by 1,100 churchwomen, was presented to the Upper House protesting against its ban on female candidates for election to parochial church councils. When the offending resolution of the previous May came before the clergy in the Lower House of

Convocation on 4 February, this protest was very much in the minds of the debaters. Another effort was made to expunge the word 'male'. The anomaly of women's eligibility for *ex officio* membership on councils as churchwardens was pressed hard. Furthermore, it was argued that country parishes would experience a shortage of suitable candidates for office were women to be excluded. Other more positive reasons were also brought forward for opening the councils to women. The dean of St Paul's (Robert Gregory) pointed out that the new bodies were to deal with 'practical questions connected with parish matters', the very issues and affairs about which women knew most and often made the largest contributions. Dean Gregory believed, too, that women were often 'the most devotional persons in the parish . . . the kind of people over whom the clergyman had most influence' and who would be most helpful to him. Members of Convocation need not fear that opening the councils to women committed them in the slightest degree on the issues or methods of the women's movement in secular politics. Gregory 'did not think that the female suffrage was the least involved' and he observed that women candidates for parochial councils

> would not be required to stand up and make speeches before they were elected, for it was hoped that the elections would be carried out on a far quieter system and would not require exhibitions of that sort.

The dean's arguments and assurances had very little effect on the ideas and fears of most of his colleagues in Convocation. Anxiety was more prominent than thought among the opponents of women councillors. Archdeacon R. P. Lightfoot feared that 'the most truly feminine women' would refuse to seek election. On the other hand if Convocation 'opened the door at all, there was no limit to the number of places on the council that women might occupy'. Would not a council 'composed very largely of women' be a weak instrument in local public affairs? Deeper questions bothered Archdeacon E. G. Sandford of Exeter. In his view women were not made by God to engage in public discussion, to debate and decide matters in a public forum, even a voluntary parochial church council without statutory powers. This sort of activity lay outside their proper sphere as it had been established by the Almighty and defined in Holy Scripture with admirable clarity by St Paul. Keen as he was to encourage women to work for the Church, he was determined to keep them out of those councils which, he thought, 'came near' to doing 'the governing work of the Church'. He saw a 'real danger lest the distinction between sex and sex should be forgotten', a danger very clear in one view 'of the position of women now finding favour in many quarters'. He went on:

> The very fact that a large body of women were agitating in this very matter seemed to show that there was something behind and beyond the mere wish that had been expressed that day.

Sandford and his allies easily won the debate and the exclusion of women from parochial church councils was maintained in the Lower House of Convocation by a vote of 39 to 18. The right of women to vote was never questioned. Sandford himself stated that 'no one would wish to exclude women from being amongst the electors for their Councils'. All voters, according to an agreed resolution, were to be '*bona fide* members of the Church of England, resident in the parish, and of full age'.[12]

By this deliberate decision of an all-male, all-clerical assembly, women were formally excluded from election to voluntary parochial church councils. The ban stood for sixteen years, although it was apparently sometimes overlooked.[13] The exclusion was much resented by Louise Creighton, wife of the bishop of London, a leading figure in the women's movement, and an exceptionally able and independent-minded person. At the Church Congress in 1899, Mrs Creighton chaired a session on 'The Training and Payment of Women Church Workers'. She asked why it was that 'in these days the best women do not devote their energies to what may, strictly speaking, be called Church work'? Among the answers she offered to her own question was the failure of Church leaders to sympathise with the women's movement. Although Church leaders

> welcomed the establishment of sisterhoods and encouraged means by which women might help the work of the clergy in their parish, they looked jealously on anything like independence of work or opinion on the part of women.

This attitude, she stated, was evident 'in the movement which would exclude women from the membership of Church councils, a movement which . . . must tend to alienate thinking women from parish work', and has had the disastrous effect of sharply separating the 'more advanced modern woman' from the Church.[14]

Church feminism was created by this skirmish over representation on parochial church councils; it was established by the protracted and confusing debate about women's right to vote indirectly for members of the Representative Church Council, the unofficial precursor of the Church Assembly.

Enthusiasts for Church self-government were encouraged when, in 1899, Arthur Balfour declared in parliament his desire to see 'greater spiritual autonomy' given to the Church of England. However, an attempt by Sir Richard Jebb to persuade the House of Commons to pass a 'Convocations Bill' providing for an authoritative Church legislature with lay representation failed in 1900, and it was clear that the direct parliamentary route to Church reform was blocked. Unwilling to facilitate self-government, parliament could not itself find time to deal with Church matters.[15] It was this parliamentary incapacity, rather than theoretical belief in spiritual autonomy, which persuaded Archbishop Randall Davidson that the Church must be enabled to govern itself, though within the framework of the Establishment. In 1902 the two Convocations and their associated Houses of Laymen decided to meet together the following July in order to create a representative legislative body. It would have no statutory power and could pass no laws for the Church; but churchmen believed it might commend itself to parliament and achieve constitutional status in the future.

The joint meeting of six 'houses' met in July 1903[16] and considered, among other things, the question of how, and by whom, the lay delegates to the Representative Church Council were to be elected, i.e. the 'lay franchise'. As a part of this discussion the women's franchise in Church elections was raised.

The issue of women serving as representatives on the proposed Council was never argued in 1903. It was agreed that 'representatives elected by the lay electors shall be of the male sex', hardly surprising in view of the ineligibility of women for the office of councillor even at the parish level.[17] On the other hand, women had been accustomed to vote for representatives in those parishes which had adopted voluntary councils, and it was not unreasonable for them to expect the vote in the election of lay representatives to higher councils, whether diocesan or national.

This was not to be. A scheme, drafted to include some female voters, was brought to the joint meeting of Convocation and Lay

Houses in July 1903. It contained a proposal for a dual 'initial franchise': men were eligible either as 'qualified to vote at the election of churchwardens' or simply as communicants; women, on the other hand, were denied the second option. Thus, fulfilment of a spiritual requirement only (communicant status) would give the vote to men. Women, no matter how committed to the Church, no matter how hard-working in parochial affairs, could achieve the parish franchise only as occupiers or ratepayers, on an entirely secular basis.[18]

Lord Hugh Cecil, perhaps the most eloquent opponent of the women's cause, launched an attack on this double standard. The proposers of the draft franchise, he argued,

> were making the household qualification the true Church qualification, because by drawing a distinction between women householders and women communicants they made out that to be a householder was more important from a Church point of view than to be a communicant.

To eliminate this inconsistency, Lord Hugh moved that the franchise be confined to male communicants only. By a vote of 90 to 60 the joint meeting of the two Convocations and Houses of Laymen accepted this amendment and so decided to exclude women entirely from any share in the selection of lay delegates to the first Representative Church Council. The success of Lord Hugh's amendment did more than this. Election of lay delegates to the Representative Church Council was to be indirect; they were to be chosen by laymen at diocesan conferences, who, in turn, were elected by parochial church councils. Consequently the 'initial franchise' from which women were excluded in 1903 was that for members on local parochial councils, a suffrage they had hitherto exercised in parishes which had established such councils.[19]

Reaction among churchwomen and those churchmen who espoused their cause was strong. At the Church Congress in October 1903 Charles Gore (then bishop of Worcester) described the exclusion of women from the Church suffrage as 'a great act of injustice'. Were it allowed to stand

> schoolmistresses, district visitors, the parson's wife, the squire's wife and many others who have been the very mainstay of the life of the Church . . . [would] be excluded from expressing their opinions in the election of the representatives.

At the same Congress Mrs Arthur Phillp, honorary secretary of the Mothers' Union in Worcester and secretary of the Ministering Children's League, representing, she said, 'women in the North and the Midlands', expressed the deep hurt and offence felt by even the most conservative churchwomen. She had no desire 'to be upon any Church Council, or to speak in any public places'; but to be denied the vote was an insult to women whose 'Churchmanship was their whole life'. She urged the men responsible to 'take . . . every means you can to get this matter reconsidered'.[20]

When Canterbury Convocation met in February 1904, Randall Davidson insisted on just such a reconsideration. He and others deplored the haste with which the question of the women's franchise had been decided, and the archbishop admitted that his request for a reconsideration of the July decision was prompted by pressure from advocates of the women's cause. Again, as at the 1903 Church Congress, Gore regretted what he described as the 'positively and definitely retrograde step' of utterly excluding women from the Church franchise, and he warned against alienating women workers whose claim was 'of the gravest and widest kind'. E. S. Talbot, bishop of Rochester, supported Gore, and explicitly drew the parallel between the movement for laymen's rights and the women's cause in the Church, urging churchmen 'to do more justice to the fundamental principle of the equality before God of male and female'. Unless the Church paid due attention to that principle, women might be tempted to insist on its indiscriminate application, demanding admission to the priesthood, seeking even to alter 'the condition under which the seat which his Grace now occupied was held'.[21]

After vigorous debate in both Houses, Convocation decided, on 4 February, to ask the first meeting of the Representative Church Council to reconsider the complete exclusion of women as electors. When that Council met on 8 July 1904, Davidson, Gore and their allies (notably two prominent ecclesiastical lawyers, Sir Lewis Dibdin and P. V. Smith) persuaded a majority of delegates to request that a committee be appointed to devise an extension of the lay franchise 'so as not wholly to exclude women'.[22]

The committee, chaired by Bishop Herbert Ryle of Winchester, included Gore, Talbot and other advocates of the woman's franchise as well as stalwart opponents such as Henry Wace, dean of Canterbury, J. L. Darby, dean of Chester, and two members of the Cecil family, Lord Salisbury himself and Lord Hugh. The committee spent more than a year on this and other constitutional problems; when it reported in November 1905, it proposed a double standard for the initial franchise very like that originally brought forward in 1903. Whereas all authentic churchmen would be qualified to vote for parochial lay representatives, only church-women who were 'entitled by ownership or occupation to vote at a vestry of the parish' received the franchise.[23]

This was somewhat unenthusiastically introduced by Bishop Gore to a thinly attended meeting of the Representative Church Council on 1 December 1905. He explained that it 'practically meant that women who would be entitled to the vote in municipal affairs should also be entitled to vote in ecclesiastical affairs', and he admitted that this was as much as could be achieved 'in present conditions'. In fact it was approved by the Council after very little debate.[24]

This reluctant concession gained women very little power. Early in 1905, while the Ryle committee was still deliberating, the *Guardian* argued that women should have the initial franchise without restrictions, 'on an equal footing with men'. Even such a relatively liberal arrangement would have given women small political might. Assuming the numerical superiority of women voters in parish elections, the *Guardian* (8 February 1905) assured its readers that

> the balance will always be redressed, because the most they can do will be to vote for men who will vote for other men who will elect the Lay House. Moreover the other two Houses of the Representative Church Council will consist of men chosen by men.

As the property qualification further limited the number of women voters in the initial elections, it is hardly surprising that church-women viewed the franchise of 1905 as less than excitingly demo-cratic. Nevertheless, it remained the basis of women's participation in the government of the Church of England until 1914.

Within the Representative Church Council itself neither the female franchise nor women's representation at any level of Church council was seriously debated again until 1911 when Charles Gore (by then bishop of Oxford) again took up their cause. On 22 November he persuaded the Council to agree that

> it is desirable that a Committee be appointed to consider afresh

the question of the Franchise of Women in the election of representatives of the laity in Ruri-decanal and Diocesan Conferences,
and consequently in the House of Laymen.[25]

The result of that committee's work was scrutinised by yet another
committee, chaired by the bishop of Southwell, Edwyn Hoskins,
which was reviewing the whole range of problems connected with
lay representation. In its report to the Representative Church
Council on 9 July 1914, Hoskins's committee recommended not
only that 'women be admitted to the parochial lay franchise on the
same terms as men', but also that women be permitted to serve as
representatives on parochial councils, although to a maximum of
one-third of the available places on each Council. In the course of
debate, the numerical limitation was removed, and women were
declared eligible for all of the available lay seats on each local
council. They remained barred from ruridecanal, diocesan and
central councils.[26]

These concessions, modest as they appeared to feminists in 1914,
were won in the teeth of fierce opposition within the Council.
Those who fought the women's battle in debate stressed their fear
that able and politically conscious women were rapidly becoming
alienated from the Church. If churchmen 'thwarted the desire of
women to work with them upon the Councils of the Church',
Bishop Hoskins was certain that they would 'drive a great many of
their best women out of the life of their Church and out of Church
work into social organisations, and into political work'. He was
supported in this view by Cosmo Gordon Lang, archbishop of
York, and by Bishop Winnington-Ingram of London, who said
that the Council could not deliver 'a greater blow to the Church'
than to bar women's participation in its political life. 'They were
face to face . . . with a new thing in the world. The women were
waking up to knowing things that they never knew before.'[27]

While the Church advanced with such extreme caution to expand
women's role in its councils, the movement for women's parliamentary suffrage moved to the centre of the British political stage,
gaining particular notoriety when the WSPU, the 'suffragettes',
adopted militant tactics. There were many ardent Anglicans in
suffragist ranks, including not only well-known activists, such as
Maude Royden and Edith Picton-Turbervill, but also that most
stable and influential of Edwardian churchwomen, Louise
Creighton, whose leading role in women's Church organisations

was matched by her national prominence in secular bodies and government agencies. Many of these ladies belonged to the Church League for Women's Suffrage, founded in 1909 by the Reverend Claude Hinscliff, who continued for many years as its secretary.[28] Although the first aim of the League was to 'secure for women the Parliamentary vote as it is or may be granted to men', and to do so by non-militant means, it also sought to draw out what its founder called 'the deep religious significance of the woman's movement'.[29] Special celebrations of the Eucharist were held for suffragists and meetings were devoted to discussion of the spiritual dimension of the cause. In August 1912, the CLWS had more than 3,000 members, and by April 1914 this had increased to 'over 5,000 churchmen and churchwomen' whose primary commitment to the parliamentary cause still left some energy to lobby for women's rights to elect and serve on Church Councils.[30] 'In Church matters', wrote CLWS member, A. Laura Hills, to the *Guardian* on 23 August 1912,

> where women are notoriously the largest givers and keenest workers the injustice of no representation is especially great, as they have no voice in Convocation, Houses of Laymen, or Ruridecanal conferences. They are not even considered persons according to the S.P.G. charter . . . It behoves all women to work together to remove such anomalies.

Archbishop Davidson, who was privately a passive suffragist in the parliamentary campaign, had considerable difficulty maintaining his customary noncommittal public stance as the women's struggle intensified. Between 1908 and 1914 militants put pressure on Davidson, particularly between January and September 1914, in connection with the effects of forcible feeding of imprisoned women and the notorious 'Cat and Mouse Act'. Those who wrote to him at this time condemned him for failing to rescue, or even to pray for, the brave persecuted suffragettes, and damned him for toadying to a heartless government. He was unjustly accused of ill-treating Annie Kenney, a suffragette who was arrested in Lambeth Palace after she refused to leave.[31] One group which took a particularly harsh line with the archbishop was the Suffragist Churchwomen's Protest Committee, whose secretary, Mrs Alice Kidd, condemned the 'servile attitude of the Heads of the Church towards an unjust and irresponsible government'. In October of that year, two months after the outbreak of the first World War, the Protest Committee sent the archbishop a letter, signed by forty-eight women, which began:

We, the undersigned women, members of the Church of England, do hereby protest against the attitude of the Church towards the Woman's Movement for reform, and towards her claim for enfranchisement, both in Church and State.[32]

The campaign for the Parliamentary suffrage thus reinforced the Church cause. Churchmen also experienced pressure directly on the ecclesiastical issue. Emma Paget, wife of the bishop of Stepney, went about talking to groups on the subject of women's representation in councils; in March 1914 she wrote to the archbishop for guidance and recommended that he push the matter forward.[33] Davidson, in turn, urged the bishop of Southwell to speed up the work of his committee on lay representation in the Representative Church Council. Long before that committee's report was accepted in the autumn of 1914, the Church press carried letters and articles pointing out both the expediency and the justice of a larger role for women in Church affairs. One such was that from 'Cornelia' in the *Guardian* of 1 December 1909. She deplored 'the depreciation of women's work and total ignoring of their status in the Church', and she thought that

it speaks volumes for the earnestness and devotion of the faithful daughters of the Church that in spite of the almost universal neglect of their interests by the clergy, and the determined ignoring of their claims to recognition on her governing bodies, they still remain loyal:

On 5 January 1912 another *Guardian* correspondent, a member of the CLWS, described an African native congregation in which the women were included in decision-making:

This infant Church evidently recognises the right and necessity of women to express officially an opinion on religious and social life — a right doubtfully debated for English Churchwomen after centuries of Christianity.

In 1915 the Church League for Women's Suffrage deliberately

concentrated its efforts on the campaign to gain for women the full rights of laity in the Church, including equal political rights on Church councils. In a petition to the Representative Church Council the League protested

1. That the exclusion of women from the Ruridecanal and Diocesan Conferences and from the Representative Church Council is an infraction of that spiritual equality of the sexes which is a fundamental principle of the Christian faith. 2. That it forbids the direct expression in these assemblies of women's views upon questions . . . upon all of which women claim the right to be heard, and upon some of which they can almost claim a monopoly of first-hand knowledge. 3. That the authority of the decisions of such assemblies is thereby weakened. 4. That a stumbling-block is thereby placed in the path of many women who regard their exclusion, deliberately decreed, as an infringement of their spiritual status . . . 5. That all women are thereby deprived of the stimulus that comes from the sense of equal opportunity and responsibility for both sexes alike.[34]

Some conservative-minded churchmen expressed alarm that Church feminists (Maude Royden among them) were taking the opportunity of wartime conditions to launch an agitation for the ordination of women to the priesthood, and in 1916 a controversy developed about the participation of women as preachers in the National Mission.[35] In these ways women's place in the ministry of Word and Sacraments became associated with the question of their rights in the councils of the Church during the war years. It was an association which anti-feminist Churchmen thought as inevitable as it was unpleasant, and one which prudent Church feminists tried to play down.

Feminist agitation was not the only 'pressure from without' felt by Church leaders on the subject of the women's franchise and their place on Church councils. The non-statutory character of all ecclesiastical assemblies containing laymen, and the absence of any national authority in the Church, resulted in a lack of uniformity and undisciplined variety of practice, carrying the threat of chaos. It is clear that some voluntary parish councils did have women members despite the action of Convocation in 1898 and of the Representative Church Council later. Sir Lewis Dibdin was alarmed to discover in 1909 that the diocese of Canterbury admitted 'women voters on the same level as men'. 'It was obvious', he thought, 'that they could not have one rule for female representation in one diocese and a different rule in another.' In the diocese of Rochester all churchwardens could be members of ruridecanal conferences, and were also *ex officio* members of the Diocesan Conferences; in that diocese women could occupy positions unattainable by their sisters in other parts of the Church. By 1913 the situation in Sodor and Man was even looser; women could vote for and be elected to the Diocesan Conference. According to one resident:

> There are at present three who have been so elected. One of them some time ago read a valuable paper before the Conference on 'Church Music' and another gave a paper on 'Sunday-School Work'.[36]

The pressure of feminists and the threat of disorder were factors in the modest concessions to women incorporated in the alteration of the lay franchise in July 1914. By that time, however, Church feminists were unlikely to be content with the concessions offered in that revision: the initial franchise and representation at the parish level only.

The year 1917 was critical both for the cause of Church self-government and for that of the Church suffragists. In November the Representative Church Council considered the *Report of the Archbishops' Committee on Church and State*, a product of deliberations begun in 1913. Its recommendations for establishing a statutory system of Church self-government, modelled on the Representative Church Council, had been public for over a year. Archbishop Davidson's inaction during that year, his expressed unwillingness to proceed with Church reform in wartime, and the conservatism of the Committee's report on the woman issue, stirred a group of impatient clergy and laity to action. Inspired by H. R. L. Sheppard, led by William Temple, the Life and Liberty movement was formed in March 1917.[37] This 'ginger group' (which included both Louise Creighton and Maude Royden from the beginning) sought Church self-government immediately as a means to further Church reform later. Among its earliest productions was a pamphlet listing several 'scandals'; one of these was 'that there should be no place for women in the councils of the Church'.[38]

When the Representative Church Council met in November 1917

to deal with the Archbishops' Committee's *Report*, it felt not only the full weight of the Life and Liberty campaign, but also firm pressure from the Central Committee on Women's Church Work, a semi-official body made up of women from every diocese and many voluntary women's societies in the Church of England, chaired by Archbishop Davidson's wife. Encouraged by Louise Creighton (the vice-chairman), the Central Committee asked the Representative Church Council for its assurance that

> women should be eligible for election to the Diocesan Conferences and to the proposed Church Council as well as to the Parochial Councils, and further that they can be granted in all administrative matters the same rights as other members of the laity.[39]

Not for two more years did women achieve complete equality of opportunity in the councils of the Church. In the meantime, the *Report of the Archbishops' Committee on Church and State* was examined, during most of 1918, by a very large committee of the Representative Church Council (known as the 'Grand Committee'); in October it recommended widening considerably the scope of women's participation by allowing them to sit on ruridecanal and diocesan conferences as well as on parochial councils. On the proposed national council, however, it maintained that only men should serve.[40] This final block to equality was swept away by the Representative Church Council on 26 February 1919 on a motion by Bishop Kempthorne of Lichfield, seconded by William Temple. No doubt the submissions of Gore and other Church suffragists over the years had some influence on this result. No doubt, too, the Council responded to pressure from without, exerted by churchwomen themselves and by their allies in Life and Liberty. In the end, however, it was the example of the Parliamentary Reform Act of 1918 which carried the day. 'It would be an anomaly', said Kempthorne, 'that women should be considered eligible for the Parliament of the nation and not be eligible for the Representative Assembly of the Church.'[41]

The Enabling Bill, providing for Church self-government, and allowing full lay rights for churchwomen in that government, passed through both houses of Parliament in the last half of 1919. As the Church of England Assembly (Powers) Act, it received the Royal Assent on 23 December.[42]

The National Assembly of the Church of England met for the first time in the following summer. Its members numbered 646, of whom 357 represented the laity; forty lay representatives were women. Among those forty were at least two, Louise Creighton and Maude Royden, whose contributions to the women's cause had been outstanding, and who continued, through the 1920s, to be leaders of Church feminism. Although the Assembly never became a female preserve, neither did churchwomen shun their new opportunity. According to Charles Gore's biographer, between 1920 and 1935 'nearly ten times as many women . . . attained membership of the Church Assembly as . . . succeeded in entering the mother of Parliaments'.[43]

II

Commenting on the removal of the last restriction on women's participation in the proposed councils of the Church, the *Guardian*, on 6 March 1919, observed that women had 'established their right to consultative rank, and when a case is overwhelming it is wise to yield gracefully'. In fact, there was very little grace exhibited by the opponents of women's right to a place in Church government, either then or in all the years since 1897. Church suffragists had to meet incredibly obscurantist arguments, and they encountered attitudes which to modern liberals seem deluded and prejudiced. Even so, these arguments and attitudes are well worth examining. In his study of the anti-suffragists, those who opposed the extension of the parliamentary franchise to women, Brian Harrison issued a useful warning:

> We are all suffragists now, but far from allowing this to silence the late Victorian and Edwardian anti-suffragist, the historian will labour the more energetically to ensure that he is fairly heard, lest history degenerate into a mere peddling of pedigrees for prosperous present-day institutions.[44]

Whether or not Church of England democracy is more or less prosperous than parliamentary democracy may be debatable. It is certain that women's place in neither can be taken for granted, and that the opponents of both should be heard and understood.

Those who fought to deny women a place in the councils of the

Church were not united either by churchmanship or political view; nor, of course, did they object to the participation of women in the same ways or at the same stages. Many were unworried by women voting for (or even serving on) parochial church councils, yet were appalled at the prospect of women electors or councillors at a higher level. In 1914 Hensley Henson, dean of Durham, was prepared to allow women the 'initial franchise', but he was utterly opposed to their inclusion in the Representative Church Council. He was contradicted in the same debate by H. J. Torr, a lay delegate, who believed women should be denied the franchise lest they swamp the male vote, but who thought it quite appropriate that women should be chosen by an all-male electorate to serve on diocesan conferences or the Representative Church Council.[45]

Several arguments were shared by those who wanted either to prevent or to restrict women's role in Church government, although they were applied differently by different men. Two points appear with great frequency throughout the whole period of debate on women's role in Church politics. One was a fear that women would overwhelm men in Church affairs, that the Church would be 'feminised'. The other was a conviction that women were peculiarly subject to clerical influence, that they lacked the independence of opinion and judgement necessary to stand up to priestly domination.

Fear of feminisation was founded on the fact of an increasing proportion of female worshippers in parish churches. 'The women, by sheer weight of numbers will be able to capture the whole government of the Church so far as representative bodies are concerned', wrote a correspondent in the *Guardian* on 22 May 1915:

> In an ordinary congregation they outnumber the other sex by at least 7 to 1 . . . It will be serious if only one-seventh of their number assert themselves. They would then be equal to the men, even if the men stand firm.

Some thought that one result of the reduction of men to minority status would be their loss of interest in Church affairs. As early as 1904 the bishop of Bath and Wells (G. W. Kennion) thought that too many churchmen regarded 'the work of the Church as women's work', and he was 'very much afraid they would find that the men would not care to take any part in exercising their franchise if women were allowed to vote'.[46] Such a transfer of control from churchmen to churchwomen, it was argued, would have an adverse effect on the influence of Church councils in the community at large. With characteristic tactlessness, Lord Hugh Cecil stated that the addition of women to the electorate would 'immensely detract from the authority and power of the [Representative Church] Council. It would be said at once that they represented the views of a lot of foolish women.'[47] If it proved impossible to keep women entirely out of Church government one Cheshire clergyman suggested that their rights be limited. 'For instance', he wrote in the *Guardian* (15 July 1915), 'women might be excluded from the vote till thirty years of age, and from taking a seat till forty or fifty years of age. And they might be given the power to speak but not to vote.'

Just as the women's opponents feared the 'weight' of Church councils would diminish as they came under female domination, so they also thought the introduction of female voters and representatives would strengthen clerical influence. Lord Hugh Cecil was not alone in thinking that women 'would do anything their parsons told them'. The prospective female lay voter was devout, 'half a clergyman', incapable of standing up to clerical pressure. 'The woman's mind', it was said, 'was more in sympathy with that of the clergy than with that of the average layman.'[48]

Clerical control of the new voters and councillors would be relatively easy, for women's minds were unsuitable instruments for forming independent political opinions, and their experience was inappropriate preparation for public debate and legislation. Dean Henry Wace of Canterbury spoke of 'the natural differences between men and women'; he considered women capable of 'administrative' duties (including 'places on boards of Guardians' and 'parish affairs'), but he denied their capacity for 'legislative duties'. Similarly, Lord Hugh Cecil 'drew a definite line between the deliberative and the administrative', declaring women incapable of the former function. Although, in 1914, Hensley Henson was prepared to allow them the vote, he still did not think that 'women generally were equipped with those powers judicial and political which qualified them for a seat on legislative assemblies'.[49]

Even in 1914 it was still possible for one churchman to write that he had never known 'a wife, or any woman, who wished to serve on a Church council herself'. It was common argument early in the debate, but one that became increasingly implausible as churchwomen made their views clear during the war years.[50] When the pressures and protests of Church feminists rose, some of their opponents began to perceive their demands for vote and voice in councils as but the first stages of a campaign for full sex equality in the Church, including the ordained ministry. In 1915 an anonymous correspondent in the *Guardian* (31 March) discovered that Maude Royden had addressed a meeting of Church feminists at which she 'declared her belief that there was no more reason why women should be kept from the priesthood than from Councils'. Fear of a 'conspiracy' to open the ordination question was the basis for Hensley Henson's last ditch vote in February 1919 against allowing women into the new National Assembly. His conviction that 'if they admitted women without any sort of limit to the whole legislative system of the Church, women would have to be admitted to the orders of the Christian ministry' was shared by no one else in the Representative Church Council, and it was swept aside by the *Guardian*.[51] Yet on 8 May 1919, hardly more than two months after Henson issued his warning, The League of the Church Militant (the successor of the CLWS) decided 'to challenge definitely . . . the custom of the Church of confining the priesthood to men'. A year later Henson continued his argument at the Lambeth Conference of 1920. 'I submit', said Henson on 8 July 1920,

> that it will be found that in the long run you cannot in your concessions to female demands stop short of the episcopate itself . . . You admit women to Councils, and what security is there that in due course those Councils will not contain a majority of women? . . . The door is being opened to a demand which cannot and will not fall short of entire admission to the ministry itself.[52]

In his Representative Church Council speech, Henson pointed out that St Paul 'taught, as a matter of principle, that the female sex was subordinate in certain respects to the male'. As a reason for excluding women from the franchise and from Church councils, the alleged Pauline principle of female subordination had played a subordinate role ever since the beginning of the debate. Its chief proponent was not Henson but the strong anti-feminist and biblical conservative Henry Wace who declared in 1904 that, although St Paul had expressed 'emancipating words' on the subject of slavery, 'there was not one . . . emancipating word in all St Paul's epistles on the subject of the authority or position of women in the Church'. Wace considered Paul's statement that women were not to speak in the Church as 'absolutely decisive for Christian men'.[53]

Wace fortified his appeal to St Paul by invoking the authority of post-biblical tradition. 'If they gave women a vote in the Representative Church Assembly,' he argued in 1904, 'the only precedents they had got for it were one-third of the colonial dioceses and the majority of the dioceses of the United States, . . . not . . . a very strong example for them to follow.' Ten years later David Howard, a layman in the Representative Church Council, asserted that 'the Church had been governed since the time of the apostles . . . by men'. 'Was it quite safe', he asked, 'to throw over all the experience of the past?' It was especially dangerous as it was irreversible; once the decision was taken to give women political rights, there would be no going back.[54]

By the time the Enabling Act had been passed, and women actually had achieved the rights and responsibilities of laymen in the new constitutional councils, Church feminists were preparing for other battles: to develop adequate training and proper recognition for women church workers, and to loosen the male monopoly of preaching in consecrated buildings and of the ordained ministry itself. These struggles proved equally arduous and even more extended than that to achieve the political rights of democratic churchmanship.

Notes

*This essay was originally published in the *Journal of Ecclesiastical History*, XXXIII (January 1982); it is reprinted here by permission of Cambridge University Press and with the kind co-operation of the family of the late Brian Heeney. ©Cambridge University Press.

1. See Michael Hill, *The Religious Order* (London, 1973); A. M. Allchin, *The Silent Rebellion* (London, 1958); The Sisters of the Church, *A Valiant Victorian: The Life and Times of Mother Emily Ayckbawm* (London, 1964); B. C. Pope, 'Angels in the Devil's Workshop', in R. Bridenthal and C. Koontz (eds.), *Becoming Visible: Women in European History* (New York, 1977); Brian Harrison, 'Philanthropy and the Victorians', *Victorian Studies*, IX (1966); Brian Harrison, 'For Church, Queen and Family: The Girls' Friendly Society, 1874–1920', *Past and Present*, 61 (1973); Diana Orton, *Made of Gold: A Biography of Angela Burdett-Coutts* (London, 1980); F. K. Prochaska, 'Women in English Philanthropy, 1790–1830', *International Review of Social History*, XIX (1974); O. R. McGregor, *Divorce in England: A Centenary Study* (London, 1957); J. O. and O. Banks, *Feminism and Family Planning in Victorian England* (Liverpool, 1964); Alan Wilkinson, *The Church of England and the First World War* (London, 1978); Roger

Lloyd, *The Church of England, 1900–1965* (London, 1966).

2. The exception to this general statement was the office of churchwarden. According to Sir Robert Phillimore, 'women may be churchwardens' (*The Ecclesiastical Law of England*, 2nd edn (London, 1895), II:1467). There do not seem to have been many females in this office in the 1890s, and the discovery of the possibility caused the bishops some unease. See Owen Chadwick, *The Victorian Church* (London, 1970), II:201; also B. Keith-Lucas, *The English Local Government Franchise* (Oxford, 1952), pp. 13, 165.

3. The two most numerous categories of women workers in late Victorian England were probably Sunday school teachers and district visitors. According to the *Official Yearbook of the Church of England* (London, 1889), there were 91,642 females teaching in Sunday schools and 47,112 district visitors (the huge majority of them female) in 80% of English and Welsh parishes.

4. *The Ministry of Women: a Report by a Committee appointed by His Grace the Lord Archbishop of Canterbury* (London, 1919), p. 22.

5. Chadwick, *Victorian Church*, II:222; Charles Booth, *Life and Labour of the People in London. Third Series: Religious Influences* (London, 1902), VII:424; Richard Mudie-Smith (ed.), *The Religious Life of London* (London, 1904), pp. 267, 443.

6. I have used the word 'feminism' in this paper to mean 'the doctrine of equal rights for women, based on the theory of the equality of the sexes'. See R. J. Evans. *The Feminists* (London, 1977), pp. 39, 63–9; Gladys Cuddeford, *Women and Society* (London, 1967), pp. 52ff; K. E. McCrone, 'The National Association for the Promotion of Social Science and the Advancement of Victorian Women', unpublished paper presented to the Canadian Historical Association Meeting in June 1979. *passim*; Keith-Lucas, *Local Government Franchise*, pp. 74, 165–8. Keith-Lucas notes that 'women, if otherwise qualified, were allowed to attend and vote at vestry meetings, and even to hold office' throughout the century (pp. 13, 165). W. J. Reader, *Professional Men* (London, 1966), Ch. 11.

7. K. A. Thompson, *Bureaucracy and Church Reform* (Oxford, 1979), p. 92.

8. Church Congress Report (hereafter cited as CCR), 1885, pp. 80ff. (speech by Miss Weston) and 164 (speech by Harvey Goodwin).

9. Chadwick, *Victorian Church*, II:359–60.

10. Thompson, *Church Reform*, p. 138.

11. Chronicle of Convocation (Canterbury) (hereafter cited as CC), 1897, pp. 227, 213. The Bishop of Salisbury was John Wordsworth (1843–1911); the Bishop of Chichester was E. R. Wilberforce (1840–1907).

12. CC, 1898, pp. 123–7; CC, 1897, p. 227 (Resolution 5).

13. For evidence that women did sometimes sit on PCCs, see *Guardian*, 29 November 1905 (speech by Bishop Gore in Representative Church Council: Report of Proceedings (hereafter cited as RCC report)); *Guardian*, 24 November 1911 (speech by Earl Nelson in RCC report).

14. CCR, 1899, pp. 127–8.

15. P. V. Smith, *Church Self-Government* (London, 1920), p. 8. Balfour was a Leader of the House of Commons in 1899. Jebb (1841–1905) was a Conservative, 'strongly opposed to legislative interference with the Established Church'. Michael Stenton and Stephen Lees, *Who's Who of British Members of Parliament* (Hassocks, 1978), II:191. P. V. Smith (1845–1929), a distinguished ecclesiastical lawyer and ardent churchman, calculated that 'out of 217 Church bills introduced into the House of Commons between 1888 and 1913, 33 were passed, 183 were dropped, and one was negatived'. (*Church Self-Government*, p. 8.)

16. The Upper and Lower Houses of both Convocations, together with the two Houses of Laymen.

17. CC, 1904, Committee Report No. 385, p. 5.

18. CC, 1903, Committee Report No. 377, p. 3.

19. Ibid. *Report of Joint Meeting of the Members of the Convocations of Canterbury and York (Sitting in Committee) and of the Houses of Laymen, held on July 9 and 10, 1903*, p. 51. Lord Hugh Cecil, Baron Quickswood (1869–1956), was a prominent and controversial Conservative MP and author of *Convervatism* (1912). A prominent member of the Representative Church Council, he continued as a leading member of the Church Assembly between the wars. He took a far more detached (to a degree even a supportive) view of women's parliamentary suffrage than he did of the parallel Church issue (see Brian Harrison, *Separate Spheres* (London, 1978), p. 242).

20. CCR, 1903, pp. 123–24, 127.

21. CC, 1904, pp. 35, 11–12, 13–14.

22. RCC, 1904, p. 42.

23. *Guardian*, 8 November 1905. Henry Wace (1836–1924) was Dean of Canterbury from 1903 and formerly principal of King's College, London. He is described in the *DNB* as 'a strong partisan', and 'an outspoken opponent of innovation'. J. L. Darby, an Irishman, was Dean of Chester from 1886.

24. *The Church Times*, 1 December 1905.

25. *Guardian*, 24 November 1911. Under the 1905 arrangement, in some dioceses parochial councils elected delegates to the ruridecanal conferences which, in turn, elected to diocesan conferences. In other dioceses the deanery step was omitted.

26. RCC, 1914, pp. 25, 63–4.

27. RCC, 1914, pp. 20, 42.

28. Claude Hinscliff to Archbishop Davidson, 5 August 1912. Davidson Papers, W16. Lambeth Palace Library. Maude Royden (1876–1956) was a prominent suffragist and editor of *Common Cause*, For a time assistant preacher at the City Temple, she was a well-known Anglican Church feminist and preacher and a member of the first Church Assembly. Edith Picton-Turbervill (1874–1958) was an officer of the YMCA in England, a suffragist, Church feminist and preacher. From 1929 to 1931 she was a Labour MP. Louise Creighton (1850–1936), widow of a Bishop of London, was an author and a leader in the missionary movement, the Pan-Anglican Congress of 1908, and of the women's movement in the Church. She was a member of the Church Assembly, 1920–30, and three times president of the National Union of Women Workers (later the National Council of Women). A member of the Joint Commission of Insurance Commissioners (1912), she was also appointed to the London University Commission.

29. Claude Hinscliff to Archbishop Davidson, 3 May 1912. Davidson Papers, W16. Lambeth Palace Library.

30. Elizabeth Metzler to Archbishop Davidson, 9 March 1912. Davidson Papers, W16; *Guardian*, 1 December 1909, letter from Elizabeth Hallowes; *Guardian*, 20 December 1912; Hinscliff to Davidson, 5 August 1912. Davidson Papers, W16; Susan Villiers to Archbishop Dividson, 3 August 1914. Davidson Papers, Women's Suffrage, 1908–14.

31. G. K. A. Bell, *Randall Davidson, Archbishop of Canterbury* (London, 1952), pp. 668–9.

32. Alice Kidd to Archbishop Davidson, 14 June and 29 October 1914, Davidson Papers, Women's Suffrage, 1908–14.

33. Emma Paget to Archbishop Davidson, March 1914, Davidson Papers, W16. See also letters in *Guardian*, 3 February 1911, and *Guardian*, 31 January and 27 June 1913.

34. *Guardian*, 25 March 1915.

35. See *Guardian*, 31 March 1915, letter from 'X'. *Guardian*, 20 July 1916, letter from Athelstan Riley; see the correspondence that follows continually up to 31

August 1916. Also Archbishop Davidson to Athelstan Riley, 11 August 1916. Davidson Papers, R11.

36. *Guardian*, 24 November 1911, speech of Earl Nelson. *Guardian*, 14 July 1909, speech of Lewis Dibbin. *Guardian*, 4 July and 11 July 1913, letters from H. W. Johnston and Ernest B. Savage.

37. F. A. Iremonger, *William Temple, Archbishop of Canterbury: his Life and Letters* (London, 1948), pp. 220ff.

38. Carolyn Scott, *Dick Sheppard, A Biography* (London, 1977), p. 93.

39. Central Committee of Women's Church Work. Minutes, 1909–19, entry for 23 October 1917. Church House Archives, Westminster, vol. 178.

40. *Report of the Committee of the Representative Church Council on the Report of the Archbishops' Committee on Church and State* (London, 1918), p. 15.

41. *Guardian*, 6 March 1919.

42. Smith, *Church Self-Government*, p. 20.

43. National Assembly of the Church of England, *Report of Proceedings*, 1920 (London, 1921), p. 6. G. L. Prestige, *The Life of Charles Gore* (London, 1935), p. 191.

44. Harrison, *Separate Spheres*, p. 21.

45. RCC, 1914, pp. 27–8. Torr (1864–1935) was a lawyer and a Lincolnshire JP.

46. CC, 1904, p. 15. See also RCC, 1911, p. 123 (David Howard); RCC, 1914, pp. 27 (Henson), 29 (Torr), 34 (Wace).

47. *Report of Joint Meeting . . .*, 1903, p. 51. See also RCC, 1911, p. 125 (Lord Halifax).

48. *Report of Joint Meeting . . .*, 1903, p. 51; RCC, 1911, p. 123 (David Howard); RCC, 1914, p. 30 (Torr). Compare this with the view expressed by Dean Gregory in the all-clerical Canterbury Convocation in 1898 (above, p. 265).

49. CC, 1904, p. 146; RCC, 1904, p. 48; RCC, 1914, p. 28.

50. *Guardian*, 30 July 1914 (letter from W. Paige Cox). See also, CC, 1904, p. 148 (Canon Bankes).

51. *Guardian*, 6 March 1919 (leading article and report of RCC debates).

52. *Guardian*, 8 May 1919, Lambeth Conference Proceedings. 8 July 1920. L.C. 106, pp. 50–1. Lambeth Palace Archives.

53. *Guardian*, 6 March 1919, RCC, debate report; CC, 1904, p. 145; *Guardian*, 20 July 1913, report of Canterbury conference.

54. CC, 1904, p. 145; RCC, 1914, p. 46; *Guardian*, 1 July 1915, letter from E. B. Trotter; CC, 1904, p. 146.

Notes on Contributors

Walter L. Arnstein is Professor of History at the University of Illinois, Urbana; among his publications in Victorian studies are *The Bradlaugh Case* (1965) and *Protestant versus Catholic in Mid-Victorian England: Mr. Newdegate and the Nuns* (1982).

Rickie Burman is an anthropologist who began her research on Jewish women while a Research Fellow at the Manchester Studies Unit, Manchester Polytechnic. She was co-ordinator of the project which established the Manchester Jewish Museum and is now co-ordinator of the Museum of the Jewish East End, London.

Susan P. Casteras is Assistant Curator of Paintings at the Yale Center for British Art, where she organised an exhibition on images of Victorian womanhood (1982); she has published studies of Millais and D. G. Rossetti.

Kenneth Corfield, educated at Birmingham University and Birkbeck College, University of London, teaches history at a secondary school in Clapham. He is now working on a book on the boycott of slave-grown produce.

D. Colin Dews is a local preacher 'on trial' in the Leeds (West) Circuit, Secretary of the Yorkshire Branch of the Wesley Historical Society, and a lecturer at Park Lane College of Further Education.

The late **Brian Heeney** was a faculty member of Trent University, Ontario; his writings in the field of church history include *Mission to the Middle Classes: The Woodard Schools* (1969) and *A Different Kind of Gentleman* (1977).

Ann R. Higginbotham is Assistant Professor of History at Eastern Connecticut State University and has recently completed a study of unwed mothers in nineteenth-century London.

Margaret Maison is the author of *The Victorian Vision: Studies in the Religious Novel* and *John Oliver Hobbes, Her Life and Work*; she is currently studying the women authors associated with the Romantic Movement in England.

Gail Malmgreen has been a Research Associate at Harvard Divinity School and is now Assistant Editor of the Papers of Elizabeth Cady Stanton and Susan B. Anthony at the University of Massachusetts; she has published historical studies of Quaker and Methodist women.

Catherine M. Prelinger, formerly a Visiting Lecturer at Harvard Divinity School and now Associate Editor of the Papers of Benjamin Franklin at Yale, has published widely on the subject of women and religion in Germany; she is completing a transnational study of the female diaconate.

Lilian Lewis Shiman is chair of the Department of History at Nichols College (Massachusetts) and author of *The Crusade against Drink in Victorian England* (forthcoming).

Index